T0340068

ILLEGAL TENDER

Gold, Greed, and the Mystery of the Lost 1933 Double Eagle

DAVID TRIPP

FREE PRESS
New York   London   Toronto   Sydney

FREE PRESS

A Division of Simon & Schuster, Inc.
1230 Avenue of the Americas
New York, NY 10020

Copyright © 2004 by David Enders Tripp
All rights reserved, including the right
of reproduction in whole or in part in any form.

FREE PRESS and colophon are trademarks of Simon & Schuster, Inc.

Designed by Joel Avirom and Jason Snyder
Design Assistant: Meghan Day Healey

Manufactured in the United States of America

10   9   8   7   6   5   4   3   2   1

Library of Congress Cataloging-in-Publication Data is available.

ISBN 978-0-7432-7435-7

For information regarding special discounts for bulk purchases, please contact
Simon & Schuster Special Sales at 1-800-456-6798 or business@simonandschuster.com

For Susan with love

———◆———

CONTENTS

———◆———

PART II: ON THE LAM

ILLEGAL TENDER

The 1933 double eagle. One of 445,500. The $7,590,020 coin.
The most valuable coin in the world, and one of the most valuable American
works of art ever sold at auction. (Courtesy of Sotheby's Inc. ©2003)

Prologue

———◆———

DR. F. LELAND HOWARD HAD BEEN STUMPED; NOW HE WAS UNHAPPY.

A narrow-eyed career bureaucrat with a reputation for playing it strictly by the book, Howard was Assistant Director of the United States Bureau of the Mint. The gray early-spring day was warming with the threat of rain as Howard sat in his spartan office on the second floor of the Treasury Building across the street from the White House. He carefully read a long memo from the Philadelphia Mint. In it was the answer to a question he had posed four days earlier, and it was not the answer he wanted.

On that Saturday, Howard had been at work, filling in, according to government protocol, for Nellie Tayloe Ross, the director, who was away. The standard work week was still five and a half or six days. As Acting Director, the most senior Mint employee present, he was checking into a seemingly minor inquiry from a New York journalist, who had asked how many twenty-dollar gold pieces, made in 1933, had been issued. The writer was curious, because an example was appearing at auction in the coming week. The description in the catalogue stated that only eight or ten existed. Could the Mint help verify the accuracy of this claim?

Similar requests for information were received from time to time, and for the most part they were easily answered by consulting the Mint's Annual Report. Checking the 1933 report, Howard learned that almost half a million twenty-dollar gold pieces had been struck. But in 1933, the same year—and month—that the coins had first been made, the government had begun the recall of privately owned gold—primarily coins and gold-backed currency. That historic event muddied the waters seriously.

Unsure of the answer, Howard had dictated a telegram to the super-intendent of the United States Mint at Philadelphia: "Does your record show that double eagles minted in 1933 were ever paid out. Your institution only one to manufacture double eagles 1933. Reported sale of same in New York scheduled for next week. Please get information by Tuesday if possible."

The first response had come by telephone directly to Mrs. Ross on Tuesday evening, followed up the next day by the extremely detailed memo Howard was now reading. The answer was unequivocal. According to the Mint's own records, *no* 1933 twenty-dollar gold pieces—double eagles—had *ever* been released to the public. If there was one in New York offered for sale, it was either a fake or it belonged to the United States Government.

Either way, it was a case for the United States Secret Service.

Thursday, February 8, 1996. Park Avenue, New York City.

A soaring forty-two-story, Art Deco palace on Park Avenue, the Waldorf-Astoria is renowned for having hosted kings, presidents, movie stars, men of wealth, and men of passion. If the Waldorf-Astoria was good enough for heads of state, it was good enough for the United States Secret Service. A suite on the twenty-second floor was wired and ready for a sting, which had been set up by a retired truck driver turned small-time coin dealer—Confidential Informant 324-15.

The informant had called in the Feds for not entirely altruistic reasons. He was planning to bank some reward money at the very least. CI 324-15 had baited the trap by offering one and a half million dollars to his mark, Jay Parrino, an American coin dealer, for a twenty-dollar gold piece, a 1933 double eagle—an elusive, mythic treasure that was illegal to own and so coveted all the more. Parrino himself didn't own the coin but was acting as middleman. The owner of the coin was an English coin dealer, Stephen Fenton. Fenton came with the golden object of the sting in his pocket accompanied by his cousin. It was not yet 9 A.M., clear and not too cold for February.

Everyone involved was anxious, some more than others. The suite was wired, and a tape recorder was running in the room next door.

At first just the three coin dealers and an innocent were assembled in the suite: the informant who had set up the sting; his mark, Jay Parrino, who had negotiated the deal; the owner of the coin, Stephen Fenton; and Fenton's bystander cousin. They were joined minutes later by two undercover United States Secret Service agents. One posed as a coin expert, the other as the informant's millionaire client—the buyer.

The scene was not quite high drama. It was awkward and poorly paced. The informant was verbose, asking leading questions and occasionally answering them himself. Parrino was agreeable, at first offering nothing but succinct replies. Soon, led on, he opened up with nervous bursts of telling information. Fenton exercising English reserve, was polite and said little—but what he said betrayed him too. The undercover men said next to nothing. Within minutes, the deal was agreed.

The next thing Jay Parrino and Stephen Fenton knew, they had been arrested and were making sworn statements to the authorities. It was barely noon.

Just over an ounce in weight and just under an inch and a half in diameter, this double eagle had been made a lifetime ago, sixty-three years before—legally. But the United States Government contended that it was stolen property—stolen from the United States itself—and it had laid claim. It was not the first 1933 double eagle the government had seized. Nor, if another ever surfaced, would it be the last.

Tuesday, July 30, 2002.
Sotheby's, 1334 York Avenue, New York City.

———

The art auction season had been over for a month. The two behemoths, Sotheby's and Christie's, were still staggering from accusations of collusion, which had cost them a combined half-billion dollars in legal settlements and the purity of their brand names. 2002 had been a tough year.

The mid-afternoon sun was fierce, the air sultry and close. A few stray green-gray clouds failed to organize themselves into a thunderstorm to relieve the city of a week-long heat wave. Sotheby's headquarters, a ten-story cracker box of steel covered in a planned misalignment of glass panels, stood largely empty except for the lobby and seventh floor, where a cumulus of the curious was assembling for the unprecedented exhibition and auction of a single coin—the 1933 double eagle, the coin seized from Stephen Fenton by the Secret Service. It had been decreed by the government the only legal one of its kind, an amazing rarity, a relic of the nation's past glories, challenges, and victories. Now the sole legitimate survivor of the near half-million that had been struck, it could at long last be displayed and admired in the light of day, without fear of confiscation by the long arm of the Secret Service. Government agents now acted as guardians, not predators.

The visitors were for the most part new to Sotheby's. They had made the pilgrimage for one reason only—to see history made. A growing host of reporters armed with stenopads, tape recorders, and video cameras diligently patrolled and interviewed the same few people.

Within the massing crowd was a handful of real bidders. Only twelve had registered and been approved by Sotheby's. Each, for his own reasons, hoped to come away with the glittering prize. Each was alone with his thoughts, calculating his odds. Some would bid from the saleroom floor. Others would relay their bids by telephone, either from a private box at Sotheby's or from the comfort of their home or office. Some had presale jitters, others were cool professionals, others still had never bid at auction before and were about to dive in at the deep end of the pool, willing—hoping—to spend millions of dollars.

The object of their desire was neatly settled within a recess made from a series of movable blue walls surmounted by two nineteenth-century American flags at either end. A single freestanding display case with sliding doors and double locks, flanked by nattily uniformed, well-armed officers of the United States Mint Police, was drenched in the luminosity of carefully aimed spotlights. Within the vitrine, perched on a carefully styled cascade of black velvet, was an oblong piece of plastic that encased a disk of gold—shimmering, glowing, waiting.

The 1933 double eagle is the most highly coveted, famous—or infamous—coin in the world. Likened to the Mona Lisa and the Holy Grail, beautiful and unattainable, it has been on the United States Secret Service's Most Wanted list for sixty years. Although it was legally made, it shouldn't exist. Its very survival is due to an unlikely convergence of luck, timing, and greed.

In 1933, in the most mournful days of the Depression, twenty dollars could support a married couple living in expensive New York City for a week or employ a farmhand lucky enough to find work for a month. Nearly half a million 1933 double eagles had come ringing off the presses at almost exactly the moment that President Franklin Roosevelt, in an effort to lift a crippled economy back to its feet, banned private ownership of gold. Millions upon millions of gold coins that had been circulating for decades were recalled.

Four years later, according to the records of the United States Government, all the 1933 double eagles were consigned to the fires of the Mint's crucibles and rendered into faceless gold bars destined for storage in the newly sanctified repository of Fort Knox. None was ever released to the public, according to these documents. But, as if by magic, within days of their supposed destruction, a few examples escaped and found their way into the hands of wealthy collectors. But how? From whom? In spite of common talk about the coins' existence in the coin world, the government was none the wiser until fully seven years later.

And so began an odyssey, a crime story, a tale of political will and international intrigue, which weaves through nearly three-quarters of a century of America's history. At times the coins have touched upon great events as well as small.

The auction that was held on that sweltering New York evening before a boisterous crowd of well over five hundred was just one chapter, and the most public, of an extraordinary saga that has been veiled in secrecy, mystery, and misunderstanding. Few who have dallied with this forbidden coin have come away richer for the experience. But rumors persist of other sister coins, cloistered in shadowy collections, and they testify that a mortal once bedazzled by its immutable rays finds it hard to turn away—whatever the consequences.

For the same enigmatic reasons that men have sought the coin, legally and illegally, for three quarters of a century I was compelled to devote more than two years of my life to investigating, unraveling, and narrating the epic of this golden disk's astonishing and, at times, unlikely tale of survival against the odds. Only one person can legally own the 1933 double eagle, but its story belongs to us all.

Forbidden, it lures, captures with its history, and captivates with its beauty. Its creation was the union of a visionary's dream with a dying artist's last supernova brilliance.

It is in 1904, just after Christmas, that the story begins.

PART I

LIFE AND DEATH

***President Theodore Roosevelt c. 1903, two years before he sprung his "pet baby"—
the redesign of U.S. coinage—on Augustus Saint-Gaudens.*** (Franklin Delano Roosevelt Presidential Library)

CHAPTER 1

The Artist, the President, and the S.O.A.B.

———◆———

"I THINK OUR COINAGE IS ARTISTICALLY OF ATROCIOUS HIDEOUSNESS," President Theodore Roosevelt thundered with his usual gale-force candor in a short personal note to Secretary of the Treasury Leslie Mortier Shaw, on December 27, 1904. "Would it be possible, without asking permission of Congress, to employ a man like Saint-Gaudens to give us a coinage that would have some beauty?"

Although federally issued paper money had circulated side by side with coins since the Civil War, in the early twentieth century Americans still placed greater faith in coins. The metal in these homely disks, whether gold, silver, or copper, held a quantifiable store of value; the value of paper money was representative at best and to many people largely illusory. Gold and silver coinage was used by governments for international transactions and to settle debts. Coins were the face of nations, and the president had hatched a revolutionary idea.

Apparently Roosevelt had not yet shared his grand vision with the artist he wanted to create it. That could wait a couple of weeks until mid-January, when Washington would be the scene of the annual dinner of the American Institute of Architects. A greater, more glittering roster of guests could not be imagined. Augustus Saint-Gaudens was one of those who would be honored, and on the next night he would be at the White House

3

for supper. There would be plenty of time for the president to birth what he called his "pet baby." And although TR didn't expect any resistance, nevertheless he wanted to find out from Shaw what the law would allow.

Wednesday, January 11, 1905. Washington, D.C.

The American Institute of Architects had provided a sumptuous meal: oysters (Cape May salts), clear green turtle soup, terrapin, Smithfield ham, red head duck, salad, and desserts washed down by Veuve Clicquot 1898 and Pommard 1889. The Dining Hall at the Arlington Hotel had been festooned with green swags, and the vast, horseshoe-shaped high table that encompassed an additional seventeen tables seated a white-tie-and-tailed constellation of artistic genius, financial wealth, and political power. The only ladies in the room were the president's wife and her party, who sat apart in a box near the entrance.

J. Pierpont Morgan (with his rubicund nose) was seated next to the artist John LaFarge; illustrator Charles Dana Gibson was two seats removed from author Henry James; and Augustus Saint-Gaudens was seated next to John Hay, the secretary of state. The three partners in McKim, Mead and White, architects who almost single-handed had shaped the look of the Gilded Age, were seated at the same table as Frank Millet, Secretary of the American Academy in Rome and one of Roosevelt's closest artistic advisors. At table after table, in seat after seat, the great and the talented sat next to the greater or the wealthier. Cigar and cigarette smoke mingled as the candlelight and electric light danced across a sea of crystal, silver, and porcelain.

In the late hours of the feast, the speeches by the president and Saint-Gaudens received the greatest applause. The artist's was the shortest, the president's the most important. He pledged the power of his office to ensure that the "capital should be enlarged, extended and made beautiful in an orderly and systematic manner" to counteract the erratic pattern of development that had begun to blight the city.

Even though the president didn't mention it in his speech, he intended that the architectural grandeur of Washington, D.C., would be visibly emblematic of the nation—and impress all who visited. So, too, as TR envisioned it, the majestic artistry of a new coinage as designed by Augustus Saint-Gaudens would reflect the wealth, maturity, and sophistication of a nation and its people.

◆ ◆ ◆

4

Augustus Saint-Gaudens on the pergola of the Little Studio, Aspet,
New Hampshire, August, 1906, one month after he agreed to redesign
America's gold coins and one year before his death. (Dartmouth College Library)

Saint-Gaudens—Gus to his friends, and the Saint to his small army of studio assistants in Cornish, New Hampshire—was the ideal choice to design a new, elegant coinage for the United States.

The fifty-seven-year-old sculptor was at the height of his fame, renowned internationally as the creator of masterpieces: the heroic, thoughtful Lincoln in Lincoln Park, Chicago, the steely-gazed, wind-blown Farragut in Madison Square Park, New York, and the brooding, haunting Adams Monument in the Rock Creek Cemetery, Washington, D.C. In New York City, across from the Plaza Hotel on Fifth Avenue, his spectacular gilt equestrian group of General William Tecumseh Sherman being led by Victory was already being compared with awed reverence to Donatello's Gattamelata and Verrocchio's Colleoni. With small, quick, gray eyes set under a heavy brow and with a sharp, curling beard, which he frequently thrust out to accent derision, the Saint was accepted as America's greatest sculptor. He was besieged with honors and turned down far more commissions than he accepted.

In 1905, Augustus Saint-Gaudens was also a man living under the shadow of death. Five years earlier, while working in Paris, the "always overworked . . . but never really ill" sculptor, recounted to his assistant, sculptor James Earle Fraser (who in 1913 would design the buffalo nickel), that he had been told by doctors that he was "in a serious condition" and had to return "home immediately for an operation."

According to his assistants, Saint-Gaudens' mood "never seemed neutral." Now, however, although he had never previously thought about dying, he became obsessed by thoughts of his mortality. Sleep eluded him, and he sank helplessly into a miasma of depression. Eventually, he told Fraser, he had "dashed out of [the studio] resolved to end things by jumping into the Seine."

Intent on suicide, the artist had run desperately through the streets of Paris, "conscious of seeing only one thing: high on every building was the word Death." But when he reached the bridge he had an epiphany. "Maybe it was the light on the river. Or the Louvre which had never looked so splendid." Saint-Gaudens there resolved to live: "Everything about me was unbelievably beautiful. The load of desperation dropped and I was happy. I heard myself whistling."

Gus returned to America, where doctors at Massachusetts General Hospital operated on him. He was told the surgery had been successful, but his wife, Augusta, was told privately that he was suffering from cancer of the rectum and that another operation would probably be needed in five years. She never let on to Gus how sick he was, as she knew his fragile temperament all too well.

The day after the A.I.A. dinner, Gus was tired. The banquet hadn't ended until 1:30 A.M., at which time he, Henry James, John LaFarge, and his valet had all piled into a cab built for two and rattled home to bed in Henry Adams's house at 1603 H Street. It had been only a week since he had been in Boston where, during a blizzard, he had undergone more decidedly unpleasant medical attention. Pain came and went as he had submitted to regular X-ray therapy, but he was stoic and now claimed that he was feeling "better than ever."

His calendar was busy that wintry day: lunch with Mrs. Theodore Roosevelt, a meeting with Secretary of War Taft, and a diplomatic reception at the White House followed by supper at 10:30 P.M. with the presi-

6

dent, the first lady, and a good portion of both the official Cabinet and unofficial "kitchen cabinet."

There were twelve small tables at supper, each seating only six. Saint-Gaudens was at the first table with the president. Next to it, at table four, was Secretary of the Treasury Leslie Shaw. And next to it, at table twelve, was Oscar Straus, a close friend and adviser of Roosevelt, and a favorite of TR's youngest son, Quentin, with whom he shared a fondness for ancient Greek coins.

Sometime during supper, Teddy, over chicken sandwiches and champagne, excitedly unveiled his scheme: a sweeping plan to have Gus create new designs for the images borne on all nine denominations of United States coins then produced, from the lowly copper cent to the lofty twenty-dollar gold piece—the double eagle. He also inveigled Saint-Gaudens to design an Inaugural Medal commemorating his coming second term in office. Because his first term had begun with the shattering assassination of McKinley, there had been no inaugural celebrations.

Gus was hesitant. To conceive designs for an entirely new coinage—from inspiration to pencil and plaster sketches to sculpting large plaster models that would be mechanically reduced to the size of the coin itself—would be a long, arduous task. Knowing the Mint and how it worked, he feared the project would be fraught with bureaucratic obstruction. He had the utmost contempt for the Mint's chief engraver, Charles Barber, as both an artist and a man. They had crossed swords more than a dozen years earlier.

Barber, the son and grandson of coin engravers, had risen to his post as chief engraver at the Mint after his father, William, his predecessor, had taken chill at the seashore in 1879 and died. A proficient engraver but an artist of faint talent, Barber made designs that were derivative and trite. Charles Barber—with a long, drooping white mustache, angry eyes under thin brows, and a hostile mouth—was pedantic and thin-skinned.

In 1889, Saint-Gaudens had enjoyed virtually universal critical acclaim for his design of a medal to commemorate the centennial of George Washington's inauguration. For it, Gus had borrowed unashamedly from the works of the fifteenth-century Italian medalist Pisanello. The reviewers noted how sharply the medal contrasted with the "banal character of United States coinage" and hoped that Saint-Gaudens' mastery of the medium would open the eyes of legislators and have a positive influence on the future look of American coins.

It did. In 1891, Saint-Gaudens, along with nine other distinguished American artists, was invited by the government to submit designs for a new coinage. But, typically, the Mint had imposed conditions, insufficient time to prepare the entries, no assurance of competent judges, and meager compensation. It was little wonder that all ten refused to participate. The Treasury Department then asked that Saint-Gaudens, who had begun his professional career as a cameo carver, together with Charles Barber and a Boston gem engraver called Henry Mitchell, sit on a panel to judge an open competition for designs for a new coinage. This interaction dissolved in acrimony. Barber claimed that only a Mint engraver was capable of preparing coin designs, while Gus told the Mint director that there were only four artists in the world "competent to do such designing," three were in France, and he was the fourth. The committee did agree that none of the three hundred suggestions submitted was an improvement on the existing coinage. Exasperated, the director of the Mint, Edward Leech, handed the job to Barber, and the tradition of banality continued.

Shortly thereafter—and solely to keep it out of Barber's clutches—Saint-Gaudens agreed to design the World's Columbian Exposition Presentation Medal in 1892. But controversy erupted over Saint-Gaudens' use of a nude figure on the reverse, and the bilious Barber was entrusted with its redesign, yielding another dreary, lackluster effort. This time Augustus Saint-Gaudens aired his disdain in public and refused to deal with the Mint again. Battling for his life was easier—and more rewarding—than dealing with Charles Barber.

But his president was asking him. Roosevelt, ever emphatic and positive, was determined that his idea would be born. "Roosevelt was like a great bell, ringing out each morning some new call to duty or devotion, with such an appeal and such a command as none could disregard," recalled Elihu Root, the former secretary of state. As Saint-Gaudens reported to his brother Louis two days later from the Players Club in New York City, "Barber is a S.O.A.B. but I had a talk with the President who ordered Secretary Shaw in my presence to cut Barber's head off if he didn't do our bidding."

During their lively discussion the president's son, Archibald, recalled—and Saint-Gaudens' assistant Henry Hering confirmed—that "Mr. Straus, Mr. St. Gaudens and father sat down and designed a coin. Mr. St. Gaudens designed it and the other two did a devil of a lot of talking."

Despite the sculptor's ambivalence, Teddy wrote to Secretary Shaw five days later and asked him how soon it would be before Saint-Gaudens could be "employed for at least one set of coins." And, he strenuously reiterated, the artist was "to be given an absolutely free hand . . . I do not wish there to be the slightest interference with Saint-Gaudens in connection with the coinage from the artistic side."

TR himself wrote to Saint-Gaudens the next day, informing him that currently only the cent and the gold coins—two-and-a-half-, five-, ten-, and twenty-dollar pieces—could be legally redesigned (coin designs had to be employed for at least twenty-five years before they could be changed). The president asked, "What would be the expense?" Gus, still unsure that he wanted to accept the commission, gently sidestepped the issue, replying instead that time was of the essence for producing the Inaugural Medal—March 4 was Inauguration Day—and that he, personally, could not do it. Instead he suggested sculptor Adolph Weinman (who later designed the Mercury dime and Walking Liberty half-dollar), who would execute it under Saint-Gaudens' guidance and to his design. "In the matter of the coinage I will write you tomorrow or the day after. . . ."

Saint-Gaudens continued to consider the commission in his own way. As with all his projects, he "began with a psychological and emotional rather than visual conception. The complete idea came only with effort on effort, perspective on perspective, growth on growth."

In April at Aspet, his house in Cornish, New Hampshire, Saint-Gaudens sat thumbing through his copy of *Coins of the Ancients* and its seventy plates of images, searching for inspiration. His pain continued to come and go, but much of it he attributed to sciatica. Months later, in July, when the Inaugural Medal was at last completed, he finally came to grips with the concept of redesigning America's coins for President Roosevelt and accepted the commission to design a new cent and all four of the gold denominations—from the quarter eagle to the double eagle.

Until the discovery of gold at Sutter's Mill in California in 1848, the ten-dollar gold piece was the nation's largest gold coin. The standard-bearer since 1795, the "eagle" was the unit of gold from which the other standard gold denominations derived their names: hence, a half eagle was worth five dollars and a quarter eagle, two and a half dollars. After the discovery of the vast California gold fields, the Mint recognized that a larger denomination would be required to meet the growing economic needs of the country. In 1849, Congress provided for a denomination of twenty dollars, called the double eagle. Designed by James Longacre, a former copperplate engraver, it first appeared in March, 1850. His new coin was adorned with a stern neoclassical head of Liberty wearing a jeweled coronet on one side, while on the other side a heraldic eagle with outspread wings had a shield emblazoned on its chest. The design, with

*One of Augustus Saint-Gaudens' preliminary sketch ideas for Liberty
on the obverse of the double eagle, c. 1906.* (Dartmouth College Library)

minor modifications, graced all of the more than hundred million examples struck from 1850 through 1907.

On July 10, 1905, Saint-Gaudens, who regularly charged up to $50,000 for his work, informed TR and the director of the Mint that he would "state $5000 . . . as my price for making the designs for both sides of the gold pieces and the penny. In fixing this amount I name a sum considerably below what I receive for work of like character." He assumed that "the same design may be adopted for both gold and copper coinage." If the Mint did not have the funds, Saint-Gaudens offered to charge less. He was committed. In doing so, he made a gift to the president and a greater gift to his nation. Perhaps too he acknowledged his own mortality.

Now Gus would sketch and compose in his head. His health was precarious. On some days he required doses of morphine to quell the pain. Still, he could conceptualize. "I make seventeen statues [for] every statue I do," he told his assistant James Earle Fraser and developed "calluses on the brain" from all his mental reconfiguring.

In November, a bursting, cheerful TR asked Saint-Gaudens how the design was getting along. He also had a modest suggestion to make for all

10

the new coins. Inspired by having seen some robustly modeled gold coins of Alexander the Great—probably gold staters, with a helmeted head of Athena on one side and a winged figure of Nike on the other—he wrote, "Would it not be well to have our coins in high relief?"

The artist, reduced by his infirmities to only a few hours a day for work, was enthusiastic about Roosevelt's radical idea but pragmatic. As it turned out, he was prescient, as well. Gus cautioned the president that "the authorities on modern monetary requirements would I fear 'throw fits,'" but nevertheless suggested that it was worth the president making an inquiry. TR, Saint-Gaudens reasoned, would not receive the antagonistic reply from the Mint that he was certain would be directed at him had he the gall to ask the same question.

Saint-Gaudens—ironically, a master of low relief—explained to Roosevelt that while he had not yet started on modeling the new designs, he was coming to terms with their composition. His inspiration came in part from antiquity, especially the coins of ancient Greece, but more so from his own body of work, either because of its innate Hellenistic qualities or because his health was so ravaged that he was simply too tired to create completely anew.

The image of the eagle that he wanted for the reverse of the twenty-dollar piece would resemble that which he had designed for the president's Inaugural Medal. It would be a proud standing bird, whose Greek antecedents were from the fourth century B.C. and the coinage of the Ptolemies of Egypt. For the figure of Liberty on the obverse, he liberally borrowed from both his own Sherman Monument and the Louvre's Winged Victory of Samothrace, which had so greatly inspired him. He wanted to express Liberty not as a staid, unforgiving goddess but as "a *living* thing and typical of progress."

Roosevelt concurred and assured Saint-Gaudens that he had "summoned all the Mint people" with the intent to "persuade [them] that coins of the Grecian type but with raised rims will meet the commercial needs of the day." The president, more a human dynamo than a realist, nevertheless proposed first testing the practicality of the higher relief. "How would it do to have a design struck off in tentative fashion—that is to have a model made?"

1906 arrived. Augustus Saint-Gaudens was increasing his use of morphine to control his pain. The scant time he was able to create was precious, and although he was eager and anxious to get on with the coinage, he asked Treasury Secretary Shaw for guidance, explaining that he would try to create "a trial between the extreme high relief of the

Greek coins and the very low relief of the modern ones." But he stressed that it "would be best to know if there [were] not some inflexible modern requirements that necessitate extreme flatness." Gus even suggested that trials in high relief would be a waste of time if this were the case.

Roosevelt, to whom Gus had sent a copy of this January 2 letter, met with Shaw, listened, and then cheerfully chose to ignore the Mint's advice. The president wrote to assuage Saint-Gaudens' concerns. He had told the treasury secretary that the project was his "pet baby," and Secretary Shaw may have thought him a "crack-brained lunatic" but did not say so to his face. Instead Shaw had told the president that even if they were good for nothing more than storage in the vaults, "he had no objection to having those coins as artistic as anything the Greeks could desire." Roosevelt informed Saint-Gaudens that despite the Mint's protestations, "we will try it anyway." One could hear the president chuckle happily as he dictated the final line of his letter to Saint-Gaudens: "I think it will seriously increase the mortality among the employees of the mint at seeing such a desecration, but they will perish in a good cause!"

Saint-Gaudens heartily agreed that the country would be well served "by increasing mortality at the Mint." But feared gloomily that "one gentleman" may have "nervous prostration," but "killed no. He has been in that institution since the foundation of the Government and will be found standing in its ruins." Gus knew his implacable nemesis, Charles Barber, all too well.

Hard at work, Gus made lightning-quick plaster sketches and had his chief assistant, Henry Hering, begin to make finished models. To help him ensure accuracy, Saint-Gaudens wrote to Adolph Weinman and asked to borrow his Indian headdress, his photographs of eagles, and models of birds' wings, as well.

The secretary of the treasury responded to Saint-Gaudens' concerns about the practicality of high relief on January 16, meticulously outlining the practical roadblocks to working in high relief and counseling against it. But both he and Gus realized that the president had already decided the issue, and high relief it would be. Shaw invited the sculptor to the Mint to examine the manufacturing process, before proceeding with his design, but Gus was too frail to accept.

In the early spring of 1906 Saint-Gaudens had a severe relapse and more surgery. Weakened and gaunt, he continued as best he could to work on the coin designs. Henry Hering became his hands, and Gus watched over him as his models took shape. Saint-Gaudens was remarkably comfortable using other artists to execute his ideas and reveled in the process. The sculptors with whom he worked in this fashion also benefited from the experience; Saint-Gaudens' sharp observations and benevolent criticism inspired them, and they strove to exceed the master's expectations. So skilled was Gus in his guidance that Frances Grimes, one of his assistants, recalled, "There was no one who had worked for him but knew he had merely been a tool in Saint-Gaudens' hand, often unconscious of what he was being used to accomplish."

Although Saint-Gaudens was striving to emulate the lush relief of ancient Greek coinage, he was a sculptor, not an engraver, and a child of the industrial revolution. The physical processes now involved in creating a coin would have been alien to the engravers of millennia past and would have seemed absurdly complex. In ancient Greece, the artists cut their designs, actual size—and in reverse—directly into the hard metal face of a die.

Henry Hering modeled large plaster reliefs from eleven to fourteen inches in diameter. These had to be reduced to the small size of the coin, for which an extraordinary machine, called the Janvier lathe, was employed. A bewildering forest of wheels, metal arms, belts, and pulleys set into a steel frame, over the course of twenty-four hours it cuts a reduced image (for the double eagle, a little over an inch and a quarter in diameter) in relief into a piece of softened steel, which stamps out the final die that strikes the actual images onto the coins. When TR's pet project began, the United States Mint did not have one of these contraptions, and so the first plasters had to be sent to Paris for reduction. By the end of 1906, however, the Mint had finally acquired the state-of-the-art lathe, but Barber had yet to master its use (and more of his acrid oaths were recorded). The Janvier is still used today by the United States Mint.

In May, Saint-Gaudens lay at Aspet and wrote to John LaFarge that he was "nailed here with pain." The ailing Gus sent Hering into the lion's den in Philadelphia, Barber's Mint, where he was treated with cool politeness and utter disdain. Roosevelt, with growing anticipation, was eager to see something and politely kept the heat on Saint-Gaudens. But the project stumbled on in gasps and gallops.

Barber's stream of invective continued, insisting that the kind of relief that Gus and Teddy wanted was just not practicable, even as an experiment. Roosevelt, infuriated by the little man, angrily wrote to the secretary of the treasury, "I direct that Mr. Barber has the dies made as Mr. Saint-Gaudens, with my authority, presents them."

This sent the resentful Barber into a fury, and he went out of his way to be obstreperous and malicious, for which he seems to have had a natural inclination. His turf had been invaded. For the first time in history an artist of fame and talent had been commissioned to design American coins. As chief engraver of the United States Mint, that prerogative had been his by more than a century's precedent. In addition to obstructing the progress of the president's project, the choleric Barber even designed his own double eagle, which was simply ignored.

Hering's models for the double eagle were ready to be sent to the Mint on December 8, 1906. The president saw them twelve days later and was rapturous. TR instructed the director of the Mint "that these dies are to be reproduced just as quickly as possible and just as they are." He told Saint-Gaudens that "I suppose I shall be impeached for it in Congress; but I shall regard it as a very cheap payment!"

Barber continued to carp and delay, but on February 15, 1907, the director of the Mint received the first four impressions in gold of the experimental double eagle. He promptly forwarded them to Saint-Gaudens, who returned them a month later, along with two additional strikes in lead.

The coin Saint-Gaudens held in his once powerful fingers was brilliantly realized. After a year and a half, the original concept had succeeded in emulating the classical tradition. The height of its relief was tremendous, far exceeding any coins then in circulation. It had taken up to nine crushing blows of some 150 tons each to bring up the detail. It was a monumental coin, belying its small metallic canvas.

On one side, Liberty, her hair whipping in the wind, seemed to burst beyond the confines of the circular tableau. The heavy folds of her gown billowed as her left foot took the last step to the top of a mountain. Her right hand held her torch aloft to light the way, while her left hand carried the olive branch of peace. In a valley below, the Capitol of the United States could just be seen, and from behind, the rays of the sun symbolized enlightenment. For the reverse, Saint-Gaudens had ultimately adapted an eagle in flight, not one from the glories of Greece, as he had planned initially, but from humble American coins, the pennies of 1857 and 1858. But he made this eagle graceful and powerful, a regal bird that soared effortlessly across a sky lighted by the same rays of the sun.

It was a majestic composition, fully sculptural in its execution, a masterpiece. But it was too bold, the relief too high, for day-to-day use, and because of the complexity of striking even the first few examples, it was almost immediately seen to be tragically impractical for commercial needs.

Even so, those within the Mint instantly recognized these few experimental double eagles as important. Their artistic bravura was also testament to the wonders that could be achieved technologically. The president waived the regulation that these be destroyed and asked to have more struck, perhaps as many as twenty, to celebrate their genius. Even the Mint director, who had not been in the president's corner, kept two of the four original strikes for himself and sent the superintendent of the Mint his check for forty dollars to cover their face value. Saint-Gaudens himself never received even one to keep. But a half-year after his death the president had one of the two in the Mint's own collection removed and sent to his widow, who in return sent the Treasury twenty dollars along with twelve cents for the postage.

By this time, Saint-Gaudens was in almost constant pain and so weakened and emaciated that on the few days he could work he was carried to his studio. There for an hour or two he could once again lose himself in the joys of creation.

In his last letter to Roosevelt on May 23, 1907, he spoke of their now mutual understanding of "how much relief can be practically stamped" on a coin and his personal preference for a standing eagle over the one he had made in flight. This stationary raptor found a home on his ten-dollar gold piece, the eagle, which, like its bigger sister, was another variation on a theme. On it, Gus had placed the head of Liberty—derived from his head of Victory modeled for the Sherman Monument—wearing a feathered headdress. Saint-Gaudens had originally conceived this design for the one-cent piece but had liked it so much that he had also suggested it for the double eagle before the walking figure of Liberty was ultimately adopted.

These designs too had faced concerns about the height of the relief, and Saint-Gaudens saw only one experimental strike of the eagle. He acknowledged its receipt in a letter to the director of the Mint on July 25, 1907. It was his last communication with the Mint. "His sickness," wrote his son Homer, "brought only feebleness of hand, none of mind." And as he saw the project nearing completion, Gus, through his amanuensis, Hering, continued to try to work within the bounds of practicality but still transcend the commonplace.

Augustus Saint-Gaudens slipped into a coma and a died a few days later on August 3, 1907. His body had been so racked with pain that Frances Grimes wrote, "I am so glad the Saint is dead. It was horrible for him to live and suffer so."

An altar, originally designed and built in plaster by Henry Hering in 1905 for a twentieth-anniversary masque given at Aspet to celebrate the establishment of Saint-Gaudens' studios, had so moved Gus when he had seen it in the twilight that he had had it reproduced in marble. Now,

15

some distance from his beloved studios, his ashes lay beneath the four simple Ionic columns surmounted by a cornice.

Unfinished projects, including the Parnell Monument in Dublin, the Phillips Brooks Monument in Boston, and the glorious caryatids designed for the Albright Art Gallery in Buffalo, which he had likened to the figures on the Erectheum in Athens, were completed by his assistants. Others had to be abandoned. But the genius of his coin designs was not allowed to die. For this last battle he had his champions: the president of the United States and Henry Hering. And they took up cudgels on his behalf.

A second set of models with somewhat lowered relief was prepared by Hering. Barber—that "S.O.A.B."—had a number of unflattering articles about the development of the coinage planted in the local Philadelphia papers. His mastery of technical minutiae and seeming delight in drowning others in it grated on both the president and Hering until the combustible Roosevelt had had enough.

October, 1907. The White House, Washington, D.C.

TR's eyes were glittering behind his pince nez. The even white line of his teeth peeked out as his mustaches bristled. But he was not smiling. He brought his fist down on his desk repeatedly, punctuating his sentences physically and shattering the calm of his office. Furious that his grand vision for a renaissance of American coinage was being stymied and sabotaged by a single malignant Mint employee, bitterly aware that his great goal would not be achieved the way he and Gus had envisioned it, Teddy was still determined to have his day. He would have the American public see what brilliance of design and execution could be applied even to everyday spending money. It was the very least he could do to honor Saint-Gaudens.

Frank Leach, the newly appointed Director of the United States Mint, recoiled but was not alarmed by Roosevelt's vigorous display. It was the unflappable Leach's first meeting with the president since he had assumed his new duties. Clear-eyed, gray-bearded Frank Leach was a former Oakland, California, newspaperman and San Francisco Mint superintendent, who had reacted with cool aplomb on April 18, 1906, during the great earthquake. Bounced from bed, his house "doing a lively jig, jumping up and down," he had escaped the "walls and ceilings twisting and squirming" and headed directly to the Mint, where he had organized his men to keep the cataclysmic fire at bay even as the searing heat

16

The metamorphosis of the double eagle design: 1907. Upper left: James Longacre's design (1849–1907); upper right: Saint-Gaudens' concept coin with extremely high relief; lower left: Saint-Gaudens' modified high relief; lower right: Barber's lowered relief.

(Courtesy of Sotheby's Inc. ©2003)

caused the sandstone and granite facade of the building "to flake off with explosive noises like the firing of artillery."

The new Mint director had listened to Teddy's tirade with interest and a touch of embarrassment. When the president had finished, Leach looked at him and said, ever so coolly:

"All you want, Mr. President, is the production of the coin with the new design, is it not?"

"Yes," he said.

"Well, that I promise you," said Leach.

A few days later Leach returned to the president's office and laid a few samples of the new coins, with slightly lowered relief, on the president's desk. These TR carefully examined and pronounced himself "delighted."

"Now," he said. "I want enough of these coins within thirty days to make a distribution throughout the country, that the people may see what they are like." Leach, not one to procrastinate, passed the order to the superintendent of the Philadelphia Mint on November 22, 1907.

The presses ran "all day and all night and Sunday" as each of the approximately twelve thousand coins took up to five blows on the medal presses to be completed. Theodore Roosevelt had, at last, his modern coin of the ancients—the most elegantly designed coin in America's history and a fitting tribute to Augustus Saint-Gaudens.

At the memorial meeting celebrating the dead artist's life, TR spoke of his partner's genius: "Saint-Gaudens gave us for the first time a beautiful coinage, a coinage worthy of this country—a coinage not yet properly appreciated, but to which the official and popular mind will in the end grow. The first few thousand of the Saint-Gaudens gold coins are, I believe, more beautiful than any coins since the days of the Greeks, and they achieve their striking beauty because Saint-Gaudens not only possessed a perfect mastery in the physical address of his craft but also a daring and original imagination."

Sadly, the distinctive relief of the originals was impossible to maintain. The need to produce a true circulating medium required simplicity and speed: one blow from the coining press, not five or seven or nine, was key. Before 1907 had ended, a third set of dies, with flattened relief, was prepared by Saint-Gaudens' old foe, Charles Barber. The brooding engraver reduced contour to line. The robust yet serene sculptural monumentality of the original was lost in the process, but Saint-Gaudens' brilliantly symbolic composition remained unaltered, splendid.

Gus's and Teddy's grand experiment had radiated the energy and exuberance of the Gilded Age. More than seventy-seven million of the Saint-Gaudens double eagles were struck over the next quarter-century, in all but three years (1917–1919) during World War I, glorifying America's ideals and fueling its seemingly endless prosperity.

When the Depression shattered the nation's optimism, however, these marvelous works of art came to be seen as mere metal. The government that had created them sought to buttress a critically weakened American economy by recalling them from private ownership. Most would be destroyed, lost forever, but not all.

CHAPTER 2

Swift and Staccato Action: The Great Depression

———◆———

"THE COUNTRY WAS DYING BY INCHES," FRANKLIN DELANO ROOSEVELT, in his second fireside chat, on May 7, 1933, reminded Americans glued to their radios. It was no exaggeration. Two months earlier, he had been inaugurated President of the United States, and the condition of the nation he had inherited was calamitous.

Much had changed since the gilded start of the century. A financial panic in 1907 had shaken confidence in the hitherto seemingly unstoppable growth of the American economy. A devastating world war from 1914 to 1918 had cruelly shorn the country of many of its young men. Prohibition had unintentionally encouraged a new lawlessness. And now, with the world in the clutches of a crippling depression, the nation's psyche had never been lower.

In the country's heartland, an agricultural depression had already lingered for more than a decade. Farmers who could only get $1.40 per ton for "old corn" (retained from the previous year's crop), stayed warm by burning it; coal, at $4 a ton, was too expensive. In 1925, twin dynamos of the economy, automobile manufacturing and residential construction, suddenly stalled and contracted, and across the nation, business inventories grew alarmingly; no one was buying. Wall Street ignored these storm warnings and went on what President Herbert Hoover labeled an "orgy of mad speculation" as he strove to turn around the failing economy. Stock prices and the soundness of the businesses they represented seemed completely alien to each other. During the summer of 1929, even though these fissures in the domestic economy continued to deepen, banks continued to lend vast amounts of money for stock purchases, and the stock market continued its giddy ascent. On Black Tuesday, October 29, 1929, the Great Crash, like a crushing body blow, brought an end to the gaiety.

While the Crash was not the cause of the Great Depression and did not mark its beginning, it was a principal indicator. By 1933, the value of stocks on the New York Exchange had crumpled from their 1929 high of $87 billion to a meager $19 billion. By comparison, during the 1920s the Federal budget was approximately $3 billion per year. The human costs were tragic. In early 1930, unemployment reached four million; by the end of 1932 the number had more than tripled to approximately twenty-five percent of the work force. Only a quarter of these people received any relief funds, however pitiful, from local government or private agencies. In New York City, for instance, those families fortunate enough to get on the relief rolls had to make do with $2.39 a week for food. Others, less fortunate, were reduced to scrabbling through mounds of garbage with sticks or their bare hands in the hope of finding fetid scraps of food.

The misery extended to those who were employed. Many people who still clung to their jobs were working shortened hours or for reduced paychecks. Coal miners' daily wages were slashed from seven dollars to one dollar. Many industries, including textiles and steel, were paying as little as twenty to thirty cents an hour, and a quarter of the women working in Chicago made less than half that.

Abroad, the world's economy was similarly shattered. Much of Europe's malaise could be directly attributed to the fiscal consequences of World War I and the crushing terms of the Treaty of Versailles. Herbert Hoover called that war the "primary cause of the Great Depression." Germany buckled under the cost of reparations, which it owed primarily to Britain and France. In a precarious international cycle of borrowing from Peter to pay Paul, American financiers lent Germany much of the money it needed to make its payments; these millions then found their way back to the United States Government as repayment by France and Britain of the loans they had been issued during the war. When the Crash of 1929 deprived the American bankers of that essential ingredient, liquidity, the Europeans as a result lacked the funds needed to service their debts, and the financial house of cards collapsed.

Bank closures and panic resulted from this "economic interdependence of nations." Austrians and Germans rioted as banks shut their doors. In the United States, where many banks had been incompetently run for years, bank failures averaged more than six hundred a year from 1921 to 1929. The rate of collapse picked up speed at a frightening pace. In 1930, 1,352 banks failed, most of them in the closing weeks of the year. The next year the number swelled to a horrifying 2,294, with more than five hundred in the month of September alone.

Confidence in financial institutions and their fundamental ability to protect their depositors' wealth was rattled and rapidly eroding. There seemed to be only one raft left to cling to in the roiling sea of economic uncertainty: gold.

"Wherever possible, depositors were asking for their money in gold so that it might be stored away as an asset no matter what was to happen to the currency system as a whole," FDR recalled.

In one form or another, most countries around the world still held to the gold standard. Essential to trade and global finances, gold backed the monetary system and guaranteed the value of most nations' currency at home and abroad. From country to country the amount of money in circulation was a fixed ratio to the amount of gold held in their reserves. When gold flowed out of a nation's coffers in the course of trade, the monetary base shrank, credit was tightened, and deflationary forces were brought into play. In 1931 the ebb and flow of "refugee" gold through the international channels grew so rapid that Hoover likened it to "a loose cannon on the deck of the world in a tempest-tossed sea."

The United States began hemorrhaging gold. Savvy investors, such as Charles Merrill, one of the founders of Merrill Lynch, had predicted the Great Crash in February, 1929, and had liquidated his positions. Now wary of the precarious state of the banks, he saw gold as a safe harbor and privately advised those of his inner circle to buy gold coins and send them out of the country. Since 1915, in reaction to huge exports of gold in 1914 at the outset of World War I, the Federal Reserve had been recording the names of people and companies withdrawing gold in quantity. To avoid being identified, sophisticated hoarders established shell companies in Canada and Europe to which they shipped gold for safekeeping— in other words, beyond the reach of the United States Government.

But all the little guy could do, as Roosevelt said, was take his money from his local bank and ask for gold coins or gold-backed banknotes, nicknamed yellow notes. The constant trickle of the little guys' withdrawals combined with a riptide of the yellow metal to companies and even countries hoping to right their own beleaguered economies created such a tidal wave of uncertainty, instability, and fear that the nation's banking system edged yet closer to the brink of total collapse.

Herbert Hoover had had the bad luck to be elected president in November, 1928. When Black Tuesday arrived, he had only served the first seven months of his term. Nevertheless the mantle of blame for the Crash and the Great Depression was unfairly draped around Hoover's shoulders, in no small part by the Democratic National Committee and its chief propagandist, Charley Michelson, who coined the phrase "the Hoover Depression." Despite compassionate and at times heroic efforts to help his citizens and nation, Hoover could not withstand the withering barrage of Democratic criticism and sarcasm: "Hoover blew the whistle/Mellon rang the bell/Wall Street got it started/And the country went to Hell—Hooray for Roosevelt." On the first Tuesday in November, 1932, Hoover was booted from office by the voting public in an even more lopsided and humiliating defeat than the one he had dealt Al Smith four years earlier.

For the next four months until the March 4 inauguration, during the interregnum—or "great void," as it was styled by some—Roosevelt was president-elect, Hoover was president, and "the bony hand of death was stretched out over the banks and insurance companies." Hoover saw it. Roosevelt saw it.

With the nation's economy being battered from so many quarters, President Hoover broke with precedent, and in November, 1932, approached the incoming president for his advice. But Roosevelt's advisers were immediately suspicious, and so began a pas de deux. Driven by a mixture of genuine concern, self-serving motives, honest collegiality, and raw-boned politics, the two men circled each other warily in the months leading up to the inauguration. Little was done to solve the mounting crises.

FDR would later recall that "for nearly two months prior to my Inauguration I had discussed with a number of people the gloomy banking situation." Even as he entered the last two weeks of the interregnum, however, Roosevelt had no secretary-of-treasury-designate. Barnard College professor Raymond Moley, "Roosevelt's alter ego, his high factotum and dark familiar," was deeply troubled, the de facto head of Roosevelt's "Brain Trust,"—a small group of largely academic advisers to FDR—"found it impossible to discover how deeply Roosevelt was impressed with the seriousness of the crisis."

In mid-January, 1933, the president-elect had offered the Treasury post to Senator Carter Glass of Virginia. Considered "the best-informed congressman on Federal Reserve banking matters," he was a logical choice. In 1913, he had ushered through Congress the Federal Reserve Bank Act, which established the nation's central banking system, and had later served as treasury secretary under Woodrow Wilson.

Now the seventy-five-year-old senator wanted to be courted, and he was, but by Moley, not Franklin Delano Roosevelt. Glass wanted to have a free hand in choosing his personnel, which FDR refused. And, as the devil is in the details, Glass also had questions about the direction of Roosevelt's economic policies. These could not be answered as they had yet to be fully formulated. Finally, there were questions of health, first his wife's, then his own. This gentlemanly gavotte took a month. All the while banks were gasping and gold was running like liquid out of the system.

At last, Senator Glass coyly indicated that he would probably say no— but remained open to those, including financier Bernard Baruch, who wished him to reconsider. On a February afternoon in New York, Raymond Moley puffed on his meerschaum and suggested to Louis McHenry Howe, FDR's gnomelike chief adviser, that William H. Woodin would be a good second choice. Howe "cocked his head . . . and nodded his approval." He thought the suggestion "swell." The more the two thought about and discussed Woodin, the more they preferred him to Glass.

On February 19 Glass finally, definitely, refused the post. Franklin Roosevelt, doubtlessly expelling cigarette smoke with his sigh of relief, instructed Moley to call Woodin. It was 10:30 P.M.

William Hartman Woodin, a highly esteemed industrialist and a director of the New York Federal Reserve Bank, would not have been bothered by the late-night summons. He was an old friend of Roosevelt's, a Republican no less, who had been a peerless fundraiser for FDR's political campaigns as well as for the Warm Springs Foundation (which Roosevelt had established to do battle against infantile paralysis), on the board of which he sat. In the months immediately following the election, he had acted as the president-elect's eyes and ears in financial and industrial circles and was consulted on a wide range of issues.

Woodin was also a composer, guitar-player, book- and coin-collector, and the walls of his library were hung with a stunning array of English watercolors by the great illustrators and caricaturists Cruikshank, Gillray, and Rowlandson. His duplex penthouse at 2 East Sixty-seventh Street, a new but architecturally undistinguished gray building with large windows that overlooked Central Park and a World War I memorial, was a short walk to Roosevelt's house at 47–49 East Sixty-fifth Street. There, at 11 P.M.,

Roosevelt made the offer. Stunned, the slightly built, self-effacing, sixty-four-year-old Woodin asked to sleep on it. Twenty-four hours later, he accepted what Raymond Moley considered "to be one of the most heroic jobs in the administration."

Will Woodin's acceptance came with the inauguration just two weeks off. Since election day, the financial crisis had gathered speed and careened out of control. Although there had been runs on banks throughout January, during the first two weeks of February withdrawals of gold and currency had accelerated to $15 million per day, triple what they had been previously. It was unsettling when Louisiana declared a bank holiday at the beginning of the month. But when, two weeks later, on February 14, 1933, Governor Comstock of heavily industrialized Michigan slapped an eight-day moratorium on the state's banks, a shiver rippled through the country and erupted in panic.

Growing numbers of banks around the country found themselves insolvent and were pushed into involuntary liquidation. One thousand four hundred and fifty-six banks had failed in 1932, but since January 1, 1933, before FDR's inauguration, almost four hundred more had already shuttered their doors. Prices fell and debt burden grew; wages plummeted as major businesses found the going rough. Millions of unemployed citizens roamed the streets and rode the rails of America in search of work, food, help.

Deeply alarmed by the unfolding catastrophe, Herbert Hoover made another approach to Roosevelt on February 17 in a lengthy handwritten letter sent to the president-elect through the Secret Service, "as obviously its misplacement would only fuel the fire and increase the dangers." The letter reeled off the litany of misery and concluded that for the nation's economy "the breaking point has come." The departing president suggested to Roosevelt that "a very early statement by you upon two or three policies of your administration would greatly serve to restore confidence and cause a resumption of the march of recovery." Despite the clearly desperate tone, wrote Moley, "Roosevelt was, to all appearances, unmoved."

In fact, FDR's reply, in an unfortunate lapse of courtesy, was not sent until March 1, supposedly, reported Raymond Moley, "because of an oversight by one of Roosevelt's secretaries." FDR rejected Hoover's advice, noting that "the fire is bound to spread in spite of anything that is done by mere statement."

Against this grimly etched landscape of despair, William Woodin went to work. Shuttling back and forth between New York and Washington, he met regularly with Hoover's treasury secretary, Ogden Mills, and listened to the proposals made by prominent New York bankers. Woodin reported back to FDR in detail, but to a stunned Moley, the president-elect appeared unfazed or unfocused and seemed to treat "details of the inaugural parade or . . . sittings for the artist who was painting his portrait as though each activity were of equal importance. . . . It was Will Woodin and I who tore our hair out over reports of mounting gold withdrawals and the growing number of bank suspensions and who sat up night after night pondering the possible remedies."

Woodin, along with Moley, the Brain Trust, and outgoing members of the Hoover administration's Treasury, burned the midnight oil during the fortnight leading up to the passing of the presidential baton. Each day, with increasing alarm, they reviewed the bank situation state by state. It was dizzying; it was dire; panic was everywhere. Twenty-one state legislatures and governors tried to limit the damage by declaring various forms of bank holiday or by limiting the size of withdrawals from a single bank account.

The Internal Revenue Service didn't help matters much by announcing on February 28 that bank holidays would not be considered an excuse for late payment of taxes, due on March 15. The recently passed Revenue Act of 1932 had reduced low-income exemptions and created a half-million new taxpayers (the total was now nearing two million). A single taxpayer with no dependents, making $3,500 a year (roughly what a doctor with a good practice might earn), could expect to owe $100 (up from $22.50 in 1931). Most Americans, who earned considerably less than this figure, didn't pay taxes.

As the inauguration drew ever closer, the situation continued to deteriorate. In Washington, D.C., the end of each day would find Woodin with Ogden Mills at the massive partner's desk in the treasury secretary's office reviewing the latest figures. It was depressing work. The numbers were painting a picture of financial desolation of inconceivable proportions. The flight of capital from the country was accelerating, and as gold went into hiding in increasingly massive amounts, the "dollar was wobbling on foreign exchanges." In the month leading up to the inauguration, $320 million in gold and gold certificates had been withdrawn, the equivalent of nearly fifteen and a half million ounces (today, at approximately $400 an ounce, this gold would be worth nearly $6.2 billion). And a staggering $226,310,000 of that amount was withdrawn in the final week leading up to the inauguration. If bold action was not taken, it "would mean the obliteration of the banking system."

President-elect Roosevelt and his advisers en route to Washington, D.C.,
to confer with President Hoover about the Banking Crisis. From left to right:
Admiral Cary Grayson, Norman Davis, Raymond Moley, Rex Tugwell,
William Woodin, and FDR. (Reprinted from Raymond Moley, *After Seven Years*)

On Thursday, March 2, a chilly day with sleet, Roosevelt and his party left New York for Washington on a Baltimore and Ohio train. Ahead of them were hours of discussion in the smoke-filled carriage. Since the election, the president-elect and his advisers had been besieged with ideas for solutions from congressmen, Ph.D.s, senators, crackpots, businessmen, and, as Will Woodin liked to joke, "the man with 147 pages of closely written manuscript elucidating a plan to save the country." But it was not until Friday, March 3, mere hours before FDR was to take office, that the momentous decisions were made. There had been an hour-long discussion at the White House between the president and president-elect, taut but gentlemanly, as to "whether Hoover would invoke emergency powers enabling him to control withdrawals of currency and gold, or whether it would be left to Roosevelt to do."

"I shall be waiting at my hotel, Mr. President, to learn what you decide." With that statement, at five o'clock in the afternoon, Franklin Delano Roosevelt left the White House. Along with his advisers—Woodin, Moley, Cordell Hull, Jesse Jones, and Senator Glass—FDR retreated to his suite at the Mayflower Hotel, where six hours of discussions and endless phone calls to bankers, governors, and other advisers ensued. Many prominent bankers told Roosevelt that they thought they could weather the storm, basing that opinion simply on the psychological effect of a change of administration. The bankers told the sitting president the same thing, and accordingly, at 11:30 P.M., Hoover called Roosevelt and told him he would take no action on his own. Any emergency action would be up to FDR. "Still the talk went on." Moley remembered. "We were all, by then, indescribably tense—even Roosevelt."

At 1 A.M. that same night, which was now Inauguration Day, President Hoover called FDR again to tell him that his own men were still at work over at the Treasury. Roosevelt then suggested that everyone get to bed, and the meeting was at last adjourned.

William Woodin had left but was too keyed up to go to bed. He bumped into Moley in the lobby of the hotel. "This thing is bad," he said. "Will you come over to the Treasury with me. We'll see if we can give those fellows a hand." The help offered to outgoing Secretary of the Treasury Mills and his second-in-command, Arthur Ballantine, was graciously—gratefully—accepted. Unlike their political masters, Moley recalled, "We had forgotten to be Republicans or Democrats. We were just a bunch of men trying to save the banking system."

The most recent figures indicated that come Monday morning, March 6, banks would have to be protected against runs, whether the bankers realized it or not, and that "the gold withdrawals were becoming unbearable." Moley fell asleep. Woodin did not, answers were falling into place, and at 4:20 A.M. Woodin got Governor Herbert Lehman of New York to agree, grudgingly, to a bank holiday. As dawn began to break, Woodin roused Moley, and the two men finally left to get a semblance of rest, their lonely footsteps echoing along the halls of the empty building, already, wrote Moley, "bowed under the same weariness" they would have to endure during the coming "week of nights."

Inauguration Day, March 4, 1933, was bleak in Washington, D.C.—gray, blustery, and misty. James Roosevelt steadied his father as FDR shuffled awkwardly to the center of the rostrum on the steps of the Capitol to take the oath of office from Chief Justice Charles Evans Hughes. The flags on the Capitol hung at half-mast in honor of Senator Thomas J. Walsh—the attorney-general-designate—who had died suddenly two days earlier. A tired, disheartened, and disgusted Herbert Hoover looked on as Franklin Delano Roosevelt was sworn in as President of the United States of America. The weather captured the mood of the day, the mood of the nation, the mood of the world.

Roosevelt stood at the balustrade, to which was affixed a wreath emblazoned with a powerfully built eagle, its wings outspread, standing on a tablet inscribed with the date, 1933. The new president paused for a moment, looked out on a sea of expectant, imploring faces, and began to speak. His inaugural address was short. His leonine head, uplifted chin, and powerful shoulders exuded confidence, but his face was "so grim as to seem unfamiliar to those who have long known him." His patrician drawl boomed across the crowd, a hundred thousand strong, and was picked up by the pewter-gray microphones that broadcast his sober words to the millions across the nation gathered round their radios.

With eyes flashing, he delivered words of Old Testament force, searing words, which announced "the time to speak the truth, the whole truth, frankly and boldly." He laid the blame for the failing economy squarely at the feet of the country's financial community. "They know only the rules of a generation of self-seekers. They have no vision, and when there is no vision people perish.

"Yes, the money changers have fled from their high seats in the temple of our civilization. We may now restore that temple to the ancient truths."

FDR grimly reminded the American people that "only a foolish optimist can deny the dark realities of the moment," but he was confident that "this is no unsolvable problem if we face it wisely and courageously." Tipping his hand slightly to decisions already made, he warned that the situation was so dire that while "it is hoped that the normal balance of executive and legislative authority may be wholly adequate to meet the unprecedented task before us," he would not hesitate to depart temporarily from the norm to combat the ills of the country.

Above all, he promised—in words that eerily echoed those of Hoover in November, 1929, "We must act; we must act quickly."

The bands played.

A half-million people lined the route of the inaugural parade from the Capitol to the White House. Many watched from rooftops and trees, and for a few hours the crowd forgot its troubles. Roosevelt, "his reassuring confident smile" returned, rode in his car "at the head of a parade of 18,000 men and women." For three hours, within a glass enclosure, "the new President," reported the *New York Times,* "advocate of a new deal, set an example of resolute fortitude and cheerfulness as he doffed his hat in deference to the colors and in greeting to old friends and supporters."

At 2 P.M., FDR had been in office for less than an hour. Even as the cymbals crashed and the "Franklin D. Roosevelt March"—composed by Will Woodin—was played by the Navy band during the inaugural parade, the United States Senate convened.

With Vice President John Nance Garner presiding, "by a pre-arranged signal, a White House messenger who had been waiting outside the Senate then delivered the messages containing the Cabinet nominations and Senator Robinson moved for their immediate consideration."

Secretary of State Cordell Hull was the first to be approved, without objection and without debate. Woodin was next.

Senator James Couzens of Michigan, a progressive Republican who had made millions from his close ties to Henry Ford, immediately took to his feet and raised the specter of Woodin's stock holdings and how they might affect his judgment. Other senators, also Republican, jumped to the defense of the nominee, arguing that his character was beyond reproach. They reminded their colleagues that, as required by law, Woodin would soon be signing a document stating that he owned no bank stocks and served on no corporate boards of directors. Nevertheless a brief debate on the floor ensued.

"Why can't we go ahead and confirm Mr. Woodin?" exclaimed Senator Reed. "If there are objections they can be studied later, but the President needs confirmation of his Cabinet so that it may function." And confirm him they did.

The rest of the nominees passed without objection. FDR had a cabinet, and the Senate adjourned. It was 2:55 P.M.

Roosevelt's promise of action was not empty oratory. As the festivities of Inauguration Day wore on, the same group of fatigued men who had worked through the previous night continued to formulate the new administration's policy. Now, on Saturday night, with the president returned from the inaugural galas, the hard decisions that had been made had to be implemented.

Two proclamations would be made almost simultaneously.

The president would call Congress to special session on March 9. Will Woodin guaranteed him that by then he would have emergency banking legislation drafted.

The second proclamation was pricklier. Roosevelt intended to invoke the Trading with the Enemy Act. First passed on October 6, 1917, it had been amended on September 24, 1918. A vestige of World War I, it was still in effect, and the president's authority to utilize it had already been vetted by the late attorney-general-designate Thomas J. Walsh and by Homer Cummings, his replacement. "This Act gave the President power to regulate or prohibit transactions in foreign exchange and in gold and silver, and also to prohibit the hoarding of gold, silver coin, bullion and paper currency." The problem was that despite the assurances of the Attorney General's office, officials of the Federal Reserve Bank harped "on the dubiousness of the President's authority to close the Reserve Banks."

On Sunday, March 5, the new president, in morning suit and top hat, along with members of his family, both personal and official, attended services at St. John's Episcopal Church. Then they all returned to the White House, where after lunch the Cabinet held its first meeting. Even as the policies were still being fine-tuned, the new Cabinet met at 2:30 P.M. to discuss the banking situation. Secretary of the Interior Harold Ickes wrote in his diary: "We considered and the President decided to issue the Executive Order . . . the effect of which will be to close every bank in the United States for a bank holiday of three days, to stop exportation of gold, and to put into effect other emergency regulations designed to stop the run on banks and to prevent hoarding of gold or gold certificates."

Ignorant of executive orders that had yet to be issued and in anticipation of the continuance of the monstrous drain of gold and currency from the nation's banks, emergency shipments—unheard-of *Sunday* shipments— were being organized at both the Treasury in Washington, D.C., and the United States Mint in Philadelphia. From the Treasury, millions of dollars in paper money was being sent out to banks. At the Mint, the employees had been called in to move gold coins out to Federal Reserve Banks, Branches, and the Treasury. It was the last consignment of gold coins that would ever leave the Mint.

❖   ❖   ❖

Throughout the day, Woodin met with hand-wringing bankers from around the country, who were scared of action but more scared of inaction. He listened patiently to Federal Reserve Bank officials who continued to doubt the president's authority to close the Reserve Banks until Raymond Moley, exasperated, finally "broke in with the remark that if two Secretaries of the Treasury, and the Governor of the Federal Reserve Board couldn't order the closing of the Reserve banks, who, in God's name, could?"

A draft of the executive order had already been prepared for Hoover by Ogden Mills and Arthur Ballantine. FDR with Woodin, Moley, and Cummings reworked this document, laboring far into the night. The proclamation of a bank holiday would "prevent complete chaos" and buy the administration time until Congress met and a concrete plan to revive the banks could be presented. On that Sunday, however, what the new plan would include was still unknown, even to those who were to propose it.

On Sunday at 11 P.M., Presidential Proclamation 2039 was released to the press. It was to take effect two hours later. It had already been another brutal, exhausting day, and there was still more to be done. Using the "swift and staccato" action he felt was essential, Woodin wired the Mints (Philadelphia, San Francisco, and Denver) to ban the payout of any gold. He dictated regulations to accompany and clarify the president's order. And because the U.S. Territories were administered by the Department of the Interior, he called Harold Ickes "just before midnight . . . to ask [for] authority to sign [his] name to cablegrams to the Governors of Alaska, Hawaii and the Virgin Islands" to alert them to the banking situation.

Eventually, William H. Woodin, his throat sore, retired to bed, where it was his habit to strum his guitar and think.

On Monday morning, March 6, 1933, America had banner headlines with its bacon, eggs, and coffee. It was the first flurry of what would be a blizzard of streamers in the weeks and months to come. "ROOSEVELT ORDERS 4-DAY BANK HOLIDAY, PUTS EMBARGO ON GOLD, CALLS CONGRESS," shouted the *New York Times*. Across town, the tabloid *Daily News* used a bigger, bolder font and was blunt: "ROOSEVELT FIXES GOLD EMBARGO." While in Philadelphia, the *Inquirer* was more expository: "ROOSEVELT PROCLAIMS 4-DAY BANK HOLIDAY, ORDERS EMBARGO TO GUARD NATION'S GOLD; CALLS CONGRESS INTO SESSION THURSDAY."

Swift and Staccato Action: The Great Depression

Bleary-eyed readers waded through the grave, official, condemnatory text of the presidential proclamation. It was loaded with a bewildering litany of "Whereas there . . . ," "Whereas it . . . ," and "Therefore I . . . ," which the newspapers and magazines boiled down to four points:

A four-day national bank holiday was ordered, and with so many states already having endured their own, it needed little explaining. In fact, as reported in *News-Week* magazine, it sounded positively cozy, "like throwing a huge blanket on top of 49 smaller blankets . . . to quench the rising conflagration of a bank-run panic [that] threatened the very structure of government."

An issuance of scrip—temporary, emergency money—backed by the assets of the banking institutions was planned to compensate for the shortage of circulating currency. Although scrip had been used successfully in New York during the Panic of 1907, it was still unofficial money that an already skittish public might reject. In the three days ahead, Woodin would seek and find a more palatable solution to be included in the Emergency Banking Act.

"Special trust accounts" could be opened at banks, which could then be drawn on at will. While this measure was explained as a means of providing a "safe depository" for those who were now holding dangerously large sums of hoarded cash, it was actually a cleverly worded ploy to encourage the most suspicious, easily panicked citizens into putting their money back into banking channels.

Finally, the most baldly dictated imposition was a complete embargo on the withdrawal of gold—not only from banks, but also, unless specifically licensed by the secretary of the treasury, from the United States Government itself. Gold exports were prohibited, and the hoarding of gold was punishable by a ten-thousand-dollar fine and up to ten years in prison. The order was dire but somewhat ambiguous. What constituted a hoard was not defined and "gold" meant monetary gold—coins, gold-backed currency, and bullion—not jewelry, although this exclusion wasn't specified.

Never before in the nation's history had a new president taken such sweeping, dramatic, controversial, and complex actions immediately upon taking office. He had invoked war powers and assumed quasi-dictatorial powers. Yet Americans across the country took a collective sigh and began to adjust accordingly. At least they now knew the rules of the game.

The Emergency Banking Bill, which was being crafted during nineteen-hour working sessions, was due in Congress in three days. Woodin was a dervish, a problem-solver, who never lost his head or his sense of humor.

"Not once did his gray toupee slip askew in the excitement," reported *Time* magazine. He felt that conventional solutions were preferable to controversial ones. It was essential that as many banks as possible be reopened as soon as possible, and he believed that in the short run "we were facing a problem of public psychology more acutely than we were facing a problem of finance." Answers to the blizzard of queries and problems had to be addressed, guidance and assurance had to be given to the American people, and to foster an unafraid citizenry, "a man-to-man appeal for public confidence by the President himself" was essential.

When help was offered to Roosevelt by Freeman Gosden and Charles Correll, the creators and voices of *Amos 'n' Andy,* he took it. The wildly popular radio program devoted an episode that week to "a message instilling-confidence" that the president felt was "decidedly effective." On March 8, smiling, joking, his teeth clenched around the cigarette holder that held a smoldering Camel, FDR held the first of his countless press conferences. On March 12, somber but soothing, he reached personally into American homes through the radio broadcast of his first fireside chat.

Even though public confidence might be growing, policy still had to be established. Woodin and Moley were legislative novices, and so they relied heavily on the sterling technical advice offered by Hoover's men, former Treasury Secretary Ogden Mills and his assistants, Arthur Ballantine and F. G. Atwalt. The plan for the Emergency Banking Act taking shape, however, was largely their own.

Woodin, his finger on the pulse of the public's fears, disliked the idea of scrip, even though the president's executive order had authorized issuing it. Unable to sleep despite the arduous hours, his sore throat growing worse, he sat in bed in the wee hours of Tuesday morning, reading, dozing, and playing his guitar. The answer hit him.

"We [the Treasury] can issue currency against the sound assets of the banks. The Reserve Act lets us print all we'll need. And it won't frighten people. It won't look like stage money. It'll be money that looks like money." It was a simple, elegant solution. FDR listened and nodded his approval after less than twenty minutes. The next two days were spent hashing out the details.

At noon on Thursday, March 9, 1933, a special session of Congress convened. Without time to print up a final version, a folded-up newspaper was used to represent the bill symbolically. It was introduced in the House of Representatives at 1:40 P.M. and was passed, without dissent, at 4:05. The Senate began debate on it at 4:30—Louisiana Senator Huey "Kingfish" Long and Carter Glass went at each other snappishly—and passed it, 73 to 7, at 7:23. At 8:36 P.M., with Will Woodin grinning at his side, the Movietone cameras rolling, Franklin Delano Roosevelt signed the Emergency Banking Act of 1933 into law.

Its provisions included approval and confirmation of the president's previous actions—the executive orders. It permitted the issuance of Federal Reserve banknotes, allowed for the progressive reopening of banks, and radically expanded the president's power over all aspects of foreign exchange, banking, and gold ownership.

The *New York Times* called it "DICTATORSHIP OVER GOLD."

Because of the complexity involved in checking the books of the nation's banks, the bank holiday was extended to March 13, when the first, healthiest, banks were allowed to open their doors and conduct business. The effect was electric. The people's confidence was renewed, and money and gold started to pour back into the system.

Moley was deeply impressed by the new treasury secretary, who, he knew, "was far from well." "Capitalism," he wrote, "was saved in eight days, and no other single factor in its salvation was half so important as the imagination and sturdiness and common sense of Will Woodin."

CHAPTER 3

Gold Rush in Reverse

———◆———

AT 1 A.M. ON MARCH 6, 1933, PRESIDENTIAL PROCLAMATION 2039 became effective and the United States went off the gold standard. Or did it? Your view depended largely on which newspaper you read, to whom you listened, and what definition of the gold standard was applied.

Perhaps not wanting to discombobulate the public further or simply unsure of the matter himself, William Woodin went on record the day the gold embargo was announced: "It is ridiculous and misleading to say that we have gone off the gold standard." His opinion was echoed by former Under-Secretary of the Treasury Arthur Ballantine and Senator Key Pittman of Nevada, who, more emphatically, interpreted the action as "a protection of the gold standard."

Others disagreed. The New York *Daily News* pointed out, quite rightly, that as the government itself had stopped honoring its obligations in gold, it was "a technical abandonment of the gold standard." In the *New York Times*, an unnamed but "noted banking authority" looked into his crystal ball and saw a bleak future for the gold standard: "Some persons may not redeposit their gold, in which case they will be forced to bury it, because it [will be] of utterly no use to them."

Two days later, during his first press conference, the president leaned back in his chair and further fanned the flames of uncertainty. He told nearly 150 reporters who crammed into his office that "as long as nobody asks me whether we are off the gold standard or gold basis, that is all right, because nobody knows what the gold basis or gold standard really is." This statement may not have been strictly accurate, but it suited FDR to say so.

Until March 6, 1933, the United States was the only country in the world that still adhered to the "full" gold standard. England had adopted a modified version in 1925, and France had followed suit three years later. The full standard specified: "The actual monetary unit is a weight of gold . . . there is free and unlimited coinage of gold . . . there is free movement of gold into and out of the arts . . . all other kinds of money are redeemed freely on demand in gold . . . there are no restrictions upon the exportation or importation of gold from or into a country . . . gold is generally full legal tender for all debts, public and private."

The argument about whether or not the United States had abandoned the gold standard, and if so, when, swirled and eddied for weeks, months, and even into succeeding years and decades. The administration, however, whether it admitted it to the public or not, knew that it had taken the nation off gold. Following a Cabinet meeting devoted to the economic situation, Secretary of the Interior Harold Ickes wrote in his diary on April 18, 1933, that the "United States, in effect went off the gold standard March 4 [sic], at the time of the banking crisis." He went on to say that this was not a conclusion he had reached by himself. "I realize that I don't have an economic mind myself, so in matters of this sort I simply listen carefully and go along."

In Will Woodin's case, the ebb and flow of the argument, along with the finality of the departure from the gold standard, was driven home once and for all on April 20. At a meeting in the White House, the president looked at him with mock severity and said, "Mr. Secretary, I have some very bad news for you. I have to announce to you the serious fact that the United States has gone off the gold standard." Woodin, ever goodnatured, "threw up both hands, opened his eyes wide and exclaimed: 'My heavens! What, again?'"

Roosevelt's proclamation "broke every historical precedent." As he assumed what the New York *Daily News* called "the dictatorial powers of a war-time President" in a peacetime battle for his nation's economic recovery, gold was in his sights. Although the language of the initial presidential order did not demand specifically that citizens immediately return their gold, it made hoarding of gold a crime punishable by up to ten years in prison and a $10,000 fine. A "hoard" was left undefined. "Gold" meant coins, bullion, and gold-backed paper money. The hesi-

36

The front page Monday, March 6, 1933. Photographs of the president and his family leaving church as millions of dollars in bills are loaded onto trucks at the Treasury to be sent to banks. A busy Sunday as Roosevelt's "dictatorship over gold" begins. (©New York Daily News, L.P., reprinted with permission)

tancy with which most Americans had embraced the use of paper currency at the turn of the century had all but evaporated by the end of the First World War. By 1933 in the United States, most gold that was used in daily transactions circulated not in coin form but as gold certificates—beautifully engraved paper notes, with portions printed in yellow to make their lofty status immediately recognizable.

With the stroke of the presidential pen that March night, gold coins could no longer be melted down to make fountain-pen nibs, the government would no longer repay its domestic debts in gold, gold certificates would no longer be redeemed for the glistening metal, gold could no longer be freely taken from the country, and the Mint would no longer sell or pay out gold to any and all who wanted it.

The only "free" movement of gold that the administration desired was one way—from the private sector back into the government's coffers.

The first step FDR and Woodin took in replenishing the nation's gold supply was to staunch the flow from the Treasury and the Federal Reserve system. Instructions poured down through the system like a waterfall: from the president to the secretary of the treasury to the Mints and the Federal Reserve system. All were issued in the early morning hours on March 6.

The secretary of the treasury wrote to the director of the Mint Bureau, Robert J. Grant, a Coloradan who had served nearly ten years: "The President of the United States has issued an Executive Order declaring a complete bank holiday in the United States for the period Monday, March 6, to Thursday, March 9, 1933, both dates inclusive, subject to such exceptions as may be permitted under regulations to be prescribed by the Secretary of the Treasury with the approval of the President.

"During the continuance of such bank holiday, unless otherwise directed, you are requested to instruct all mint and assay offices to pay gold in any form only under license issued by the Secretary of the Treasury. This does not prohibit the deposit of gold and the usual payment therefor."

As instructed, Grant wired all the Mints and Assay Offices with a verbatim transcript of Woodin's communication. In effect, the Mint would continue to accept deposits of gold coins, bullion, and gold certificates, for which the depositor would be paid in paper currency or coins that were neither backed by, nor made of, gold. The Mint was prohibited from paying out gold in any form—coin, currency, or bullion—without written permission from the secretary of the treasury.

Identical orders—permitting the deposit of gold but banning its withdrawal—appropriately tailored to fit each institution's specific function, were sent to the Treasurer of the United States as well as Federal Reserve Banks and Branches around the country. Each bore the signature of the president.

All of these instructions forbade the egress of gold from the government. Now it only remained a question of how to encourage—chide, bully, and coerce—citizens to take their own gold coins and yellow notes back to the Treasury. In theory, the recall of gold seemed simple. The imposition of penalties for gold hoarding, without defining how much gold constituted a hoard, was a start. The language of the internal orders was direct by government standards but still confusing to the citizens it affected. And Woodin, new to government, quickly learned the hydralike character of legislation and its practical consequences. Every simple directive the Treasury issued was met with a barrage of questions from the public as well as from the affected government agencies. Answering them bred yet more queries. Within twenty-four hours the Treasury was besieged by inquiries on every imaginable issue, all begging for immediate interpretation. Woodin had his "officials . . . working at top speed to

38

ILLEGAL TENDER

prepare additional information" and suggested to the public that they direct their questions not to the Treasury itself but to the specific institutions from which the answers would, in good time, be provided.

But confusion reigned for days. For every letter of inquiry sent to the Treasury or the Mint, there seemed to be a new or different answer, often appearing contradictory (but echoing the constant fine-tuning of the edicts), as seen in the following internal Treasury Department wires to the Philadelphia Mint. March 7: "AUTHORIZED TO ISSUE GOLD COIN OR BARS IN EXCHANGE FOR GOLD BULLION RECEIVED." April 12, to the same institution: "ISSUE OF GOLD COIN OR BARS IN EXCHANGE FOR GOLD BULLION *NOT* [italics supplied] AUTHORIZED UNDER PRESIDENTS EXECUTIVE ORDER APRIL FIFTH."

Regulations were being written, interpreted, and amended on a near daily basis, and the replies from the director of the Mint to the public reflected this fluidity. A March 15, 1933, letter to Lewis A. Froman, a Buffalo, New York, economics professor, clarified a recent exception made for unmanufactured gold needed by industry. "If a depositor presents gold scrap in the form of jewelry or dental scrap and asks to have the equivalent in gold returned, this would be done." On March 17, 1933, F. H. Jackson, Atlanta, Georgia, received the most basic of answers: "No gold or gold certificates may be paid out."

The questions, answers, and pressures were unrelenting. But Woodin, a small man who liked to chuckle, was keeping up with the demands and enjoying himself, despite the sore throat that had been nagging him since before the inauguration.

Roosevelt kept gold on the front pages day by day. In this way he also kept the pressure on the public. The ban on the export of gold was enforced vigorously. On March 7, the *New York Times* reported that the French Line steamship *Paris* had been due to sail with $9 million in fleeing gold but was caught in the nick of time. The shippers were not identified but were said to be a number of banks and one well-heeled individual.

March 8 headlines around the country called for hoarded gold to be returned to the Federal Reserve Banks, but the president continued to be vague about what or how much gold counted as a hoard, and this frightened people. The papers reported what the administration already knew, that the Federal Reserve Bank had kept records of all the larger gold withdrawals since 1915 and that recently, "all those who went to the Reserve Banks to get gold coin were asked to fill out withdrawal slips giving their names and addresses." Whether this practice was legal or not was apparently a moot point in those perilous times. Banks were clamoring for the imposition of taxes on gold hoards as a means of smoking them out.

The administration's tattoo to force the return of gold continued. Everyone from the increasingly nervous little guy to the indignant wealthy was affected. Roosevelt imposed an arbitrary time limit: all those who had withdrawn gold since February 1 and not returned it by March 13 would be reported.

The flow back to the Federal Reserve vaults started as a trickle.

Within the first forty-eight hours, although the actual amounts of gold returned by citizens and companies across the country were not precisely known, a few million dollars was reported; it was an encouraging start. But Woodin's directives had neglected certain fundamental needs, and dentists suddenly "found their supply of twenty-four-carat gold from the United States Assay Offices almost completely cut off . . . except for what might be obtained for deposits of sweepings and old or salvaged gold."

On March 10 the passage of the Emergency Banking Act the previous day, in record time, was the banner news across the nation. It was also the first time the extent of the deluge of gold back to the Federal Reserve was reported in depth, and the news was astonishing. More than $65 million had been returned in the three days since the president's initial decree. On March 9 alone, $30 million in gold was turned in: $700,000 in Philadelphia, $163,000 in Richmond, and about a quarter of a million in Cleveland alone. The rush had just begun.

Newspapers reported that it was not just businesses and wealthy skeptics redepositing their golden hoards. Law-abiding, everyday citizens went to the banks not thinking of themselves as hoarders but wanting to do the right thing. "They came with little bags, briefcases, paper bundles, boxes or bulging pockets. Many had only a few coins, while others had bags of thousands of dollars of double eagles." These bags would have included examples of Saint-Gaudens' designs dating from 1907 and those they had replaced, which had been in circulation from 1850 through 1907. People brought in souvenir gold coins that had been given to them as commemorative gifts, the "few odd coins left over from Christmas," and "one important banker, informed of the new law, reflectively drew from his pocket the gold piece he had received at the last meeting of directors he had attended and fingered it gingerly." The fear of prosecution was spreading, even though only days earlier it had been legal to be paid in gold.

Next the government broadened its reach for the precious metal to include withdrawals made over the past two years. But FDR still did not define what hoarding meant. Even during the hurried Senate debate on the Emergency Banking Bill, Roosevelt's ally Carter Glass commented on the arbitrary nature of the gold-hoarding provision. "I do not know who

*March 10, 1933. Unhappy but law-abiding citizens heeding Roosevelt's orders
and returning their gold coins to the Federal Reserve Bank of New York.*

(General Research Division, The New York Public Library, Astor, Lenox & Tilden Foundations)

there is with wit or wisdom enough to define hoarding. Under that pro-vision of the bill any Senator who drew his salary [about $173 per week] three or four days ago and kept it in his pocket might be regarded as a hoarder and fined $10,000 and put in the penitentiary for ten years."

The Emergency Banking Bill, once passed, not only confirmed but also expanded the president's powers. It was the first time the recall of gold was so bluntly and officially stated. It required "any and all individ-uals . . . to pay and deliver to the Treasurer of the United States any or all gold coin, gold bullion, and gold certificates." In return, "an equivalent amount *of any other form* [italics supplied] of coin or currency coined or issued under the laws of the United States [would] be given in exchange for [the] surrendered gold."

On March 10, 1933, the "gold stampede in reverse" was on. In New York, men and women, frightened by the draconian punishments threat-

Gold Rush in Reverse

The Federal Reserve Bank of New York in the 1930s. Appropriately located at 33 Liberty Street.
(Federal Reserve Bank of New York Archives)

ened by the government, braving gale-force winds and temperatures in the 20s, nervously descended at dawn on the Federal Reserve Bank of New York at 33 Liberty Street. They quietly lined up outside next to the massive rusticated stone walls and waited to enter between the two enormous iron lanterns that flanked the entrance. Police and bank guards kept a close eye on the scene, inside the building and out. Taxis and private cars pulled up. Carrying the gold in satchels, boxes, and bags, some people struggled under the dead weight of the metal. They waited until 8 A.M., when at last the doors opened. Tellers at twenty-two receiving windows beneath elegantly vaulted ceilings counted as fast as they could, paying out banknotes in exchange and scribbling receipts, which patrons—now relieved of their gold and guilt—carried away patriotically into the wind-whipped canyons of downtown Manhattan.

By 10:30 A.M., an estimated fifteen hundred people had made deposits; by 2 P.M. it was three thousand; and by the time the cages closed

ILLEGAL TENDER

at 5 P.M., two hours late, at least four thousand people had visited the bank. There had been "little smiling, virtually no laughter and no disorder."

It was a scene repeated across the nation, and, as the grip of the Depression was unyielding, etched a stark contrast with the grim reality that so many other Americans faced with resignation. As the haves lined up in frustration to deliver their golden bounty to the government and were compensated in return, the millions more—the have-nots—waited shivering in the endless breadlines for a scrap of crust and a bowl of thin soup merely to survive.

On that Friday the New York Fed took in $20 million in gold, more than half of it in coin; in Philadelphia it was $907,000; $257,000 in Minneapolis. The drama was repeated across the country, in Kansas City, Cleveland, Atlanta, and San Francisco. Deposits of gold large and small flooded back into the system—into Federal Reserve Banks, commercial banks, and post offices. The total for the first week was $100 million, approximately 1.25 percent of all Federal spending in 1933. Americans were supporting their new leader.

The banking emergency continued, but there were signs of abatement. The banks, at last, began to reopen, the most fiscally sound first. Confidence as well as gold was flowing back into the system. With a bit of bait and switch, the president extended the deadline for gold returns by another four days, until St. Patrick's Day. Perhaps a rainbow would emerge from these pots of gold.

March, 1933, wore on. Los Angeles was rocked by a deadly earthquake. Lou Gehrig and Babe Ruth, now near the end of his career, came to terms with the New York Yankees (the $23,000 cut in pay the fading Bambino took still left him with more than the $21,500 Gehrig, then in his prime, signed for and substantially more than what remained after the $500 pay cut United States senators accepted). The Senate hearings into "bad banking"—cozy insider dealings and speculative manipulation of the stock market—were getting under way. On the funny pages, Ignatz continued to hurl bricks at Krazy Kat (who loved it). Excitement was brewing with the anticipated legalization of beer, although the complete repeal of Prohibition was still months away. And returning gold to the government was becoming increasingly chic and patriotic.

During the first seven days following FDR's initial proclamation, the total gold returned to the Reserve Banks was $300 million. Ship passengers were warned by customs agents, but "there were no orders from Washington to search for gold." The postmaster general reminded citizens that shipping gold out of the country through the mail was forbidden. Maryland threatened to publish lists of known hoarders whose names had turned up on the carefully monitored gold withdrawal slips. But in spite of the government's threats, no famous hoarders came to light. The returns proceeded with resigned calm.

Slowly some of the kinks were ironed out of the system and order began to replace chaos. No longer would dentists—or, more to the point, their patients—have to worry; until formal licensing procedures were developed, Regulation Number 25, signed by Woodin and Roosevelt on March 13, permitted them and other businesses to get a supply of "unmanufactured gold" upon submission of an affidavit proving their need. Even the Internal Revenue Service magnanimously reversed its earlier decision and extended the income tax filing date by sixteen days— but it would charge late filers six percent interest on the extra time.

Yet many people were still uncertain about what they should do. The government continued to send mixed signals. Woodin went to the press and explained that the government was primarily after big hoarders and that they would be hunted down. "The fellow who has $10, $20 or $50 in his pocket will not be bothered." But days later, the White House released a letter to the press from "An Italo-American" that made the front page of the *New York Times.* An unemployed Brooklyn girl had sent Franklin Roosevelt a five-dollar gold piece and a little gold chain, her only jewelry, "which [she] was keeping for the sake of its sentimental value." Unaware that the government would exchange cash for her gold but believing that she was a hoarder and had "been harming the country right along," she had sent them to her president. "This little offering of mine is just like a drop in the bucket, but every big sum is made of little ones." She closed by noting that "a healthy America means a healthy world."

Roosevelt himself was tickled with the letter. He made it known to the press that the government would try to find the anonymous writer and return the gold chain, which didn't fall into the hoarding category. But the coin, apparently, did, and its return was not considered. Both items were sent to the Treasury with a note: "The enclosures speak for themselves and I am delighted that the Treasury has a spot for such things."

The increasingly cheerful president was also exceedingly pleased with the actions of his Treasury Secretary, William Woodin. He freely sang his praises and acknowledged that the industrialist, collector, and composer had borne the brunt of the enormous burdens of the new administration. When, at his first news conference, FDR suggested to a reporter that the specifics of a question on controlled currency would be best addressed to Woodin, he gleefully joined in the explosion of laughter when the newsman shot back, "He's too busy." A week later, in summing up the early successes of the administration's first ten days, he told the gathered journalists: "Off the record . . . there is one person responsible for its working so well and that is Bill Woodin. He has done a perfectly grand job and has been up day and night, literally. It is really wonderful the way Bill came down here and took a hold of a thing he had never had any experience at before and I think what he has done would be a credit to anybody."

His sentiment was shared by many. During the crisis, Woodin's now chronically sore throat had continued to bother him and worsen, but he maintained the sense of humor and wit that, with his boundless energy, slight frame, small mustache, pointed chin, and bright, sparkling eyes, caused many to describe him as elfin. The *New York Times* wrote, almost with a sense of disappointment, "One of the curiosities of the new Secretary's personal and official triumph is that he is one of those men who laugh constantly . . . [and] that his good-nature does not mask incapacity."

Indeed not. By March 20, the gold haul was up to $400 million—and the deadline was extended yet again, this time for another week. Patriotic women's clubs started running "swap shops" purchasing old gold, including jewelry, trinkets, old eyeglass frames, school pins, Phi Beta Kappa keys, and even a few gold teeth. In Hastings-on-Hudson, New York, one club took in $300 the first day, while the American Women's Association, on West Fifty-seventh Street in Manhattan, came in at $210. The gold was all turned in to the Federal Reserve Bank in New York.

On March 22, Woodin visited the Fed for the first time since stepping down from its board just after Roosevelt had asked him to serve as Treasury Secretary. He told the assembled press it seemed like a hundred years, not mere weeks, and thanked them for their cooperation, which had helped make his difficult problems easier. But, he told them, with a puckish grin, he was surprised by how much was expected of him. When he got to Washington, he said, he assumed he would rise at 10 A.M., have "luncheon with an Ambassador," dictate a few letters, and leave the office for a round of golf at 4 P.M. "Instead," he said, "we all work until 4 o'clock in the morning and get back to the office by 9 next morning."

As March closed, other news items started crowding the gold stories. Speakeasies were getting bolder, thirsty citizens couldn't wait for the legalization of 3.2 percent beer after thirteen years of Prohibition. The Collegiate School in New York, the oldest school in the country, was celebrating what it said was its three hundredth anniversary (it was in fact its three hundred and fifth). The *Akron,* the finest dirigible in the world, tragically crashed in a lightning storm. And a new appointment for the government was announced. Nellie Tayloe Ross, vice chairman of the Democratic National Committee, former governor of Wyoming, was reported to be "slated to be made United States Treasurer," a job she did not get. Instead she was appointed Director of the Bureau of the United States Mint, a post she would hold for the next twenty years.

But on April 5, Roosevelt's and Woodin's patience with the gold hoarders ran out. $633 million had been returned in a month, but the government estimated that a billion dollars in gold was still outstanding: $600 million in currency and $400 million in coin and bullion.

On April 3 the president forwarded to Attorney General Homer Cummings a copy of a new "Executive Order which I have under consideration forbidding the hoarding of gold coin, gold bullion and gold certificates." He asked Cummings, "Please give me your opinion as soon as possible as to whether this order complies in all respects with the provisions of the Constitution . . . and all other applicable laws." Within twenty-four hours the attorney general gave the thumbs-up, and on April 5, 1933, Franklin Delano Roosevelt issued Executive Order No. 6102.

The White House lauded the "many persons throughout the United States [who] hastened to turn in gold in their possession as an expression of their faith in the Government and as a result of their desire to be helpful in the emergency." But it chastised those "who have waited for the Government to issue a formal order for the return of gold in their possession. Such an order is being issued today."

For the first time the order spelled out what constituted a hoard of gold in the government's eyes: anything more than one hundred dollars. It also gave a nod to coin collectors, who had been wringing their hands with nervous anxiety for a full month, wondering if their cherished possessions might be included in the recall. William Woodin, himself a renowned numismatist, had assembled—and sold more than twenty years before—one of the finest collections of United States gold coins ever known. It was no surprise therefore that Secretary Woodin weighed in on behalf of his fellow collectors. The executive order included language that provided an exemption for "gold coins having a recognized special value to collectors of rare and unusual coins."

The news of this recall was not given the same urgent coverage as the previous pronouncements. Hoarding was becoming stale news, and, like the boy who cried wolf, the deadlines were forever being extended—now it was May 1. The order made the front pages, but barely. It was

ILLEGAL TENDER

Two presidents who had an effect on America's gold coins: the only known photograph of Theodore and Franklin Roosevelt together. 1914, Syracuse, New York. The man they are flanking is one of TR's attorneys.

(Franklin Delano Roosevelt Presidential Library)

shoved off to a corner on the broadsheets to make room for a more important headline: "BEER IS LEGAL AT MIDNIGHT."

Throughout the rest of 1933 another dozen executive orders, radio addresses, and joint resolutions of Congress followed. More tightening of the noose around gold. More closing of loopholes. Less flexibility. Finally, as the new year dawned, these moves culminated in the Gold Reserve Act of 1934, which was signed by FDR on January 30. In the end, it was decreed, all gold, with very limited licensed or stipulated exceptions, belonged to the Government of the United States of America.

With this act, gold coins were no longer a part of the American monetary system. It was the end of a grand tradition. The birth of America's gold coins had been an integral part of debates by founding fathers Alexander Hamilton and Thomas Jefferson over the establishment of a United

47

States Mint in the eighteenth century. It had been Jefferson who had first suggested issuing a ten-dollar gold piece in 1784 and Hamilton who a few years later had named it the eagle, because, he admitted, he could think of nothing better. Now, 139 years after the Mint's first meager delivery of 744 five-dollar gold pieces (half eagles) on July 31, 1795—which had on one side a charmingly homely, naive Liberty wearing a turbanlike cap and on the other an underfed eagle clinging precariously to a branch—the nation's unwavering reliance on the uncorruptible yellow metal as a circulating medium was over. Gold was the fuel the discovery of which in 1848 in vast amounts in California had created great personal fortunes—including those of Leland Stanford, Collis Huntington and Darius Ogden Mills—and had helped to propel an awkward, insular, and adolescent nation into the ranks of some of the wealthiest countries on earth.

Ironically, Franklin Roosevelt rang the death knell for the coins whose innovative designs his exuberant cousin Theodore had battled so zealously to achieve. Will Woodin, the passionate collector, was extinguishing the very coins he loved. But in the battle to save the nation's economy, there is no record that either man gave these ironies a moment's thought.

FDR and Woodin had overlooked something else. In their first urgent rush to right the foundering economy in March, 1933, the president and his treasury secretary had ordered the Mint not to pay out any gold. But nobody had instructed it to stop making gold coins. So the Mint had kept to its bureaucratic schedule striking twenty-dollar gold pieces—double eagles—bearing the date 1933. From March through May, as the new coins rang to life, they were massed in the blackness of the Mint's vaults, sequestered from their sisters. They were the last gold coins struck by America. Her last treasure.

In Baltimore, in the late winter of 1934, while reading and rustling though the pages of newspaper reports in the huge, elegant, American-walnut-lined library of his mansion, Evergreen, the Honorable John Work Garrett, a collector of coins, recognized the historic ramifications of the passage of the Gold Reserve Act of 1934. If it was possible, he thought, if it was legal, he would make the last gold coins struck by the United States a welcome, important addition to his cabinet.

Garrett's family had expanded the Baltimore and Ohio Railroad, and his grandfather had essentially run the railroad for the North during the Civil War. Lincoln had called him "the right arm of the Federal Government." Wealthy beyond imagination and acknowledged as the owner of one of the greatest coin collections in existence, John Garrett was a career diplomat. He had served five presidents and was well acquainted with most of those in the corridors of power, past and present—William Woodin and he had served together on the board of the American Numismatic Society for years.

Garrett's coin collection had grown through two generations. From dealers and auctioneers the Garretts had taken their pick of the finest, the rarest, and the most expensive. From the United States Government the Garretts had added new, everyday coins to their collection, first directly from the Mint and later, as the regulations changed, from the Treasurer's office. They paid face value, postage, and, for special issues, a trifling premium.

John Garrett, gray and bald, with a Vandyke beard and piercing pale blue eyes, walked awkwardly with a cane. When he was a child, a tubercular hip had made him focus on less strenuous activities than those of his brother Robert, who became America's first gold medalist in the first modern Olympics. John would collect a different kind of gold. Coins, books, and natural history exercised his mind; through them the world was his.

The events and proclamations of 1933 and their effect on gold ownership, which had culminated only days earlier on January 30, intrigued him and awakened his curiosity. On February 2, 1934, Garrett wrote to Wayte Raymond, America's foremost coin dealer:

> It might be interesting for me to add to my collection, if it is not against the law, the last gold pieces. $20.00/$10.00/$5.00/$2.50.
>
> I do not know whether any or all of these were struck last year, but perhaps if you can come across the actual last ones, in [proof] or uncirculated condition, you might put them aside for me.

Raymond, whose contacts were legion, checked around, certainly with his well-connected sometime partner in Philadelphia, James G. Macallister. All in vain. He finally replied to Garrett on March 29, 1934: "In reference to your inquiry about gold coins, would say that 10's and 20's were struck in 1933 but I have never been able to get them."

No one could.

Yet.

The Third United States Mint in Philadelphia. Where the 1933 double eagles were made. (Author)

CHAPTER 4

Just a Factory: Making Money

———◆———

IN 1933, THE BUILDING THAT HOUSED THE PHILADELPHIA MINT WAS entering middle age. It bore the weighty gravitas of the nineteenth century with dignity but was showing its years. Clad in yellow-gray Maine granite flecked with pink, the three-story building was a city block long and half as deep; it faced northeast on Spring Garden Street between Sixteenth and Seventeenth streets. At the top of the front steps, massive bronze doors studded with snarling lion's head protomes greeted the few visitors that still came to call. The three-bay arched entrance supported four two-story fluted columns of no strict architectural order—an Ionic scroll uneasily rubbed shoulders with some Corinthian acanthus leaves. The entablature above read: UNITED STATES MINT.

The foundations for the Mint, Philadelphia's third, were begun in 1897, dug by hand on swampy land that had once been part of an estate owned by Alexander Hamilton's family. Built at a cost of more than $2 million, the third Mint was opened for business in 1901, very much a product of the Gilded Age.

The halls of the ground floor were covered in heavily veined white Italian marble. A cascading formal double stairway flanked by brightly gilt torchères and guarded by marble eagles with spread wings led to a two-story rotunda, which was faced with porphyry-red marble from Vermont. There the Mint's own fabulous collection of coins and medals was initially displayed in elaborately carved, glazed mahogany cases.

The lobby's squared columns and the stepped pilasters supported a web of vaulting, groin and barrel, which led off to long corridors, left and right. The vaulting was covered in gold-backed Tiffany glass mosaics edged with patterns of olive leaves, so the electric light that came from the garlanded, frosted suspended glass globes danced, reflected, and dazzled.

In the lobby, above the doors to the Visitors' Waiting Room and the Guides' Room, was a pair of lunettes also decorated with mosaics. The designs were freely adapted from frescoes discovered in Pompeii in the House of the Vettii. They had been painted some time after 62 A.D., buried and preserved by the eruption of Vesuvius in 79 A.D., and excavated in 1895. In the originals, a merry band of chubby, naked, winged *erotes* illustrated the process of making coins in ancient Rome—melting, weighing, and striking. Here in the Mint they were metamorphosed into clean, tunic-wearing children happy in their work (apparently the nudity of the *amorini* was more offensive to the early twentieth-century eye than the specter of child labor and pre-pubescent youth pouring molten metal). Designed by William B. Van Ingen for Louis Comfort Tiffany, whose firm had been commissioned by the Mint, their cost was included in the staggering sum of forty thousand dollars for the ceiling and walls of the entry hall and flanking corridors.

When first built, the opulence of these public areas, their creative brilliance and excess drew visitors from far and wide and shouted to the world that the streets of the United States must be lined with gold—certainly the Mint's ceilings were. This gilded Mint was a far cry from the original Mint, the first public building authorized by the Congress of an infant American republic in 1792. It had been plain, a three-story brick building with dormer windows and a standing-seam tin roof, that had served the fledgling nation well for nearly forty years. By 1903, when the new Mint became fully operational, the first Mint building still stood, forlorn, soon to be razed, its glory days three-quarters of a century past. Stripped of its dormers and its pride, it no longer housed an engine of the nation's economy but Fauth and Ogden's Cosmos Cigar Factory and the Chambers Umbrella Factory.

By 1933 the original interior opulence of the third Mint had also faded somewhat. Tiffany's art had fallen out of favor, and the now dusty halls were no longer admired. Ten years earlier, because of security fears, Secretary of the Treasury Andrew Mellon, founder of the National Gallery and a firm believer in a monumental, imperial Washington, D.C., ordered that the irreplaceable Mint collection, cases and all, be removed to the Smithsonian Institution. Absent the collection, the Mint contained little to draw visitors. It had become nothing more than a factory.

Like virtually every other business in America, the United States Mint was not immune to the Depression. When people were broke, there was little reason to make new money, and year after year as the demand faded, production followed suit. In 1929 the Philadelphia Mint had produced over a quarter of a billion shining new coins, copper, silver, and gold. By 1932 it was down to just over twenty-five million, and in 1933 it would make even fewer. The branch mints faced similarly bleak conditions. The old Granite Lady, as the San Francisco Mint was lovingly nicknamed, had opened for business in 1874, another child of the Gold Rush, but had not struck gold coins since 1930. In 1933 its entire output would be limited to half-dollars worth less than $900,000. Denver, which had been operating since 1906 and had last struck gold in 1931, would mint little more than pocket change, $62,000 in pennies.

By mid-February at the Philadelphia Mint, production of the new year's coins was moving along languidly with only one-cent pieces and Saint Gaudens' Indian head ten-dollar gold pieces having been struck.

Saturday, February 18, 1933. The Philadelphia Mint. Birth of the 1933 double eagle.

On February 18, work finally got under way on the 1933 twenty-dollar gold pieces, still the country's largest, grandest, and most beautifully conceived coins. It was the twenty-fifth year Saint-Gaudens' design was struck—and it was to be the last.

On the second floor of the building, in a corner room bathed in pale northern light, John Sinnock, the chief engraver, and his staff were finishing work on the new dies, of which each coin needed two: one for heads (obverse) and one for tails (reverse). During the process of striking thousands or millions of pieces of metal under extreme pressure, dies wore out or broke, and so numerous sets had to be prepared for each denomination. In 1922, for example, the San Francisco Mint reported that for double eagles, the average obverse die was good for 48,190 coins, while the reverse die led a harder life and was only good for 32,292 coins.

In 1933, as Sinnock's men in the Engraver's Department were preparing the more than a dozen pairs of dies that would be needed for the striking of double eagles, the hot work was under way on the ground floor and at the other end of the building in the Melting and Refining Department.

There workers prepared special coining ingots in a time-honored process that had scarcely changed in centuries. Vulcan would have been right at home and able to slip easily into the activities of this department with its brawny men mixing searing-hot metals. In the seventh century B.C., when melded precious ores first took shape as coin, this elemental process was only a single step toward the interaction of disparate peoples through commerce. While the technique of making coins one at a time with the crushing blow of a hand-held hammer on a simple punch had given way over the milennia to machines that churned out more than one a second, little else had. Coins were wrought as utilitarian objects but could be works of art, and they have ever been an alchemical mixing of metal with a nation's symbols and spirit—a reflection of a people's temperament and the face they wish to show the world.

Where the gold used for the 1933 double eagle was mined is impossible to say, but it is probable that it was mined in California. In 1932, the United States was the world's third largest source of gold, and California, though output was well down from gold rush days, still led the nation.

The gold alloy was to be exactly nine parts gold and one part copper. To fuse the two metals properly, the crucibles in the Melting and Refining Department were kept at 2,000 degrees Fahrenheit, and the alloy was cooked for three-quarters of an hour. Then, like batter, the molten mix was poured into two-part molds, which had been greased, like bread pans. Almost immediately, as the flames licked out of the molds, they were opened, and the searing, red ingots, about the size of a thick foot-rule, were chilled in cold water and then dipped in a mild acid bath. A deviation of only one- or two-tenths of a percent was allowed in the purity of the alloy. If the assayer, who took little chips to test, found the purity to be greater or less than permitted, the process was begun all over again. Large four-hundred-ounce bars were used for international trade, but these coining ingots only weighed about six pounds and were tapered at one end to help in the rolling process that followed.

On that Saturday, February 18, 1933, during the late-winter thaw, light streamed into the Rolling and Cutting Room from the south through the nine heavily barred windows that backed up on Buttonwood Street. Men with their sleeves rolled up, wearing aprons and heavy leather gloves, stood before the rolling machines, feeding gold ingots through two giant rollers. Driven by a fifty-horsepower electric motor, the rollers acted like giant pasta-makers. Again and again the strips were sent through to be flattened as the distance between the two rollers was reduced. Up to two

The Rolling and Cutting Room at the United States Mint, c. 1903.
(Reprinted from James Rankin Young, The United States Mint at Philadelphia, 1903)

dozen passes through the heavy, or breakdown, rollers were required. By the time this phase was complete, the ingot, once a foot long, was a noodle: more than three times as long and one-quarter as thick. The yellowy-red alloy had become brittle from repeated exposure to the crushing weight, so it had to be softened by the next process, called annealing: the strips were reheated to fifteen hundred degrees Fahrenheit, after which they were cooled in water, dried, and rolled yet more. Another four to twelve more trips through the finishing rollers yielded a ribbon of metal more than five feet long and just over an inch and a half wide. A test blank the size of a finished coin was then punched out from either end to ensure that the weight and thickness were consistent.

Five-foot strips of gold are unwieldy, so massive shears cut the strips down to usable lengths, which were then sent to the cutting presses, great belt-driven engines that were nothing but massive hole punches. A plain steel die descended about a 170 times a minute, and gold blanks the size of double eagles—just over an inch and a quarter in diameter and each weighing a hair over an ounce—poured into plain oak boxes. The waste, a golden Swiss cheese, was returned to the refinery, where it was melted down and the process begun all over again.

The new blanks were taken upstairs to the second floor, where weighing machines, hand-fed, weighed the blanks one by one. The process sorted flans of the right weight from those that were too heavy or light. The underweight pieces were condemned and sent back to the fiery furnaces. Those that were overweight were sent next door to the Adjusters Room, a long room with high windows along one side and two bare-bulbed spiderlike chandeliers dangling from the ceiling. For decades the adjusters, traditionally women, seated in row upon row of high-backed clerks' stools, had taken fine rasps and scraped off tiny filings from the edges of the offending blanks, but by 1933 machinery did their work. Afterwards the blanks were weighed again. If they were over-adjusted and now too light, they were condemned to the crucible. Those that made the grade were put aside for the next stage.

This first day yielded just over five thousand blanks. The failure rate from each ingot approached ten percent, and since gold was then still the store of value by which the country's wealth was measured, there was no tolerance of error. The faceless pieces of metal were taken to the coiner's vault on the first floor and stored. The next day was one of rest, but until the end of the month, day after day, the process would repeat itself.

On March 1, 1933, Hibberd Ott, the assistant cashier of the Mint, recorded an over-the-counter transaction. One of the few visitors to the Mint came to the Cashier's window, to exchange an old ten-dollar gold piece or ten-dollar gold certificate for one of the freshly made 1933 ten-dollar gold pieces, or "new coin," as it was termed then.

The 1933 eagles were struck and delivered to the Cashier between January 19 and March 3, 1933—all before FDR's March 6 proclamation beginning the recall of privately held gold. One hundred had already been sent to the Treasurer for sale to the public and so, in the eyes of the government, had been issued for circulation.

Historically, trading an old, worn coin for a bright new coin had been an integral part of a Mint tour, and whoever was manning the Cashier's window would have thought nothing of it. Over the years, whether it was a humble cent or an elegant double eagle, the clerk who made the transfer would have duly noted it in the Cashier's Daily Statement. The brilliant 1933 eagle, now exchanged, was but one coin from a total mintage of more than three hundred thousand. The striking of its big sister, the double eagle, would not begin until the next day. The clerk could not have known that this eagle would be the last United States gold "new coin" ever to pass through his grille. Assistant Cashier Hibberd Ott dutifully recorded the transaction, made by Mr. J. Pomerantz of Philadelphia, in his daily records.

March 2, 1933, was a Thursday. The weather was turning, and a dank threat of rain hung in the air. It was to be a short work week at the Mint. A number of the Mint's employees were headed down to the Capitol to watch the president-elect be sworn in that Saturday. The banking crisis was in full swing.

The superintendent of the Coining Department now had a stock of about sixty-five thousand double-eagle-sized blanks in his vault, and his men had started on the next phase of work.

To protect the design of a coin from excessive wear during day-to-day, pocket-to-pocketbook use, the circumference of the coin, its rim, was raised in the curiously named upsetting machine, which was something like an amusement park ride. This contraption had a horizontal spinning steel plate in the center between two grooves; one stationary, the other moving onto which the blanks were fed. As they whipped around, usually about three times, the pressure between the grooves raised an even rim on both sides of the disc, which then dropped into a box.

The intense pressures of the second round of rolling, the punching, and the upsetting had made the coins-to-be brittle again, so they were sent back to the Annealing Room for another round of softening. The coiners liked to get the blanks to a glowing "cherry red," after which they were washed in a weak sulphuric acid bath and dried in another carnival ride—the revolving riddler. Then, having been tumbled about in bass-wood sawdust, the blanks were treated to a gust of hot air, which finished the drying process. The discs poured out, gleaming and ready to be impressed with the images that would make them recognizable as coins, each to be a stunning work of art that the government valued at twenty dollars.

The Coining Room ran two-thirds of the way along the Seventeenth Street side of the Mint. Two stories high, it was pierced by eleven tall, arched windows, facing south and west. At the mezzanine level, a visitors' gallery allowed for a bird's-eye view of the two dozen "knee joint" coining presses: massive, sleek-looking machines with huge six-spoked steel flywheels at their sides. Ten had been made for the opening of the new building at the turn of the century by the T. C. Dill Manufacturing

Company of Philadelphia, and they would still be operable sixty years later. They produced a nation's money and, when they were all running at full tilt, an unimaginable din.

March 2. The newly prepared double eagle dies bearing the Augustus Saint-Gaudens designs that had been used since 1907, his monogram, and the date 1933 had been carefully fitted into one of the coining presses. They would be used to strike the first batch of the last issue of American gold coins.

Gauging the proper distance between the dies to ensure a clean, sharp strike was a finicky job that required experience. If the dies were too close together, too much stress would be exerted as they came in contact with the metal blank, and they would soon break. Too far apart, and the design would not be clearly defined; though freshly made, the coins would look old and worn. Elsewhere on the floor, the metallic rattling of copper cents being produced echoed sharply like sleet on a tin roof.

The freshly softened, clean blanks were fed into a tube. At the bottom, a pair of mechanical fingers carried off the glittering disc to where it was set within a collar between the two dies.

In the blink of an eye the two hard steel dies came together on the malleable 21.6 carat piece of gold. A hundred and seventy tons of pressure, applied with lightning speed, crushed and spread the blank. Nature abhors a vacuum, and the metal sought every cavity. Up and down into the intaglio designs of the dies the metal flowed. Simultaneously, as the punishing force flattened the disc, it stretched horizontally until it was stopped by the collar, which encircled the disc, and like a third die bore the engraved legend E PLURIBUS UNUM, which was pushed into relief, punctuated by six-pointed stars. The dies released the coin, and more mechanical fingers plucked it away and ejected it into a waiting bin. Ninety times a minute the process repeated itself. In less than an hour, the entire supply of more than four thousand readied blanks was now fully struck, looking for all the world like coins (which legally they were not). The day's output was wheeled to the coiner's vault and locked away.

The production of the 1933 double eagles had begun, but the process that would make them coin of the realm was not yet completed.

Monday, March 6, 1933, dawned with a new president and headlines screaming about his first acts in office. Refreshed from having had an unusual two-day break from their labors, the men of the Coining Department were unconcerned. To be sure, the events of the last two days in

The United States Mint's Coiner's Record, indicating that the first 1933 double eagles were struck (but not delivered) on March 2, 1933. (National Archives and Records Administration, Mid Atlantic Region, Center City, Philadelphia)

Washington were a hot topic of conversation, but so was news from Florida and baseball spring training.

Over the weekend, with Assistant Mint Superintendent Fred H. Chaffin in charge, the Mint workers in the Weigh and Deposit Room had worked without respite. On Saturday and Sunday both, they had been hard at it in the basement, men with powerful, sinewy arms, hauling sacks of gold coins, each worth five thousand dollars, regardless of the denomination, and with a heft of more than twenty-two pounds, out of the concrete-, brick-, and steel-lined Mint vaults and into the hemorrhaging Federal Reserve system. Armored trucks drove down the narrow ramp, through heavy gates, and into the East Court Yard, where under the watchful gaze of the Mint Police, they were loaded up with their precious cargo: 2,450 bags—767,500 coins (five-, ten-, and twenty-dollar denominations)—with a face value of $12,250,000. The trucks, laden with their transfusion of gold for Federal Reserve Banks in Cleveland and Richmond, Branch banks in Louisville, Baltimore, and Charlotte, and the United States Treasury in Washington, D.C., then lumbered up the slight incline past the crisscross ironwork and fluted "US"-emblazoned stanchions, where they pulled out into Seventeenth Street and hurried away like ambulances carrying a critically ill patient. They contained no 1933 double eagles.

59

A reporter from the *Philadelphia Inquirer* was curious about the effect on the Mint of the president's proclamation of a bank holiday and embargoed gold. He stopped by that Monday, asked a few questions, and watched, rapt, as the gold and copper blanks were given faces. The item he filed that night ran the next morning on the front page and confirmed to the people of Philadelphia that "it was business as usual."

"MINT NOT AFFECTED BY BANKING HOLIDAY; BUSY MAKING MONEY."

"The busy artisans of the plant wholly unconcerned with the President's emergency proclamation continued to turn out gleaming piles of $20 gold pieces and 1-cent pieces. . . . Thus far officials of the Mint have received no orders from the Treasury Department or elsewhere affecting the money-making machine.

" 'This is just a factory,' one official stated, 'and we only send out money on orders from the Treasury Department. We have no orders with regard to the present situation.'"

Down on the floor, when at last the cacophony of the coin presses and the ringing waterfall of metal bouncing off metal was stilled for the day, the coiner calculated that finally he had enough double eagle product to take to the next stage.

To make sure nothing, not a single piece, was missing, the entire output of the past three days' work was taken back upstairs and passed through the automatic weighing machines. About 750 pieces didn't pass muster and were tossed into the discard bins like undersized fingerlings. The shifting piles of glistening discs that had made the cut were returned to another of the Coiner's vaults, a substantial holding cell just off the Counting Room. Over the next two days, the coins were reviewed for quality control and then counted—not mechanically like the one-cent pieces but, because they were gold, by hand.

Neat, sturdy piles of ten pieces each were lined up like soldiers on parade. Each phalanx of twenty-five piles, 250 pieces, would be destined to fill one heavy canvas bag. These sacks were printed with bold black lettering: the bag's serial number, the total face value of its contents ($5,000), the denomination (double eagle), place of manufacture (Philadelphia), and the date—1933. When each bag was filled, a stiff hemp cord was drawn about the neck and tightened sharply and repeatedly, like a garrote. A blob of dead gray lead was threaded onto the ends of the twine, slid into place like a bolo tie, and crimped to keep the bag shut. Tags with the date of the count and the scribbled initials of the clerk responsible were tied in place. The bag was tossed onto a dolly, and the counting began again.

The physical process of making money was precise. Every separate act was carefully scripted, each dependent on the other yet independently executed. All along the way differences were carefully noted in the Coiner's record.

By the end of business on Wednesday, March 8, approximately twenty-two thousand 1933 double eagles had been made—not yet enough to pass on to the cashier. Coiner William Bartholomew recalled in 1945 that "it was always customary to deliver gold in $500,000 or $1,000,000" (groups of twenty-five or fifty thousand coins). And so, ever patient, the bags once again went into the Coiner's Vault.

Finally, a week later, on March 15, 1933, the magic number was fulfilled. With no fanfare, with nothing more than clerks scribbling away in ledgers and on receipts, the 1933 Gold Delivery Number 7 was made from the Coiner to the Cashier: twenty-five thousand shimmering new 1933 double eagles. The handover was *pro forma* but tinged with suspicion. According to a senior official in the modern Mint, the mutual distrust between the Coiner and the Cashier was not only a time-honored tradition but also one of the best protections the Mint had against pilfering.

During their manufacture and birth, the 1933 double eagles had been the Coiner's concern. Now Cashier Harry Powell, a long-tenured employee, eyeing retirement, accepted the delivery, more than a ton in weight, on behalf of the superintendent of the Mint. Working with him was Hibberd Ott, the assistant cashier, a sickly man, who had hopes of becoming Cashier when Powell retired. The Cashier's Office, on the first floor, was immediately to the left of the front entrance and was small, but much of Powell's work was done with no natural light at all, in the Cashier's Working Vault—called Vault E—in the basement almost directly beneath his office. It was his job, in the dingy-yellow light of his subterranean lair, to organize and account—cent by cent—for the tons of riches that entered and departed his domain.

To ensure that coins reaching the public were of the value and purity guaranteed by the government, a two-tier system of testing existed. The first, and arguably the more important, was the Mint's own "special" assay. The second, more formal and to some degree more ceremonial, was the annual meeting of the Assay Commission.

As required by the Mint's Rules and Regulations, Powell selected one of the sacks of the newly received double eagles at random, slit the cord, opened the bag, and took out two coins. He placed them in a heavy, linen-backed envelope and sealed it with wax. These he "forwarded to the Director of the Mint by registered mail for assay by the Assayer of the Bureau of the Mint." This was an essential part of the internal fail-safe system to make sure that no errors, honest or otherwise, had been made in Philadelphia.

These two specials, as they were known, would be tested by the chief assayer, Timothy J. Quirk, in Washington, D.C., to ensure that the gold was of the stipulated weight and purity. If they failed, the entire group from which they had been removed—all twenty-five thousand pieces—would be sent back to the superintendent of the Melting and Refining Department and destroyed. Until they were tested and approved, the just-struck coins were in limbo. Under the Mint's regulations, the coinage from which the samples were taken could not be released into circulation until the specials passed their test.

From this same bag, an additional twenty-five coins (one piece for every thousand in the delivery) were taken at random. They were to be placed in the Pyx Box for the official testing by the Annual Assay Commission—an honored trial, the roots of which extended back to medieval England, and which was part of the law establishing the Mint in 1792—which would meet almost a year later. Two keys were required to open the massive padlocks that sealed the three-foot-square rosewood Pyx Box: one was held by the Cashier, the other by the Assayer.

Every step of the way, clerks scratched entries into their departmental books. Some, like Powell's, bore a florid copperplate hand, some showed tight but neat columns of figures, while others still demonstrated nearly illegible penmanship and a questionable command of arithmetic. Checks and balances, double-entry accounting, and dual control of vaults—these were security, records of the wealth of America. In mints and banks, then and now, nothing has changed. All has to be balanced at day's end. If a loss exceeding that allowed for wastage was found, "then the employees in that department [were] kept until the shortage [was] accounted for, or the error in calculation discovered."

The number of coins made each year and their denomination were based on what the Federal Reserve Bank anticipated it would require to feed into the arteries of commerce. Meetings between Mint, Treasury, and Federal Reserve officials calculated the numbers, which to a great extent were based not on the previous year's production but on what was actually used.

For the entire calendar year of 1932 a total value of $8,890,540 in double eagles (444,527 pieces) had been pumped from the Mint into circulation in spastic shipments ranging from massive fifty-thousand-piece commercial tranches to minuscule orders of one or two pieces at a time for collectors, museums, or, occasionally, for official presentations. Based on these figures, and the fact that virtually the entire double eagle mintages of 1931 and 1932 (some four million coins) were still sitting in the Mint's vaults gathering dust—a mere hundred of each had been sent to the Treasurer for sale to the public—the number of double eagles to be produced in 1933 was set at $8,910,000, or 445,500 pieces. As the political firestorm in Washington raged and gold lost its place as a medium of exchange, the Mint in Philadelphia, seemingly oblivious to the real world, lethargically cranked out its golden product.

The process that had begun on February 18 with the first rolling and cutting of the double eagle blanks was concluded on May 19, 1933, when the last group of finished product was delivered to the Cashier. 1933 double eagles had been struck on nineteen days in March, twelve days in April, and ten in May. There had been ten deliveries from the Coiner to the Cashier, beginning on March 15—all after Roosevelt had begun the recall of gold. Dutifully Cashier Harry Powell noted his entries—totaling 100,000 in March, 200,000 in April, and 245,500 in May. On the date of each delivery, two specials were pouched off to Washington and a book entry was made to account for the number that would be required for the Assay Commission.

Although the regulations required that the coins to be tested were to be randomly taken from each delivery, in practice this was not done, and shortcuts were taken, rules certainly bent, if not actually broken.

In all, only *two* bags—stored in the cashier's office vault—containing a total of five hundred coins (from the March 15 and April 26 deliveries) were actually opened and used to draw down from until the numbers balanced. Twenty coins were sent to Washington for assay as specials, and 446 were reserved for the Assay Commission. Whether these last coins were physically segregated and placed in the Pyx Box as required by regulations is unclear. Powell may have simply made a paper transfer to be completed when the coins were physically needed for the meeting of the commission in February, 1934. This was a breach of the strictest reading of the Mint's Regulations but must have been common practice, as the entries in the Cashier's ledger made no attempt to disguise the procedure.

The first six special coins, representing the first three deliveries in March, were tested together by Assayer Quirk, and his report confirming they met the stipulated requirements was signed and forwarded from Washington to Philadelphia on March 29, 1933. The day that report was physically received in Philadelphia was the first day that in normal circumstances the law would have permitted the issuance of 1933 double eagles.

Just a Factory: Making Money

The Coining Room at the Mint in Philadelphia, c. 1904. The same presses were still operable sixty years later. (Bowers & Merena Galleries and Q. David Bowers)

But did it ever happen?

Roosevelt's recall of gold had begun three weeks earlier, on March 6. Tens of thousands of Americans, responding heroically to their president's repeated urging and his view that "hoarding [had] become an exceedingly unfashionable pastime," had already turned in nearly a half-billion dollars in gold to the government. In such a charged, warlike atmosphere, in which gold returns and patriotism were whispered in the same breath, the cashier would hardly have considered blithely paying out one of the new coins. Within a week of Quirk's report on the specials being submitted, on April 5, FDR issued his formal edict commanding the return of all privately held gold. Whatever crack in the door might have existed for the issuance of a 1933 double eagle was slammed shut. And even if the Cashier had thought to do so, the Cashier's Daily Records indicate that he never did.

ILLEGAL TENDER

Tuesday, June 27, 1933. The Phildelphia Mint.

June had been blistering, one of the hottest in recent memory, and the humidity hung heavily in the air like a damp rag. Four hundred and eighty 1933 double eagles remained in two bags in the cashier's private vault on the first floor, and the bulk, 445,000 1933 double eagles weighing nearly fifteen tons, lay underground in the cool of the Cashier's Working Vault, Vault E. Under the supposedly watchful eyes of the three members of the Settlement Committee, the mountain of sealed canvas, 1,780 bags, was removed from this vault and wheeled on squealing dollies a short distance to the left and down an off-white glazed-tile-lined corridor and taken to Vault F, which, like all the Mint's vaults, had three steel doors, the outermost one weighing approximately eight tons. Each bag was checked under the auditors' gaze for the last time and heaved onto the growing piles in Cage Number 1, a steel-grated compartment. Once every bag was accounted for, the cage was closed and sealed. Vault Custodian Edward F. McKernan duly noted the formality in his ledger. On one side the contents of the cage were neatly typed or handwritten, beneath which each member of the Settlement Committee signed his name. An additional signature appeared, as the duly authorized representative of the Mint superintendent. It was that of a thirty-eight-year-old employee, George A. McCann.

A heavy red silk grosgrain ribbon was looped across the cage door and sealed with wax. Each member of the committee had his own seal matrix bearing his initials. Some were crudely made. Others, including McCann's, bore sweepingly elegant monograms and were probably made by the Mint's engravers. All four applied their signets to the hot red wax as it was dripped onto the ribbon.

Caged, the 1933 double eagles, America's last gold coins, lay dormant, facing extinction. Never to be collected, spent, or saved. Gathering dust, not interest. Yet some would be sprung, and spirited well beyond their dungeon, drawing after them a fury of dragons intent on their return

CHAPTER 5

The Great Melt
and the
Great Escape

—◆—

Wednesday, St. Valentine's Day, 1934.
The Philadelphia Mint.

A DAINTY FIFTY-SEVEN-YEAR-OLD WOMAN WITH A NARROW FACE, dancing blue eyes, and plain homespun features made history. "Ever feminine, never a feminist," Nellie Tayloe Ross, Director of the Bureau of the United States Mint, called to order her first meeting of the Annual Assay Commission. It had been 142 years since the commission had been established and the first time it had been chaired by a woman.

Mrs. Ross, born in Missouri, was a stalwart Democrat with deep roots in the Washington, D.C., area. Nellie Tayloe married William Bradford Ross and moved with him to Cheyenne, Wyoming, where in 1924, while he was seeking reelection as governor of the state, he dropped dead. With only three weeks left before the elections, Mrs. Ross was pressed to stand in his place and was duly elected. Her inauguration, which occurred only a few days before that of "Ma" Ferguson of Texas, draped upon her the mantle of being the first female governor in the nation's history. It was a distinction she wore with pride but surprise. "As long as my husband lived," she said, "it never entered my head, or his, that I would find any vocation outside our home."

Following her defeat for reelection two years later, she headed to Washington, D.C., where she became an active vice chairman of the Democratic National Committee, in charge of women's activities. Her unstinting efforts helped elect Franklin Roosevelt, and the new president showed his thanks by offering her the appointment Director of the Mint—the first time a woman had been so honored. Initially she was leery of accepting the job: "It all sounded so cold, dealing with metal." But on April 28, 1933, she accepted and expressed her gratiude to Roosevelt: "I am deeply grateful for the privilege of serving in your official family." The Senate confirmed the appointment, and on May 1, as 1933 double eagles were still shooting out of the presses, Mrs. Ross assumed the post she would hold for the next two decades—longer than anyone before or since.

The rules regulating the Annual Assay demanded that samples of all the gold and silver coins produced at each of the nation's mints—Philadelphia, San Francisco, and Denver—during the previous year be submitted for the trial. In 1933, the only silver coins made were half-dollars, and the only gold denominations produced were the eagle and double eagle.

On February 2, 1934, in anticipation of the meeting of the Assay Commission in twelve days' time—as ever, the second Wednesday in February—the 1933 double eagles required were taken from storage. The 446 examples of 1933 double eagles to be submitted for the trial had been physically segregated from the total held in the Cashier's vault since their delivery. The additional thirty-four 1933 double eagles that would not be needed for the Assay Commission's meeting were turned over to Vault Custodian McKernan and signed for by him. The 445,000 in Vault F, Cage 1, remained untouched, with the seals applied in June, 1933, still intact.

The meeting of the 1934 Assay Commission has never been considered ironic, but it should be. Two weeks earlier, when Franklin Roosevelt put his signature to the 1934 Gold Reserve Act, gold coins had formally ceased to be an instrument of exchange in the United States. The six individuals appointed by President Roosevelt and the three ex-officio members required by statute to serve would be testing and hoping to affirm the quality of gold coins that were now illegal tender.

The Assay Commission met in the long conference room on the second floor of the Mint, directly over the front entrance to the building. Pilasters broke up the expanse of walls, and an enormous table ran down the center of the room. Portraits in carved gilt and ebonized black frames of the

Mint Director Nellie Tayloe Ross with Assistant Superintendent of the Philadelphia Mint Fred Chaffin (one of the "Four Horsemen"), in the lobby of the Philadelphia Mint, June 29, 1933. (Bettman/CORBIS)

once high and mighty—previous mint directors, superintendents and others, now gone—stared straight ahead. Standing at the far end of the table, Mrs. Ross, who for such formal occasions wore a small hat, dark suit, and string of pearls, made her opening remarks. She charged the commissioners with their responsibility, as elucidated in the Act of April 2, 1792, which was the Mint's birth certificate. Three committees were appointed: Counting, Assaying, and Weighing. With businesslike dispatch the "commission adjourned until 9 o'clock Thursday morning, that the several committees might perform their respective duties."

There were not many gold coins to test. The rule of one coin selected for every thousand struck yielded a meager 313 eagles and 446 double eagles. Each denomination was checked separately. The Committee on Counting opened ten envelopes of 1933 double eagles and sent them on to the Assaying Committee, where they were subjected to two sets of assays. The first tested four 1933 double eagles, each ostensibly taken from a different delivery (one in March, one in April, and two in May). The coins were rolled flat, mutilated, melted, and tested. All were found to be of acceptable purity. Five more double eagles, drawn from what was believed to be five different deliveries from Coiner to Cashier, were selected for a mass melt and assay, along with five 1933 eagles. The mixed group was melted into a mass and its purity tested. The resulting fineness, .900, was the ideal.

The final test was administered by the Weighing Committee. Put onto a fine Troemmer balance, which belonged to the Philadelphia Mint, the coins were weighed against a sealed set of coin weights supplied by the Bureau of Standards. Three double eagles were selected for weighing from each of the ten envelopes. All fell well within the deviation allowed by law.

At 11 A.M. Thursday, February 15, 1934, the commission once again met as a whole. The committees tendered their reports, which were duly accepted, and the report of the proceedings was signed by all the members. The arcane ritual was over.

Like stagehands breaking down a set after the last performance, the Mint's clerical staff busied itself with tidying up after the meeting of the Assay Commission. On February 20, Hibberd Ott, as Acting Cashier, received the remaining coins in the Pyx Box and entered them back onto his books. Of the 446 double eagles that had been tendered to the Assay Commission, nine had been destroyed and 437 returned. These were fully accounted for on the Cashier's Daily Statement and once again were stored in the Cashier's Vault.

The aftershocks of the 1934 Gold Reserve Act rumbled for months. The price of gold was revalued by the government from $20.67 per ounce to $35 per ounce, hugely increasing the worth of the nation's hoard. The new law created an infant bureaucracy that was busily designing and happily numbering the multitude of special forms that all the freshly invented gold licenses would require.

The Act stated: "All gold coin of the United States . . . shall be formed into bars of such weights and degrees of fineness as the Secretary of the Treasury may direct." On June 29, 1934, after months of discussion, Nellie Ross was given orders to begin the gargantuan task. To simplify and speed the onerous work, it was agreed that the coins simply be melted and not refined. "Coin bars" of .900 fine—in contrast to "good delivery bars" of .998 or better—would be permissible. These were to be stamped with the identifying marks of the Mints or Assay offices doing the melt, as well as the weight and fineness of the ingot. Additionally all the bars were to be numbered serially. Mrs. Ross fought this last requirement, in the interests of time, and lost.

On August 4, Nellie Tayloe Ross wired the superintendents of the Mints at Philadelphia, San Francisco, and Denver "to proceed with the melting of the general stocks of domestic gold coin." It was the beginning of the end for all the gold coins stored in the government's vaults. The furnaces at the Mint would now blaze. Each day, eighty-four thousand ounces of gold coin was metamorphosed into bars. The smoke that issued from the tall stack that loomed above the Mint added to the hazy pall that hung over the city. At this rate, it would take more than two and a half years to melt the nation's vast hoard of gold coins.

Two weeks later, almost as an afterthought, Mrs. Ross ordered the Philadelphia Mint to send sample coins to the Smithsonian Institution for the national coin collection. Almost two months later, on October 9, Acting Superintendent Fred Chaffin acknowledged the instructions and informed the director that her will had been done. The deposit, which was recorded two days later by the curator as having been received, included cents, nickels, dimes, quarters, half-dollars, silver dollars struck in 1933 and 1934 at Philadelphia and Denver, and two bronze medals of Franklin Roosevelt (probably his Inaugural Medal designed by American sculptor Paul Manship). It also included two 1933 double eagles but—curiously—no 1933 eagles.

These two double eagles had been withdrawn from the Cashier's Vault by the new cashier, George A. McCann. Four hundred and sixty-nine remained under his personal control. The canvas-clad dune of 445,000 1933 double eagles remained under seal in Vault F, untouchable.

As the great melt continued, a new bunkerlike facility for storing the nation's yellow bounty was being constructed in the rolling bluegrass country at Camp Knox, Kentucky. The spot had been selected by Roosevelt not for its superior security but because he felt that having the riches in one spot in America's heartland would be psychologically comforting to Americans. And who can say he was wrong? The Gold Depository at Fort Knox—a small, squat building, constructed of concrete, steel and granite, which looks as though it has been dropped from above and simply sunk into the ground—has entered the vernacular as symbolizing the invulnerability of the enormous wealth of the United States.

That wealth was in the form of bars of gold. Ton upon ton, each ingot had been formed from gold coins. Once gleaming works of art, the gold was now rendered into plain, utilitarian bricks that were not adorned with

The Great Melt and the Great Escape

symbols of a nation's great ideals but furnished with a series of numbers that coldly stated the country's bottom line.

Almost two years later, early in 1936, Congress was getting impatient and the House Appropriations Committee called on Nellie Ross to give them an update. "It has not all been melted," she told the gathered legislators, "but we are melting it steadily, just as fast as we can." The headline to the article, printed in the *Numismatist,* the house organ of the American Numismatic Association, put a slightly different spin on her comments: "MANY GOLD RARITIES NOW REPOSE IN BARS."

By February 3, 1937, the monstrous task—destroying America's gold coins—was nearing an end. George McCann broke the temporary seal on Vault F, Cage 1. Months earlier, on October 20, 1936, when the Mint had installed a new protective system, the cage had been briefly opened—for the first time since June, 1933—and resealed the same day, "with former values (1933) intact."

Now the vault was being emptied of its gold coins for the last time. The cage had held in total 3,733,400 five-, ten-, and twenty-dollar gold pieces with a face value of over $50 million. In addition to the 445,000 1933 double eagles, there were more than 900,000 other double eagles, most of them struck in 1928 and 1929. Between February 6 and March 18, 1937, like condemned prisoners being taken to the executioner, bags of 1933 double eagles were rolled down the echoing corridors of dully gleaming, specially hardened brick, and into the Melting and Refining Room. Thousands of double eagles, each dated 1933, were consigned to the glowing heat of the crucible, reduced to anonymity.

When at last the deed was done, the shipments to Fort Knox began. The newly made bars were placed in massive crates made of inch-thick planks of seasoned oak. These were reinforced with heavy straps of cast iron that encircled the lower three-quarters of the crate and looped outwards so that bars could be fitted on either side to carry the fiendishly heavy boxes. Each had stenciled on its side, US MAIL.

Eighteen armored trains made up this granddaddy of mailings. Each shipment carried over three million ounces of gold and was meticulously accounted for by the number of bars, and the melt from which they had come. Tommygun-toting Mint Police rode shotgun with the precious cargo. Nothing got lost. By the end of June, 1937, the great melt of America's gold coins and the transfer of the gold ingots to Fort Knox was over.

Four hundred and forty-five thousand 1933 double eagles from the lower vault and 469 from the Cashier's Vault had met their scalding end in the previous weeks. Twenty-nine others had been destroyed during the assays in earlier years. The columns in the ledgers balanced. The only two extant 1933 double eagles resided in the national collection at the Smithsonian Institution. And as far as the United States Government was concerned, the books on the 1933 double eagles were closed for good.

Early February, 1937. Philadelphia.

Israel Switt, a forty-one-year-old jeweler and old-gold dealer in Jewelers' Row, sat in his shop and looked at his latest purchase. In the gloomy half-light of his office, the small group of gold coins glinted alluringly. He picked one of the coins up and examined it. It was a double eagle and bore the date 1933.

Somehow a few had survived.

Two months later, the April, 1937 edition of the *Numismatic Scrapbook* reported the latest scuttlebutt in the coin-collecting hobby. Concerning the fate of 1933 double eagles: "It has been reported that a few escaped the melting pot and those in the hands of collectors and dealers are being held at a fancy price."

Their time had come.

The Great Melt and the Great Escape

PART II
ON THE LAM

CHAPTER 6

A Double Eagle Flies to Cairo

———|———

Friday, February 25, 1944. Washington, D.C.

THE WEATHER WAS UNSEASONABLY WARM AND HUMID. THE STREETS
teemed with traffic. Old, cranky, exhaust-belching automobiles easily
outnumbered the new. The sidewalks were a crush of government workers, more women than men. Girls who worked at typewriters, wearing
their smart, matching sweaters and skirts, headed to their crowded, clattering warrens. The men wore uniforms, either those of the armed
forces, neat and well-tailored, or that of the new bureaucrats, cheap, off-
the-rack, disheveled, and ill-fitting. Of the few taxis in town, none was
ever in sight. The war was entering its third year, and the engorged government of FDR's New Deal its eleventh.

The strain of growth was everywhere. Along the Mall new "temporary" office space had sprung up like mushrooms next to the old "temporary" buildings built in 1917 for the last war. The sleepy city on the
Potomac had died. In its place was a city that according to some wags
combined the charm of the North and the efficiency of the South. But of
the many things that had changed in Washington, D.C., the weather was
not among them.

Accustomed to a dry desert heat, a perspiring Mr. Fahim from the
Egyptian Royal Legation walked unhurriedly up the granite steps of the
Treasury Building and, as he likely had done many times before, headed

77

to the Bureau of the Mint on the second floor. He was there to do the bidding of his king, Farouk I of Egypt, and to obey the laws of the United States of America.

In his pocket was his monarch's latest purchase, a 1933 double eagle. If not fully worth a king's ransom, it hadn't been exactly cheap either. Farouk had paid $1,575; more than the $1,440—equivalent to about $15,000 today—living wage the government typists got annually. King Farouk had bought it two days earlier from arguably the largest and undeniably the most flamboyant coin dealer in the country, B. Max Mehl of Fort Worth, Texas. The king had been told the coin was rare, extremely rare, one of only two or three the dealer had ever handled.

Born in Lithuania in 1884 and settled in Texas with his family at age eleven, Mehl was the first coin dealer to recognize the value of spending money to make money. Though a dull, runtish man with slicked-down hair, he became a P. T. Barnum-like character. His eyes darting suspiciously behind rimless glasses, he always stared straight past the camera, tight-lipped, unsmiling, seemingly bereft of humor—except in print. There, even his unkindest critics admitted, he was a genius. A shameless self-promoter, he advertised coin collecting and himself to the general public in grandiose terms as no one before or since. By 1919, he was spending $5,000 a year in advertising, by 1924 ten times that. Though hard to believe, throughout the Depression years he was spending a sensational $100,000 per year.

He bought space in *Colliers,* in the *Saturday Evening Post,* and on the back page of the Hearst papers' Sunday magazine section, the *American Weekly* (at a cost of $17,500), and time on the Mutual Radio Network. With over a quarter-million inquiries per year, he was quite simply the best known coin dealer in the United States—ever. And he got the goods. In the 1940s he was selling some of the very finest coin collections to come to auction—some approaching, later exceeding, then unheard-of sale totals of $100,000. King Farouk, who habitually sent unlimited bids, was one of his best clients. Even so, from Mehl there were no bargains, no preferred client discounts—especially for royalty—and the $1,575 Farouk paid for the 1933 double eagle was high, very high. Even more so when compared to what the average Egyptian was then living on. Three-quarters of the population lived in the country, where peasants eked out an existence on about a nickel a day, while skilled workmen in the cities made a princely dollar.

Mr. Fahim had come to the Treasury to fill out paperwork. Under the Gold Reserve Act of 1934, gold coins could be exported from the

United States only if they met certain criteria defined as having had "a recognized special value to collectors of rare and unusual coin" prior to FDR's April 5, 1933 Executive Order. The form that had to be completed was Treasury Gold License Number 11—better known as "Form TGL-11."

Initially a simple, two-page affair that had been created from the afterbirth of the 1934 Act, the form had been updated, improved, and complicated in 1937 at the behest of Nellie Tayloe Ross. At first the form required no more than the name and address of the applicant, a basic description of the coin—including the denomination, date, and country of issue, from where it was to be exported, and to whom it was to be sent. The revision insisted on greater detail, including the coin's condition, its mint mark, its design, and a "representation that the particular coin is to be exported for a historical, scientific or numismatic purpose."

The responsibility for authorizing the export rested solely with the Bureau of the Mint, which originally specified that a duplicate of the form be filed with the director of the Mint. Mrs. Ross, exposing herself as a political appointee and not a career civil servant, was ever mindful of excessive paperwork and eliminated this last requirement. The legation would have been well aware of all the nuances, as their monarch had been collecting coins for years, and all the major American dealers conducted their business directly through Farouk's representatives in Washington, D.C.

Farouk I of Egypt was in all things excessive—a glutton, voluptuary, and collector. In February, 1944, twenty-four years old, he was still recovering from a harrowing car accident that had totaled his red Cadillac convertible, nearly killed him, and cracked his pubic bone—giving rise to endless rumors and snickering about his love life that followed him to his grave. During his rehabilitation, with women most definitely on the back burner, he focused on his collections, and, already portly, he ballooned to 245 pounds as his gross appetite became prodigious. Curiously self-conscious about his corpulence, he kept his tailors busy figuring out ways to camouflage his expanding girth. He looked decades older than his age but exhibited the maturity of a petulant teenager.

A passionate collector since his childhood, Farouk had started with aspirin bottles, paper clips, and, even more strangely, razor blades. When he ascended the throne in 1936 and found his wealth suddenly limitless, he set about making his collections limitless as well.

Farouk's tastes leaned heavily toward ostentation and vulgarity, but if something interested him, he bought it—in quantity. Stamps, cars, glass paperweights, Gallé glass vases, Fabergé imperial eggs, gold boxes, watches, automata, and an astonishing, voluminous collection of erotica and pornography, which, though tame by today's standards, was of sufficient importance for the British Museum to express a strong interest in acquiring it in 1953.

Then there were his coins. His collecting tastes were not governed by borders–the entire world intrigued him. Distant history seemed to intimidate him, however, and Farouk was generally interested only in coins that had been made in the nineteenth and twentieth centuries, with rare exceptions. Nearly all coins of the United States nestle comfortably into this tidy time frame, and they infatuated him. He hungrily devoured the greatest rarities offered to him–price be damned.

Farouk's unlimited bids to auctions inevitably got him what he wanted, though how much or how often he was gored by frequently greedy dealers will never be known. Every dealer's dream client, he was every dealer's nightmare as well. While his pockets were bottomless, the exchequer attempted to keep him in rein by setting limits to the amounts he could spend without consultation. Ten thousand dollars was the magic number. With more expensive purchases, dealers had to contend with receiving a multitude of checks, none of which individually reached the forbidden figure and few of which were ever tendered on time.

But Farouk was a collector and a king, not an accountant. In 1950, New York coin dealer Hans Schulman–who was utterly charming, if slightly roguish–when the king's guest, tried to work the conversation around to quicker payments. Farouk "brushed [it] off with a wave of the hand" and said, cocking an eyebrow, "the bookkeeping department handles this; I don't ever know if you are paid or not." And he couldn't have cared less.

Yet he did care intensely about his collection and was, according to Schulman, "completely different from what the newspapers and later books reported him to be." Farouk liked to talk coins in an American English that he described as "just like in the American drug stores" and, much to Schulman's surprise, was up on the latest trade gossip as well. He kept his coins and numismatic library tucked away in a special study in the Koubbeh Palace and always put aside a part of the day to spend with his newest treasures. In this habit Farouk was much like his fellow collector Franklin Roosevelt, who, regardless of the day's pressures, whether at home or abroad–FDR always traveled with an album or two–found time for his stamps, some of which had been presented to him by the Egyptian king. With a large cigar inevitably guttering in a gold ashtray, Farouk made " 'coin time' between 10 P.M. and 1 A.M., after which he went night-clubbing."

Schulman knew the peculiarities and idiosyncrasies of those touched by the collecting bug and recognized them in Farouk: "He was as normal as any other coin collector."

Fahim completed the paperwork, surrendered the 1933 double eagle, and took his leave. He would await the government's decision. The Bureau of the Mint had the authority to issue the export license, but no one there had the necessary expertise to pass judgment on whether or not the coin qualified. Mint Director Ross, who had developed the vetting process and whose office was directly responsible for approving all gold coin export licences, knew this and she dictated a letter to Theodore Belote, the Curator of History at the Smithsonian Institution, asking for his opinion.

Mrs. Ross asked if the coin that the Egyptian legation wished to export from the United States had been recognized as a coin of special value to coin collectors since before FDR's Executive Order of April 5, 1933, which demanded the return of gold, and ever since. With the letter and coin tucked into her pocketbook, Ross's assistant, Mrs. W. D. Fales, headed across the Mall to the Smithsonian's Arts and Industries building, hidden off to the side and just behind the Institution's famous "Castle."

Belote, with a shock of streaky gray hair combed straight back and wistful small pale blue eyes, had come to the Smithsonian in 1908 after teaching history at the University of Cincinnati for a number of years. His responsibilities were wide and varied, but until 1923, when the Mint collection was conveyed to his division—coins absorbed only a fraction of his time. Not a numismatist by training, the task of receipting nearly twenty thousand coins made him one by necessity. Regarding coins and their history, the Harvard-educated Belote was more dilettante than scientist, more collector than curator, and—having a healthy dose of eccentricity—he was said to have wandered about the museum with still uncatalogued coins tucked into the pockets of his jacket.

Belote met with Mrs. Fales in his office. He unfolded and quickly scanned the letter, slipped the comfortably heavy gold coin out of its small, stiff paper envelope, and slightly arching his eyebrows, gave it a cursory glance. He rolled Mrs. Ross's letter into his typewriter and banged out a hasty answer at the bottom, which he signed: "The reply to each of the two questions above is 'Yes'. The coin is returned to the Treasury Department herewith in the possession of Mrs. W. D. Fales, by whom it was brought to the Museum."

He was wrong.

Of course he couldn't have known that none had been issued. Seven years after the 1933 double eagles were melted it appears that few did. Perhaps, since he had two in his care in the national collection, he thought they had been issued. Belote would also have been unaware that it was not until after the crucial April 5, 1933, Executive Order stipulated on the export license that the majority of the 1933 double eagles were even made. But more starkly wrong still was his opinion that they had been of "recognized special value" at any time in 1933. He would have been wrong even if any *had* been issued.

In years past, up to 1916, specially struck samples of the nation's coinage, called cabinet coins or proofs, could be purchased by collectors from the Mint at a modest cost above face value. For a double eagle the added charge was twenty-five cents. However, all of the nearly half-million 1933 double eagles had been struck with the intention of their being circulated as spending money, not as special, collectible, "souvenir" coins with added value. If the double eagles had been issued in 1933—like the millions of 1933 one-cent pieces that were released—they would have been worth nothing more than face value—twenty dollars, just as the 1933 pennies were worth only one cent. It was an opinion shared by the Mint itself. On January 9, 1934, Mary O'Reilly (Acting Director of the Mint on that day, filling in for the absent Mrs. Ross), making no mention that the coins had never been released, wrote to T. H. Lillard in Graves Mill, Virginia, about exactly this issue. "Twenty Dollar gold pieces were made at the Mint in Philadelphia in May 1933 . . . and these pieces are worth only their face value at this time."

Belote might have been swayed by knowing the coin was intended for the king of Egypt, but there is no evidence for this. Certainly if preferential treatment was to be afforded by the United States Government, having Belote vet the coin in the first place would have been unnecessary. Most likely he simply rendered his opinion as an academic. A coin worth $1,575 in 1944 must have been worth more than face value and so must have been of special interest a mere eleven years earlier. Understandable reasoning—but incorrect.

Mrs. Fales, her outing for the day completed, thanked Mr. Belote and hurried back to the Treasury. The predicted rain was growing imminent as wispy pale clouds were being chased away by thickening gray ones. Once back at her office, she reported the findings to Mrs. Ross and took the coin to the office of the Assayer, Timothy Quirk, in whose vault the coin would be kept. The paperwork officially granting permission to export the coin was now under way. It was ready by the following Tuesday, February 29,

1944, and the legation was duly notified. J. E. Graf, the associate director of the Smithsonian, sent a formal letter to Director Ross, confirming Mr. Belote's opinion—a week after the license had already been authorized.

Two weeks later, on March 11, 1944, Mr. Fahim returned to the Mint offices, where the 1933 double eagle was returned to him along with the newly issued License TGL-11-170.

Just how or exactly when Farouk's double eagle left the country is lost to time. Crossing the Atlantic during the war was hazardous, whether by air or by sea. It could have been mailed, carried in the Egyptian diplomatic pouch, or it could have been hand-carried by an American. There was precedent. Just over a year earlier, Farouk had bought "a $3 set of medals" that would have cost $80 to airmail. Instead, in the interests of international harmony, Ambassador Extraordinary and Plenipotentiary of the United States of America to Turkey, the Honorable Laurence A. Steinhardt, dropped them off in Cairo on his way back to his posting.

Eventually, though, the 1933 double eagle successfully journeyed to the king's coin room, where it was cloistered for the next ten years, to be caressed by the thick-fingered Farouk—just a collector like any other. There it bided its time as its sisters, thousands of miles away, bewitched a legion of collectors and bedevilled all those who sought them.

CHAPTER 7

A Routine Inquiry

◆

Saturday, March 18, 1944. New York.

ERNEST KEHR WAS A STAMP MAN BY INCLINATION, AND A GOOD ONE. He was also the Stamp and Coin editor for the *New York Herald Tribune,* a position he had held since 1939 and one he would keep until the paper folded in 1966. Ernie went through life with the knowing, lightly amused look of a man who loved what he did, the outer reflection of the contented inner man.

That Saturday, Kehr was flipping through the pages of a blue-covered auction catalogue issued by a relatively new coin dealership in New York: Stack's. The catalogue was devoted to a highly disparate collection of gold coins formed by Colonel James W. Flanagan, of Toronto, New York City, and Palm Beach.

The seventy-two-year-old politically well-connected Flanagan had made his fortune as a petroleum engineer and banker. He had given generously toward the establishment of the presidential library at Hyde Park and in 1936, on a more personal level, had given a Haitian tomtom to FDR himself. In 1944 the rather portly colonel was getting on and changing his lifestyle, either by design or necessity. Within a one-month period he sold his library and collection of antique firearms in two separate single-owner auctions at Parke-Bernet Galleries on Fifty-seventh Street and Fifth Avenue and his collection of coins at Stack's. This last sale was by far the most important of the three offerings and had the makings of being one of the most valuable coin collections ever sold at auction. Getting it and selling it well would cement Stack's place as one of the preeminent firms in the country, having been in the auction business for nine years.

Brothers Joseph and Morton Stack knew it. In 1944, New York was the center of the coin trade, and it offered plenty of rough-and-tumble competition. The two shortish, bald men, both snappy dressers, were well suited for it. Aggressive, innovative, and determined, they reveled in the scrum and with increasing frequency came out on top, much to the dismay of their rivals.

Pounding the drums of PR loudly, Stack's began advertising the sale in January. In the *Numismatist* they shouted: "ANNOUNCEMENT EXTRAOR-DINARY." "WE EXPECT THIS SALE TO REALIZE THE WORLD'S RECORD IN TOTAL AMOUNT OF DOLLARS!" Buried deep within the advertisement was a titillating piece of information: the sale would include the "rare" 1933 double eagle.

Kehr had been following the upcoming auction for months. Its contents were astounding—almost 1,700 lots of gold coins from around the world, common, rare, and exceptional. But it was the last item in the auction that caught Ernie's eye. Lot 1681 would be offered sometime in the late afternoon on March 25, exactly one week away.

> THE EXCESSIVELY RARE 1933 DOUBLE EAGLE. 1933 Brilliant uncirculated. Perfect gem with full mint bloom, the last year of issue. Although this is the first one that ever came up in any public auction and there is not a price set on this in the standard catalog we know that 8 or ten of the pieces were sold for privately from $1,000.00 to $2,200.00. This piece has cost the Col. the tidy sum of $2,200.00 which has set a new high for this coin. He paid this price to one of our leading dealers in the south. Excessively rare and in great demand, no buy orders on this particular coin will be accepted.

Ernest Kehr's curiosity was piqued. The price Flanagan had paid was enormous. Only the great historical rarities—classics—brought that kind of price. An 1804 silver dollar, long considered the king of American coins, was sold the following year for $3,150, and the all-time record auction price for an American coin was $6,200 for the famous Brasher Doubloon in 1907, the first American gold coin ever struck. Old Master paintings and Picassos could be had for less, and this coin was only eleven years old. Although Kehr had published a small coin price guide for the newspaper in 1941—available on receipt of a three-cent stamp—he would have been the first to admit that his knowledge of numismatics was wanting. How many of these coins could there possibly be to make it so valuable? The catalogue might be little more than dealer's bombast. The stamp man prided himself on being a diligent newsman as well, so he started asking questions. The most logical source for information was the Mint, and so Kehr directed his inquiry to the office of the Director.

Dr. F. Leland Howard, Assistant Director of the United States Bureau of the Mint, was a sour man whose mouth was perpetually drawn down at the corners. A graduate of the University of Kentucky, he had joined the government in 1934, two years prior to taking his Ph.D. from the University of Virginia. But he was scrupulous in all things, strictly by the book. Howard approached his work in a straight-backed, blinkered sort of way and angered many. Over the years he had earned the undying enmity of coin collectors and dealers—a group not only as narrow-minded as he at times but also jam-packed with its own idiosyncratic foibles—for being "anti-numismatist."

Doc Howard was in the office that Saturday to answer Kehr's inquiry. Off the top of his head, he couldn't.

Scowling and going to the most basic source, he would have plucked off his shelf a copy of the 1934 *Annual Report of the Director of the Mint,* which had a breakdown of the coins produced in 1933. No double eagles were listed as having been made in 1933. Instinctively he knew that was wrong. A perusal of the 1933 annual report provided his answer: 445,500 double eagles had been struck. So the 1934 report contained a glaring error. It omitted the production of 1933 double eagles entirely. At least it hadn't happened on his watch.

The report didn't answer the newsman's underlying question, however: how many were out there and why were they so rare? Howard needed help to answer the question. Something didn't feel right to him. He knew every gold regulation and its timing inside and out—it was part of his job. But 1933 was before he had got to the Mint, and who knew what chaos existed before he arrived and imposed his strictly ordered world.

Doc Howard fielded Kehr's question like a sharply hit double-play ball, touched base in Washington, and fired it on to Mint Superintendent Edwin Dressel in Philadelphia. He had had enough for one day and went home. The fuse he had lit with his telegram would flame up, catch, splutter, then refire and set off strings of small explosions for the next half-century and more.

On Monday, March 20, Howard briefed Director Ross on Kehr's question, his response, and what it all might mean. Late that day, in the early evening, Helen C. Moore, the assistant superintendent of the Philadelphia

A Routine Inquiry

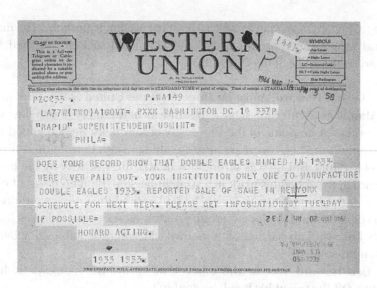

The Match that Lit the Fuse: Telegram from Acting Director of the Mint F. Leland Howard to the Superintendent of the Philadelphia Mint, March 18, 1944.
(National Archives and Records Administration, Mid Atlantic Region, Center City, Philadelphia)

Mint, called Mrs. Ross direct and filled her in briefly on the findings. She gave a cold accounting exercise: dates and numbers, a countdown of what had been made, tested, and destroyed. She didn't give an unequivocal answer to the question but said instead that she would put all the particulars on paper and send it to Washington. They could expect the report by Wednesday and make their own judgment.

Wednesday, March 22, 1944.

In Italy, allied troops were stalled at Monte Cassino in a hellish battle with the German army, while just a few miles to the south, in San Sebastiano, Mount Vesuvius, erupting, was unleashing a hell of a different sort. Over Germany, 1,400 U.S. bombers pounded Berlin, having warned German citizens to evacuate. In New York, Ringling Brothers Barnum and Bailey Circus was coming to town; Frank Sinatra was starring in the "year's laugh, song and music sensation" (the utterly forgettable *Higher and Higher*), and on the radio, *America's Town Meeting* asked the question, "Is There Too Much Censorship in War News?"

In Washington, D.C., Dr. Leland Howard had cleared his desk and was poring over the ten-page memorandum he had just received from the Philadelphia Mint. Rain splattered on the window as he analyzed the unvarnished facts provided by Mrs. Moore. His face settled into a frown. Something was wrong.

Each page told the same story from a different angle. The first page was a summary breakdown of the number of double eagles that had been made in 1933 and those assayed and destroyed by testing. On September 13, 1934, all 445,471 1933 double eagles had been declared uncurrent. The difference between the number struck and the number accounted for in September was correct. The books balanced.

The report continued, page after page, a life-and-death story told in figures, not prose: The date and quantity of every delivery from the Coiner to the Cashier. The contents and destination of the last shipments of gold coin from the Mint on March 5, 1933, a full ten days before the first 1933 double eagles were even delivered by the Coiner. The Vault Custodian's records of what came to him, where it was put—Vault F, Cage 1—when it was sealed, unsealed, resealed, and broken for good. The fact that two 1933 double eagles, "value $40," had been sent to the Smithsonian was also duly noted, although the date of the transfer was not. Everything added up—sort of.

There were a few inconsistencies. The weight of the gold scrap returned to the Mint from the special assays in Washington, D.C., didn't add up to twenty double eagles. It added up to more. But this was later easily explained. And exactly where the Vault Custodian, Edward McKernan, had put the thirty-four coins not sent to the Assay Commission was unclear.

But to Howard it was grim reading. The entire mintage of almost a half-million 1933 double eagles was laid out for him in black and white. As far as he could see, every last one of the coins was accounted for. None, not one, had ever left the official control of the United States Government.

Doc Howard's assessment was confirmed by the Office of the Treasurer. In checking through its records, it could find no mention of any 1933 double eagles having been issued to them by the Mint for release to the public. Glowering, Howard dashed off a terse wire to Ernest Kehr, which his secretary, Miss Hayden, signed. "Miss McNutt [of the Treasurer's office] says No double eagles for 1933 received in Treasurer's Office. Consequently none paid out."

Shaking his head, Howard left his office and marched down the long, opulent halls of the Treasury Building and into the impressive office of the Chief of the United States Secret Service, Frank J. Wilson.

Howard settled into one of the leather upholstered chairs and told the Chief what he knew. Wilson, ever studious and polite, listened. What notes he took were done in his large, ragged hand, while he occasionally puffed on one of his habitual nickel stogies.

After eight years in the job, Wilson was comfortable in his grand office with fifteen-foot ceilings and a Sarouk rug, which had been seized from a smuggler, on the floor. Four massive windows overlooking the White House's East Gate were accented by heavy rose-colored velvet drapes. The glistening mahogany desk at which Wilson sat had been made for secretary of the treasury, William Gibbs McAdoo. Lincoln's secretary of the treasury, Salmon P. Chase, stared down at the two men from within the heavy gilt frame that surrounded his portrait.

Howard, a midlevel functionary, poured out all the information supplied by Kehr and the Mint. He was concerned, very concerned. Somehow, the coin going up for sale on Saturday—in only three days—had escaped from the Mint, apparently with others. Or it was a counterfeit. Something had to be done and done quickly, but without making waves. The coin was expensive; it had cost some $2,200 and was expected to bring $3,000 at the auction. And the owner was connected. He was, said Howard, "a close friend of President Roosevelt and Secretary Woodin and Secretary Morgenthau."

Frank Wilson shifted slightly in his chair. "Proud custodian of about four gallons of one degree above freezing water in his veins," he took it in, unperturbed by well-heeled political cronies. He was, after all, directly responsible for the life of Franklin Roosevelt. In the last year he had gotten FDR across the Atlantic and back, with U-boats patrolling the seas and Messerschmitts the skies—twice. That had been a job. He was used to tough assignments and was a top-notch investigator.

Early in his career, while working for the Internal Revenue Service, Wilson was the point man in the case to finally settle with Public Enemy Number One, Al Capone, once and for all. Scarface ended up behind bars. That conviction paid double dividends when after Pearl Harbor FDR was suddenly in need of a bulletproof limousine. A federal regulation prohibited "buying any car that cost more than $750," and so Al Capone's huge, armored car was "washed, lubricated and driven to the White House." Roosevelt's grin was broad, he loved it.

Frank Wilson was also the man who had insisted on spending the night at J. P. Morgan & Company at 23 Wall Street in New York, recording the serial numbers of all the banknotes used to pay the ransom for

Charles Lindbergh's kidnapped baby. Fourteen thousand, six hundred dollars of those bills were discovered in Bruno Hauptman's garage and helped usher the convicted man to the electric chair.

"Frank J. Wilson [was] a big, slow-moving, slow-speaking man, with a round kindly face, and round moonlike glasses and a slow smile," wrote journalist Adela Rogers St. John. He might not look the part of a Special Agent, nor "measure up to any fiction detective," but if you were in his sights, "you would never be safe, never be out of the reach of that relentless glacier. . . . You could no more shake him nor reflect upon his honesty or his sureness of his facts than you could melt a glacier with a blow torch."

As Wilson looked down at Leland Howard, smiled quietly, and asked to have all the relevant information sent to him. He would not only launch an investigation; he would oversee it personally.

Doc Howard left. He had done his job.

Frank Wilson exhaled a slow plume of blue smoke after Howard left. Lazy tendrils snaked their way upward and tickled the ceiling. He gazed distractedly at the model of the *Albatross,* a yare little schooner he had sailed on Lake Erie years ago.

Why had he agreed to oversee the case himself? Dr. Howard was certainly agitated and persuasive enough. But the Secret Service had a vast docket of criminal investigations: 26,470 cases in 1944, up considerably from the year before. And they had to protect the president. And a world war was being fought.

This whole matter was over a handful of coins. Wilson's department was charged with enforcing violations of the 1934 Gold Act, but as more and more gold was firmly in government control, these had become fewer and fewer over the years. Thefts of Treasury property were up, however. The Secret Service's initial responsibility, going back to its founding in 1865, was first and foremost protection of the nation's money. Keeping politicians alive had come later.

Besides, something about the case intrigued Wilson. Gold still backed the wealth of the country, and if gold had walked out of the Mint it was not only theft, it was embarrassing. Something must have told him there was more to it than Howard had let on.

He picked up the phone and got in touch with the New York office. The Supervising Agent, John McGrath, a good man who got things done and would later be promoted to assistant chief of the Service, listened as Wilson laid out the background and told him what he wanted. Because Wilson himself would have oversight of the case, he wanted McGrath to give him a solid investigator. More information would follow by teletype.

The next day flew by in preparation. The boss was calling the shots, and McGrath put his best people on the job. U. E. Baughman, who would take over as Chief of the Secret Service in 1948, put a call in to Superintendent Edwin Dressel at the Philadelphia Mint. He started asking the background questions that would guide the direction of the investigators.

Special Agent Harry W. Strang was assigned to the case. Powerfully built and of average height, with a ruddy complexion and an easy way about him, he had the confidence of his superiors. Although all Secret Service agents were trained for both protective and investigative work, Strang seemed more suited to the latter. Perfect for the job, he knew New York City well. Enforcing the 1934 Gold Reserve Act was part of his beat, and so over the years he had got to know the denizens of the old-gold and coin worlds.

Friday, March 24, 1944. Manhattan.

Accompanied by Special Agent James Haley, the Custodian of the Contraband Section in Washington, D.C., Strang headed uptown to the offices of the *New York Herald Tribune* to see Ernest Kehr. Haley, who had been in the Secret Service since World War I, was considered the government's authority on currency and securities. Kehr met with them briefly. His desk was part of the bullpen, where other writers and columnists, hats perched on the back of their heads, hammered hard at the keys of the massive Royal typewriters favored by so many newsrooms. The atmosphere had urgency. Deadlines never let up.

Kehr had little more to offer the two men. He showed them his copy of the auction catalogue, but everything he knew had already been forwarded on. He pointed out that later that afternoon the second session of the auction would begin. Strang and Haley headed to Stack's.

"Scarcely 50 paces from fabulous Fifth Avenue," Stack's was becoming a destination of choice for coin collectors of all stations and stripes. At 12 West Forty-sixth Street, a shallow canopy emblazoned RARE COINS greeted visitors, who could gaze through two windows and see a sampling of the cave of riches that awaited them inside.

Stack's was eons removed from the typical musty, cluttered coin shops that brought on claustrophobia. The brothers had designed their gallery, as they liked to style it, after a gentleman's club, which in time it came to resemble, particularly on Saturdays, when men from all walks of life gathered. Bankers, librarians, actors, industrialists, politicians, or shopkeepers, anyone who wanted to talk coins, relax, and add to their collection was welcome. The shop was forty feet wide. Wood paneling ran the length of both sides to a height of seven feet. Along one side were display cases and leather-backed chairs; on the other, a few private booths, where transactions could be carried out with a modicum of privacy.

As Strang and Haley doffed their hats, they were politely greeted by Stack's receptionist. Both Stack brothers were busy. They had held the first session of the auction the previous afternoon, and the second portion was to begin in hours. The two partners were making calls to potential bidders, answering their last-minute questions, and recording the mail bids that had been received that morning. Joe and Morton entrusted these chores to no one. They did the work themselves, and their business, as usual, was frantic.

Strang and Haley showed their five-pointed stars and soon found themselves escorted to the back of the store. The agents were ignored by the collectors seated at the vitrines, prospective bidders, every one of them intently examining the coins, some with magnifying glasses screwed up to their eyes. Their time was nearly up, since in minutes, the staff would start moving furniture, pushing the cases against the walls and setting rows of chairs down the center of the room to transform the shop quickly into an auction room.

As one Joseph and Morton Stack rose from either side of their partners' desk to greet the agents. Strewn with catalogues and papers, their desk was a small, ornate English affair of deeply polished walnut, with barely enough room for the telephones.

The T-men got to the point without hesitation: Lot 1681. The 1933 double eagle. They asked to see the coin and wanted to know what the Stacks knew about it including the catalogue's claim that only eight to ten were known.

As one brother expounded, the other excused himself momentarily and came back with the coin and a letter. As the agents listened, Haley, the expert, picked up the coin and looked at it. Although he would have it checked, it looked absolutely genuine. This didn't have the makings of a counterfeit case.

Joe, the elder of the two brothers, liked to talk. Strang and Haley learned that the number of pieces believed to be in existence was common knowledge in the trade. Others were around. Personally, the Stacks had never handled one until now, but the coins existed. Max Berenstein, Stack told them, a jeweler over at 435 Madison, had one. It was no secret.

Nonetheless, the Stacks admitted they had made a mistake in the catalogue. The coin had not cost Colonel Flanagan $2,200—only $1,250. B.

Max Mehl, who had sold him the coin, had sent the Stacks a note just a week ago to correct the error. He even mentioned that the coin had been invoiced to Flanagan on November 26, 1937. A copy of the letter would be given to the agents.

Harry Strang carefully explained to the two brothers that according to the Mint's records, none of these coins had ever been issued. And if they hadn't gone out through the front door, they had slipped out the back, potentially stolen property. Until the case was solved, they would have to take the coin.

Joe and Morton looked at each other in dismay. They had no option but to comply. Frustration from losing their star lot gave way to the urgent need to get on with their sale. Strang seized the coin, pulled out his thick-nibbed fountain pen, and signed his florid signature to a receipt, which he gave the Stacks. It was 2 P.M. The auction was due to start. Harry Strang and Jim Haley left to pay a visit on Max Berenstein.

It was a short walk, a block east and one uptown, to small, chic, Bern's Antiques just off Forty-seventh Street, a classier extension of the Diamond District. Green-painted buses chugged wheezingly north and south on Madison Avenue, coughing up sooty gray-brown clouds, their brakes squealing.

Max Berenstein couldn't have been pleased that the Stacks had offered up his name so freely to the Secret Service, but he answered Strang's and Haley's questions expansively and specifically. And just as the Stacks had shared Berenstein's name without a moment's hesitation, he provided other names and addresses.

A jeweler, antique dealer, coin collector and dealer, Max Berenstein handled a little bit of this, a little bit of that. The collector in him had bought his 1933 double eagle from "James G. MacAllister [*sic*], 3400 North Fifth Street, Philadelphia, Pa., on February 17, 1937, for $1,600." A very hefty price for a four-year-old coin, especially in the black days of the Depression. But it was the first one he'd ever seen or heard of.

As Berenstein, like the Mad Hatter, breathlessly rattled on, Strang could scarcely keep up. "MacAllister had three of these coins," one he sold to a New York collector called Taylor, who had then sold it to Berenstein (the dealer), "who resold same to R. H. Smith, 2267 Clybourne Avenue, Chicago," who then sold it on to "Ira Reed, 37 South Eighteenth Street, Philadelphia, Pa."

He didn't specifically mention Macallister's other two coins. But he "also advised that Mr. Fred C. C. Boyd, 59 West Twelfth Street, New York

City, President [*sic*] of the Union News Co., also had one of these coins as did Mr. J. F. Bell, 100 North LaSalle Street, Chicago, Ill, as well as T. James Clarke, President of Clarke's Box and Label Works, Jamestown, N.Y."

Berenstein was running late, but he could meet with the agents again the following morning. Anything to help. Strang and Haley graciously took him up on the offer—and then seized his coin. It was 3 P.M. Max Berenstein had saved the agents a lot of shoe leather.

The agents had made a promising start. The coins were genuine. A quick trip to the New York Assay Office in the bowels of the city at 32 Old Slip, nearly in the East River, had confirmed that. They had been weighed "and found to be within the weight range of perfect coins." The alternative that this might be a counterfeiting investigation evaporated. Strang and Haley sent out a teletype to the Chief to let him know that two of the coins were in hand and they had leads on others.

Saturday, March 24, 1944. Manhattan.

The floodgates opened and a torrent of information poured forth. As Berenstein had promised, he met again with the two agents in his shop. That chill morning he offered one useful crumb, that a "New York dealer named Kasoff [*sic*] . . . had distributed several of these coins," including one that had been resold "to a man named Williams, the head of a large insurance company" in Cincinnati, and one tasty morsel: Messrs. Boyd, Bell, and Reed could all be found this instant at Stack's, where they were awaiting the final session of the Flanagan auction.

Stack's was crowded. The last section of the auction was devoted to the United States series, which had the widest audience and greatest financial potential. The Stack brothers offered Strang and Haley their library, where they could conduct their interviews in private. It was a small room but served their needs. Bookshelves, some open, some glazed, lined the walls with framed displays of currency, coins, and medals perched along the top.

Frederick Cogswell Charles Boyd, an urbane executive, chatted affably with the agents, but in him they would meet with their first resistance. The vice president of the Union News Company, the newsstands of which had the concessions at both Grand Central and Pennsylvania stations and drug stores, cigar shops, and luncheonettes all over the city, he was a wealthy man. A fifty-eight-year-old, kinetic New Yorker, with a full head of hair brushed straight back, Boyd had started out at thirteen as a printer's devil in St. Louis and had worked his way back east and up the ladder of the Union News Company's purchasing department. Now he was the entire department, seeing up to fifty-eight salesmen a day, and possessed an uncanny ability to make the right selections from the cigars, candy, toys, magazines and books he was offered (the *Rockefeller Center Weekly* wrote in 1934 that he reviewed ten books a night and "has made only two major mistakes in 10 years."). He was also rumored, without foundation, to be a friend of FDR's (according to his obituary published in the *New York Times* in 1958, he had served on the boards of the National Recovery Administration and the Office of Price Administration).

Fred Boyd lived in a smart new apartment building off Sixth Avenue in the upper reaches of Greenwich Village and maintained a separate apartment for his collection. A passionate, exceptionally knowledgeable collector, he dabbled in coin dealing on the side. He collected expensive coins, cheap coins, banknotes, tokens, and medals; he knew what he had and was only too happy to share. Boyd supported every major numismatic organization in the country, giving of his time, considerable financial resources, and collections.

F. C. C. Boyd was happy to talk about his 1933 double eagle. But that was all. He bluntly informed the agents that until they could prove "to him that this coin had been illegally taken from the Mint," he would not surrender it. They didn't press the point. They listened.

Boyd told the agents he had bought the coin from James Macallister "and that it was his understanding that all of these 1933 Double Eagles had been secured by a collector or a coin dealer, possibly MacAllister, from the son of the President of the Federal Reserve Bank of Philadelphia." When the recall of gold was ordered, Boyd continued, "by former Secretary of the Treasury Woodin . . . [someone] instead of returning the bag intact to the Mint" removed "ten of these coins . . . leading to their subsequent distribution."

If it occurred to Boyd, Strang, or Haley that even this explanation alleged some form of theft, no one brought it up. Boyd had bought the coin in February, 1937, the same month Berenstein had bought his, from the same source. But Boyd had paid Macallister only $1,100. If nothing else, it proved that the coin market was fluid and that Macallister gave preferred clients a break, unlike B. Max Mehl.

Ira Reed was next. A small, weedy man with glasses too big for his narrow face, beneath his smooth, bland exterior he was a most unwilling participant. Yes, he admitted to having sold two of the coins, but beyond that his memory failed him. Reed did not recall to whom he had sold them but promised to consult his records and get back to the agents.

James F. Bell was next. His real name was Jake Shapiro. A collector-dealer or dealer-collector, his collection expanded and contracted as the need arose. Dollar value held a sweeter attraction to Bell than historical or artistic merit. His real business, in Chicago, might have been a bit murky—loan-sharking was whispered—but as far as the Stacks were concerned, he was a good customer who had some astonishing coins.

At 2 P.M., as the last session of the auction began, thoroughly unhappy, Bell handed over to the agents one newly purchased, brightly shining 1933 double eagle. As Harry Strang wrote out a receipt for the coin, Bell, with a frustrated, rueful sigh, gave him an interesting bit of information. He had bought the coin only two days earlier—from Ira Reed.

A Routine Inquiry

CHAPTER 8

Assistance, Resistance, and Stalemate

———◆———

Monday, March 27, 1944. Manhattan.

HARRY STRANG SAT IN HIS OFFICE AND STARTED ON FOLLOW-UP, MAKING lists, jotting notes, isolating pieces of the jigsaw. He made a column of the coins surrendered and from whom: Berenstein, Bell, and Flanagan. A column for known but unseized pieces: Boyd. A column for those believed to be owners: Clarke and Williams. Six so far. Another page, more columns, the dealers: Stack's, Mehl, Berenstein, Smith, Reed, Kosoff, Kaplan, and Macallister. Finally, a past owner: Taylor.

Boyd's story about the coins coming out of a bag sent to the Federal Reserve Bank in Philadelphia sounded good or at least plausible and needed some checking. Strang made a call to a successful local coin dealer, Louis S. Werner, who told Strang that Boyd's story had wide circulation and that it had been freely discussed by coin collectors at the annual meeting of the American Numismatic Association in New York in 1939. Apart from that he knew nothing.

New York Supervising Agent John McGrath received a telephone call from headquarters in Washington. He told Strang to pack a bag and wired Chief Wilson to confirm that Harry was headed to the Philadelphia office on "temporary assignment in connection with the investigation of $20 Gold Coins date 1933." Strang completed his initial report to Wilson and turned it in to McGrath.

At 2:45 P.M., the teletype bell rang: "REFERENCE TO GOLD MATTER ON WHICH AGENTS STRANG AND HALEY WERE WORKING, PLEASE USE FILE NUMBER CO-10468. WILSON END."

The New York office responded: "OK MCGRATH END."

The case had a number. It was official.

When Strang got to Philadelphia the next morning, he immediately headed over to the local office in the new Custom House, a limestone and brick monolith that towered over the historic district of the city. The austere, uninspired exterior of the building hid a lobby of multicolored marbles, brushed steel, and gleaming brass. With sweeping staircases, elaborate metalwork, and a domed atrium, its interior resembled one of the great transatlantic liners rather than a government workplace.

The Secret Service offices were in room 407, where Strang met the local agent assigned to assist him. George C. Drescher was a twenty-five-year veteran in the Secret Service who had spent a spell protecting Herbert Hoover. They discussed the case and decided to head out immediately and tackle James G. Macallister, at 3400 North Fifth Street.

Tuesday, March 28, 1944. Philadelphia.

No Macallister was at the address provided by Berenstein, which looked like a grocery store. Drescher suggested they head down to the financial district, where there were plenty of coin dealers. Reed of course was one, but first they tried Stephen K. Nagy, a well-known authority on coins and antiques.

Nagy, whose shop was on South Eighteenth Street, was closing in on sixty. Years earlier he had inherited great connections at the Mint and with his partner, John Haseltine, had used the Mint as a made-to-order shop. Odd and curious concoctions, rare coins, unique coins, the likes of which no one had seen or heard of before—all seemed to emanate from Nagy.

Two of the most infamous—and valuable—were the 1884 and 1885 silver trade dollars. According to the Mint's records, neither issue was ever made (dies for the 1884 were prepared, however), and none was known to exist until Nagy and his partner magically appeared with a handful of each beginning in 1907. The first of these was sold to the greatest coin collector of all time, Virgil Brand, a reclusive Chicago beer baron who had accumulated a staggering collection exceeding 368,000 coins at the time

100

Secret Service Special Agent George C. Drescher (rear left) with Harry S. Truman in 1945, months after being reassigned from the 1933 double eagle investigation. Drescher became head of Truman's protection detail.
(Herbert Hoover Presidential Library)

of his death in 1926. Brand, who eventually owned at least five of the ten known, bought this first 1884 trade dollar for a mere $50 (examples are worth up to $400,000 each in 2004), and the first of his two or three (of five known) 1885 trade dollars cost him $750 in 1912 (specimens have flirted with a million dollars in recent auctions). Were they genuine? Restrikes? Authorized? Or just elaborate fakes? No one knew and nobody cared to ask—including the authorities, then or since. The sharp-featured Nagy, who many numismatists consider "the top crook of them all," got rich.

Now a wealthy dealer in manuscripts, silver, Americana, paintings, and of course coins, Nagy liked to talk. A spinner, a dissembler, perhaps a bald-faced liar, he always knew something about everything and always said he knew more than he could say. But Strang and Drescher did not know of this reputation.

Always happy to cooperate, Nagy, his deep-set eyes darting, told the two agents that he had been acquainted with former Secretary of the

Assistance, Resistance, and Stalemate

Treasury William Woodin. It was the truth. Well before his appointment, William Hartman Woodin, industrialist, friend of FDR, had been a collector of coins at the loftiest levels.

In 1909, Nagy and Haseltine had orchestrated one of their special inside deals. Woodin, in return for a numbing $10,000 apiece, received two massive gold coins. Nicknamed "half unions" with a face value of fifty dollars (a union would have carried the value of $100), they were experimental coins—patterns—made in 1877, that were never adopted for use. Where the two coins truly came from (one article, published in 1886, reported that they had already been melted) is lost in the pea soup of numismatic lore, but Nagy claimed to have gotten them from the estate of his partner's father-in-law, William Idler, from whom indirectly Nagy had come into the thriving Mint concession.

Woodin, an enthusiast whose numismatic weakness had long been gold coins, reacted like an addict—without thinking. He bought them. But when word of their sale became public, the hullabaloo was deafening. "The coins were rightly the property of the Nation." Woodin wouldn't argue, couldn't argue. He agreed. He returned the coins to Nagy and expected his money back. But in 1909, $20,000 was an enormous sum and possibly already spent. Instead of providing the refund, Nagy and Haseltine went back to their private well, the United States Mint, and produced several trunks of other pattern and experimental coins that had been littering one of the vaults. Perhaps these thousands of coins were leftovers, originally made to be sold to collectors, or perhaps they too existed in the murky twilight of quasi-legality, but no issue was made of their legitimacy. Woodin accepted the swap, which not only pleased him enormously but redirected his collecting habits from gold coins to patterns.

Nagy smoothly continued, "While Woodin was still secretary [I] visited him in Washington and during this visit, Secretary Woodin exhibited [to me] five 1933 Double Eagles." Strang and Drescher shifted forward with interest. Woodin supposedly had made an offer of one of the coins to Nagy. But unaccountably, the Philadelphia dealer, whose stock in trade was getting the rarest, priciest and most unusual of coins, said that he had declined. Instead, he said, he had asked Mr. Woodin "whether he had more than five, to which Mr. Woodin replied with a knowing wink of his eye."

That was the end of Nagy's story. Intriguing, even shocking, it provided another lead to be investigated. The agents thanked Nagy and headed a few doors down to meet with Ira Reed at 37 South Eighteenth Street.

Nagy had been effusive and forthcoming, but he had not been a focus of the investigation. Ira S. Reed had already been implicated and so was only grudgingly responsive. As Strang tossed questions at him, new information seeped out from Reed's replies. When he had been interviewed in New York on Saturday, he had admitted only to having handled two coins; now it was *three*. Conspicuously, his memory had improved and he remembered to whom he had sold them: one to T. James Clarke and two (*not* one) to James F. Bell.

No new coins had been added to the list. Strang knew about the Clarke coin, but, Reed explained, he had purchased it over the counter of his shop in 1941. Both Bell's coins were also known examples, but Reed revealed more of their history. The first was the Taylor coin that Berenstein had mentioned; Reed said he had sold it in 1942 to Bell, who had in time moved it on with a collection to B. Max Mehl in Texas. The second coin, now in Secret Service custody, was identified as the Hammel specimen, which Reed had sold to Bell only days earlier and hadn't remembered when first interviewed by Strang just the previous Saturday.

Ira Reed produced no backup for any of these transactions. As the questioning wore on, he inadvertently "intimated that he had disposed of others" but quickly recovered and "declined to give further information." He then coyly suggested to Strang and Drescher that if the present owners of other examples could be "assured that the coins would be ultimately returned to them," there could be greater cooperation and more information forthcoming. The agents firmly told the dealer that they could make no promises to that effect.

Reed promptly clammed up.

Strang and Drescher dug their hands into the pockets of their coats and trudged through the cold a few blocks over to dealer Macallister's current address on the tenth floor of another expensive-looking Deco confection in the heart of the tony financial district on Walnut. A pale, glazed-brick exterior with slightly darker terra cotta triglyphs between each floor housed a lobby of brass and steel, starkly severe geometric metalwork reflecting off highly polished marble walls. The Philadelphia Stock Exchange was just down the block, and Macallister's primary clientele worked in this neighborhood: stockbrokers, bankers, and industrialists, men of extraordinary wealth. Many thought that Macallister, "Gentleman Jim" as some called him, was a product of the same privileged world to which he catered so successfully. Not so. Although James Macallister's family had deep roots in Philadelphia—his forebear John Macallister, an optometrist, had been caught on canvas by James Peale in 1812—they

Assistance, Resistance, and Stalemate

James G. Macallister. He bought the first five 1933 double eagles from Israel Switt and stopped when he thought they were too common to justify the price!
(James T. Macallister)

were of modest means. Macallister's father was a grocer who had let his son deal in coins from the second floor above his store.

Without a college education but with an exceptionally gifted eye for coins, a terrific sense of humor, a fair golf game, and great skills at bridge, Macallister forged a successful career. He had worked originally in real estate but had dabbled in coins for years and begun dealing full time about 1930. His success grew steadily. He forged an alliance with Wayte Raymond, a legendary New York City dealer and auctioneer, whose annual turnover quietly approximated that of the extrovert Mehl. By 1944, Macallister was a pillar of the coin business, respected for his knowledge, his contacts, and his manners. King Farouk, who occasionally called Macallister at home, and dilettante collector Franklin Delano Roosevelt (who had 402 coins, compared to his 1.25 million stamps), whom Macallister had cut off for not paying his bills, had numbered themselves among his better-known clients. Mac kept rooms at the Waldorf-Astoria and generally spent Thursday and Friday in New York City, working on the well-regarded auctions that he had conducted with Raymond since 1932.

Jimmy Macallister liked good cigars and cats, moved easily in monied circles, and lunched regularly at the Union League. His prosperous appearance—a bowler and chesterfield coats, shining benchmade shoes, and bespoke suits from the most expensive tailor in Philadelphia—did nothing to belie his peers' belief in his equal social standing. Macallister at fifty-two was a successful man who enjoyed life. But in March, 1944, he had just over a year to live.

He graciously met with Strang and Drescher in his small but thoroughly civilized office. Wearing his trademark double-breasted suit with vest, the well-fed Macallister looked bigger than his five-foot eight-inch frame suggested. Sitting behind his desk, which dominated the front room, he offered the agents leather club chairs.

Macallister had nothing to hide. He answered all of the agents' questions directly, fully, and offered more than they asked. They found it a welcome relief.

On February 15, 1937, he had purchased the first of the 1933 double eagles from Israel Switt, a jeweler and scrap gold dealer. Just to be sure, he went to his files and dug out old receipts. He had paid $500. It was an important purchase, an exciting one. It was the first time Macallister had seen a 1933 double eagle, and he had never before even heard rumors of their existence. It was pristine. Prior to Switt's offer, said Macallister in his rich baritone, "no 1933 double eagles were circulated."

Macallister peered at the Secret Service men through his rimless glasses and recalled that after he had purchased the coin from Switt, he had made one call to sell it—to Max Berenstein in New York. It had been an easy sale. Berenstein had run an ad in the *Numismatist* back in February, 1936, offering to buy any number of differing dates in the double eagle series, including the 1933. He may have been fishing. Berenstein snapped it up and paid Macallister $1,600, a handsome profit indeed.

With such an easy sale under his belt, Macallister called Switt and bought another one four days later, again for $500. Fred Boyd eagerly added that one to his collection within days, together with two of the elusive 1933 ten-dollar gold pieces as well. The price for the double eagle was $1,100. In 1938, Boyd and Macallister found out that the national collection was lacking an example of the 1933 eagle and jointly donated one of the two included in this transaction to the Smithsonian.

Assistance, Resistance, and Stalemate

Macallister told Strang and Drescher about three other '33 double eagles he had purchased. Another at $500 he bought on July 1, 1937, which he sold to a collector, B. L. Taylor. But, he understood, it had changed hands since. In the middle of July, he recalled, the price from Switt went up to $550. The first of the two that he bought at that price he had sold to B. Max Mehl, from whom it had gone to Colonel Flanagan, and it was now safely residing in a Secret Service vault. The last one Macallister bought, again for $550, was in early December, 1937. Again he dealt the coin to Mehl, this time for $1,000. In all, he bought five coins from Israel Switt, but none after December, 1937.

It wasn't that Switt wouldn't sell him more. Macallister was worried about his own reputation. "It became apparent," he sighed, "that there were too many of the coins obtainable to warrant their being represented as rarities." Something was wrong, and he was becoming uneasy. Every time he asked Switt where the coins came from, he got a different answer: "An old lady who was related to a high official in the Treasury Department . . . a man called Norris connected with the Federal Reserve Bank of Philadelphia."

"In view of Switt's reputation as a gold-coin bootlegger," said Macallister, "[I] was not disposed to place any credence in Switt's stories." It had been a good run, though. In 1937, James G. Macallister had moved up from an Oldsmobile to a Cadillac.

Strang and Drescher interviewed the prosperous Macallister at length. In addition to his own sales, he provided information about other examples, both of which were already known to the agents: the Hammel coin and the one said to belong to Frank Williams, the president of the Western and Southern Insurance Company in Cincinnati. Both, said Macallister, had been handled by New York coin dealer Abe Kosoff.

Strang and Drescher returned to the Custom House. Over a full day, they had stirred up a blur of information. As they mounted the steps to the main entrance, they couldn't have helped but notice the cornerstone just to the right. William H. Woodin's name was carved into the yellowy-gray cornerstone, as Secretary of the Treasury, with the date—1933.

Another suspect.

Tuesday–Thursday, March 28–30, 1944. Washington, D.C.

On Tuesday afternoon in Room 115 in the Treasury Building, F. C. C. Boyd was conferring with Special Agent James Haley, whom he had met three days earlier with Harry Strang at Stack's. They spent "a very interesting couple of hours" together, discussing the 1933 double eagle.

Boyd was one of most prominent and revered of American coin collectors and had assembled storied collections that abounded in the rarest, most valuable, and most perfectly preserved specimens known to exist. F. C. C. Boyd was one of only three men (John Garrett, who had sought a 1933 double eagle in vain was another, and Virgil Brand the third) who had once owned not one but two examples of what was America's most famous coin: the legendary Brasher doubloon. Privately struck in 1787 in New York, five years before the establishment of the Mint, by Ephraim Brasher, a goldsmith and neighbor of George Washington's on Cherry Street, it was the first gold coin made in the young nation and worth sixteen dollars, the value of the Spanish doubloons that freely circulated in the colonies. With the sun rising behind a mountain on the obverse (and with a charming conceit, Brasher's own name just below), and a heraldic eagle on the reverse, only seven survived and were considered to be the most valuable of all American coins. Garrett owned the finest example, which had been sold at auction for a record-breaking sum. (When re-offered in 1979, it again set a world record: $725,000. In his 1942 novel *The High Window*, Raymond Chandler had detective Philip Marlowe on the trail of one.) Boyd's collections ranged from colonial to modern, paper money to patterns (a vast number of which he acquired from William Woodin's estate), and many of his finest treasures ultimately ended up during the 1940s in the hands of the voracious collector from Cairo: King Farouk.

Boyd lived and breathed coins. The previous Saturday he had made himself abundantly clear to the Secret Service about his '33 double eagle, and his view hadn't changed one iota: the coin would remain in his custody until the government gave him a satisfactory rationale for its return.

Yes, he had indeed bought the coin in February, 1937, from Jim Macallister. It was a great purchase. He had never seen a 1933 double eagle before, nor had he heard of their availability. Boyd was one of the most active participants in collecting circles, and if he hadn't heard of something, it was unlikely to exist.

While the purchase price, $1,100, wasn't cheap (his salary during the Depression years was approximately $27,000 a year), it had nearly completed his collection of twenty-dollar gold pieces. He had even purchased along with it two 1933 ten-dollar gold pieces. Boyd had known there were a few of the eagles around, but they were hard to find, and so, when Mac had offered him two, he grabbed both.

107

F. C. C. Boyd, c. mid-1950s. He bought his 1933 double eagle from Macallister in February, 1937, for $1,100, and exhibited it publicly three times.
(Eric P. Newman Numismatic Education Society)

Like a kid with the newest and best toy that no one else has, Boyd had been thrilled by his newest acquisition and had immediately shown it off to other collectors. Barely three weeks after buying it, he first exhibited his 1933 double eagle at a meeting of the New York Numismatic Club, along with the one of the two eagles. Not only was it no secret, but the sudden appearance of this amazing rarity had made news. The *Numismatist,* with a few thousand subscribers, twice mentioned Boyd's display in its April issue. A smaller but feistier publication, the *Numismatic Scrapbook,* went further and got the gossip: There were more 1933 double eagles out there.

A year later, in August, 1938, in Columbus, Ohio, Boyd had exhibited the '33 to an even wider audience at the American Numismatic Association convention. The convention report called it "the last of the gold series." In 1939, Fred Boyd's wife exhibited the coin at yet another A.N.A. convention at the Pennsylvania Hotel in Manhattan. There was no subterfuge. It was the talk of the convention, as Lou Werner had told Agent Strang.

In February, 1941; Smith and Son, 2267–69 Clybourn Avenue, Chicago, had even run a full-page ad in the *Numismatist* with a photograph of the coin dead center. Smith called it one of only three known to exist at the

Rarities That Are Seldom Offered For
Sale Is Our Specialty.

MOFFAT & CO.

San Francisco, Calif., 1849

$16.00 Ingot, extremely fine. Price on application to interested buyers.

DOUBLE EAGLE, 1933.

1933 $20.00 Uncirculated, the rarest of all Double eagles with the exception of the 1849; only 3 pcs. known to exist at the present time. Price on application to interested buyers.

CLARK GRUBER & CO., 1861.

1861 $20.00 Clark Gruber & Co. Strictly very fine $300.00.

Drop us a line if you wish to buy, or if you wish to sell. We are in the market to purchase all worth-while Numismatic material in any series.

ESTABLISHED 1920

Smith & Son

2267-69 CLYBOURN AVENUE
Chicago, Illinois
DIVERSEY 2097

Advertisement for the sale of a 1933 double eagle, February, 1941. There were no immediate takers, no interest from law enforcement, and Ira Reed bought it months later.
(The *Numismatist*: American Numismatic Association)

present time; the price revealed only to interested buyers. In the March and June issues, minuscule one-line, unillustrated ads followed. The coin was said by Max Berenstein to have been purchased by Ira Reed. No Treasury men had come knocking on the door then. Why now?

Haley offered no answer but instead rattled off the list of 1933s that the Secret Service had confirmed and asked Boyd if he knew of any other owners. He did. James Stack, of New York City—no relation to the coin dealers—had one.

The meeting concluded on a cordial note, and the two men agreed to stay in touch. Boyd sent him James Stack's address at the Roosevelt Hotel. Haley thanked Boyd and invited him to visit "any time you are in Washington."

For Boyd to relent and relinquish his great prize, the Secret Service would have to prove their case. For the time being they had a gentlemen's standoff.

109

Frank Wilson held a hurried meeting in his office. Jim Haley was there. He had brought the Flanagan coin along from New York so the boss could see what all the hubbub was about. Dr. F. Leland Howard was also there—with a chip on his shoulder. The gleaming oval mahogany conference table was at the far end of the Chief's office.

Haley briefly sketched out the opening gambit of the investigation. Strang was still in Philadelphia following up, and teletypes were rattling back and forth with the Dallas, Texas, office, checking up the Mehl angle.

All was pretty mundane, but Leland Howard was embarrassed, defensive, and combative. In a memo that Howard wrote to Chief Wilson following the meeting, the reasons for his attitude were readily apparent. He revealed that only a month earlier, on February 25, 1944, a 1933 double eagle had been submitted to the Bureau of the Mint as part of an application for an export license for the Royal Legation of Egypt. The license was granted on February 29, the coin destined for King Farouk of Egypt. The Secret Service men could only have stared at Howard in stunned disbelief. Their efforts to retreive the coins were already undermined by the very institution that had asked them to begin the investigation.

The coin had been shown to Smithsonian curator Belote. Doc Howard reported that "as far as I know, Mr. Belote did not have information in his possession which would indicate whether or not these coins had ever been paid out by the Treasury." How could he? Even *he* hadn't known.

Where the gold coin was now was unknown. The '33 had been physically removed from the Mint vault and returned to the Egyptians only a week—exactly a week—before Ernest Kehr's question had been fielded. For all Howard knew, it was sitting in Cairo by now.

Howard reiterated his blamelessness and in so doing all but accused Nellie Tayloe Ross of having made the blunder. "As you will recall," he informed Wilson primly in his memo, "the discovery of these coins in circulation came about through a routine inquiry as to the number of these coins that had been placed in circulation. I checked . . . and discovered none was ever legally paid out by the Mint. With this information at hand," he continued, "I called on you and informed you of the situation." The implication was clear.

Officiously he changed the subject, said he would forward copies of the two authorizing letters from the Smithsonian and the "Philadelphia accounting for the entire coinage of $20.00 gold pieces in the year 1933." In return, he requested self-importantly that he would greatly appreciate being kept fully up to date on the investigation at all times. Apparently Mr. Strang had called on Mr. Dressel, the Mint superintendent, without his knowing, and he would like the "full details of Mr. Haley's visit to New York . . . and a copy of his report as soon as he submits one."

A career bureaucrat to the core, Howard's densely worded memo to the Chief was clearly intended to protect himself.

Equally clear was that at least one 1933 double eagle—residing in a king's coin room—was well beyond the grasp of the law, at least for the time being.

Thursday, March 30, 1944. Philadelphia.

Nobody liked Israel Swift. One either loved him or loathed him. Regardless, his customers did business his way or not at all. His obituary, a half-century later, described him as short and round, but he was of average height and pudgy. Prickly enough to flay the hide off anyone who crossed him, he was generous to charity but not to his tailor, if he had one. Izzy Swift couldn't care less about the way he looked. Sloppy, balding, with errant wisps of red hair, he looked more like a hobo than the wealthy man he was. His shop reflected his dress code.

130 South Eighth Street was in the heart of Philadelphia's Jewelers' Row, the oldest diamond district in the nation and one of the largest. Signs and placards hung helter-skelter from the fronts of the buildings and shops, inviting, encouraging, begging for customers to cross their thresholds.

Swift's plain-fronted four-story building in the middle of the block was singularly uninviting. The CLOSED sign that perennially hung at the door whether he was open or not didn't help to dispel the lack of welcome. It was a short walk from the Custom House. Passing the elegantly pointed brick facade of Independence Hall to the tumble of low commercial buildings on Sansom Street was a trip through time and cultures. The window of Swift's shop was dirty. The cheap, tawdry items on display looked as if they belonged in a down-at-the-heels hockshop, not the store of a jeweler of substance—just the way Swift liked it.

Although Strang and Drescher turned up at Swift's without an appointment, Swift was expecting the visit. Ira Reed, tight as a piano wire, had called Swift on Monday morning and told him the Secret Service had confiscated three coins in New York, had his name, and was sure to be knocking on the door to his shop. Just a heads-up.

Assistance, Resistance, and Stalemate

Their visit was the start of a tiring day for both Switt and the agents. The shop was long and dark, divided into thirds. Two tall framed cases with sliding glass doors ran two-thirds the depth of the shop, separated by a narrow aisle. A wooden Chinese tall case loomed to the left of the entrance, and a long, low glazed counter protected the three large safes behind it. Above them, encircling the shop, were paintings, prints and photographs, some framed, some not, all of questionable artistic merit with the exception of a nineteenth-century photograph of the Roman Forum. A huge, ornate National cash register indicated that some money must have changed hands at some time. The stock in the cases was almost as unimpressive as that in the windows, but upstairs and in the safes, unseen, unshown, and unknown, was an embarrassment of riches, if the Secret Service had the right information.

Following up on what they had been told in New York, what they had learned from Macallister and at the U.S. Mint, Strang led Switt through the interview. The middle-aged jeweler readily remembered and admitted to selling nine 1933 double eagles. Five to Macallister in 1937. Two to Abe Kosoff and two to Ira Reed two or more years later. After that his memory faded, became selective, and grew dimmer and dimmer as the day wore on.

Strang pressed him. Where had the coins come from?

"I do not remember when, where or from whom I purchased them, as they were received by me in collections with other coins at other times," replied the jeweler.

Neither Strang nor Drescher believed him.

Switt told them, "On my oath . . . I do not have any records which show the time, place and identity of the persons from whom I obtained these coins."

That, they believed.

They took another tack to shake him. Macallister had told the Secret Service agents that Switt had been arrested a decade earlier for illicitly trafficking in gold coins. Their official records jibed.

Switt had been lugging an unusually heavy briefcase in the Thirtieth Street train station in August, 1934, when wary policemen had stopped him. They found over a hundred gold coins, mainly double eagles from the nineteenth century. Switt was arrested and prosecuted under the 1934 Gold Reserve Act and lost his license to deal in gold. The case dragged through the courts for four years, and ultimately Switt was ordered to forfeit the coins as a fine. Pretty stiff for those Depression years, it was calculated at an even $2,000.

Switt shrugged it off. He was wealthy and, he said, the coins in the briefcase hadn't been his, even though in 1934 he had said otherwise. That episode hadn't even slowed down his trade in gold. His brother-in-law and silent partner, Edward Silver, simply took out a new gold license, and the business thrived. Probably the biggest scrap gold dealers in Philadelphia by a long shot, they were rumored to have their own melting pot in the back room.

Doggedly the agents kept pushing. They took Swift for a drive. Halfway across town at the Corn Exchange Bank on Chestnut Street, Izzy opened his safe deposit box for examination. Strang found nothing of interest, but learned that Ira Reed had warned the canny jeweler days earlier. Who knew what had been there before the timely call?

The agents tried questioning Swift in their Custom House office, but he was a tough egg to crack. The interrogation, like haggling over the price of a piece of jewelry, may have bothered him, but it didn't show. He didn't like it, but this was the law, not customers. He couldn't just show them the door, as he was renowned for doing if an unsuspecting client committed the heinous crime of negotiating.

In doing some homework the day before, Strang had spoken to Edwin Dressel, the Mint's superintendent and got some names of those who might have had peripheral or intimate dealings with Israel Swift over the years. He went at Swift.

Swift was firm. He said that he'd been in the business of buying and disposing of scrap gold for forty years and that the only Mint employees he had got to know were Jack Pepper, in charge of the Receiving Department, and Robert Graham, who had retired from the same department.

No one else?

He had briefly spoken to former Head Clerk Fred Chaffin in an attempt to get his revoked gold license renewed.

What about Assistant Superintendent Ralph Roland? asked Strang.

No.

Head cashier George McCann?

No.

Swift was emphatic: "I never had any conversation about or obtained any gold coins from or through any employees of the U.S. Mint at Philadelphia or elsewhere."

Did he have any more of the 1933 double eagles? attempted Harry Strang.

Swift's answer was to be expected. He did not, he said, have any of these coins in his possession or under his control at that time. It was a pat answer that left a warren of openings.

Strang, exasperated, wrapped it up. Switt agreed to have his accountant open what books he did keep, along with his tax returns. He gave the agents a sworn statement, reiterating the day's questioning.

Neither Strang nor Drescher found Switt's statements, sworn or otherwise, to be convincing. Switt's wandering and inability to remember the details of the purchase of the coins were suspect, especially as "his memory was entirely clear on all other particulars as to these transactions."

A stalemate after four hours. It had felt longer.

CHAPTER 9

The Crooked Cashier

———◆———

ISRAEL SWITT WAS THE NEW ROME—ALL ROADS LED TO HIM, AND ALL 1933 double eagles had come from him. They hadn't suddenly materialized out of thin air, and Switt hadn't made them himself. He had had a source. But who? And from where had the source got them?

One thing was clear: the fable that Switt had spun—different coins from different sources—was made from the flimsiest of threads. Each alone would be blown to tatters by the investigators, but seeing through all of them woven together was tough.

Superintendent Dressel extended every courtesy to special agents Strang and Drescher when they visited the Mint and settled them into a room set aside for their use. The long Reception Room on the second floor, used annually for the meeting of the Assay Commission, was the perfect room in which to spread out, dig through files, and conduct interviews. In the coming days and weeks, the Secret Service agents would become familiar, if not always appreciated, faces.

The initial interviews in New York and Philadelphia with the front-and-center protagonists had been telling. The responses, ranging from complete cooperation to evasion and veiled hostility, gave Strang a sense of the problem's parameters. The foot soldier in the van, he was tracking the golden spoor in two directions: to the current owners and to its origin.

The trail to the owners was the easier. They were collectors, men of substance with reputations to uphold, and now, he had found out, even the King of Egypt. These men were not criminals but single-minded with a mania that had led them to part willingly with a thousand dollars or more for a mere ounce of gold. They may not have liked surrendering such fruits to the Secret Service, but neither, it appeared, had they obtained them by nefarious means.

The road less traveled, pitted and potholed with false exits and blind alleys, would lead to the wellspring somewhere within the looming granite edifice of the Mint. In the piles of linen-tied files laid out on the long table, somewhere lurking in the yellowed correspondence and records straight-pinned together, the buckram and leather-bound ledger books, lay an answer.

An unintentional shipment? A simple accounting error? An official request? Or plain and simple malfeasance? Greed? Theft for profit? If so, how? Then, who? And when?

Agent Strang started with the same ten-page memo accounting for the total mintage that had led Leland Howard to the Secret Service. But he wasn't looking to balance columns of figures. He was looking for names and opportunities. It was a short list, and possibilities blossomed immediately.

The vast majority of the 1933 double eagles had been stored together. On June 27, 1933, all but five hundred of the total production of the coins were removed from the Cashier's Working Vault and rolled on ponderously laden dollies down the enameled brick hall and into the massive bullion-holding Vault F on the Sixteenth Street side of the building. When the Mint was constructed, it was considered to be one of the largest vaults of its kind in the world, second only to the cavernous Silver Dollar Vault at the other end of the long subterranean corridor. Between them were four smaller vaults. The hardened steel doors of each were stenciled with an identifying letter. Each was protected by time locks, and the metal of the inner workings was etched with elaborate foliate designs—a touch of spring enlivened the stygian halls.

One thousand, seven hundred and eighty bags, all containing 1933 double eagles, each printed with a consecutive serial number, had been heaved into tidy piles on the floor in Cage 1. They joined the piles of other gold coins deposited there in previous years. The heavy steel-grated enclosure was shut, sealed, and its contents would sleep uninterrupted for three years.

At 9:20 A.M. on October 20, 1936, to install a new protective system, the cage was briefly opened, promptly closed, and resealed. All in the same day. The records of the auditors indicated that nothing had been touched.

On February 3, 1937, Vault F, Cage 1 was invaded for the last time. The contents of the cage included nearly seventy-six tons of gold coins, and all had an appointment in the Melting Room.

Strang saw that one name cropped up twice in this chronology: George A. McCann. In June, 1933, then an assistant in the Cashier's Office and representing the Superintendent of the Mint, he had applied his red wax seal to Cage 1 when the 1933 double eagles were first put into long-term storage. Then, in February, 1937, it had been McCann again, now risen to the post of Cashier of the Mint, who had broken the seal for the last time on the same cage when the last of the nation's gold coins were removed for destruction. On that dark, late-winter's day, it was discovered that an entire bag of double eagles valued at $5,000–250 coins–was missing from Cage 1 in Vault F, which had a four-combination door and three-foot walls lined with millions of pounds of specially hardened steel. Houdini couldn't have done better.

A Secret Service investigation had immediately ensued. William Landvoight, a former Olympic athlete, then the Philadelphia Supervising Agent, led the inquiry, which concluded that the double eagles that had disappeared were probably struck in 1929. There had been thirty bags of them stored in one bin in Cage 1, and only twenty-nine were accounted for in 1937. Landvoight studied the pattern of dust on the floor and other bags in the cage and deduced that the missing bag had been taken in 1933. This despite the official record, which said that the contents of the cage had been fully intact as recently as October, 1936–during an examination that was obviously cursory and flawed. How the bag had disappeared and who had taken it remained a mystery, but not who was held accountable.

One of the Mint's oldest, most effective security devices was to make those responsible for oversights, mistakes, losses, and malfeasance in their department personally liable. In 1937, the missing bag of 1929 double eagles–thought to have disappeared in 1933–was charged to Edwin Dressel, even though he had not even been employed at the Philadelphia Mint until 1935. Dressel was distraught.

On assuming the superintendency, Dressel, should have insisted that the Settlement Committee audit the holdings prior to his taking the reins of office, which was the traditional procedure. Even though a full stocktaking would have been a gargantuan and costly task during the Depression, it would have saved Dressel considerable suffering.

Superintendent Dressel was not merely charged the $5,000 face value of the coins; the January, 1934, gold revaluation had upped the ante from $20.67 to $35 an ounce, so he was on the hook for a whopping $8,465.62.

The Crooked Cashier

Dressel was not an independently wealthy man, and it was an enormous sum of money for anyone at the time, especially a government employee. For eight years the charge had been a fearsome Damoclean sword dangling over Dressel's head from an ever-fraying thread. Finally, in 1945, at the urging of Nellie Tayloe Ross, a bill passed by both houses of Congress eliminated the superintendent's debt.

Even though Dressel had been expected to bear the financial responsibility, he was not the thief, not a suspect, and the actual culprit had never been conclusively identified. But as Strang continued to sift through the piles of documents, one individual, in retrospect, seemed to fit the bill: George A. McCann. Strang followed his career with interest.

The former Cashier of the United States Mint at Philadelphia had been a veteran employee of the Mint who had first been employed in 1917 and had risen quickly through the ranks. Early in his career, as the fair-haired boy, he had found favor with three men who controlled the Philadelphia Mint according to their own pleasure: then Head Bookkeeper Ralph Roland, Chief Clerk Fred Chaffin, and Assayer Chester "Doc" Ziegler. The ambitious McCann "was their whippersnapper or did their bidding." In 1926, however, as foreman of the Weigh Transfer Room, McCann "lost" ten thousand dollars of gold in his records in a month. John Carey, a bookkeeper, who aimed to become superintendent, caught the discrepancy and immediately reported it to the then Assistant Superintendent and Chief Clerk Fred Chaffin. Carey flatly called McCann "a crook."

But Carey had complained to the wrong man. Chaffin, one of McCann's patrons, called a meeting with Roland and Ziegler at their regular watering hole, a hotel on the corner of Catherine and Broad streets, far from the Mint itself. Carey, by some twist of fate, was the manager of this hotel and knew of the meeting—and of others. But McCann was exonerated. The loss of five hundred ounces of gold was put down to "wastage" and forgotten. McCann was now one of the "Four Horsemen,"— as Helen Moore, the assistant superintendent of the Philadelphia Mint called them in 1944—fully insulated, and his stock continued to rise.

By 1933, as the last of the double eagles were being struck, McCann, now an assistant in the Cashier's Department, was positioned for his major move. Cashier Harry Powell, who was not part of the special circle, was due to retire at year's end, and his assistant, Hibberd Ott, in failing health, was next in line. When the frail Ott missed work, Roland flexed his patronage muscles. McCann filled in for Ott and was eventually appointed to the post permanently. It was March, 1934, and now the Four

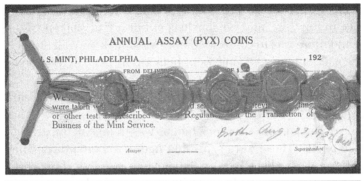

United States Mint Cage Seal: Vault F, Cage 3. A similar one—now lost—would have been used to seal Cage 1 (containing the 1933 double eagles) on June 27, 1933. Note signatures of George A. McCann, Edward McKernan, and Timothy J. Quirk.

(National Archives and Records Administration, Mid Atlantic Region, Center City, Philadelphia)

Horsemen controlled the Cashier's, Chief Clerk's, Book-Keeping, and Assaying Departments—a stranglehold on the Mint. The historical distrust between the Coiner's Department and the other side of the building could not have been greater.

McCann was working in the right place. He liked money and, considering it was the depths of the Depression, he was making good money: $2,421.79, twice what a schoolteacher earned. Even with a wife and child he had enough money to buy a house in Westmont, New Jersey, a solid middle-class neighborhood, with lots of Irish names on the mailboxes. He even had money to gamble in the stock market and went on a four-year winning streak.

Life had been good—until 1937. On February 3, they broke the seals and opened Vault F, Cage 1. The loss of the bag of coins was discovered, and the Secret Service had descended on the Mint like a pack of hounds

The Crooked Cashier

from Hell. There was no proof that McCann had been involved, slight evidence of any sort, and no conclusion, but it had shaken his perfect world, and more was to come. McCann's good luck on Wall Street began to wane suddenly in 1937 and went belly up in 1938. By year's end, his financial worth was $170.73, down from a high of $20,297.68.

McCann began to get desperate. He had lived beyond his means and now, stretched financially, he began to get careless.

One of the Cashier's responsibilities was to take in uncurrent coins from the public. These were coins that had seen better days. They had been damaged or so heavily worn that not only was there little design left but also so much metal had been rubbed away that the coin didn't meet the minimum weight standards. These would be exchanged by the Cashier for coins of full weight and value, which protected the integrity of the circulating medium.

Usually the coins came in bags from shopkeepers, businessmen, banks, and others who had accumulated enough to make the trip to the Mint worthwhile. The coins were weighed and quickly counted, and the appropriate equivalency returned to the depositor. The old coins would be sent to the refinery, rendered down, and the metal reused. The process was simple, direct, and gave McCann a chance to supplement his flagging fortunes. Beginning in 1938, he began diverting a few of these coins at a time for his personal use. He was not the only one.

Pilferage was a problem as old as the Mint. With the vast volume of material passing through, and the chance of being caught seemingly slim, even workers who didn't have financial problems occasionally succumbed to the temptation to steal. In June, 1939, for instance, Mrs. Elizabeth Gook, "A 71-year-old worker at the Philadelphia Mint had been indicted . . . on a charge of stealing $11.55 from the nickels, dimes and quarters which she inspected." She had been due to retire and receive a pension in November. "We are not in financial straits," the mother of five said, "and I didn't have to do it."

Any theft, regardless of size, was alarming and an affront to the security of the nation's wealth. In the spring of 1940, Edwin Dressel, already feeling flames from the Comptroller General's office over the loss of the bag of double eagles, had the quantities and weights of the defaced and worn coins that had been deposited double-checked. Dressel's audit found shortages, and the beleaguered superintendent "immediately went to Washington, and in the absence of the Director, took up the matter with Mr. Howard the Acting Director." Together they went to Chief Wilson, who promptly launched a Secret Service investigation. It was mid-May.

To ferret out the leakage, Philadelphia's Supervising Agent Landvoight, well aware that the intense investigation over the missing bag of double eagles in 1937 was still fresh in everyone's memory, brought in agents from Detroit, Washington, and New York, who would not be recognized by the Mint employees under scrutiny.

"As an aid to trapping the person(s) guilty of peculations, bags of silver coins were treated with a fluorescent chemical." An agent was assigned to become a barfly in the local establishment where thirsty Mint workers hung out. He sat at the bar and traded stories, the latest jokes, and baseball scores, and occasionally stood his new pals a drink or two. He listened, watched, and waited. Other agents checked toll booths to see if any of the fugitive coins turned up.

It was a quick, effective investigation. On May 29, 1940, the foreman of the Cashier's Counting Room, Charles P. Rumpp, was arrested and confessed to taking about $250 in beat-up, worn-out coins.

Quite separately, George A. McCann, Cashier of the United States Mint, was also arrested, for "defalcations" to the extent of approximately $1,200 over a two-year period. A fraction of that was found under his control at the time of his arrest, secreted throughout the Mint. Most was in the pockets of clothing stored in his locker, "$16.75 he had placed in the Mint pay envelopes of May 31, 1940," and $1.50 was found fluorescing at a toll booth.

By this time there was no longer a cabal to break McCann's fall from grace. Two of the Horsemen, Fred Chaffin and Doc Ziegler, were dead, and Ralph Roland, now an assistant superintendent, distanced himself in haste.

"GEORGE A. McCANN did knowingly, willfully and unlawfully embezzle, steal and purloin from the United States Mint at Philadelphia aforesaid, certain valuable things of the property of the United States, to wit: two coins each of the value of twenty-five cents and of the denominations of a quarter dollar:

"Contrary to the form of the Act of Congress in such case made and provided and against the peace and dignity of the United States of America."

All six counts of the indictment read similarly. The total of the losses he was charged with amounted to $339.90. The ongoing investigation opened up McCann's murky financial history and gave the peculator and his lawyer little wiggle room.

On March 24, 1941, McCann pleaded guilty to the charges. At the sentencing, Assistant United States Attorney James P. McCormick asked Federal Judge Guy K. Bard to impose a stiff penalty on the thieving Cashier as an example of how an individual who had been "held in the highest esteem by his superiors at the Mint" would be dealt with. McCann was sentenced to serve a year and a day at Lewisburg Federal Penitentiary in Pennsylvania, was fined $500, and would face further repercussions in the years to come.

It could have been worse. The original Act of April 2, 1792, authorizing the birth of the Mint a different idea: "*Section 19* fixed the death penalty for any employee who debased the coinage for profit or other fraudulent purpose, or who embezzled any sum in coins or bullion left in his control."

McCann, disgraced, had been led from the court house to prison in shackles.

Three years later, Harry Strang quietly smiled to himself. He had a tried and convicted thief as one of his suspects.

Monday, April 3, 1944. New York City.

It was no way to start the week. James Aloysius Stack looked grimly at Special Agent Edward Connors, who was following through on a lead phoned in from Washington earlier that day. There was little Stack could do but be polite, and he offered the investigator a chair in his Broadway office, a leisurely walk from the Roosevelt Hotel on Madison Avenue and Forty-fifth Street, where he had lived since his wife died. Stack had made his money as a textile importer and spent much of it buying coins, seeking out quality as much as rarity. Unlike other collectors, he had not been forewarned of the flowering Secret Service investigation. He was wary and not particularly forthcoming.

Yes, he admitted slowly, he had purchased a 1933 double eagle about two years ago but he had given it to his daughter. Stack said he had "purchased it from a reputable dealer in rare coins" who had told him "that a number of these coins had been shipped to a small country bank apparently in error." End of story.

When asked by Agent Connors who the dealer was, Stack stubbornly refused to answer without the advice of his lawyer. The meeting ended.

Connors headed back to the office, where he reported to Supervising Agent McGrath. They teletyped Wilson in Washington for further instructions. Frank Wilson already knew from whom Stack had bought the coin and told Connors to get back in touch with Stack with this information to see what his reaction was.

James Stack swiftly admitted that he had bought the coin from Ira Reed.

Tuesday, April 4, 1944. Fort Worth, Texas.

B. Max Mehl had not been evasive, but his hectic business schedule had made him elusive. From the outset of the investigation, the Secret Service knew that Mehl was an integral component and Wilson wanted his cooperation. For the past week teletypes from Washington to the Dallas office had been peppered with questions to ask of Mehl's office. In return, the answers were incomplete.

Mehl had just returned to Fort Worth from Chicago when he met with Agent Ralph Oates at an address then known to most numismatists simply as the Mehl Building. From here all of B. Max's advertising, catalogues, and hoopla had emanated since 1916. "Mehl" was carved into the facade above the doorway in stylish, funky lettering.

Barely over five feet tall, the stiff-lipped but courteous dealer met with Oates in his private office, a large wood-paneled room, where he would talk about many things but never sell a coin. Mehl preferred the mail.

The stream of Secret Service inquiries to his office over the past days had given Mehl's efficient secretary, Mary Ferguson, plenty of time to assemble the information requested. As in all aspects of his life, Mehl was rigorously organized. He had nothing to hide and answered all the questions to the best of his ability. There was no hint of deceit, no uncomfortable body language; he had the facts at hand.

He had purchased only three 1933 double eagles over a seven-year period, beginning in 1937. They were, he reminded the investigator with a small smile, rare. Two had come from James Macallister, both in 1937. The first of these he had sold to Colonel Flanagan, but as to the second, he was not positive and offered to comb his records and get back to the Service. The other '33 he had bought from Ira Reed only a few weeks ago, on February 23, 1944, and had sold it the same day to King Farouk of Egypt through his Legation in Washington, D.C. The king had paid him $1,575.

Agent Oates then asked the dealer about the '33 that James Bell had sold him. Mehl produced a list of the collection he had bought from Bell in 1943. There was indeed a 1933 double eagle listed, but it had a pencil line

1933 eagle. First struck and issued to the Treasurer in January, 1933, and legal to own. The design is a variation on that preferred by Saint-Gaudens for the double eagle.

(Courtesy of Sotheby's Inc. ©2003)

drawn through it. Other coins were similarly cancelled, and Mehl explained that none of those coins had been included in the transaction. Mehl was unequivocal in his denial. Why admit to others and not this one? He offered to call Bell to confirm his statement. Oates took him up on it.

As Oates reported to the Chief: "Mr. Mehl placed a telephone call to Mr. Bell in Chicago and invited me to listen in on a connecting telephone. In response to Mr. Mehl's direct and opening question Mr. Bell stated positively that one of these coins was not included in the collection sold to Mr. Mehl. Mr. Mehl then questioned Mr. Bell as to what disposition was made by him of such coin . . . and Mr. Bell refused to give him this information, countering with the question 'Is the Secret Service after you about these coins too?' To which Mr. Mehl replied 'I understand they are checking on them.'"

Oates thanked Mehl and filed his report with Washington. Wilson got in touch with Chicago to do some checking on James F. Bell.

The first week of April had brought cold, dreary weather to Philadelphia and new questions. In addition to the 1933 double eagles, the investigation was to be expanded to include the eagles, which, though perfectly legal to own, might lead back to the shadowy fountainhead.

The official history of the 1933 ten-dollar gold pieces was perfectly straightforward. The first batch had been delivered to the Cashier on January 19, 1933, when Herbert Hoover was still sleeping in the White House and FDR was still a New Yorker. A hundred pieces were reserved that day and shipped to the Treasurer of the United States; they were, therefore, officially issued.

A total of 312,500 eagles had been made and delivered in six shipments between January 19 and March 3, 1933. After the meeting of the 1934 Assay Commission, those not destroyed were returned to the Cashier's Department. George McCann had control, and Israel Switt had subsequently sold some, including the one (purchased with a 1933 double eagle) given by F. C. C. Boyd and James Macallister to the Smithsonian. An ironic trail.

Although the investigation was only days old, with every new question asked of each Mint employee, coin collector, and dealer, the wall of reticence seemed to become higher, deeper, and more resilient. Strang and Drescher knew the inquiry would reach an impasse unless they could get more cooperation. They sought some cloak of immunity from the local United States Attorney's office to offer in return for information. The attorney general's evaluation of their options was at once cheering and depressing. Edward Kelley advised the T-men that in his view "the time element was such that any prosecution statute that might be invoked would now have expired." So, he said, now Strang could safely assure those he was interviewing that no criminal charges would be brought. This would be a boon, surely.

For Strang, however, the opinion must have carried the force of one of Joe Louis' fists. If time protected the cooperative, it also protected the guilty. The case could be over before it had fully begun. But Strang reported the findings to Wilson, and the investigation continued apace. Without the ability to threaten prosecution Strang might now be a toothless, clawless tiger. But then again, maybe not. After all, Frank Wilson had put Capone away not with a bullet hole but with some mislaid assets.

The agents interviewed anyone whose involvement had touched on McCann or Switt. A few still worked at the Mint, but years had passed; many had retired, and others were dead. The only two employees that Izzy Switt had admitted to knowing, despite daily trips to the Mint year in and year out, often with his then-chubby little daughter Joan in tow, were Robert Graham, the retired Deposit Weigh Clerk, and his successor, Jacob Pepper.

Strang and Drescher drove north. The roads glistened with the ugly sheen of black ice. Roslyn, Pennsylvania, where Robert Graham lived, was not far out of town. Graham had known Switt for years and had nothing bad to say about him. He had nothing much to say at all. He admitted that he had been "more or less friendly" with Switt as a depositor of gold for years but said he had never had any dealings with him over coins. He shrugged. His only dealings with him now were over a couple of watches he had over at Switt's shop for repairs.

McCann? Well, as far as he knew, McCann and Switt may have known each other, but he was unaware of any dealings between the two. As for McCann himself, Graham thought about it. He "admitted a close acquaintance" with him and had even been to his house in Westmont, New Jersey. But he hesitated and didn't speak in glowing terms of the former Cashier, noting wryly, he "was a coin collector, aside from the peculations that led to his arrest."

Strang asked, what else?

Graham told the agents that he really knew very little about McCann's activities. But it was apparent that McCann had some money and even more apparent that he liked having it. Graham denied that he knew anything about the source of McCann's income but noted one somewhat unsavory possibility. McCann, explained Graham, "was said to have profited considerably at his brother's expense in the administration of their dead father's estate."

If true, it spoke volumes about the man. Graham offered any help he could and suggested that Strang might talk to his successor Jacob Pepper, and also the man who had been McCann's assistant for three years, Willard Boyce.

The next day Strang and Drescher sat down with both men at the Mint. Jacob Pepper said of course he knew of Israel Switt as a gold depositor, who didn't? But he denied any dealings with the man.

Strang asked him about one name after the other to no avail—except for Ira Reed, who "was familiar to him as a coin dealer." People frequently contacted the Mint for information about their coins, especially their value, and in the Deposit Weigh Room there were a few names recorded as dealers to whom to refer the questioning public. Ira Reed was one of those listed, and Robert Graham had been responsible for it being posted.

Cashier Willard S. Boyce was interviewed next. He had gone to work for McCann in early 1937 and had succeeded to his current position at the end of 1940. If McCann hadn't been arrested, Boyce might have still been his assistant. Once again, money and McCann entered the same sentence. Boyce stated that his old boss "had many activities in which money was involved such as promoting dances and social affairs." No harm, just interesting.

But at work, noted Boyce, he had no idea of McCann's interest in coins until "[I] observed a quantity of silver dollars of old mintage in the cashier's money tray." These, McCann had told him, he kept for "persons wishing coins for commemorative purposes." It was a peculiar observation, especially coming from the current Cashier, because such exchanges had been commonplace for decades.

After Boyce had replaced McCann, he was approached by Ira Reed. Boyce twisted in his chair, clearly uncomfortable, both about Reed and about his subsequent dealings. Only a year ago, in January or February, 1943, recalled Boyce, Ira Reed had contacted him and "wished to secure a quantity of the zinc coated [steel] pennies before they were officially circulated." For his trouble, "Reed promised to compensate him" and stated that "another employee of the Mint had, in the past, made himself quite a piece of money" in doing so. The ever-cool Reed had not identified that individual to Boyce but had "intimated very strongly that person had been McCann."

Boyce had apparently rebuffed Reed's overtures. But the coin dealer was persistent and decided to be Willard Boyce's buddy. He invited him out to dinner, to his office, and to meetings of coin collectors, all, reported Strang, with the express purpose of "endeavoring to cultivate [Boyce] for Reed's business purposes." Had it worked? Boyce admitted that yes, he had sold Reed a number of obsolete proof coins—coins specially manufactured to the highest standards for presentation and sale to collectors. But, he insisted, it was in the regular course of Mint business. The implication was clear: Boyce had not profited, but McCann had.

Willard Boyce didn't particularly like Ira Reed and was unhappy in having to admit his dealings with him. He told Strang and Drescher that he would be willing to "rope" or entrap Reed if they so desired. He also suggested that they might want to talk to Alexander Zimba, who had also known McCann and who might be able to help them with their inquiries.

Zimba was a powerful skilled workman at the Mint, which meant he had done a lot of the heavy lifting. From May 28, 1934, until December 31, 1937, Zimba had been regularly employed in the backbreaking physical movement of the gold from the vaults to the melting room. One stop along the way was weighing the coins and, he told the rapt agents, he had frequently seen McCann "running his hands through the gold coin and handling the coins separately."

127

This was revealing. McCann's tactile excursions were totally unnecessary and "could permit the removal or substitution of coins if so desired." They asked Zimba if he had ever actually seen McCann take any of the coins. He shook his head, rubbing his thick, calloused fingers together. Alexander Zimba looked at the two agents and tried to explain. He had known the Cashier and had known of the Cashier for years, and he said, with eyes wide open and a sense of awe, "[I] regarded McCann as a 'magician' who could get away with anything."

CHAPTER 10

Working the List

———◆———

Thursday, April 6, 1944. Washington, D.C.

SECRETARY OF THE TREASURY HENRY MORGENTHAU, JR., LEANED BACK in his chair and began the wrap-up of his 11:00 A.M. staff meeting.

"Anything else?" he asked the seven men and his indispensable, long-suffering secretary Mrs. Klotz, who was furiously scribbling on her steno pad.

Herbert Gaston, the assistant secretary of the Treasury, who liaised with the Secret Service on a regular basis, smiled. He had been sent a memo by Chief Wilson three days earlier. Gaston, an ex-newspaperman, had been in the Treasury Department since the first fraught days of the Roosevelt administration, during Will Woodin's heroics and the banking crisis. Had he still been the night editor of the New York *World,* he might have run with this one. It was serious, but compared with the war crises that they confronted with wearying regularity, it counted as leavening.

"You might be interested to know that a twenty-dollar gold piece of the 1933 issue was offered up for sale in New York." He paused for effect. "There weren't any of the issue issued. There shouldn't be any in circulation, but quite a large number were coined. [The] Secret Service has been spending some time trying to run it down."

Gaston continued, "There probably was crookedness at the Philadelphia Mint. They first got the story that it was an official of the Federal Reserve Bank of Philadelphia who got them as a favor and sold them, but that seems not to have been true."

Morgenthau, "Henry the Morgue" as some dubbed him, peered absentmindedly through his pince-nez—something may have jogged his memory.

"What did they bring," he asked Gaston, "a couple of thousand dollars?"

"Well," replied Gaston on uncertain ground, "they are worth a good premium, of course, if they can sell them, but I think . . ."

"Gold dollars?" a voice interrupted.

Gaston said, "They are twenty-dollar gold pieces, the issue of 1933, and none were issued legally."

Another voice jumped into the fray. "They were minted."

"There appear to be three or four that got into circulation," said Gaston. Morgenthau interrupted, and the conversation veered off at a tangent.

A decade before, in early February, 1934, just a month after he had officially taken over the Treasury Department, Morgenthau had received a note from the diminutive, wizened Louis Howe asking about 1933 gold coins. Although this letter is lost, it is apparent from the tenor of the reply that Howe was hoping that the Treasury Secretary would be responding with more than just a polite note. Morgenthau had written back to the president's most intimate advisor at the White House and told him that "during the year 1933, we coined $10 and $20 gold pieces." He carefully pointed out that under the new law, passed only days earlier, the nation would coin no more gold. A heavyset man who had wanted for all the world to be the Secretary of Agriculture, Morgenthau squinted, but he had an eye for detail. He sent Howe a copy of the new law, just to make sure there was no misunderstanding. Morgenthau, "who was honest: far too honest," closed his note with a joking reiteration of what he had just said: "I would love to coin a few for you personally, but I am afraid that this is impossible." If Howe had been expecting a few 1933 eagles and double eagles, he was sorely disappointed.

In the same building, just a corridor or two away, Frank Wilson sat in his office, rather less opulent than the big boss's, and reread a memo on his desk from Assistant United States Treasurer Marion Barrister. It was succinct:

"In compliance with Mr. Haley's recent informal request, please be advised that the records of this office do not show that any payments of 1933 Double Eagles were authorized to be made by the United States Mint, Philadelphia, to any Federal Reserve Bank or Branch."

The tales of a handful mysteriously turning up at a country bank or

The man who put Al Capone away: United States Secret Service Chief Frank J. Wilson. He directed the hunt for the 1933 double eagles. (United States Secret Service)

a few neatly slipped out of an inadvertently sent bag by the son of a Federal Reserve Bank president were illusory. Mr. Reed was spinning fables. Mr. Boyd and other collectors had bought in to them either honestly or knowing they were false but wanting to believe them to be true—it made no difference to Wilson.

Still, the Chief was a careful man. He rubbed his square jaw. He would want Strang to double-check all the stories himself. Wilson had been in law enforcement a long time and had come a long way by covering all the bases.

In light of the growing influx of information he thought it best that he sit down with Strang and Drescher to see what they really had, if they were reading the clues properly, and how he might help map their future strategy. He asked Assistant Chief James Maloney, to set something up.

The two agents reported to the Chief's office on a cool, sparkling Friday morning, April 14.

In anticipation of the meeting, Strang and Drescher, working from their notes and an ever-changing handwritten chart, neatly typed up a comprehensive list of the known "1933 Double Eagle Gold Coins."

The list of the known '33s was hazy, unsatisfactory, and occasionally had contradictory connections. It was more detailed than the first list the agents had sketched out only ten days earlier, but it was, Strang knew, still imperfect.

D-E No. 1:
July 1, 1937—Sold by Israel Switt to J. G. Macallister, Philadelphia, then to B. L. Taylor, New York City, then to Ira Reed, Philadelphia, then to J. F. Bell, Chicago, who claims to have sold same in a collection to B. Max Mehl, Fort Worth, Texas, who denies receiving the coin. (This may be coin described as No. 10.)

D-E No. 2:
About 1939—Sold by Israel Switt to Abe Kasoff [sic], New York City, then to Hammell, New York City, then to Ira Reed, Philadelphia, then to J. F. Bell, Chicago, on March 23, 1944, and seized by U.S.S.S. at New York City on March 25, 1944.

D-E No. 3:
About 1939(?)—Sold by Israel Switt to Ira Reed, then to T. James Clark [sic], Jamestown, New York.

D-E No. 4:
February 16, 1937—Sold by Israel Switt, Philadelphia, to J. G. Macallister, Philadelphia; then to Max Berenstein, New York City, on February 16, 1937. Seized by U.S.S.S. at New York City on March 24, 1944.

D-E No. 5:
February 20, 1937—Sold by Israel Switt, Philadelphia, to J. G. Macallister, Philadelphia; then to Fred C. C. Boyd, New York City.

D-E No. 6:
July 1937—Sold by Israel Switt to J. G. Macallister, Philadelphia, then on July 15, 1937, to B. Max Mehl, Fort Worth, Texas; then to Col. J. W. Flanagan on November 26, 1937. Seized by U.S.S.S. at New York City on March 24, 1944.

D-E No. 7:

December 6, 1937—Sold by Israel Switt to J. G. Macallister, Philadelphia, then to B. Max Mehl, Fort Worth, Texas; then to C. P. and C. M. Williams, Ohio. (See Chief's IOC [Inter Office Communication] to AAIC [Acting Agent In Charge] Cincinnati, April 12, 1944.)

D-E No. 8:

About 1939(?)—Sold by Israel Switt to Abe Kasoff [sic], New York City, then to Sol Kaplan, Cincinnati, Ohio; then to C. Frank Williams, Cincinnati, Ohio.

D-E No. 9:

About 1939(?)—Sold by Israel Switt to Ira Reed, Philadelphia, then to James Stack, New York City. (See Agent Connor's report, New York City, dated April 5, 1944.)

D-E No. 10:

February 23, 1944—Sold by Ira Reed, Philadelphia, to B. Max Mehl, Fort Worth Texas, then to Egyptian Legation on same date for forwarding to King Farouk of Egypt. (This may be Coin No. 1, whose whereabouts from Bell to Mehl is disputed.)

The day's meeting covered who had been cooperative, who had not, and what, if any, pressure to apply. All agreed that Switt, Reed, and McCann were at the center of the web. The answers of the first two individuals had proved singularly unsatisfactory, while more and more evidence pointed to the former Cashier as the spigot from whence the stream of golden coins had poured. Wilson wanted McCann interviewed but not until they could ask him tougher questions.

They reviewed the list. The Chief looked up from the page in his paw. Numbers 7 and 8, for example: one coin or two? Strang raised an eyebrow, but Wilson was ahead of him. He had already sent a memo to the Cincinnati office to straighten things out and see if perhaps Williams had not one but two '33s. The Chief shook his head. The list's tangle of pedigrees still needed combing. Wilson suggested that Strang and Drescher continue to double-check to see if there were any overlaps, deviations, or duplications. He told the two men to keep on the track they had been following inside the Mint, and he would get the field agents around the country to interview all the suspected owners, other dealers, and see how far the leach field extended. The progress thus far had been satisfactory, but there were still too many loose ends.

Philadelphia.

Harry Strang and George Drescher once again headed up to their new office in the Mint. Their well-worn shoes clicked and shuffled on the marble steps of the grand staircase, which was bathed in flat, undirected light from bulbs set into the coffered ceiling above. A few had burned out. On the mezzanine level, the Treasury seal, carved in marble, hung heavily over the doorway that had once opened onto the display of the fabulous Mint collection. The agents passed the heavy bronze doors that now only protected a huge leaded chandelier, memories, echoes, and dust—all that remained in the once glorious rotunda.

The investigation had led the agents to three primary suspects more quickly than expected, but the ownership trails were still rutted. Right now they wanted background. McCann, Reed, and Switt were firmly in the crosshairs, and the agents wanted the facts with which to confront them, "as past experiences with these persons [had] shown them to be very uncooperative and evasive." They would interview anyone who had dealt with the three or who might have seen something without knowing it or who just might be involved as well.

Charles P. Rumpp, a former Mint employee, was a sad loser, sixty-six years old and an ex-con. The day after George McCann had been made an example and sentenced to prison for a year and a day, Rumpp had been sentenced to six months. For twenty years he had worked at the Mint and been trusted, but then unaccountably he had begun to steal: "I would take a little at a time, and I have never taken very much at any one time." Over three years he took a total of about $250.00, which left his life a shambles. He was fined $250, had to make good on the stolen amount, and was cast out from the Mint family. Now he was only too willing to help the two agents who had dug him up.

Rumpp had been the foreman of the Deposit and Weigh Room a decade earlier, in the spring of 1934, when the first of the gold coins were being reduced to gold bars. He remembered the men removing the gold stored from the big bullion vault, F–Cage 3–and that Edward McKernan, the Vault Custodian, and his assistant, Louis Frizzle, had been there as well.

Third Philadelphia Mint lobby interior, decorated by Louis Comfort Tiffany at a cost of $40,000. (Author)

They had found five miscellaneous double eagles loose in a bin—unbagged, orphans. The three men did what they were supposed to do and turned the coins over to the Cashier, George McCann, but as far as Rumpp knew, "No subsequent accounting or disposition has been found of them."

Strang and Drescher took notes. Two days after Rumpp had been arrested back in 1940, he had made a second statement. Four years later, he readily confirmed to the two inquisitors what he had said then: "I can recall several instances which now look suspicious to me in the actions of Mr. McCann." Rumpp explained that "the employees of the Mint are so used to handling coin that they do not play with it in their hands." But McCann, "while standing at the boxes filled with uncurrent coin on the trucks, would be handling the coin."

It was not just an occasional idle instance: "He would tell me to phone him when the uncurrent coin were ready to be counted."

"It now occurs to me," Rumpp had said, in a simple, understated way, "as suspicious."

Strang and Drescher visited Louis Frizzle at his home in Delaware Gardens, New Jersey. He looked tired, ill. Accompanying them was one of the Mint's accountants with the original vault records clutched tightly under his arm. The Secret Service agents had been having a bureaucratic tussle with Superintendent Dressel, who allowed them to look at the books but absolutely refused to let them make photostats. They had appealed to Washington for help, but in the meantime, if the records were needed off site, the accountant tagged along with them.

Frizzle had taken charge of the vaults in October, 1936, and the only substantive information he could offer was confirmation that he had been with Edward McKernan and Rumpp when the five double eagles had turned up loose in 1934. He knew they had been turned over to McCann but had no idea what had happened to them subsequently.

The three men thanked Frizzle and left. It had taken only a couple of hours, but Frizzle had seemed exhausted. He died two weeks later.

Between interviews, as new information was gleaned, Strang kept charting, refining and updating the number of coins known and who owned or had owned what. The chart remained a work in progress and was constructed like a family tree stretching back to an unknown progenitor. It had a big black question mark in a box on the left and Switt's name in another next to it. From there the graph paper on which it was drawn was crisscrossed with arrows and marred by cross-outs and erasures.

Numbers were changed, prices were added. The chart looked like something physicists on the Manhattan Project might be proud of, but Harry Strang wasn't.

Cashier Willard Boyce got in touch with Strang and Drescher again. His antipathy toward Ira Reed had apparently grown, and he again offered to set up the coin dealer. He was rebuffed, but something else he remembered about George McCann held the Federal agents glued to their hard wooden chairs.

Boyce recalled that "on at least one occasion he had seen McCann (then Cashier) come into the Deposit Weigh Room with a number of gold coins and weigh them."

The two agents looked at each other. It was more than significant information. It was critical—possibly damning.

Since the Mint's books balanced, and all the coins that had been struck were accounted for appropriately, Strang and Drescher wrote, "the 1933 Double Eagles which are known to have gotten into the hands of collectors, may have been substituted as to weight and value on the cashier's books, by Double Eagles of prior years mintage and having no numismatic value." The Cashier, McCann, would not "ordinarily have any occasion to weigh gold coins, especially a handful of them . . . unless he had been unduly interested in weights."

In other words, McCann might have palmed common twenty-dollar pieces while running his hands through piles of gold coins and later swapped them with the 1933 double eagles under his control. A quick switch. The books would balance. Just as important, the scales would balance. Any discrepancies discovered during the melting process would be minor and well within the acceptable range allowed for wastage. Pretty clever.

The disgraced Cashier had made an indelible impression on everyone agents Strang and Drescher interviewed, and the mounting rash of testimony left little doubt that the question mark on Strang's working chart might soon be replaced with a name: George A. McCann.

The evidence continued to grow. The retired former assistant superintendent, Ralph Roland, one of the Four Horsemen, had been McCann's old mentor and instructed him in his duties when he had taken over as Cashier on March 19, 1934. When interviewed by the two agents at his home in West Philadelphia, Roland appeared to want to help, but "owing to the lapse of time . . . professed not to have a clear recollection." He confirmed, however, that McCann had had access to the 1933 double eagles (kept, he believed, "either in a cage of a basement vault accessible only to the Cashier or in the Cashier's Office Vault") and would have been the one to forward the two coins to the Smithsonian. If Roland was shielding his former protégé, it was a half-hearted effort. There was only one other Mint employee who might have had unfettered access to the '33s—Edward McKernan. The Vault Custodian until October 16, 1936, McKernan had then retired. The peppery Irishman was asked by Strang to explain inconsistencies in the vault records, specifically regarding the whereabouts of the thirty-four 1933 double eagles that hadn't been needed for the Assay Commission and which had supposedly been delivered to him by the Cashier on February 2, 1934.

McKernan looked long and hard at his own records, sloppy, slipshod, and barely legible, colored slightly, and said point-blank that he had never received the thirty-four coins from the Cashier. "He admitted that the entry was in his writing but denied that the initialed acknowledgment appearing at the lower right hand corner was his." He grew restive, and "either unable, or unwilling to explain the balancing entries . . . stat[ed] that he could not say at this time just why these entries had been made or what they represented."

As Strang continued the questioning, the old vault keeper became increasingly agitated. He protested that he knew nothing about the circulation of the 1933 double eagles, insisted that he did not know Israel Switt or Ira Reed, and stated emphatically that apart from the tons sealed in Vault F, Cage 1, all the 1933 double eagles had been under the sole control of one man: the Cashier, George McCann. Again.

Other Mint staff who had worked with McCann offered the burly Strang what little they knew, but it was still telling. The former Cashier's clerk, Thomas Golden, hadn't seen "anything about McCann's actions which might be considered irregular," but back in 1937 he had "observed gold coin being kept in the vault connected to the Cashier's office" and those bags had been "under the Cashier's seal." On this crucial point, Roland, McKernan, and now Golden, all agreed.

McCann could have opened and closed the bags at his leisure and taken, replaced, or swapped at will. No one would have known. It was not until April 26, 1937—well after the 1933 double eagles had been sent to the melting pot and the first had appeared in commercial circles—that the Mint closed that barn door. From that date forward, a new regulation required that all bags required not one but two seals to bind them shut. Dual control. Simple, effective security—a time-honored deterrent. But, for the 1933s, a little late.

Then there was John J. Carey. Following through on specific instructions from their relentless Chief, who had his own contacts, Strang and Drescher headed out to Glassboro, New Jersey, on April 17 to interview the retired bookkeeper. Hardly at the nexus of the shenanigans, Carey had left the Mint in November, 1933. But if it was a cool gray day outside, Carey supplied the heat. He was kinetic, he had accusations galore and vitriol to spew.

First he told the agents, even though he had no "direct knowledge of the circulation of the 1933 double eagles," he was "reasonably certain that McCann had a hand" in it. Chaffin, Ziegler, and Roland had always covered for him, and as long as they were around, McCann was untouchable. Their little cabal planned and plotted together; they were up to no good—ever.

Strang took a breath and tried to direct the proceedings.

What about Ira Reed? he asked.

Carey had never heard of him. When Carey had been at the Mint, a coin dealer called Henry Chapman had been "a personal friend of Ziegler's [and] had exclusive numismatic privileges at the Mint." But, Strang soon discovered, Chapman had been dead since 1935, well before any of the targeted double eagles had hit the market.

The agents then asked Carey if he knew anything about the missing bag of five thousand dollars' worth of double eagles.

Carey responded that the Settlement Committee that was responsible for auditing the comings, goings, and contents of the vault "was not a vigilant one . . . [I] knew the members of this Settlement Committee personally, and they were more concerned with their own affairs than with their duties."

Strang knew this comment was on the mark, since it echoed Agent Landvoight's investigation back when the bag had first been discovered missing. His next accusation, however, was a horse of a different color.

Carey reckoned "that in view of their lethargy, McCann could have easily taken the missing bag from the bin, [which was] located in the back of the cage." Then, posited the increasingly excited Carey, his quarry in sight, McCann could have "place[d] it in his shirt," sealed the cage, and taken "the bag to a place of concealment in his own department," where he could have taken "the coins in small quantities from the Mint."

Strang and Drescher, trained investigators, took down the statement as it was given. Keeping a straight face must have been tough. Carey had clearly come from the bookkeeping side of things and must never have hefted a bag of 250 double eagles, which would have weighed about

Working the List

twenty-two dense, unwieldy pounds. McCann would have had to have been extremely fit and worn a reinforced shirt. Even the sleepy members of the Settlement Committee might have cottoned to the muffled jangling of the big coins.

Nevertheless, Carey had given them some interesting observations, a lead or two, a little light entertainment, and was another who viewed George McCann with cold suspicion.

The case was building well in Philadelphia, and the Chief had intervened and talked to Leland Howard, who had overridden Dressel: the agents would now get the photostats of the records they wanted. But Strang and Drescher were still frustrated by broken links, incomplete and inaccurate information on the master list of the escaped '33 double eagles. They needed answers about the Williams coin and all of Bell's. Who had gotten what and from whom? Harry Strang needed help from New York. He needed help from Cincinnati and Chicago.

Cincinnati.

Acting Agent in Charge Ralph W. Robuck got in touch with Charles M. Williams, the vice president of the Western and Southern Life Insurance Company in Cincinnati, Ohio. The coin collector admitted to Agent Robuck that he had paid B. Max Mehl $1,500 for three coins. One was the 1933 double eagle and the other two were double eagles of 1931 and 1932, also rare, he told the agent. The '33 had cost him a cool $1,000, and the other two coins only $250 apiece.

It was the only one he had, and he took the agent to his safe-deposit box to prove it.

He had, he recalled, "first tried to secure one from Joseph Barnet," a Brooklyn dealer, "but before he could get it, Mr. Barnet had sold [it]." Williams couldn't remember the exact date he had bought his. He would check, but it would have been some time in 1938.

Robuck saw but didn't seize the coin, and he asked Williams to "hold the coin until further notice." The insurance man agreed.

Agent Robuck made a quick check on Sol Kaplan, a short, stocky local dealer with a small mustache and big ideas. He had only been in the coin business for about a half-dozen years, making the transition from stamps, but Sol was a quick learner and had become very close to a prominent New York coin dealer, Abe Kosoff.

Kaplan admitted to Robuck that he been warned by Kosoff a week earlier about the investigation, specifically, about the coin Kosoff had supposedly sold him. No, he told Robuck, not only had he never bought one of the 1933 double eagles from Kosoff, but two years earlier, in the midst of negotiating for one, he had broken off the deal "upon learning-there was something shady about the issue." Kaplan went even further. Not only had he "never had one of the coins." He had "never even seen one of them."

Chicago.
————

James F. Bell had not only seen one, he had owned two or maybe three 1933 double eagles. His business was on paper a commercial banking concern, but he was not above making loans with "waterfront interest," and in later years had some scrapes with the law. The erratic nature of his business caused his collection to expand and contract like a beating heart. If Bell needed funds, he bled off part of his collection, and when the fiscal cloud cleared, he started right up again, buying back what he had just sold. For a dealer or an auction house, he was an ideal, if demanding, client: a source of material to sell and an aggressive bidder willing to buy at top prices.

Visited a number of times by Chicago-based Special Agent Samuel Goldman, the five foot seven inch collector with a fringe of white hair, displayed reticence bordering on evasion and proximating belligerence when asked direct questions. A domineering individual, who Abe Kosoff called a *nudzh* (noodge), or pest, Bell thought nothing of calling on dealers after hours, on weekends, or on religious holidays if they had something he wanted.

A fanatical collector who liked playing pitcher, Bell wasn't so keen about standing at the plate, fouling off high and tight questions from a government agent. The answers he gave Goldman were perfunctory, incomplete, and occasionally contradictory.

The 1933 double eagle that the investigation had intitially indicated Bell had sold to Max Mehl had been purchased by Bell in 1942 from Ira S. Reed, for a sum he refused to disclose. He told Goldman tersely that he had sold the coin in the spring of 1943, because he was in need of funds, not to Mehl, but to F. B. Trotter, Jr., of Memphis, Tennessee. Bell would not reveal the amount he obtained for the coin, but Trotter told the Secret Service two days later that he had paid $900 for the coin in the fall—not the spring—of 1943 for L. G. Barnard, president of the Memphis Sash and Door Company, who had no intention of disposing of the coin.

Agent Goldman, following his orders from D.C., next asked Bell about his latest purchase of a '33—just last month.

141

Working the List

From Ira Reed again, admitted Bell. It had cost $1,000, had been "taken up by Harry Strang" and now "Reed [was] pressing him for his money." In fact, continued Bell, only a week or so earlier he had written to Frank Wilson about it. If the Chief would let Bell "hold the coin in [his] possession" until its legal status was determined, he would pay Reed, who was insisting on payment. The plea fell on deaf ears.

A month later, in an attempt to properly correlate the transaction dates, costs, and disposition of all the '33 double eagles, Agent Goldman again contacted Bell, whose statements just got murkier. At first, as usual, "Mr. Bell was evasive in giving information," but eventually he said that he purchased yet another '33 "from Mr. Reed . . . on November 6, 1943." Again he could not or would not tell Goldman how much he had paid. Gold coins, not clarity, were J. F. Bell's strong suit.

New York.

Abe Kosoff, one of the numismatic trade's standard-bearers, had dark eyes and dark hair—a lot of it—and he parted it high. With an easy grin that pulled to the right and an eyebrow that arched on the left, his good looks were in the Hollywood mold of the period, *film noir,* a Sheldon Leonard or George Raft heavy. His wide-lapeled, double-breasted, gray wool pinstripes fell neatly and looked great. Kosoff knew it.

By 1944 Kosoff, a butcher's son, had already been in the business for the better part of fifteen years. In those first years his shop had moved from the Bowery to East Fifty-seventh Street and finally to East Fiftieth Street, or, as he liked to put it, "right around the corner from the famed Waldorf-Astoria."

Kosoff was sharp, charming, and lucky, a man of whom one competitor said, "I'd play golf, have cocktails, or go to dinner with him, but never do business with him." Kosoff was the first to admit he had been fortunate. From strictly buying and selling coins privately, he had expanded into the auction side of the trade. The way had been paved by Wayte Raymond and his Philadelphia partner, James G. Macallister, who had offered him the chance to sell the material that they didn't need or want for their own auctions.

Kosoff had welcomed the opportunity, and over the years he ended up selling the collections of F. C. C. Boyd, T. James Clarke, and C. M. Williams—all on the Secret Service list of 1933 double eagle owners. Kosoff had also supplied King Farouk with a raft of his most fabulous numismatic possessions, many of them once in the collection of William Woodin.

The "Dean of Numismatists" Abe Kosoff, c. 1950. In 1944, Israel Switt said he sold him two; he told the Secret Service he only sold one. In 1982 his story changed again.
(Bowers & Merena Galleries & Q. David Bowers)

Kosoff was connected all right. On April 24, 1944, he greeted thirty-one-year-old New York Special Agent Milton "Mitch" Lipson—who had campaigned for Fiorello LaGuardia and was one of the first Jews to serve in the Secret Service—with ease. In fact, he said with his infectious grin, he'd been expecting the call for some time. The numismatic community was a small one and word traveled a lot faster, but no less noisily, than the Sixth Avenue El.

Only two days ago, on Saturday, at the Stack's sale, said Kosoff, the 1933 double eagle "was the main topic of conversation."

With typical bravado, Kosoff reckoned the best defense was a strong offense and with no prompting from the natty, well-spoken, politically connected Lipson, launched ahead. The New York born dealer said he was aware that the Service believed that two 1933 double eagles had passed through his hands.

It "was not so," said Kosoff seriously. He "had only received and had possession of one coin," which "he had purchased in 1937 from Switt," when his shop was at 82 Bowery, not far from Canal Street, an area where many scrap-gold and more marginal jewelers had shops and offices. Izzy "had called with the coin and after much dickering," he left it with Abe on approval. If Kosoff sold it, he was to give Switt $600, part cash, part coins.

Abe said he sold the coin to a collector, Walter Hammel, in a swap. Hammel, who Kosoff said had "an unbalanced mentality," decided a few months later that he didn't want the coin and tried to sell it back to Kosoff for $1,000. They bargained, Kosoff lost out, and Hammel sold the coin to Ira Reed.

Kosoff said "the truth of the matter" was that he had only handled the coin once but had negotiated for it *twice*. "This is the reason," he concluded, "that it was understood that he had two '33 [Double] Eagles." He also admitted that he had talked to Sol Kaplan but said that he had never sold him any contraband coins.

Ever the charmer, Kosoff continued. "All these '33 Double Eagles emanated from Switt." He had known the jeweler "for some time since Switt appeared at his office with rare coins of American origin, usually accompanied by a 'tall story' of how he got them from a banker or other similar personage." According to Abe, Switt usually shopped around for the best price and dealt primarily with the Philadelphia dealers. Most of the '33s had gone to Macallister, along with "some of the single Eagles issued in 1933."

In parting, the dapper Kosoff told the agent, "off the record," that the investigation into the '33 double eagles was creating a stir in numismatic circles.

Special Agent Lipson, finished with—or finished off by—Kosoff, hopped on the BMT subway line, which lurched and shrieked to Brooklyn, where, from 2025 Ocean Avenue, Joseph Barnet, a kindly, high-waisted "coin dealers' coin dealer," conducted his business. At seventy-seven he was not in the best of health, and he was not the biggest of dealers, but he was a man of rock-ribbed integrity and universally liked.

Aware of the frailty of the elderly man's health, Lipson trod lightly. Barnet responded gently and firmly that he had only "seen the '33 Double Eagle once" when James Macallister had shown him one in Philadelphia; he had "never had any . . . nor did he ever sell one."

Staring through his thick lenses, Barnet added that he had *almost* sold one. Charles M. Williams of Cincinnati had called him and, as Barnet regularly advertised to sell 1931 and 1932 double eagles, asked if he might have a '33. Old Joe got in touch with Macallister, who offered him one at $800. Barnet, however, advised Williams not to buy it as he suspected "that more of these coins would appear on the market" and drive the price down. In the middle of 1936, for example, 1931 and 1932 double eagles, once exceptionally rare, had started showing up in quantity (also from Israel Switt), and had become increasingly less expensive. Barnet had first advertised them in 1938 for $150 and $175 respectively, but within four years they had become a drug on the market, and Barnet was having a hard time moving them, even as he dropped the price. By 1942 they were being offered for as little as $80 and $85 each, with few takers.

Barnet's honestly offered advice to C. M. Williams was ignored, and the collector went to Mehl, who profited handsomely. The old man shrugged.

There is not much of New York State farther west than Jamestown, where T. James Clarke, sixty years old, lived. Stout, short, and florid, he wore his hair slicked back under a generous coating of brilliantine. The company he owned made boxes, and Jimmy Clarke collected stamps, coins, watches, precious stones, firearms, antique glass, and curios the rest of the time. He seemed to live comfortably within the sweet gray-blue haze emanating from his ever-present pipe, and he "rode the hobby horse hard." The exceedingly knowledgeable collector met with Acting Agent-in-Charge Edwin Manning, from Buffalo, and confirmed that he owned a 1933 double eagle. He recalled that he had acquired it from Ira Reed by mail order, but he couldn't remember exactly when and offered to check his records. He did remember the price, however: $550. Clarke's reputation as a hard bargainer—or, depending on whom you spoke to, cheapskate—was no fable. He had bought the coin at a wholesale price. Manning didn't seize the coin but instructed Clarke to hold on to it.

Philadelphia.

Harry Strang and George Drescher shuffled through the reports filtering in from around the country and built the framework for a double helix of ownership. Swit had told them that he had sold only nine coins, and they wanted to make sure the numbers balanced. It still wasn't altogether satisfactory. There were too many conflicting dates and stories, particularly concerning Ira Reed and J. F. Bell, whose explanations were a knot of incoherence.

Working the list was like cleaning the Augean stables. It just kept coming.

CHAPTER 11

Wondering about Woodin

———◆———

Washington, D.C.

THE WEALTHY COLLECTORS WHO HAD SURRENDERED THEIR PRIZES TO Harry Strang were starting to get restless, and the drumbeat began.

J. F. Bell was being dunned for payment by Ira Reed, who had been at Stack's when the coin had been expropriated from Bell. Reed had been interviewed at length by the Secret Service concerning his involvement in the distribution of the '33 double eagles and knew that the cloud of impropriety hovering over the coin was getting blacker and angrier. Still, Ira Reed had nerve; not only had he sold a potentially illegal coin to Bell but was now insisting on payment.

Chief Wilson must have smiled. Reed certainly wasn't shy. But such bravado bordered on hubris. Reed would bear more investigating.

On April 18, 1944, the same day Bell had asked for the return of his coin, and a week later, Assistant Chief James Maloney received a letter from Colonel Flanagan's attorney, also asking "that some arrangement should be made to facilitate the prompt return of the coin."

Both pleadings received the cold shoulder, a form letter above Wilson's signature:

"A criminal investigation relating to the source of this and other coins is being conducted and until the investigation is completed, which we hope will be at an early date, it would be inadvisable to return the coin."

Wilson would be hearing from James W. Flanagan's advocates, Green-hill & Greenhill, Attorneys and Counsellors at Law, again. And again.

Friday, April 28, 1944. Philadelphia.

Strang and Drescher were at a crossroads in the investigation. From all appearances, Switt, McCann, and Reed were shaping up to be the trio of villains requiring the closest scrutiny. Israel Switt had already agreed to meet with the agents again, so Strang would shuffle back along that obfuscatory path. A couple of days earlier, the Chief had sent a memo suggesting that "serious consideration should be given to having all these men (or any of the three who will agree to it) submit to the lie detector test." Strang would give it a shot.

But these three suspects were not the only possibilities. The agents were also nagged by other alleged avenues of exit that they needed to test, like a bothersome shoelace that won't stay tied. One other theory—the possibility of a mistaken delivery from the Mint to a Federal Reserve Bank or Branch and the subsequent distribution of a handful of coins from a wayward bag—had been carefully investigated in both Philadelphia and D.C. by the Mint, the Treasury, and the Secret Service. It had been plowed under like Carthage by Chief Wilson. The second possibility concerned William Woodin, his "five coins," and his "knowing wink." That one required some research.

Of course, it was easy to accuse the dead and tough for them to respond. Stephen Nagy, the ferret-featured authority with a well-known reputation today as a purveyor of queer coins of indeterminate parentage, had Zola-like pointed an accusatorial finger at William Woodin. And what about Woodin? Straight as an arrow? Or bent like a hairpin?

William Hartman Woodin had always been described as puckish. He had a clear twinkle in his eye and a small white mustache that seemed to quiver with nervous energy, like the White Rabbit in *Alice in Wonderland*. But he was also an individual of substance, born to wealth, who hadn't let the silver spoon choke him. He succeeded in the many disciplines to which he set his mind, from music to philanthropy to collecting to industry, and ultimately to rescuing a grievously wounded banking system.

Born in 1868 in Berwick, Pennsylvania, Woodin had little denied him. His father, Clemuel, ran Jackson and Woodin, a firm he had founded, which had developed an exceptional reputation for building railway equipment. Although young Woodin was to have graduated from the Columbia

School of Mines in 1890, the urge to travel overwhelmed him and he headed to Europe. His father had given him the stunning sum of ten thousand dollars to do with as he pleased, as long as he didn't go into debt.

Will Woodin traveled to the East, to Armenia, where, for reasons either "musical or mystical," he at once played the part of "a playboy who lived for a time with the gypsies" and worked as a newspaper stringer, sending back grim stories about the Armenian massacres to papers such as the London *Times,* the New York *Herald,* and the Philadelphia *Press.* His life as a newspaperman was short-lived. Having run through his money in a scandalously short six months, he was back in Berwick, working in the family company, not as an executive but as a laborer. He might have been slight of stature, but his father "forbade any member of the family holding an office position until he had won his spurs on the lowest rungs of the ladder in the shops." He was paid 90 cents a day for work he later described as "hard, dirty and unpleasant."

For three years, until 1892, he toiled in the superheated air of the shops, sweat running off him, as he learned to cast plates, make molds, and pour red-hot liquefied iron. By 1899 he was president of the firm, beloved by the men on the floor, to whom he cheerfully referred as his teachers and who, in return always called him their Billy.

The family firm merged with the American Car and Foundry Company in 1899, and Will Woodin rose from district manager of the larger firm to assistant to the vice president to assistant to the president to, in 1916, president. The meteoric climb continued with the chairmanship in 1922. Woodin later added the chairmanship of the American Locomotive Company to his resume as well.

At the time, railroads were king. The bright, shining ribbons of steel meandered across the continent, and on them, rocking and swaying, was the fleet of cars that Woodin's twenty-five plants and twenty-five thousand men produced: seventy-five thousand freight cars and fifteen hundred passenger cars in 1922 alone.

Woodin made time for many pursuits besides work. Alcohol didn't agree with him, so he avoided it. In the evenings he gravitated to a comfortable velvet-covered armchair next to a fabulous, huge, richly sculptured chimneypiece in his panelled library, smoked a cigarette, and read. For escapist reading he preferred the works of H. Rider Haggard, gripping adventures such as *King Solomon's Mines, Allan Quatermain,* and *She.* On the more serious side of his library, he included works by Dickens, Shakespeare, and according to family lore (perhaps apocryphal), a Gutenberg Bible.

149

But after dinner was the time for his remarkable collection of rare gold coins. His youngest daughter, Elizabeth, recalled that "he would take them out and fondly inspect them," while reminding her that "the only time it's good to have money is when you need it for your health." He collected for relaxation and, blessed with intuition, and a searching intellect, he adored his coins for the richness of history that was captured in each piece. "Coins," wrote Woodin, "are the metallic footprints of nations."

An extremely active and familiar face in the New York numismatic scene, Will Woodin ventured down to Keen's Chop House for meetings of the New York Numismatic Club, where he would break bread, talk coins, and show off his latest sterling acquisitions to other great collectors, dealers, and connoisseurs, F. C. C. Boyd, Wayte Raymond, John H. Clapp, and Stephen Nagy among them. But in 1909, his purchase of the two incredible half unions from Nagy and their subsequent return to the government under duress seemed to cool Woodin's ardor for gold coins somewhat, at least publicly.

Pattern coins were struck to see how new designs might look or how new metals might bear up to the rigors of coining. The two controversial gold patterns had been designed by William Barber—father of Saint-Gaudens' nemesis, Charles—in 1877. Each bore a cold, starchily drawn head of Liberty in profile staring blankly ahead, a coronet over untidy tresses that cascaded heavily to her neck. The reverse design was no more than a swollen rendering of the heraldic eagle on the then-circulating twenty-dollar gold pieces. Each pattern was subtly different from the other, neither was timeless art, but each was unique. Both had a face value of $50 and were the largest gold coins ever struck by the United States Government—from whose collection they had inexplicably departed.

Woodin used the massive hoard of United States patterns and trial coins he received in return for the two great coins as would an archaeologist. With Edgar Adams, one of the singularly talented numismatic experts of the period, he assiduously recorded each and every type, and in 1913 the American Numismatic Society published the result. Although only two hundred copies were printed, *United States Pattern, Trial and Experimental Pieces,* which was largely about the contents of the trunks of coins he now owned, became the standard work of reference on the subject for almost a half-century.

The exchange also transformed Woodin's collecting tastes, and he auctioned off his gold coins in a three-day auction in March, 1911. But Woodin kept his patterns, "the finest collection . . . in the United States," a cabinet so vast and complete that it needed little addition, so while he

Meeting of the New York Numismatic Club, January 1908, at Keen's Chop House.
William Woodin seated second from right foreground, across the table from Stephen K.
Nagy. Also seated at the table, left foreground, is Wayte Raymond. The bearded man in
the middle left is Victor David Brenner, designer of the Lincoln penny.
(American Numsimatic Society)

continued to pop up at auctions, his activity as a buyer dwindled. In 1915, Woodin agreed to serve on the council of the American Numismatic Society in New York, the preeminent research center and museum devoted to coins in the United States. He sat on the board and gave generously to the society for the next nineteen years, his interests increasingly focused on the knowledge to be gained.

By 1930, William Hartman Woodin was one of America's great industrialists. "A man of extraordinary executive ability . . . with a brain capable of grasping all the details of an industrial or other problem almost at a glance, and working out a solution with lightning-like rapidity."

Even though he seemed frail by most standards, Woodin was a champion golf-putter, and liked tennis and fishing. His wealth and social standing afforded him his own private railroad car for traveling and an eighty-foot yacht, while he sat on the boards at one time or another of

Wondering about Woodin

more than fifty companies, and was a member of no fewer than eight exclusive private clubs. He lived with his wife, Annie Jessup Woodin, "a large, imposing woman," whom he had married in 1889, in a Manhattan apartment building on the site of the old Elbert H. Gary mansion. Gary's widow occupied the seventh floor, and the Woodins' neighbors included two partners of J. P. Morgan and the widow of another. Will Woodin's American Locomotive Company paid a post-Crash dividend of $8 a share, so he could well afford the twelfth floor and penthouse, which he had purchased for a breathtaking $310,000—reportedly the second most expensive apartment in New York City.

A great collector of the illustrated books and drawings of the great English visual satirists, he expressed in this collection his amused outlook on the world and his wicked sense of humor.

Woodin's deepest, most abiding love was music. Although he had played the piano a little as a child, he was drawn more to the guitar, and spent the richest hours of his day, every day, not merely listening to music but "endeavoring to create it." He was self-taught and talented. Besides the "Franklin Delano Roosevelt Inaugural March," he wrote "Twelve Viennese Waltzes," collaborated with the great Johnny Mercer, and with Johnny Gruelle wrote the "Raggedy Ann Songs" and "Raggedy Andy Songs."

Somewhere along the way, this Republican became a close friend of that Democrat Franklin Delano Roosevelt. Woodin and the New York governor laughed hard together, and the small, natty man raised money for FDR's philanthropic and political causes. He personally gave thirty-five thousand dollars in cash to the presidential campaign. When Woodin, a "director over the destiny of great industries," was tapped as Treasury Secretary, he was entering the final chapter of a remarkable life.

Officially William Woodin was secretary of the treasury from March 5, 1933, to December 30, 1933, but his actual time in office was much less than that.

From the instant of his surprise appointment, he was a lightning rod rising into the seething tempest of New Deal politics. His superhuman efforts in the first weeks of the Roosevelt administration won him instant national and international kudos. His face adorned the cover of the March 20, 1933, issue of *Time* magazine, looking haggard, the skin wasted, but with the bright words, "We are not going any lower."

Sadly, although the nation was not going lower, the sixty-four-year-old Woodin himself was. Seemingly, the moment Woodin started solving national problems, his personal world began to crumble, slowly at first.

152

During those first critical days, as he came to grips with the banking crisis, endless meetings in closed rooms—the air stale and blue from cigarettes, cigars, and pipes—eternal phone calls, stressful cajolings, and little sleep strained Woodin's throat, which became increasingly sore. He tried not to let it worry him or color his humor. When the Emergency Banking Bill was at last submitted on March 9, 1933, Woodin was asked by eager reporters, "Is the bill finished, Mr. Secretary?" "Yes," was Mr. Woodin's weary reply. "The bill's finished. My name is Bill and I'm finished too."

He wasn't—yet. A month later, just days after the Roosevelt's April 5, 1933, Executive Order forbidding the hoarding of gold, Woodin was rocked by the death of his mother in Berwick, Pennsylvania. The president sent his condolences. Woodin grew sicker. All that month Woodin continued to labor long and hard in public and behind closed doors to halt the ghastly gold hemorrhage and get Americans to respond to the president's plea to consider the greater good.

Woodin the ardent, private numismatist, as secretary of the treasury suddenly became a very publicly known coin collector and took some ribbing for it. A newspaper panel cartoon by Cecil Jensen entitled "Some People Get All the Breaks," run during the early days of the gold recall must have given him a hearty, if wistful, chuckle because he clipped it from the paper and his family saved it. A caricature of the collector, neatly identified "Numismatist—W. H. Woodin" is seen seated at the desk of the secretary of the treasury. His eyes are aglow like a kid's on Christmas morning as he holds a gold coin in his hands and, surrounded by piles and bags of more, exclaims with delight: "Ah! A rare one!" Outside, looking in through the window, stands a crowd of glowering men, labeled "The Rest of Us Collectors."

It was Woodin, concerned for his beloved hobby, who had language inserted in the April 5 antihoarding order that specifically excluded "gold coin having a recognized special value to collectors of rare and unusual coin" from confiscation by the grasping talons of his own department. No one offered him thanks.

As April faded to May, cherry blossoms dropped gently to the bright yellow-green grass of early spring, crises continued to mount, and Woodin's health continued to fail. He spent much of his time in bed at home in New York, not in his office in Washington, D.C. The end of May nearly saw the end of Woodin's term in office, not as a result of his weakened condition but because of the Pecora Hearings.

This Senate Banking and Currency Committee investigation, which had begun with Hoover in early 1932, examined potential improprieties, alleged shenanigans, and manipulation of the markets on Wall Street, by the "money changers." In January, 1933, a former New York assistant district attorney, Ferdinand Pecora, took over the investigation and was given a free hand by the committee's chairman, Senator Duncan Fletcher of Florida. In the late spring of 1933, Pecora, a Sicilian immigrant with a "defiant pompadour of gray-black hair," closely and very publicly examined the financial doings of near-titan J. P. Morgan, Jr. (Jack), and his cronies. In a room humming with expectation and excitement and bristling with journalists, Morgan admitted to Pecora (who made $255 a month) that despite his millions in income he had "quite legally paid no income tax in the United States" between 1930 and 1932.

This was scandalous enough to Depression readers, but what set the nation on fire was the revelation of Morgan's "preferred list," and the few "good, sound, straight fellows" to whom the "House of Morgan occasionally sold stock at figures far below market price." Charles Lindbergh was one, Calvin Coolidge another—and so was William Woodin.

From across the nation newspaper articles, columns, editorials demanded Woodin's head on a platter. Letters and telegraphs blanketed the White House in a blizzard of grievance. A few were supportive of the treasury secretary, most were not. "Discredited," "Exposed," "Forfeited Confidence" read the litany of invective. Moviegoers at the Ziegfeld in Manhattan, "a class audience," hissed exuberantly when Jack Morgan's face appeared on the screen during the newsreels. Dr. C. S. Horton, an optometrist from Lincoln, Pennsylvania, summed up to his president what many of his fellow citizens now felt: "We are still with you, but for Heaven's sake tie the can to Woodin."

Woodin's daughter, Elizabeth, was ashamed of the whole affair, which came to a head on Friday, May 26, 1933. A beleaguered, distraught Woodin "told the President he would like to have an expression of opinion from 'members of the family,'" as he referred to the Cabinet. They met, and with the notable exception of Vice President John Nance Garner, no one felt Woodin should resign. FDR stood staunchly behind his treasury secretary. What he had done had been as a private citizen, it had not been against the law. In a delightful example of temporal ethics, Roosevelt pooh-poohed the entire affair, saying that "many people had done things in 1929 they would not think of doing now."

Still, it was another blow, and Woodin's health rapidly weakened that spring and summer. On the last day of June, Press Secretary Steve Early wrote a memo to the president: "Will Woodin is, I believe, more of a sick man than anyone suspects. . . . He has been in his bed in his New

York apartment for the last week or so." It was no understatement. On that day, during an urgent conference call to London to stabilize the dollar, with Bernard Baruch and Dean Acheson at his side, Woodin lost consciousness, and those with him "feared the end had come."

A week later, on July 5, Woodin tendered his first resignation to the president, "through the insistence of my medical advisors." He fought through his misery, and his old humor shone brightly. "This old boy Staphylococcus is one of the meanest ever, and hangs on even worse than the man with 147 pages of closely written manuscript elucidating a plan to save the country."

Although Sir Alexander Fleming first observed the effect penicillin had on bacteria in 1928, it was not until 1941 that scientists developed the antibiotic in a form that might have helped Woodin. In 1936, just over three years later, FDR's own son, Franklin Delano Roosevelt, Jr., stricken with a deadly strep infection, would be one of the first Americans to be given an experimental drug, sulfa, that saved his life.

FDR would have none of Woodin's resignation. In August, "after a severe illness," Woodin quit again, and again his president rebuffed him. Secretary of the Interior Harold Ickes noted in his diary on September 15, 1933, that Woodin, having "been away for three or four months," was looking better. But it didn't last, and on October 27, Will Woodin, his once strong hand growing spidery, wrote to FDR and again resigned, for if he didn't, his doctors told him, it could have "dangerous and probably fatal consequences." Roosevelt again demurred but told him to take a leave of absence, which he did, with his son's family in Tucson, Arizona. His health did not rally, and after a flurry of letters with FDR, he submitted his final resignation on December 13, 1933. It was at last accepted, to take effect on the last day of the year. But it was all too late. Woodin was mortally stricken and died in May, 1934.

On paper Woodin had been in office ten months. The first two or three of those had been a maelstrom. The last half year or more, torpid misery.

Could William Hartman Woodin, collector extraordinaire and financial savior of the nation, possibly have had the fistful of 1933 double eagles that Stephen Nagy had allegedly seen?

Yes, it was possible. The battery of proclamations, executive orders, assumption of war powers, and passage of draconian acts gave the President of the United States dictatorial powers over the ownership of gold. By extension those same tightly worded, ever-changing, hard-to-understand documents also mightily built the muscle of the executive branch of government, in particular that of the secretary of the treasury. He too had assumed autocratic powers and answered only to the president. In all likelihood, if Woodin had wanted, he could have obtained as many 1933 double eagles as he desired. He might even have done it legally.

But did he? It was unlikely. Assuming that Woodin had wanted a 1933 double eagle, amid the turmoil of the first month in office, the imposition of war powers to prevent private ownership of gold, the death of his mother, a nagging illness that would ultimately kill him, and questions of his probity being bandied about in the papers and the halls of Congress, what would he have done?

Seated atop the Treasury's bureaucracy, he could have written a memo to the superintendent of the Philadelphia Mint or called him. The superintendent would have passed the request down the line to the Cashier, who would have taken the number required from the bag stored in his office vault and sent them on to Washington, D.C., to the secretary of the treasury's attention. It would have been simple, and would have resulted in nothing more than a ledger entry.

Special Agent Harry Strang had all of the handwritten Cashier's Daily Settlements and cleanly typed Cashier's Daily Statement of Receipts, Disbursements, and Balances at his disposal. In 1933, the Cashier had been Harry Powell, an honest man with no apparent ties to any of the Mint's cliques, who was soon to retire after years of exemplary service.

The pages of the ledgers day by day reveal the story of a tidy mind keeping meticulous records of dreary comings and goings. Large, small, and minuscule receipts and disbursements were all entered: from a million dollars in double eagles, to twenty cents for "Unofficial use of Official Telephone" to two cents for the Treasury's authorization of the release of two new 1933 pennies. Throughout the year, every day was similar, every transaction recorded. When the last shipment of 1933 double eagles arrived on May 19, 1933, the total holding of the denomination at the Mint was $143,439,700. On January 18, 1934, it was $143,439,720. Someone had turned in, not taken out, a double eagle. If Woodin had requested any 1933 double eagles, there was no record of it, official or otherwise.

If he had, it would have amounted to "issuance" of the coin, and a ledger entry would have been essential to the Cashier, who was personally liable. In 1907, for example, Treasury officials—and the president—had paid by check for each and every piece of the new Saint-Gaudens coinage. In 1933 it would have been no different. If Woodin had wanted to swap or exchange twenty-dollars for a 1933 double eagle, there would have been a ledger entry for that, as well, and if he had wanted to make an official withdrawal for Treasury Department business, a line in the Cashier's Daily Statement would have been essential. But there was no record at all, and so that theory of exit from the Mint was unlikely—at best.

Another possibility was that Timothy Quirk, who was in charge of the Special Assays and whose office was in the Treasury Building in Washington, D.C., had given or exchanged some of the '33s that had been sent to him for testing with Woodin. But he was on record and had assured Agent Strang "of the improbability of any . . . having been circulated after being received by his department."

None of Woodin's friends, coin collectors like him, men of significant wealth, is known to have contacted him about the elusive double eagles. Perhaps in 1933 they didn't consider them special or perhaps, at the time, they simply didn't care. Woodin had served with John Work Garrett of Baltimore on the council of the American Numismatic Society for a decade, and they were both Republicans. But it was not until 1934, when Garrett asked for a 1933 double eagle from Wayte Raymond, another old pal of Woodin's from the early days at the New York Numismatic Club, that the dealer told Garrett he had never been able to get any. James Macallister, Raymond's partner and a fellow member with Woodin of the tony Union League Club of Philadelphia, had said he hadn't even seen a 1933 double eagle until 1937—when, he also said, they had first appeared. Similarly, F. C. C. Boyd, who had known Woodin well for a score of years and was also politically well connected, only got a 1933 double eagle when he shelled out $1,100 to Macallister—in 1937.

Woodin could have acquired a few for his family if it had been legal, but that was questionable, and apparently he never did. He had reveled in the issuance of banknotes with his signature on them and could be seen across the land in wire photos, a huge, delighted grin on his face, clutching piles of uncut sheets. Some of these banknotes he kept as souvenirs. He gave some to his children. And when on that last long trip to Arizona he stayed with his grandson, he autographed one of the one dollar silver certificates and gave it to his young namesake. The largesse did not include 1933 double eagles.

Although Woodin had disposed of his collection of gold coins in 1911, Strang discovered that he had "retained a quantity of coins until his death"—the pattern collection—which had gone to his wife, Annie, who kept them intact until her death in 1941. The executor of her estate, James Wade, of Chase National Bank, a coin collector himself, had consigned Woodin's wonderful library and watercolors to Parke-Bernet Gal-

Wondering about Woodin

No Scrip: Treasury Secretary William H. Woodin grinning gleefully with piles
of uncut currency, April 17, 1933. To left and right: Assistant Treasury Secretary
James H. Douglas and Director of the Bureau of Engraving and Printing, Alvin W. Hall.
(Bettman/CORBIS)

leries in New York. The coins were sold privately to "Fred C. C. Boyd of
New York City," but when Strang checked, Macallister told him that "no
1933 Double Eagles were contained in Woodin's collection when sold to
Mr. Boyd." Boyd later sold parts of the collection piecemeal to Abe Kosoff,
who packed off the best of the best to King Farouk in Cairo.

Every possibility of removal of the '33s by Woodin was considered.
After the opening salvo of FDR's assault on gold ownership, everything
changed. By April 5 much of the apparent confusion that had run ram-
pant during the first month had sorted itself out. Gold was no longer permitted to be exchanged or swapped for coins. The Cashier of the Mint no
longer kept extra gold coins jangling around in his trays, as he had done
for scores of years.

William Woodin was a man of intellect, wit, and most of all integrity
and character. When Roosevelt invoked war powers over gold, Woodin
was by his side. To have played fast and loose with still amorphous law

for strictly personal reasons would have smacked of hypocrisy at any time but most especially at the outset of the new administration and during a grave national crisis. Woodin and his family were honorable—at a time when honor was still considered a virtue—and while being one of "Morgan's preferred" was in no way illegal, the public reaction to his inclusion shamed, humbled, and appalled him.

His job, his service to his country, cost him his life. This "Peter Pan in the Treasury," had "held the controls of the Treasury and brought us safely through. This labor cost him years of peaceful twilight, and since he had the means and talent for happy leisure, his sacrifice was very great."

And the only person who had ever claimed to see William Woodin raising his eyebrows, and winking with five 1933 double eagles in his small hands was Stephen Nagy—"the biggest crook of them all."

CHAPTER 12

The Red-Headed Philadelphia Sucker and the Deacon

———◆———

AS A COOL, DAMP APRIL DRIZZLED INTO A RAPIDLY WARMING MAY, Harry Strang's and George Drescher's dogged hunt for the source of the "1933 Double Eagle Gold Coins" (DEGC, as they were known in all official correspondence) continued in Philadelphia, while special agents fanned out across the country to identify all those who had owned or trafficked in the suspect coins. Collectors still in possession were advised that the coins were under investigation and subject to seizure. But one collector and his coin were far away amid the ostentatious precincts of the Koubbeh Palace. He was also, officially, of no concern. Treasury General Counsel Joseph J. O'Connell, Jr., wrote that "the coin held by King Farouk does not in my opinion present a problem that this department should consider at this time."

In Washington, D.C., as reports from agents around the country landed on his desk, Secret Service Chief Wilson noticed that when a 1933 double eagle had been purchased, a 1931 and 1932 double eagle had frequently been part of the same transaction, as had the occasional 1933 ten-dollar gold piece. It seemed a little too convenient, and on April 29, the Chief got Strang on the telephone and instructed him to check and see if his hunch was a clue or coincidence.

The agents found the official records were exceptionally complete and detailed.

Between October 16, 1931, when one hundred 1931 double eagles had been issued to the Treasury, and February 23, 1933, only eighteen had been purchased by collectors, dealers, and museums around the country, and all their names were recorded. The American Numismatic Society sent in its twenty dollars and got a new 1931 double eagle on December 11, 1931; the Connecticut State Library bought two on February 1, 1932; and the last one had been sent to Clarence N. Reynolds of Morgantown, West Virginia, on February 23, 1933, nine days before FDR's inauguration. An additional two had been sent out directly by the Mint to S. R. Earl of the Federal Reserve Bank of Philadelphia for presentation to another Federal Reserve Bank governor. In all, twenty coins had been officially circulated by the Treasury.

The records on the 1932s told a similarly direct tale. One hundred were sent to the Treasury and thirty-two were sold. The American Numismatic Society and Connecticut State Library were again purchasers, as was C. F. Childs, a well-known collector in Chicago; and Clarence Reynolds purchased the last example in February, 1933, just before the fulminating over gold in Washington began. Others had been sent out directly by the Mint on orders from the Treasury, including fifty to Spencer S. Marsh of Newark, New Jersey, who had returned them all on November 26, 1934, during the gold recall, making the total remaining in documented circulation fifty-seven.

Finally, according to the official record only five 1933 eagles had been officially circulated: four from the Treasury and one from the Mint.

The remaining stocks of all three issues had been sent back from the Treasury to the Mint on February 21, 1934, and were received by the Cashier's Department in whose vault they would be stored. The coins were entered on the books by the Acting Cashier, Hibberd Ott, who was replaced a month later by George A. McCann.

When Strang and Drescher then sought out James Macallister about the apparent connection to the '33s, the bespectacled dealer nodded his affirmation of what Chief Wilson had intuited. The '31 and '32 double eagles had been rare, hardly if ever seen in the marketplace until 1936. Then, like worms after a quick downpour, they started popping up everywhere, and Israel Switt had been the source.

Max Berenstein had got the best deal of all, perhaps because of his

AM IN THE MARKET

FOR THE FOLLOWING U. S. $20.00:

1920 S	1925 S	1931 Phila.
1921 Phila.	1926 D	1931 D
1922 S	1926 S	1932 Phila.
1924 D	1927 D	1933 Phila.
1924 S	1927 S	

Will also pay a good price for the 1883 Phila., 1884 Phila. and the 1885 Phila., and also the 1856 O.

BERNS ANTIQUE SHOP

71 East 59th Street, New York City.

Proprietor, Max Berenstein, A. N. A. 4103.

Solicitation advertisement by Max Berenstein, February, 1936. It yielded cheap 1931 and 1932 double eagles a few months later from Israel Switt—and an expensive 1933 double eagle, in a year's time. (The *Numismatist*: American Numismatic Association)

offer in the February, 1936, *Numismatist* to buy the two dates. Switt had shambled into the classy shop on Madison Avenue in May, 1936, and sold a half-dozen of each date. Max had paid Izzy forty dollars a coin—dirt cheap, only barely more than the most common, beat-up double eagles on the market and only six dollars above their gold value.

Berenstein hadn't been able to contain his good fortune and had crowed to Jack Rubin, a gregarious runner for the Forty-seventh Street jewelry and gold trade, that Israel Switt was "a 'red-headed Philadelphia sucker'" for having sold him the coins for "their bullion instead of their numismatic value." Rubin, a known receiver of stolen goods, with a long, thin face and a Jimmy Cagney cockiness, stirred things up by passing the comment on to Switt.

The cantankerous "sucker" Switt had learned his lesson and when it came to business, seldom made the same mistake twice. He upped the price on the '31s and '32s from then on. Rubin himself bought a few, Brooklyn dealer Joseph Barnet some, Reed others, and Macallister remembered buying one each "from Switt for $75 apiece" in July, 1937, selling them on to Max Mehl for a hundred dollars each.

These dates had been legally issued by the government and were not subject to confiscation, but they did form a golden link among the 1933 double eagles, George McCann, and Israel Switt, who once again met with Strang and his partner.

The Red-Headed Philadelphia Sucker and the Deacon

Accompanied by his accountant, Israel Rubin, Switt surrendered a mass of documents, including all his income tax returns for the years 1936 through 1943, but notably lacking his business records for 1937, the crucial year in which he had begun selling the 1933 double eagles. Rubin and the two agents agreed to search for the missing papers the following Monday.

During their sparring session, Switt told Strang that he and Kosoff had conferred and he realized his memory had been in error. Izzy now told the agents that he had only sold *one* '33 to Kosoff. The other coin, Switt now recalled, "the ninth coin may have been sold to Reed." At the end of the lengthy interview the taciturn jeweler then stunned Strang by agreeing to make himself available for a lie-detector test.

With Switt's latest revelation needing digestion, Strang and Drescher again looked to James Macallister, whom they considered one of the leading numismatists in the United States, for confirmation. They seemed to enjoy his good humor and help in equal proportions. His candor was refreshing, the cigars he smoked were better than Chief Wilson's twofers, and the clubby atmosphere of his office, lined with bookshelves, always yielded information.

Macallister was dubious about Izzy's latest version. He told Strang that "he [was] positive that Kosoff and Kaplan [had] acted as Agents for the disposal of a second coin," and suggested that they check with another Cincinnati dealer, who later proved to have no connection with the case. As Strang and Drescher settled into the Walnut Street dealer's comfortable club chairs, Macallister turned over his cancelled checks to confirm his purchases from Switt and again reiterated that the high price of sixteen hundred dollars he had charged Berenstein was because it "was the first 1933 Double Eagle to make its appearance as a collector's item."

Monday, May 1, 1944, dawned balmy but turned hot. Harry Strang and George Drescher could not have been comfortable in their customary wool suits as they assisted accountant Israel Rubin research through piles of rank, moldy, dog-eared files, looking for Izzy Switt's missing business records for 1937 and anything at all prior to 1939. They found nothing incriminating but enough to spark more questions.

All the checks Macallister had written to Switt had been endorsed twice. The second name was Edward Silver, who owned "a gold-buying concession at 130 South 8th Street," the same address from which Izzy Switt did business. In a masterpiece of understatement, the agents reported to the Chief later that week that because they were "feeling that there might be collusion between Switt and Silver, the latter was included in the investigation." As accountant Israel Rubin conveniently also kept Silver's records, the agents requested that they be allowed to investigate his business and tax records as well. Silver's lawyer was contacted for permission.

In the meantime, the two agents dug through records at the Philadelphia Mint and unearthed more damning evidence new to them. In 1934, two weeks after Swit had been arrested with the gold-filled suitcase and had lost his license to deal in gold, his "silent" partner—and brother-in-law—Edward Silver was granted one and had deposited $758,003.23 in gold at the United States Mint over the next nine years.

It was an astonishing sum. It made Silver one of the largest scrap-gold dealers in all Philadelphia. More interesting still, Mint employees Robert Graham and Jacob Pepper recalled that while the deposits were made in Silver's name, Israel Swit had "actually brought the gold to the Mint." On some days Swit would turn up at the Mint three separate times, each time with a pound or two of gold. No wonder he knew the Mint personnel so well. And no wonder they would occasionally take Swit and his daughter back to the Melting Room—supposedly off-limits to the public—and occasionally give little Joan a shiny new penny or two.

"While Swit and Silver," wrote Strang, "profess to operate individually, the facts indicate that there is a working relationship between them." Since 1933 Israel Swit and Edward Silver had leased the space on Eighth Street together. A decade later they bought the building from the owner's estate at a fire-sale price. With $5,500 in cash and a mortgage of $7,500, the deal was reckoned to be far below that of neighboring properties. Theirs was a cozy, profitable arrangement.

The two men complemented each other perfectly. Whereas Edward Silver was a big, tall man who preferred to tend to the shop, the smaller Izzy, more active, acquisitive and volatile, preferred the road, looking to sell—looking to buy—anything. Part gold buyer, part pawnbroker, part jeweler, part junkman, Israel Swit was born to the trade.

The Switts had come to the United States from Latvia, where Israel's father had been a spy for the Germans in the 1860s or 1870s. The family continued their Old World business as pawnbrokers and jewelers without pause upon their arrival in Philadelphia. A shop at the corner of South and Seventh streets was one of their earliest locations, and before long Israel, youngest of thirteen children, and his brothers all ran separate shops. They were not franchisees of the same business, but nor were they rivals.

In a brutal, highly competitive business where failure was easy, Israel Swit succeeded. Strang and Drescher looked in amazement at some of his

The "Red-Headed Philadelphia Sucker," Israel Switt (center), July, 1944,
clearly unconcerned about the investigation into 1933 double eagles.
(Harold Carter, appeared in *Life*, July 14, 1944)

income tax returns. In 1937, deep within the Depression, Switt's business had grossed $60,634.80, and "he had paid no tax for that year, nor for any year until 1940, when he paid a total of $50.79 on a gross income of $59,850.41." Strang carefully noted that all this information would be "brought to the attention of the [Treasury Department's] Intelligence Unit."

Israel Switt finally decided that he had wasted enough time fending off annoying questions from the Secret Service, so he settled back to work in the cluttered murk of his shop and let his attorney be his mouthpiece. On May 8 Emanuel Friedman, who was also Edward Silver's lawyer—and Switt's cousin by marriage—contacted the Secret Service and requested that any further negotiations be conducted through him. Friedman was friendly enough, offered his cooperation, and permitted Edward Silver's books to be laid open for the agents to examine. Once more there was a gap for 1937—that year again—and there was little of substance in the rest, but Harry Strang could only hope for the best, even if he realistically expected less.

Strang and Drescher sat down with attorney Friedman and reviewed the issues at length. The counselor clucked sympathetically, "promised to consult with his clients," and assured Strang they would "cooperate with the Government in every way to clear up the manner in which the 1933 Double Eagles became circulated."

Shortly after the meeting with Friedman ended, Strang and Drescher were contacted by a Philadelphia city detective, Jacob Gomborrow, a friend of Israel Swift's. Lawman to lawman, a little too comfortably, perhaps, Gomborrow sought to convey to Strang and Drescher "the impression that Swift did not know from whom the coins were obtained." Izzy's attitude would not have been at all unusual; in fact, it was in the nature of Swift's cutthroat profession. People brought bits and pieces into Swift's shop all the time. If the price was right, Izzy bought it. If he didn't, one of his rivals would. Swift neither asked nor cared particularly where the goods came from. It was just part of doing business, no big deal.

But Swift's friend, Gomborrow, and his attorney, Emanuel Friedman, were not on the same page. A few days later, Strang sat wrangling with the lawyer, whose easy manner and readiness to help in any way had changed. Now his "attitude was anything but cooperative." But what Friedman had to say was news, and he flatly contradicted Detective Gomborrow's knowing winks.

Friedman had discussed the case with both his clients, who had told him a lot. But he would only confide a little, including a startling revelation that turned Swift's own sworn statement to the Secret Service—that he couldn't remember from whom he had received the coins—on its head. The Philadelphia lawyer informed Strang and Drescher that his clients had told him that "they had not obtained the coins directly from a Mint employee [and] there were others involved." He would not divulge their names. He then jolted the two lawmen and "intimated that his clients had handled a considerable quantity of [the] coins."

The lawyer stopped there. He flatly, adamantly refused to enlighten the agents further. If this new information was true and not a red herring meant to sidetrack the investigation, it was a stunning turn of events. Strang and Drescher argued with Friedman. They "used all of the persuasive powers at their command" to have Friedman reconsider his stonewalling, but to no avail. They broke up the meeting. Friedman had successfully given them a new, roaring headache, and all they got from him in return was the promise of another meeting.

✦   ✦   ✦

Needing a sympathetic ear and straight talk, the agents gravitated to James Macallister's office. They needed to know if there were any truth to Friedman's latest story. Mac listened carefully and was able to fill in some blanks.

His first recollection was innocuous, interesting, and fit with the appearance of the two signatures on the back of Macallister's checks. When he had been buying the '33s from Switt, Macallister said, the sale price "on each occasion had to be passed on by Silver" before Izzy would commit to the deal.

Macallister reminded Strang that he had given up buying the 1933 double eagles at the end of 1937 when he felt that the supply was too abundant for the coins to be considered rare much longer. What Switt had told Macallister he now recalled in vivid detail: "My partner Ed can get all he wants of these, as we had 25 and only sold 14." Indeed, Macallister was told, Silver "was keeping two for his daughter."

It was not what agents Strang and Drescher wanted to hear, and Macallister wasn't finished. He reminded the two attentive men yet again "that no 1933 Double Eagles were circulated with coin collectors of the United States prior to the sale by Switt to Macallister on February 15, 1937." He also mentioned that Switt had boasted to him that somewhere along the way the jewelers had acquired and "melted up a whole bag of $20 gold pieces," although he hadn't mentioned their date.

In the silence that must have followed these startling pronouncements Strang could have only gloomily calculated a few of the new permutations. His investigation had accounted for nine of the gold coins, but *fourteen* coins were now claimed to have been sold. If what Macallister had been told was true, an additional eleven, unsold, were still out there, somewhere. Maybe Switt and Silver had melted them as the heat from the investigation had been turned up, but maybe not.

And that whole bag of twenties: could that have been the missing bag of 1929s that had been investigated without a solution in 1937? Another link to McCann?

Although much had already been revealed about the Cashier's checkered past and his activities by the ongoing interrogations and reams of official files, Strang and Drescher had no intention to interview McCann quite yet. Not until all possible information had been gathered from Switt and Reed, and they could confront the former Cashier with hard questions.

They had done more background on him and learned that McCann now worked for a realtor in Westmont, New Jersey, in a clerical capacity.

Paroled after serving four months of the one-year sentence at Lewisburg Penitentiary, the ex-con had sold his house on a quiet, tree-lined street and moved his family into a four-family apartment house that he owned in an untidy, noisier neighborhood. George McCann was still paying the price for his admitted defalcations, and would again.

On May 16, 1944, a stifling hot day in Philadelphia, Emanuel Friedman allowed Strang and Drescher one shot at Edward Silver. The air was still and heavy. The mercury flirted with ninety, while anvils in the sky built, waiting to crack and wash away the fetid air. At 2:30 P.M., the four men met in Friedman's office in the Fidelity-Philadelphia Building. Photostats of Silver's tax records were produced, none for 1937. If Izzy Switt was Croesus, Ed Silver was Midas. Between 1936 and 1943 his business grossed close to $200,000 annually and, like his brother-in-law, "he paid little or no income tax during those years."

To the agents' obvious, harmless, softball questions, Silver was responsive. He had been a gold dealer since 1934. He went to the Mint four or five times a week but also sold gold to others, all reputable firms that met the smell test except for one: Kushner and Pines in New York City. Bernard Kushner, its owner, and Jack Rubin, the Forty-seventh Street runner who had worked for him, had criminal records and were currently serving time, Kushner four years at Lewisburg for receiving smuggled bullion from Canada and Rubin seven years at Sing Sing for receiving stolen jewelry from a theft at the Waldorf-Astoria. Switt and Silver had some interesting business acquaintances.

When it came to the touchier questions, Edward Silver was unresponsive but consistent. He admitted that he had known Mint employees Pepper, Graham, and Roland, but he denied knowing George McCann. He stubbornly dismissed ever having had "any coin transactions with the Cashier's office." But Strang later put the lie to this assertion. The current Cashier, Willard Boyce, said that he "had seen McCann and Silver frequently in conversation," an observation corroborated by Jacob Pepper.

Thunder rumbled outside. Strang, in light of what James Macallister had told him, asked Silver pointedly about the 1933 double eagles.

The big jeweler responded that he had no "financial interest in the 1933 Double Eagles disposed of by Switt" and he "denied that he had ever handled any gold coin."

What about his endorsements on the back of Macallister's checks? Strang shot back.

A banking accommodation only, was the calm reply.

169

Friedman then abruptly lowered the boom and brought an end to the meeting. He would allow Silver to answer no more questions until they had consulted with Switt, but the jewelers' attorney smoothly tried to mollify the Secret Service men. He assured them that he would yet again consult with his clients and "determine if they could be of assistance in clearing up the disappearance of the 1933 Double Eagles from the Mint," without, he added pointedly, "incriminating or unduly involving themselves, or others." It was no admission of guilt, but it was certainly an indication of involvement.

Fat drops of rain smacked against pavement as the two special agents left the meeting. "It was obvious," Strang and Drescher agreed, that Silver "was not telling the truth, especially with regard to Switt's transactions with Macallister." And taking no chances, Friedman had "declined to permit either Switt or Silver to take a lie detector test." The leaden skies matched their mood as they trudged back to the Custom House.

If the agents' questioning of Switt and Silver and the trail of paper indicating their activities could be said to be yielding up vital information, the same could not be said of their progress in unraveling the activities of Ira Reed. The coin dealer, who "profess[ed] to keep no records of his coin transactions," had been singularly elusive and unavailable to be interviewed by the Secret Service, due, he said, to "being confined to home by illness." In the absence of Reed's cooperation and records, Strang requested of Washington that all the clients to whom Reed admitted selling the 1933 double eagles be contacted to get copies of their checks.

When Strang and Drescher finally got to interrogate Ira S. Reed at length in early May, if they learned anything new, it was well camouflaged. Reed was clever, evasive, and apparently fearless, even in the face of two increasingly exasperated agents of the United States Secret Service. It was a game. Reed toyed with Strang, telling obviously conflicting tales, vaguely intimating that he had sold more '33s, but steadfastly refusing to give out the details.

An enigma to the investigators, Ira Reed operated a coin business that catered to a small, wealthy, select clientele, and he occasionally held auctions the only distinction of which was the speed at which he conducted them, not their content. Reed seemed to sail very close to the wind, thumbing his nose at clients and the Treasury men alike, badgering Jake Bell for payment even though he knew Bell didn't have the coin and the Secret Service did.

To top it off, Ira Reed, a lifelong member of the Evangelical and

The great enigma: Philadelphia coin dealer Ira S. Reed, August 1942 (seated second from right with unnamed friends). How many 1933 double eagles did he handle?
(The *Numismatist*: American Numismatic Association)

Reformed Church, was continuing to deal in 1933 double eagles. Had Harry Strang or Frank Wilson known of Reed's defiant trafficking, there would have been hell to pay—but they did not.

Only weeks earlier, on April 15, 1944, Ira Reed, with full knowledge, charged an innocent and unsuspecting collector, Louis E. Eliasberg of Baltimore, one thousand dollars for the privilege of owning a coin that was the object of a Federal criminal investigation and subject to confiscation. Louis Eliasberg was a model of decorum, a scrupulously honest, modest man who owned the Finance Company of America and was one of the founding directors of the Maryland National Bank. Blessed with extraordinary business acumen, which had made him very wealthy, he was no shifty-eyed collector living in the shadows, looking over his shoulder, worrying about who might be catching up to him.

Eliasberg's devotion to coins was all-encompassing. His goal was to have them all, an example of every circulating coin struck by the United States federal government—every date, every denomination, every mint. The 1933 double eagle was one of the ten thousand coins he would one day own. To Ira Reed it was just another sale, and the Secret Service, along with Louis Eliasberg, were none the wiser.

Two days of questions and answers with Reed was like dodge ball. Reed admitted to Strang, with his small smile, that he had given "original circulation among coin collectors" of three 1933 double eagles, but this was old news. Clearly there were others, but Reed wouldn't say, and because of the United States Attorney's opinion that too much time had lapsed for prosecution of a crime, the Secret Service agents had no bludgeon with which to threaten him.

Ira Reed's records were as incomplete as his explanations. Somewhere within the blur of equivocations he had told his inquisitors that he had paid Switt by check. But the canceled checks he produced for 1937 to 1943 showed only one check, for $150, made out to Switt. That was for silver coins, recalled Reed, nothing for 1933 double eagles. Strang asked him about his previous statement, to which Reed replied unprofitably, that "he [had] evidently paid Switt in cash." And there was "no record in his books [that] would identify such purchases or payments." None of his books indicated "the name of the person from whom an article was purchased or to whom it was sold." And as none of his income tax returns "for 1937 to 1943 inclusive" had been kept, an income tax inquiry could not be far away.

Nothing about Reed seemed to add up right to the agents. He said he had only done business in Philadelphia since 1937, when he bought the shop on Eighteenth Street, but Macallister had said that Reed had "engaged in coin dealings in Philadelphia" before moving to the city. Reed said he hadn't met Switt until 1939, when Switt purchased some pewter from him, but Macallister's impression was that when the 1933 double eagles "were first circulated in February, 1937, Switt was acting in collusion with Reed." And although Reed admitted that he had contacts at the Mint, Superintendent Dressel, and Cashier Willard Boyce among them, he denied knowing McCann or Robert Graham of the Deposit-Weigh Room and had no idea how Graham had come to record Reed's name there.

It was all thoroughly unsatisfactory to Strang and Drescher, but there was little they could do. In the meantime Ira Reed, the beneficent member of the board of trustees of the Bethany Orphans' Home, who in 1930 had built for them the Reed Baby Cottage, continued as a pillar of his local community, revered, esteemed. But this deacon of the church seemed to derive a devilish pleasure from skirting the bounds of the law.

Strang and Drescher sat down in the Secret Service office to write their latest report to the Chief in Washington. Earlier in the month, Nellie Tayloe Ross, deeply concerned about gold vanishing from one of her facilities, had asked to meet with the two agents. On a glorious day with the sun glinting off the mica flecks in the row of carved granite lions' heads that ran along the Mint's roofline, the tidy lady with the riveting azure eyes had listened intently as Strang and Drescher took her through the investigation step by step. The "past developments and [the] proposed handling" of matters in the future were all discussed. The director would continue to follow their progress.

Now, while they had assembled a volume of new information, any fresh, solid leads were becoming scarcer. Hurdling and slaloming over and around patently false statements, curiously short-circuited memories, and obstreperous lawyers, with no legal muscle of their own to flex, was certainly impeding a quick solution to the puzzle. An interview with the two incarcerated gold traders might provide some new insight. But not until a week later. 1933 double eagles were not their only responsibility, and both agents were scheduled to give court testimony in other cases.

CHAPTER 13

Grounds for Recovery

———◆———

ON MAY 10, 1944, STAMPS, NOT A FUGITIVE 1933 DOUBLE EAGLE, WERE the subject of a government missive from dusty Cairo to Washington, D.C. The Honorable James K. Landis of the American Legation to Egypt forwarded to the President of the United States a sheet of stamps for his collection. They were a gift from fellow philatelist King Farouk and were a special issue, valid for only fourteen days, that depicted the king's father "without the characteristic tarbouche."

Wednesday, May, 17, 1944. Washington, D.C.

———

Secret Service Chief Frank Wilson, as was his habit, looked out his window and down at the East Gate of the White House. Even when little was happening and his number-one charge was safe in his office, Wilson liked to look across the street just to make sure.

The 1933 double eagle investigation had bogged down. Lawyers' tactics were taking their toll, and the Secret Service did not have much leverage to counter them. Wilson knew his men in the field must be growing weary in their often thankless and occasionally ridiculed task. They were soldiers in the Secret Service's defense of the nation's money and enforcement of the Gold Act, their primary responsibility. Strang, Drescher and all the other agents in the field were grunts, just like the GIs getting shot at Monte Cassino. This was their war. Digging into the whos, whys, and wherefores of a double eagle may have seemed unimportant to others, but Frank Wilson, their general, intended that they would do it right.

Messrs. Greenhill and Greenhill, Colonel Flanagan's attorneys, had sent another demanding epistle to Chief Wilson. The colonel, it appeared, had actually sold the '33—after it had been seized by Harry Strang—and was now being "pressed for the delivery of the coin." The colonel's counsel complained that their client was now in "a very embarrassing situation." Small wonder. Unaware of Ira Reed's continued covert activity, Wilson must have wondered who would sell a confiscated coin in the first place. And who would buy it? His response to the New York lawyers, echoed his first letter—but more tersely.

Wilson wasn't about to tip his hand to Flanagan's advocates, but the Treasury Department was actively considering what further action to take on the 1933 double eagles. To date nine had been positively identified by the Secret Service. Three had already been seized—or "recovered," as the government liked to style it—from their owners. Five others were still in the possession of collectors who had been alerted by agents not to part with them. And one, not forgotten, remained thousands of miles away in the cabinet of King Farouk, who was completely unaware of its murky status.

On May 4, 1944, Treasury General Counsel Joseph J. O'Connell, Jr., had sent a lengthy memorandum of opinion to Assistant Secretary of the Treasury Herbert E. Gaston, which was now making its rounds. Wilson focused on it through his wire-rimmed glasses and meticulously absorbed the carefully crafted reasoning.

Gaston had asked for "advice in the matter of nine $20 gold pieces minted in 1933, [and] purported to have been stolen from the Mint at Philadelphia." Could the Treasury recover them and if so, by what authority?

O'Connell provided a menu of choices but pointed out, presciently, that the path of recoupment was sure to be rutted. He cautioned that "particular attention must be given to the evidence needed under each method of recovery." The attorney considered it most unlikely that the owners of the coins, all wealthy men, would cheerfully hand them over without being required to do so by court order.

The counsel mapped out three courses of recovery, each with the applicable legal statute, a description, and his opinion pro and con. The first option, which he considered the most expedient, was also the simplest; he telescoped the lengthy section of criminal code by underscoring:

"Whosoever shall receive, conceal, or aid in concealing, or shall have

His was the first 1933 double eagle seized by the Secret Service:
Colonel James W. Flanagan (far right) with (from left) Henry Stimson and Jesse Jones.
(Center for American History, University of Texas-Austin)

or retain ... any money ... of the United States, which has ... been, stolen ... knowing the same to have been ... stolen ... shall be fined ... or imprisoned."

O'Connell explained that the courts had held that "it was unnecessary to prove that the accused knew that the property was stolen at the time it was received." All that was necessary for conviction was to "establish that it [had been] retained" while known to be stolen.

To seize the coins, he reasoned, inform the current owners that their 1933 double eagles "were stolen from the United States" and that they could either return them or be prosecuted for knowingly holding stolen property. The only proof needed by the government was that coins had in fact been stolen and "not lost or mislaid." In light of the direction the Secret Service investigation was taking, this seemed a mere formality.

The other variants he offered were more tenuous, put a greater burden of proof on the government, and allowed wide latitude for argument.

The first involved invoking articles under the Gold Reserve Act of 1934. The confused year of 1933 had produced some byzantine law and

O'Connell was wary of entering into that maze. His negative arguments significantly outweighed the positive. To prosecute successfully and obtain the forfeiture under one densely worded provision, "an intent to violate the Act" was required. That, thought the lawyer, was unlikely, at best.

The other twist was that under the Gold Reserve Act coins "of recognized special value to collectors" got a pass. The Treasury's counsel prophesied, accurately, as it turned out, that owners of the double eagles would argue "that they acquired the coins in good faith" and that numismatic opinion would support their special collectible status.

O'Connell pointed out that Curator Theodore Belote at the Smithsonian had been of this opinion and, in the mistaken belief that the coins had been legitimately issued, had allowed the issuance of the export license to King Farouk. It would be hard, if not impossible, he warned, for the government to prevail if the coins were seized on these grounds—a minefield at best.

The final option was a variation of the first. Again it was "based on the contention that the coins are property stolen from the United States and that the [collector] did not acquire valid title." Even a good-faith purchaser could not take "title to personal property from one who is not the owner."

However, money—cash—"even if acquired from a thief," was the single exception. If the coins had been purloined after August 28, 1933 (the date of another of FDR's executive orders concerning gold), then the valid title could not be acquired because they had ceased to be negotiable and had been acquired from the thief as "rare coin and not money." But if they had been stolen earlier, the gumbo of laws and proclamations might protect the owner and not the state. O'Connell thought that this was another treacherous path and counseled avoidance.

General Counsel O'Connell also understood market forces and cautioned that the Treasury Department should take the safest path to regain its stolen property. It was essential that the grounds of seizure be fully enforceable. He warned that if the process was "only partly successful it [would] merely serve to multiply the value of the coins remaining outstanding." He warned Gaston in the conclusion of the memorandum that if the government decided to recover the 1933 double eagles it had to be all of them—no exceptions. Even the one that had "been exported to King Farouk." Contrasting his opinion of only a week earlier, he wrote that "it would be only proper to attempt by diplomatic representations to have that coin returned to the United States."

The document on Frank Wilson's desk was a legal blueprint for the future, and the decision to implement any of the options was wholly dependent on the case his men were building around the country. Recovering the coins in the United States would be his job, but dealing with King Farouk would fall to the State Department.

Friday, May 26, 1944. Lewisburg, Pennsylvania.
———

A bucolic college town on the west bank of the Susquehanna River, Lewisburg was distinguished by its Federal and Victorian architecture, which, for Bucknell University's students, had an idyllic charm. For the inmates of the United States Penitentiary at Lewisburg, however, there were no vistas and nothing remotely enchanting.

The warden gave Harry Strang and George Drescher a private room in which to interview Bernard Kushner, the fallen scrap-gold dealer, who was only too happy to dish the dirt on Switt and Silver. Eager to help, he would "do anything which might help his application for parole," which was coming up in a few months time.

Melting gold coins privately had become illegal after the government had called them in at face value, and then, after passing the Gold Reserve Act of 1934, revalued the metal from $20.67 to $35 an ounce. Thus in 1944 a double eagle could still be surrendered to the Mint for twenty dollars in return, but the same coin melted down was worth nearly thirty-four dollars in gold value. It was a good if dodgy business for scrap-gold dealers to profiteer by buying old gold coins and melting them. If Switt had, as he bragged to Macallister, melted a whole bag of double eagles, he had increased his investment from $5,000 to $8,465.62, a pretty fair profit.

Bernard Kushner had met Izzy in New York around 1937. The convict took a dim view of Izzy Switt's business integrity. Switt had been dealing with Jack Rubin, who then sold the scrap gold to Kushner's firm. When Switt discovered this, he approached Kushner, cut out the middleman, and from then on did business with Kushner and Pines directly. The firm's gold dealings with Switt and Silver were in the neighborhood of $2,000 weekly, and the kind of gold he was buying from Switt was *not* the sort that the canny redhead could take to the United States Mint.

Izzy wasn't brazen enough to bring in gold coins. But, Kushner related, he knew that Switt and Silver had once operated a melting pot and "that he [had] received a considerable quantity of melted gold from Switt, the fineness of which was in the neighborhood of .900"—21.6 karat—exactly the purity of United States gold coins. Most scrap jewelry was closer to .500 fine—12 karat—gold. Switt, he reckoned, would thin out the purity of melted coins with some bits of old jewelry and dental gold.

Kushner had looked the other way. If he hadn't taken the gold, someone else would have, and he would have lost a customer.

At the end of the four-hour interview the convict promised to get in touch if he recalled anything further.

Their questioning of Jack Rubin at Sing Sing yielded nothing. Even though he had a long prison term facing him, he had little to offer. He admitted he had bought 1931 and 1932 double eagles from Israel Switt in 1936 as numismatic items, but "he denied having bought gold coins or melted gold" coins from Switt, despite Kushner's more believable statement to the contrary. The Secret Service files in New York indicated that both men had been melting gold coins illegally back in 1935 and 1936.

During another meeting with Strang and Drescher, attorney Emanuel Friedman essentially admitted the involvement of Switt at some level and certainly seemed to agree that the coins had illicitly disappeared from the Mint. He informed the agents that he knew "the correct version of the affair" and that there "was another principal involved" who was not his client. While it might not provide "the entire solution of the disappearance of [the] Double Eagles from the Mint, [it] might nevertheless prove helpful in solving the problem." But again he divulged nothing more. Promise, renege, delay, and obfuscate—he used tried-and-true legal tactics.

Since nobody was telling Strang and Drescher much more than they already knew, they needed a meeting in Washington with Frank Wilson.

Saturday, June 5, 1944. Washington, D.C.

The war was about to take its most dramatic turn within hours, but President Franklin Delano Roosevelt, ever the enthusiastic hobbyist, wrote to thank King Farouk with "keen delight" for the sheet of stamps he had just received. He felt they would make a wonderful addition to his collection and expressed hope that the king's leg, injured in the car crash months earlier, had entirely recovered. There was no mention of the 1933 double eagle.

Monday, June 7, 1944. Washington, D.C.

The big push, Operation Overlord, had been made the day before. On the beaches of Normandy, 150,000 troops were digging in. The sands were damp with salt water, sweat, and blood.

By contrast, Washington was calm. Traffic bustled, horns honked.

Life went on. The sky was gray and the air temperate, a welcome change for June. Frank Wilson met with special agents Harry Strang and George Drescher in his office. The massive granite and marble building's grand corridors and rooms seemed bearable on hot days and chilly on cool ones.

The agents' recent reports, despite their dispassionate lawman's language, reflected their sense that the walls of the investigation were narrowing and few corridors remained to be followed. Strang and Drescher greeted their boss grimly. Before getting down to the matter at hand, Wilson, as was his habit, walked them over to the ship model of the "famous American sloop, *Ranger,* which [he] had seen win the International Cup Race off Newport." The Chief found it calmed his visitors.

The slow-moving, inexorable glacier of a Chief then sat them down, and they raked over the case yet again. The greatest hindrance was their lack of clout. If the government lawyers had latched onto the statutory lapse of time and the impunity it imparted to the suspects with such ease, Emanuel Friedman, a smart lawyer, tough negotiator, and no fool, would have come to a similar conclusion and advised his clients accordingly.

Ira Reed was playing them. Switt had buttoned up. Nine coins were all they could locate. The tom-toms beat steadily and loudly in the coin world, and the dealers and collectors always seemed to be one or two steps ahead of the agents. Despite Macallister's help and Friedman's and Reed's indications and intimations that there were more examples out there, none had been traced.

George McCann remained the most likely source of the coins. The other theories had come up empty. The records proved that none had been sent to any Federal Reserve Bank. The Cashier's records proved that none had gone out legitimately through that office.

The Chief instructed Strang and Drescher to pull the drawstrings on Switt, Silver, and McCann. Check into withdrawals and deposits. If a link emerged, they would see it. The former Internal Revenue man needed numbers. He wanted more. Numbers had tripped up crooks before.

Philadelphia.
———

The path to gold was paved with cancelled checks. Almost. Strang and Drescher sank their gumshoe personae, rolled up their sleeves, donned metaphorical green visors, and became forensic accountants. If there were a link, however tenuous, between any of the current roster of alleged malefactors, then numbers, deposits, withdrawals, and checks would be the clues.

The work was time-consuming, but as the agents had no other ready clues, they dug through the paper. If McCann was accepted as the likely insider and Switt, or his silent partner, Silver, the acknowledged distributor—fence was such an ugly word—then there should be, must be, a few threads to start them weaving the connections.

Switt's records yielded nothing with the shadow of pattern. Edward Silver's checks, four years' worth, were their task at hand. The bridge to George McCann was made easier by the escapade that had landed him in Lewisburg four years earlier. Back then, in an effort to correlate the discredited Cashier's infusions of cash with the Mint's unofficial excretion of coin, Secret Service Agent Harrington had peeled back the onion skins of McCann's finances.

In 1940 the investigators hadn't known what they were searching for, and when they crunched the numbers, even though the results looked screwy, they hadn't realized why. With the benefit of the passage of time, fresh facts, a broader canvas, and a more significant crime, Strang and Drescher could see that more had been expropriated from the government than just nickels and dimes. A larger, more complex cast of characters—conspirators—was involved.

Cashier George McCann's salary had risen steadily, if unspectacularly from $2,421.79 in 1934 to $3,087.84 five years later, but his financial worth had twitched erratically, like a seismograph's needle. Much of the movement of these financial-worth figures could be laid at the feet of the spastic stock market that dominated the 1930s. But three years of additional income, deposited into his brokerage account—beyond his salary—was most provocative. A little over a thousand in 1934 grew generously and blossomed into nearly ten thousand dollars in 1936. After 1937 it dropped to nil. Such relatively mammoth amounts, growing exponentially over a three-year span, had needed explaining, and back in 1940 McCann had been interrogated about their source.

At first he easily offered up "statements with respect to the source of [the funds]," which the Secret Service investigated and found to be lies. When the agents had confronted McCann with the fabrications, he backtracked, fessed up, and admitted they were false, but then brought the shutters down. Asked again where the money had come from, he sat mulishly quiet—no answer. They dogged him repeatedly, but he was unyielding and went to jail having never explained the source of his funds.

Nearly a decade after those first subtle swellings of McCann's bankbook, the view was now panoramic. McCann's "personal transactions," read one Treasury memo, "were in magnitude far beyond his salary, or any property the acquisition of which he was willing to explain." McCann still needed to explain the source of all that kale.

In 1940 the Secret Service had been investigating pilferage of what amounted to pocket change, thefts that were used to buy beers and pay tolls. The apparent disappearance of the 1933 double eagles had not even been discovered, and the redoubtable ensemble of Israel Switt, Edward Silver, and Ira Reed had not yet gathered on stage—although it now appeared they had been lurking in the wings.

The agents sorted through the dense fog of financial numbers until there seemed to be a clearing. In 1936, from an active account at the Central-Penn National Bank, Edward Silver had made a series of withdrawals. Ten of them: each for a thousand dollars or more. The first had been made on January 9, 1936, the last less than six months later, on June 1. Strang compared these to the profile of McCann's unexplained income: the aggregate for 1936 was $9,837.50, a total similar to Silver's withdrawals. McCann's first cash deposit had been on February 25, 1936, the final one on June 2. A piece of the jigsaw dropped neatly into place— the timing overlaid the amounts.

It was about time the two government sleuths had got a break.

They reviewed Switt's checking activities. His account at the South Philadelphia National Bank showed minimal activity and nothing of sufficient size to be relevant to their task at hand. But the agents discovered that Israel Switt held "held a Power of Attorney to sign checks against" Edward Silver's bank account. Evidence that the brothers-in-law were using a common account in Silver's name, was confirmed by Kushner and Pines in New York, which provided cancelled checks from 1938.

Here the agents' luck spluttered. The Central-Penn National Bank had copies of all the checks, but the copying method used, the "Recordak" system, photographed only the face of the check, not the endorsing signature on the back. There was no way to tell if it had been McCann who had cashed Silver's checks.

Trained in the structure of the country's banking system, the agents knew that all transactions were recorded on transit sheets that were kept on deposit at the Philadelphia Clearing House. But fate dealt them another poor hand. The sheets had been destroyed only months earlier; the seven years the law required them to be held had lapsed in January. Timing was everything, and again it was working against the investigators.

The run of bad luck was particularly infuriating, as a solution to their quest was tantalizingly within reach. Although Israel Switt and Edward Silver vehemently denied ever having met—let alone known—

George McCann, there was sworn testimony from numerous witnesses to the contrary. Now the fiscal trail of crumbs went beyond the obvious who knew whom. The suspects' activities of 1936 looked like a living, breathing organism. McCann's inhalations of largess were perfectly timed to Switt's or Silver's exhalations of nearly identical funds.

At the Mint in the latter part of 1934, as the first of the gold coins headed to the melting pot, George McCann, the newly appointed Cashier, suddenly had an unexplained influx of cash. The following year McCann was physically running his hands through the endless stream of gold currency that continued to be poured into the crucible, and his income grew bounteously. George McCann had enjoyed a veritable bonanza during the first six months of 1936 that had abruptly stopped on June 2.

Only ten days earlier, on May 21, Israel Switt had sold Max Berenstein a dozen of the 1931 and 1932 double eagles cheaply—forty dollars apiece—indicating both the Philadelphia jeweler's unfamiliarity with the current coin market prices (the 1936 edition of the *Standard Catalogue of United States Coins* listed them at seventy-five dollars apiece) and his ready access to both issues. Macallister, Joseph Barnet, and Berenstein himself had all commented on their rarity until they had been circulated in quantity by Switt and Silver in 1936 and 1937.

George McCann had these coins under his personal control along with the 1933s that would become exceptionally rare when the bulk of the mintage was melted a few months later. The timing of these events was too close to be coincidental, but it was still only circumstantial, and why McCann's income stream had then dried up remained unclear. Many questions waited to be asked, but blanks were being filled in.

Tuesday, June 27, 1944. Washington, D.C.

In summer, any politician who could do so deserted the swamp of a city, which was considered a hardship posting by some diplomatic services. In Europe, Cherbourg had fallen to the United States army, and a vital foothold had been gained. The president, looking grayer and more haggard by the day, labored at his desk across the street, and so Frank Wilson had no escape. His high-ceilinged office was some relief from his modest house on Tennyson Street, but there was no avoiding the oppressive blanket of heat and humidity. He wearily dictated another letter in response to Colonel Flanagan's attorneys. They were nothing if not persistent, but they weren't getting back the coin.

A month later the obsessed Colonel Flanagan tried again. Now his lawyers wrote with their backs up: "Surely by this time your investigation has been completed. We cannot see how the government, in this particular instance, was able to take possession of this coin which was not its property and we do not see why the government insists on retaining it for so long a period."

Wilson responded laconically.

The unhappy colonel then got in touch with his senator, Claude Pepper of Florida, and pressed him to get answers. Pepper wrote Wilson and asked politely to be kept abreast of any developments, and the Chief promptly replied with a "My dear Senator" letter that brought the legislator up to date and promised nothing.

From the Abdin Palace in blistering Cairo, on August 5, 1944, King Farouk wrote to Roosevelt to thank him for his thank-you note. He was glad the president had received the stamps, rejoiced in the "recent victories of the American troops" and "still cherish[ed] the hope that we shall some day meet."

A month later Frank Wilson wired Fred Gruber, the Supervising Agent in Phildelphia, to reopen the investigation. The case had been suspended since mid-July, when Emanuel Friedman, whose hints of others' involvement, if not phantom, were critical, had been called away, and Harry Strang had been requested by the United States Attorney to prepare for a lengthy trial.

Fall fell, time melted away, and the bulwarks rose once again. Friedman vamped, indicated he would like to cooperate, and promised to get in touch once his clients agreed to "advance any information, if they actually possess[ed]" any. But all pretense was dropped a few weeks later when the lawyer, brought to heel telephonically, informed the Secret Service that Switt and Silver had nothing more to say and "intimated that no further cooperation could be expected." The game was up. Emanuel Friedman had run out the clock.

It was October 10, 1944. On this high note, Harry Strang was back on the case. Summer was little more than a warm memory, and it was George McCann's turn to answer some questions—finally.

CHAPTER 14

A Clumsy Liar

---◆---

Tuesday, October 10, 1944. Westmont, New Jersey.

ORANGE, YELLOW, AND RED FLECKED THE EDGES OF TIRING GREEN leaves in a kaleidoscopic blur as Harry Strang, back on the case, and his new partner, Charles Rich, headed out to confront McCann. George Drescher had been reassigned during the summer, and would, within a few months time, become the head of the protection team for the new vice president, Harry S. Truman.

Westmont was a healthy suburban working-class village, and, like so many small towns, was dominated by the local movie palace, which had soaring pointed-arch windows above a long, low marquee. Haddon Avenue was the main drag, a broad boulevard flanked by a long line of tiny two-story shops. Some were freestanding, shoehorned in next to one another; others were little multishop buildings; tidy, dried-blood-red brick structures, a storefront below and triple window above, several had shingle canopies to protect shoppers from the elements.

Muller's Real Estate office was at the other end of the strip from the movie theater, an ordinary shop front in an ordinary town. The war raged abroad, but things were looking up at home; meat rationing had been eased. The clear crackle in the air stood in stark contrast to the dark fug with which George McCann greeted the two unexpected lawmen.

He was suspicious of them and edgy. If he had been warned by Switt, Silver, or any other target of the investigation, he didn't let on. His actions and replies to Strang's questions were opaque and unhelpful. As McCann sullenly answered questions, he was regularly interrupted by real estate business. It was tough going.

Strang started with the 1933 double eagles and walked McCann through the Cashier's responsibilities, flicking him questions along the way. The former Cashier, to hear his side of it, had seemingly never touched gold and was certainly untouched by evil.

McCann's gospel was that he had not had "custody at any time of the 1933" double eagles returned by the Assay Commission in February, 1934. Instead, he pointed at Edward McKernan, the Vault Custodian, who, he said, received the Pyx Box and had the only key. McCann claimed that when the coins were removed from the box, "they were placed in the gold coin stock of Vault F." He charged that only McKernan and his assistant, now dead, had access to the '33 double eagles. "At no time," he maintained, "were these gold coins placed in the Cashier's Vault," where he could have had access to them. After the January 30 passage of the Gold Reserve Act of 1934, McCann said, "he had no gold coin in his actual custody" apart from that which was turned in by the public. McCann also claimed that Vault Custodian McKernan had sent the two examples of the '33s to the Smithsonian Institution. McCann insisted that his own role was limited to merely relaying the instructions.

The discredited Cashier admitted that he knew of Switt's fall from grace and his run-in with the police more than a decade earlier, but he maintained he did not know him personally, only as a gold depositor. As for Edward Silver, McCann said, he had never heard of him.

If, asked Strang, McCann as Cashier had no access to these coins, then how, in his opinion, had the 1933 double eagles become circulated?

McCann could conceivably have claimed that he had paid them out or exchanged them with collectors perfectly innocently over the counter, but he didn't. He might have said that the Secretary of the Treasury had requested them, but he didn't, and the daily ledgers would belie such a claim. Instead he fell back on familiar territory. He "professed to have no knowledge" at all and again suggested Edward McKernan. McKernan had "carte blanche authority to enter the gold vault" and, according to McCann, held the only key to the Pyx Box.

As Strang scratched down his notes, he knew from previous interviews and sworn statements that McCann was lying.

Harry Strang turned his questioning away from 1933 double eagles and to the missing bag of 250 double eagles believed to have been struck in 1929 that had been discovered missing from Vault F, Cage 1 in February, 1937. Accounting for the bag had been the Cashier's direct responsibility, and its disappearance had occurred on McCann's watch.

On January 27, 1942, mere months after McCann's emergence from

United States Mint in Philadelphia:
Vault E—the Cashier's Working Vault.
(Author)

prison, he was informed by the Secretary of the Treasury's office that his retirement funds had been garnished by the government and that it was attempting, through his bonding company, to recover the balance of the gold value of the bag—nearly $6,500 more. McCann became apoplectic and by this point in 1944 had already been in legal skirmishes with the government for two years. (He would continue to do battle for another three, only to lose.)

This issue had been festering, and when Strang addressed it, McCann became extremely agitated and proceeded to spew accusations and theories to get himself off the hook.

The first allegation was that McKernan had once been arrested for spending gold coins outside the Mint. Strang knew this, but the investigation had gone nowhere, and no charges had been filed. The second was that the vault custodian had the opportunity to steal the bag of gold coins during the last emergency shipment on Sunday, March 5, 1933. According to McCann, that was the only time prior to the installation of protective devices in 1936 that Vault F, Cage I had been opened.

Strang had caught the former Cashier in another lie. "McCann said nothing regarding the opening of the Vault on or about June [27], 1933." On that day the 1933 double eagles had been sealed into Cage 1. The

189

work had been shoddily done, and the contents of the Vault were "certi-fied to but apparently not checked by" the Settlement Committee, so anything was possible. During that lackadaisical exercise, the records showed, George McCann acted as "the representative of the Superinten-dent of the Mint, and had free access to all parts of the Vault."

Strang didn't challenge McCann on this singular omission "in the interest of possible future litigation." After two hours of business inter-ruptions and occasional fulminating exchanges, Strang asked McCann for another appointment.

The aggrieved McCann declined until he could consult with his attor-ney, Thomas J. Minnick, Jr., who was battling with the Treasury Depart-ment over the attachment of the ex-Cashier's monies. Minnick spoke to Strang the next day and refused to allow the Secret Service any further contact, arguing "that McCann's health would not permit it." McCann claimed to be suffering from epilepsy. The agents had had their first and only interview with their prime suspect.

Wednesday, October 11, 1944. Philadelphia.

Agent Strang dutifully headed back to question former Vault Custodian and Shipper, Edward McKernan, anew. During their first tangle McKernan had been wary and not especially cooperative. Now, in an interview at McKernan's modest dwelling in West Philadelphia, Strang dealt the same questions he had asked McCann. But McKernan's answers were in direct contradiction to those of the crooked Cashier. A short time later officials at the Philadelphia Mint would corroborate McKernan's statements.

Regarding the lost bag of 1929 double eagles: when the last, March 5, 1933, emergency shipment of gold had gone out, it was the late Assis-tant Superintendent of the Mint, Fred H. Chaffin, who had supervised. McKernan had come in late that day, having attended the inauguration of Franklin Roosevelt the day before. The coins had been removed from the vast underground cavern called Vault F and rolled the short distance to the Shipping Office. McKernan hadn't even reported to work yet. McCann's accusation was false.

There were two keys, not one, and two locks to the Pyx Box, McKer-nan said, which was tradition. One was kept by the Cashier, the other by the Assayer. One could not open the box without the other. McCann was one holder. The rule was ages old, and the same system was still in use. Strang checked. McCann was a clumsy liar.

McKernan had a theory about the circulation of the 1933 double

190

eagles. It might have happened after the death of Fred Chaffin in June, 1936, who was supposed to have "accumulated a quantity of numismatic coins." Doc Ziegler and Ralph Roland had helped out with the estate. They had been in cahoots for years.

The specter of conspiracy within the Mint having been raised by McKernan, Strang met with Superintendent Edwin Dressel and Helen Moore, the assistant superintendent, the next day to clarify this angle.

Mrs. Moore was direct about the tight, powerful clique of Chaffin, Roland, Ziegler, and McCann—the Four Horsemen. She admitted they had run things the way they liked. This was an open secret. No one challenged them. It was almost a Mint tradition. Each generation had its own group that used the Mint as their factory for their products, for their gain. Today, some consider them Robin Hoods, others thieves. Over a century earlier, Chief Coiner Franklin Peale had taken private commissions, while more recently, coin dealers such as John Haseltine, Stephen Nagy, and Henry Chapman had murky inside contacts who provided the unusual, the rare, the specially made coins—strictly illegal, but largely ignored by law enforcement. In the intervening years, a similar roster of corrupt employees had been producing and peddling unofficial metallic myths to line their pockets. Until 1885, this shadowy manufacture had been on a vast scale, but then the reins of authority had tightened, and these ventures had gone even deeper underground.

Some of the most valuable coins in the world owed their very existence not to great art, stunning history, and chance survival, but to Mint employees' after-hours legerdemain. The 1804 silver dollar was first made for diplomatic presentation in 1834 (thirty years after the date it bears) perhaps illegally but nevertheless officially. When word of their existence enthralled mid-nineteenth-century collectors the entrepreneneurial underground workshop at the Mint got to work some twenty-five years later and illicitly made still more for private gain. Both the 1884 and 1885 trade dollars and the 1913 Liberty Head nickel, five examples of which had been illicitly made, quite probably not in 1913, were fabrications from the start, intended for collectors only. Hundreds, thousands, of others—including patterns, coins struck in the wrong metals, and complete fantasies—all led back through generation after generation of similarly enterprising cabals. Seldom, if ever, were the malfeasants prosecuted, and the coins themselves were eagerly, avidly, sought by collectors, who spent increasingly more and more money on them. The government's attitude, with an occasional half-hearted grumbling exception, had been one of benign neglect. With a nod

A Clumsy Liar

and a wink, it averted its eyes and allowed the now legal trade in illegal coins among collectors to flourish.

If such a clique still existed in the wake of the Four Horsemen, Dressel and Moore did not say, and Strang did not ask.

This comfortable brotherhood had started breaking down in 1936. Fred H. Chaffin, then sixty-five and ready to retire, had been seconded to serve on a Settlement Committee at the San Francisco Mint. On June 17, 1936, while his train sped west through the vistas of Wyoming, he suffered a massive heart attack and dropped dead.

When Mint Assayer Doc Ziegler handled the coins in Chaffin's estate, which he sold to an unnamed New York dealer for $134, there was said to be no gold. Chaffin, even with his sidelong look at rules and regulations, had taken FDR's gold recall seriously and had at that time "redeemed his gold coin collection." Strang checked the records carefully and came to the conclusion that there had been no double eagles involved in his estate. But the Four Horsemen had become three and more vulnerable.

Chaffin had died within days of McCann's last mysterious deposit of funds into his brokerage account. And Ziegler had died a couple of years later. In the wee hours of February 16, 1938, the third-floor night supervisor at the National Stomach Hospital in Philadelphia had heard a noise from one of the rooms at the far end of the hall. She hurried toward the source and found an empty room; cold winter air whistled through the open window. Moments later her knees buckled slightly as she looked down from the window. Splayed on the pavement below was Chester W. Ziegler, Chief Assayer of the United States Mint since 1929, a suicide. Hours earlier he had handed power of attorney to Ralph Roland.

The former assistant superintendent of the Philadelphia Mint, Ralph Roland, met with Strang on October 17, 1944, at his country house in New Holland, Pennsylvania. Roland assumed the post of assistant superintendent upon Chaffin's death in 1936 and served until his retirement in 1942. He freely discussed his administration of Ziegler's estate, which, he confirmed, had no gold coins. He also discussed George McCann.

Strang asked the guarded Roland about the return of the coins from the 1934 Assay Commission. Roland, surprisingly, did not back his former whippersnapper. Instead he confirmed the Mint's official versions and that of Edward McKernan. These three corroborating statements "gave direct lie to McCann's account."

Mint employees were a family; it was a tradition, it was pride. Philadelphia was a small city, the Mint was a neighborhood. Fathers, sons, wives, and daughters all found employment there. When Doc Ziegler had been appointed Assayer by Herbert Hoover, he had been the first, since the establishment of the Mint in 1792, to hold that position whose surname was not Eckfeldt. The first Eckfeldt had been appointed to the post by George Washington.

As in most extended families, there were disagreements, feuds, clannishness, and the occasional black sheep at the Mint. While they fiercely protected their own and a degree of laxity was accepted, certain transgressions were not countenanced. The Four Horsemen had protected McCann in the 1920s when his ledger balances hadn't tallied. But when he got caught with his hand in the till, there was no net to catch his fall. Two of the mutual protection group were dead, and the last, Roland, protected his own hide first. Getting caught was the unforgivable crime. From that point on, George McCann became a pariah.

Roland bluntly gave Strang his opinion. The 1933 double eagles, he felt, "could not have become circulated without collusion" from George McCann. It was that simple. McCann, he elaborated logically, "had the only coins of this mintage not under seal" and had evidently substituted double eagles of other years so "that his records would show sufficient weight and value."

It wrapped it up pretty neatly, thought Harry Strang. It was his theory too.

Monday, October 23, 1944. Philadelphia.

James Macallister asked Harry Strang about the current status of the 1933 double eagles. Max Berenstein was getting nervous about the sixteen hundred dollars he had paid for his '33 double eagle and was wondering if Macallister would return his money. The dealer said he had no issue with refunding the money if the government was planning to keep the damned thing, but he would like to know so that he could "in turn call upon Switt and Silver to reimburse him." If the Secret Service agent couldn't give him an answer, he would be happy to go straight to Mint Director Ross or Treasury Secretary Morgenthau "to obtain a prompt decision in the matter." Macallister seemed to have connections he didn't usually trumpet.

Later that week, Nellie Tayloe Ross came to the Mint, met with the two investigating agents, and again reviewed the case in depth. Mrs. Ross had the advantage of historical perspective, having been at the Mint, admittedly as a rookie, when the saga had all begun and 1933 double eagles were still hurtling from hammering presses.

When Strang completed his recitation of the facts as he understood them and had answered her questions, the director sat and thought. Then she drew breath and expressed her view. While it was clearly up to the Treasury Department's General Counsel to render a "definite decision in the matter," it was her opinion "that the Government should recover and keep the coins as they were illegally in circulation."

Saturday, November 4, 1944. Philadelphia.

The election was to take place in three days. Roosevelt was running for his fourth term, and the Republicans were now sacrificing the chilly Thomas Dewey. It was eleven tempestuous years since FDR had taken the nation and the world by storm. He looked old now, thin and ill. Through his sweeping actions in 1933, Roosevelt, the man Harry W. Strang's agency was sworn to protect, had created the very problem that the heavy-shouldered agent had been struggling to solve for the better part of a year.

A smudge of gray mist overhung the city. Harry Strang and Charles Rich sat quietly and read the four-page report to Chief Wilson they had just rolled out of the typewriter. It was a cold, spare document with no literary license, no soaring metaphors, just a recitation of facts known and inferences drawn.

Their investigation was headed toward its finale. Strang had interviewed all the primary players—more than once, when he hadn't been rebuffed. The plot needed no more tweaking.

The typed pages now lying on Strang's desk in the Custom House represented his synthesis of the case, the four most likely possibilities of how he deduced the coins could have wandered into "unauthorized circulation."

The first prospect, that the vast quantity of the '33 double eagle mintage that had been stored in Vault F, Cage 1 might have been tampered with between June, 1933, and February, 1937, he demolished. The vault records and cage seals had been carefully examined, and there was "no account of any discrepancy or irregularity." The second possibility, that during the Assay Commission of 1934 Doc Ziegler might have substituted 1933 double eagles for coins of another date was deemed unlikely. Yet Strang noted that it might be "a coincidence of importance" that nine double eagles were to be destroyed during the assay, and nine 1933 double eagles were known to be in "unauthorized circulation."

To disprove the possibility that the coins had been appropriated from the tons of double eagles undergoing the final melt, Strang had contacted the Mint's retired Refiner, who had explained the process in detail. Twelve melts per day of seven thousand ounces each was the norm. The coins were weighed before and after melting, and while the weight of nine coins would not have been noticed "if divided throughout the total melt," the supervision was so tight that there would have been little opportunity for theft. Any such discrepancy would have triggered an investigation. The average melt had produced little more than .025 ounces per thousand of shortage, far less than the weight of a double eagle and fully attributable to the melting process.

Then there was the Cashier: George McCann, the clumsy liar.

During the three years he had had exclusive control of the 1933 double eagles his unexplained income had risen majestically. He said he hadn't sent the coins to the Smithsonian; the Mint's records and officials, McKernan, and Roland said he had. He said he had no access to the Pyx Box; McKernan, Roland, and Mint tradition said he did. He denied having had access to any 1933 double eagles; repeated testimony said he had them in his office under his sole control. He said he didn't know Switt or Silver, and they said they didn't know him; but witness after witness had seen them talking knowingly. And in 1936 his nearly ten-thousand-dollar windfall neatly matched Edward Silver's withdrawals. Some of his denials were more outrageous than others. All were demonstrably false. McCann had opportunity, motive, and means.

Strang closed the report with a request to meet with Chief Wilson "for the purpose of discussing ways and means by which the investigation may possibly be brought to a successful conclusion."

Monday, November 20, 1944. Washington, D.C.

All of Washington seemed on the move around them as Harry Strang and Charles Rich headed up the rain-slicked steps of the Treasury Building. Frank Wilson's cavernous office had become familiar territory for Harry Strang and on such a filthy day it was welcoming. The boss sat with his agents, and together, carefully, they walked through the intricate melodrama.

Strang knew the routine. He knew his case. If he proved it to Chief Wilson, then the investigating would end and hopefully the litigating would commence, and the guilty would be convicted. In 1944 the Secret Service ran a 97.9 percent conviction rate.

In the end it was a tidy leach field. After McCann—the "magician"— spirited the coins from the Mint, probably in his pocket, one at a time—

he was senior, trusted, and there were no metal detectors—it was: McCann to Switt. Switt to Macallister, Reed, and Kosoff. Macallister, Reed and, Kosoff to their bevy of connections—dealers, collectors, and, of course, King Farouk.

Having listened to it all, Frank Wilson stood up with agents Strang and Rich and asked for the final report.

After the Chief had received it, a heavily pruned version of it was submitted to the United States Attorney about a month later. It "set forth the facts in the case involving Israel Switt and Edward Silver, Old Gold Dealers, and George A. McCann, former Cashier of the United States Mint."

Five paragraphs later it asked humbly for an opinion, having considered the facts, if "any criminal action might at this time be taken."

Wednesday, January 17, 1945. Washington, D.C.

The answer was no. The case was strong enough, but the clock had run out.

Frank Wilson might not care for the decision—lawmen never like losing to felons—but he knew it was the law. Justice protected the innocent, but it also shielded the accused, guilty or not. It wasn't the first time it had happened, and it wasn't going to be the last. But it was disappointing.

If the crooks couldn't be brought to heel, then at least the fruits of their craven enterprise could be returned to the government, he hoped. Wilson sent a memo to the Treasury's counsel and attached a copy of Strang's summary report. "We are awaiting," he wrote, "a letter from the United States Attorney at Philadelphia, indicating that criminal procedure can not be brought against the persons responsible for the sale of the coins to collectors or against the person who is believed to have taken them from the Mint, [because of the] Statute of Limitations." Timing was everything. His memo also asked the Treasury counsel for "an opinion as to whether libel proceedings can be instituted to regain possession of the nine coins now held by collectors."

On January 15, 1945, Messrs. Greenhill & Greenhill, attorneys for Colonel James Flanagan, wrote again to Frank Wilson. "Is there anyway this matter can be brought to a conclusion at the present time and the coin returned." In a few months they would get their answer.

CHAPTER 15

Seizures, Suits, and Surrender

———◆———

SHROUDED IN SECRECY, FRANKLIN DELANO ROOSEVELT QUIETLY departed from the Bureau of Engraving at 10:30 P.M. on Monday, January 22, 1945. Secret Service Chief Frank Wilson had ten of his agents traveling in the president's company and another ten in advance positions. FDR, looking small, his great midnight-blue cape enveloping him, was assisted onto a Chesapeake and Ohio train, which swayed and hissed through the darkness to Newport News, Virginia. From there he set sail across the Atlantic aboard the U.S.S. *Quincy.* The sleek cruiser, its gray silhouette almost invisible between the leaden skies above and the tempestuous iron depths below, cut an erratic path to avoid the German U-boats, which "were showing more initiative and fight in the Atlantic."

Winter did not impede the American forces in the Ardennes or the Russian winter offensive in the east. In Italy the combatants had ground to a bloody stalemate. From February 3 to February 11, Franklin Roosevelt, Winston Churchill, and Joseph Stalin met at Yalta. They argued furiously, compromised resignedly, and decided the fate of the post-war world. Countries were to be carved up to suit the three great powers, which smelled victory on the bitter blasts of winter.

On Tuesday, February 13, 1945, FDR was exhausted but back at work aboard the *Quincy.* Its great chains, streaked with rust, groaned as it swung gently at anchor in the Great Bitter Lake in the Suez Canal. Smoke from a Camel curled and eddied while he briefly studied the political notes prepared for him in anticipation of the arrival of his guest, King

Farouk. Besides the sheet of stamps Farouk had sent his fellow philatelist, they had little in common.

Egypt was chafing under the British yoke. Despite its having acquired full sovereignty under treaty with Britain in 1936, certain rights, such as the maintenance of British troops to defend the Suez Canal, had not been ceded. These acted as a burr, itching and inflaming Egyptian nationalistic tendencies that would reach critical mass in a few years. Mixed into this stew was the presence, since 1939, of British and Allied troops fighting the war from Egyptian territory. Their demands—martial law, strict censorship, and a state of siege in an officially neutral country—further exacerbated now festering sores.

Before Yalta, Roosevelt had intended to confer with Farouk "in hopes of arranging accommodations for a Palestine homeland for the Jews of the world." But afterward, crushingly worn and unfocused, "he could not answer simple questions and talked what was close to nonsense." On the chilly morning of February 13, Farouk arrived, wearing oversized sunglasses, a fez, an admiral of the fleet's uniform, and a bewildered expression. The weary FDR, wearing his blue cape and a gray homburg, simply talked and talked. He wished His Majesty a happy, if belated, twenty-sixth birthday and launched into a largely one-sided conversation about trade and tourism. Long-staple Egyptian cotton and sightseeing around the Pyramids were the extent of Roosevelt's monologue. Farouk smiled; he had expected more. He nodded politely.

It was reported that the "conversation was animated and friendly," even if nothing of substance was discussed. Egypt was vital to security in the region, Farouk had no personal animosity for Jews, and stable control of the Suez Canal was essential for maintaining American world interests. Farouk had long liked Americans and still yearned to visit. If not a meeting of profound importance, it was of diplomatic essence. When the two men took their leave of each other, FDR presented Farouk with a framed presentation copy of his most recent inaugural address and a gold medal to commemorate the same event.

As the two men made diplomatic small talk for two hours, neither was aware that they were inextricably linked by a single object: the 1933 double eagle. Roosevelt's laws had destroyed them, but Farouk's mania had saved one, now, seemingly, the only one.

The president returned to the United States at the end of February, drawn, listless, nearly comatose at times, and with lines deeply etched into his once beaming face. The harsh ordeal of Yalta and the strain of the long journey had drained him of his customary optimism and zeal

ILLEGAL TENDER

Two collectors, linked by the 1933 double eagle. King Farouk of Egypt meets with FDR aboard the USS Quincy after Yalta and two months before the president's death. Standing right: Anna Roosevelt Boettiger.

(Signal Corps: Franklin Delano Roosevelt Presidential Library)

and, ultimately if not clinically, his life. Days before Roosevelt's death, King Farouk sent the president another sheet of stamps and expressed his "greatest enthusiasm and pleasure" in their having met. FDR never saw the gift, probably the last addition to his beloved stamp collection. The sheet would be sold for forty dollars a year later with the rest of FDR's fabled holdings of more than one and a quarter million stamps.

Tuesday, May 15, 1945. Washington, D.C.

It was just over a year earlier that Assistant Secretary of the Treasury Herbert E. Gaston had lightly informed his boss, Henry Morgenthau, Jr., that the Secret Service was investigating the theft of 1933 double eagles. It seemed a lifetime. Franklin Roosevelt had died on April 12. Hitler had outlived him, just, but now that monster too was dead. Days later, the war in Europe ended.

A chilly form letter, ready for Gaston's signature, contained news critical only to a few exceedingly wealthy men. The owners of the 1933 double eagles or their legal representatives were about to get a blandly worded notice that decisions had been taken. The Secret Service investigation had determined that the "coins were embezzled or stolen from the United States." The government attorneys, like habited monks, had cloistered themselves, struggling to come to a resolution: to seize or not to seize, and if to seize, on what grounds. The letter coldly informed owners that under the Criminal Code (section 48), "retention, with knowledge" of stolen property was unlawful and that the 1933 double eagles fit that description. It had taken lawyers five months to adopt the tack Treasury Counsel Joseph O'Connell had suggested to Gaston more than a year earlier.

If a coin had already been seized, it would not be returned. If it hadn't already been seized, then "an agent of the Secret Service will call upon you in the near future." It was so direct, impersonal, simple. But, as Harry Strang augured in his final report: "It is possible . . . that there may be some litigation in the matter."

Upon receiving this unwanted piece of official foolscap, James F. Bell, who had written twice during the past year to Chief Wilson, pleading piteously for his coin to be returned so that Ira Reed's demands for money could be met, dropped the issue cold. Perhaps he fretted that a battle might open the rest of his collection to seizure or his business to scrutiny. Either way, the Secret Service already had his coin. How he made out with Ira Reed is unknown, but the odds were with Reed.

Max Berenstein was out the most, a hole sixteen hundred dollars deep. In December, 1944, his attorney had arrived unannounced at the Treasury Building in Washington and tried in vain to get a simple, plain update on the issue. Berenstein wanted to get back the 1933 double eagle or go after James Macallister for recompense.

Macallister had already told Harry Strang that if the '33s were determined to be officially taboo, then he would return owed monies and go after Switt. But by May, 1945, Macallister, only fifty-three years old, was losing weight, in hideous pain, and mortally ill with bladder cancer that would kill him in October. Ever a man of his word, he made amends, but when his son tried to recoup from Israel Switt, all he got was a baleful glare and the bum's rush.

Colonel James W. Flanagan of the Waldorf-Astoria, New York City, and Palm Beach, Florida, the self-styled friend of the late President of the United States, with legions of political connections, had been pestering Frank Wilson for the past year, but when Gaston's letter was received by his solicitors, Greenhill & Greenhill, he disappeared without a trace. If funds had changed hands between the colonel and the man to whom he had purportedly sold the stolen coin, it remained just between gentlemen.

F. C. C. Boyd's ties in the nation's capital ran deep, and he had established a welcome dialogue with the Secret Service during the early days of the inquiry. From the outset, Fred Boyd had simply asked for proof positive that the double eagle was illicit before he turned it back to the government. The flatly worded letter from Gaston could not have fully satisfied the inquisitive collector, but neither did he believe he was being flimflammed by the Treasury. "I do not care to have anything in my possession," he wrote to Gaston, "that has been embezzled or stolen. However," he continued, "as a collector I should like to keep this coin." Boyd's request that a receipt of his own composing, assuring his heirs some rights if the government ever changed its mind, was rebuffed by Gaston, and the gentlemanly Boyd acquiesced. At 3:00 P.M., on June 18, 1945, at the Union News Company offices on Varick Street in Manhattan, Fred Boyd gloomily handed over his 1933 double eagle to Special Agent Harry W. Strang.

Boyd then made a suggestion that, had it been heeded by the Secret Service, might have changed history. The collector thought either the Secret Service or he should write an article about the troubled status of the 1933 double eagles "for the American Numismatists." It was important, he felt, so that if in the future "any other coins of like character," came to the attention of collectors, they would react immediately and notify "the proper people since the coins might have been embezzled from the Government." Boyd received an official receipt, a handshake, and thanks from the agent who was tidying up the case. His proposal, however, was recorded, filed, and ignored.

Charles M. Williams didn't like it one bit. The insurance man took enormous pride in his collection, and he wasn't about to give up one of its jewels willingly. In his view he had bought the coin perfectly legally. On June 1 he informed the Secret Service that he was not going to surrender the coin and the government would have to start proceedings against him. Then Williams sought counsel from his fellow collector Fred Boyd, who commiserated about the injustice of it all but who wired Williams several weeks later to inform him that he had surrendered his '33 to the Secret Service the previous day. Williams, seething and truculent three weeks earlier, showed up unannounced and contrite at the Secret Service office in Cincinnati on June 21 with a 1933 double eagle, which, with sighs of regret, he returned to the United States Government.

Previously unpublished photographs of a 1933 double eagle, believed to be F. C. C. Boyd's. Purchased late February, 1937. Seized June 18, 1945. Destroyed August 21, 1956.

(Ex F. C. C. Boyd estate)

Special Agent Robuck accepted the coin and forwarded it to the Chief via registered mail in its official jacket, Form 1548.

The rest chose to stand and fight—and lose.

In Jamestown, New York, T. James Clarke read and reread the thickly official piece of paper from Washington, D.C. Concerned that he might have to forfeit the $550 he had paid Ira Reed and troubled also about the validity if the government's argument, he called Harry J. Stein, an attorney and astute collector of ancient Roman coins, in New York City.

The hustling but soft-spoken Stein, ever so politely at first, advised Assistant Treasury Secretary Gaston that while he would cooperate in every possible way, including surrender of the offending double eagle, he was knowledgeable in the way of coins as well as law. In vaguely condescending tones, he informed the Treasury man that he knew as much as they knew, since he was well traveled in "numismatic circles." Advocate Stein found it hard to imagine how "one coin of an issue of 445,500" could be identified as stolen and pressed for the proof that had so branded Mr. Clarke's coin. He received a boilerplate reply from Gaston.

On June 19, Stein laid the 1933 double eagle on his desk, insisting that it be a permissive seizure. Strang, who had come to pick it up, pulled out his fountain pen and embellished a receipt with his luxuriant signature. He left with the gold piece in his pocket, and the next morning Stein, on behalf of T. James Clarke, fired his first salvo in court.

Down south, in Memphis, Tennessee, L. G. Barnard tossed Gaston's letter onto his desk. He had also decided that the coin was still his, and he was going to prove it. On May 28, 1945, his attorneys filed a petition with the United States District Court in Memphis, Tennessee. "L. G. Barnard vs United States of America" requested a "declaratory judgment by the court to clear the title of the coin." Uncompromising in its brevity, the suit claimed Barnard had bought and paid for the double eagle legally and that he didn't know, never knew, and the government had never shown proof that the double eagle was illegal.

The battle would soon be joined.

When Harry Strang strode into James Stack's office on June 20, 1945, Stack politely handed over the 1933 double eagle he had bought from Ira Reed for a thousand dollars two years earlier, with a letter. It was terse. He delivered the coin "under protest and under legal duress" and reserved the "right to institute legal proceedings as may be necessary for its recovery." Attorney Harry Stein had asked Stack to join the fray, but he chose instead to wait, watch, and keep his options open.

Eight 1933 double eagles were now in government custody. Harry Strang's quest had identified nine. Farouk's remained untouchable.

Like ships of the line, ponderous, creaking in agonizing slow-motion, the two sides, the government on one side, the collectors on the other, arrayed themselves, readying for the first ranging shots.

On July 28, 1945, as the two sides continued to eye each other warily and the government continued its excavation of archival evidence, a B-29 bomber, hopelessly off course and lost in a blinding fog, slammed into the side of the Empire State Building. Thirteen people were killed. Fiery debris rained down from the seventy-ninth floor and destroyed the penthouse and studio of Henry Hering, Augustus Saint-Gaudens' former assistant, the man who had brought life to the dying artist's final inspiration. Elsewhere, their last coins were under siege.

At the Mint in Philadelphia, as she was organizing the squadron of dates, names, and numbers, all in tight formation needed for the case, the assistant superintendent discovered to her great distress that, according to the Coiner's records, the first 1933 double eagles had been struck on March 2, not on March 15. The Treasury was just as troubled: "that's bad for us . . ." and, had more than a handful been minted, the government's case would have been in trouble. But the minimum delivery to the Cashier was twenty-five thousand pieces, a quantity that was not met until March 15. Under the law, under the arcane regulations of the Mint, still in force today, until the coins passed through the magical gate, Coiner to Cashier, they technically didn't even exist.

There were no other nasty surprises, but combing through the Cashier's Daily Settlement sheets revealed that, despite the order that no gold coins were to be paid out after March 6, 1933, without a license from the Secretary of the Treasury, seven double eagles had in fact been exchanged for gold. None was a 1933 double eagle. Five had been "circulated" coin, and two had been from the "prior year" (1932). The names of the recipients were all neatly logged, the last on March 17, 1933.

T. James Clarke's case was supposed to have been first to the plate, but with stays, delays and continuing orders neither it nor the Barnard trial saw the light of day in 1945. All the while the Treasury lawyers bided their time, and the Mint loaded more and more documentary ammunition into its barrel.

On June 27, 1946, Harry J. Stein, the Fifth Avenue lawyer with New York *chutzpah,* offered to drop the suit and cease to be an annoyance if the Treasury simply acquiesced and returned Mr. Clarke's double eagle. His gambit was met with a firmly written letter that reminded him that a similar case was pending in Tennessee and that no settlement was in the wind. The Treasury was scrupulously polite and confided to Stein that "while the Department felt it regrettable that coin collectors, including [Mr. Clarke], had paid high prices for the coins in question, it was the clear duty of the Department to obtain a return of the stolen or embezzled coins."

Stein was also in contact with the Memphis law firm that was handling the case for the aggrieved L. G. Barnard and agreed to lend his numismatic savvy to their cause. T. James Clarke, who didn't like throwing good money after bad, now agreed to abide by the decision rendered in Tennessee and saved himself a passel of legal fees.

Nineteen forty-six faded into memory and two players left the stage. Secret Service Chief Frank J. Wilson, after nearly a decade in the nerve-jarring position, passed the baton to James Maloney at the end of the year. Wilson's retirement was short-lived, and within months he was recruited to be the first Director of Security for the newly established Atomic Energy Commission. Maloney had been involved in various stages of the 1933 double eagle investigation and continued as Chief to have a personal interest in the case.

The second, Ira S. Reed, departed with no fanfare but, as legal issues were ginning up, with exceptional timing. Ever cool, ever vigilant of his own needs, he quietly sold his shop and retired to help orphans and to assist his pastor as deacon to tend the flock of his church, until his death in 1954. Perhaps it was to assuage his conscience—or maybe he never gave it a second thought.

In June 1947, Barnard's fight against government confiscation finally came to a head. The two sides agreed only that apart from the two '33 double eagles in the Smithsonian, the rest had been melted, and that the weights had balanced, before and after melting.

The government's case was backed by reams of official documents and bolstered by an all-star cast of employees who had worked at the Mint in 1933. It contended that the double eagles had been "removed illegally from the vaults," probably replaced with other coins, and that in any event they were not currency, but property of the government.

Barnard's attorneys countered with a laundry list of arguments that tried to have it all ways: their client had purchased the rare and unusual coin in good faith; it had been minted as currency, "issued as such" and was therefore negotiable and transferable; even if stolen, it was cash, and therefore their client's claim was protected as he had acquired it legitimately; and since the government's weights all balanced, it couldn't have been stolen in the first place.

On July 22, 1947, in Memphis, Tennessee, two weeks after the end of the trial, Judge Marion S. Boyd's decision on *United States of America* versus *L. G. Barnard* was filed. In the jurist's opinion, the facts tilted inexorably toward the State. He found that the 1933 double eagle, never left the Mint legally. At no time, opined Judge Boyd, was it "money or currency" but "chattel, or an article of virtu." Thus good title had never passed. The 1933 double eagle, in the view of the court, was now legally illegal: the property of the United States of America, *not* L. G. Barnard.

It was a crushing defeat. Barnard considered his options. He might be right but not in the eyes of the law, and perhaps it wasn't worth the mounting costs. He chose not to appeal, but the loss continued to rankle, and Abe Kosoff reported that he later went broke, possibly even insane. On August 13, 1947, the Secret Service retrieved the Barnard coin from the District Court Clerk, who had held the coin for the past two years, and forwarded it to Washington, D.C. For Harry J. Stein it was a similarly devastating defeat—doubly so, as T. James Clarke's coin was also forfeited. His case was dismissed with prejudice on August 26, 1947.

James A. Stack bided his time for three years. Then, unexpectedly, on March 16, 1950, he went to New York State court and after his 1933 double eagle, naming bluff Harry W. Strang as defendant. Strang must have thought this incandescent piece of metal had a life of its own and would follow him to his grave. Instead, in 1951, James Stack went to his. The complaint against Strang as an individual was dismissed in 1950, and the United States Government was named as defendant instead. For half a decade more, like the *Flying Dutchman,* the case would silently sail into dim view in the form of memoranda exchanged and drift back into the mists. The government now had case law on its side and, even better, the coin itself.

In May 1945, King Farouk of Egypt did not receive a demanding letter from Assistant Secretary of the Treasury Herbert Gaston, nor did a Secret Service agent come to call. A man ill-equipped to deal with the real world, Farouk had begun his ignominious political descent, a painful one of short, broken falls. Egypt had emerged at the end of the war as one of the wealthiest of countries in the region and no longer thought of itself as an ancient entity, different from its neighbors. It was now an "Arab" country. This newly discovered self-awareness spawned fresh dynamism in political parties, the army, and the Moslem Brotherhood. Appealing to a desperately poor populace had two goals: elimination of the British presence and overthrow of the monarch and his class.

Farouk's wild escapades and his publicly lecherous lifestyle, the interminable and increasingly lurid stories, his grotesque appetites and bloated appearance, his monstrous expenditures, and his corrupt circle of advisors merely added fuel to the fires of nationalism and revolt. The trouble began slowly and gathered momentum. Farouk was "intelligent enough to be cynical," but he "lacked the intellectual and moral stamina" to battle the rising tide against him.

In the late morning of January 26, 1952, a seething cauldron of mobs washed into the streets of Cairo. As if choreographed, destruction rained down: a Jewish school, four hotels, four night clubs, eighteen cinemas, and countless other buildings were left shells. While seventy people were killed, the indolent Farouk gave a banquet. Cairo was in flames, and Farouk was at lunch.

The British and the Americans were sorely tested but held back from sending in their troops. Farouk finally moved late in the day, but by the time the army had restored a semblance of order, more than twelve thousand people were without homes or work. Blame for the rioting was laid at many feet. Farouk proclaimed martial law and began shuffling prime ministers like one of the decks of cards in his famed collection. He was drowning politically, and those around him knew it, even if he did not.

"In the palace a seedy clique of Levantine procurers and Nubian valets organized the King's entertainment brought down governments and made army appointments." Farouk's time was up.

It was a sweltering 117 degrees on July 22, 1952. The Free Officers, led by General Mohammed Neguib and his corps of colonels, including Gamal Abdel Nasser and Anwar el-Sadat, began the coup d'etat that was over almost as soon as it had begun. All the essential buildings were seized, tanks and armored vehicles took up strategic positions, and proclamations were broadcast in Neguib's name.

Two days later Farouk gathered his family and told them to pack. It was the end. He got behind the wheel of one of his Mercedes and headed to Montazah, his palace on the Mediterranean coast, to be closer to his yacht. But escape was impossible. Troops closed in around them.

On July 26, 1952, the Free Officers debated Farouk's fate: execution or exile. Nasser's tempered words, "Let us spare Farouk and send him into exile. History will sentence him to death" prevailed, and by a single vote Farouk was given his life.

Farouk sailed away on his yacht, with gold ingots in its hold, to luxurious, dissipated oblivion in Capri and Rome. There were rumors of Swiss bank accounts bulging to the tune of $40 million. But he did not have his precious collection of coins including the elusive 1933 double eagle. It was one of the few things he had begged, in vain, to keep.

Late August, 1952. Philadelphia.

Edwin Dressel shook when he realized what he was holding. He instantly called Leland Howard in Washington. The assistant director paled and knitted his brow. Unannounced, unexpected, and addressed to the Superintendent of the Philadelphia Mint, a registered mail package had arrived, postmarked August 21, 1952, Baltimore, Maryland. Inside was a double eagle, a golden ounce of rare beauty. The familiar, majestic image of Liberty striding forth, her right arm raised, holding aloft the torch. Her left hand held Peace, the olive branch, and below it the date: 1933.

Of the nine Harry Strang had tracked down this was—the *tenth.*

Two weeks later Leland Howard, still in a state of chagrined disbelief, read the letter from the owner of the coin, Louis E. Eliasberg, the Baltimore financier who had a complete collection of United States coins. In 1951, the financier had been in the process of mounting a display of his stupendous collection at the Baltimore National Bank, which he exhibited anonymously. During the preparations, Eliasberg, who had never been involved in the Secret Service investigation, learned that there was a cloud to the title of one coin and dutifully checked its status with the Baltimore branch of the Federal Reserve Bank. It was on their advice that the rigorously law-abiding collector forwarded the double eagle to the Mint.

The now gray-haired Eliasberg, whose collection would soon grace the pages of *Life* magazine, garnering an astonishing seven thousand letters from readers, closed his letter to Howard on a wistful note. He wrote that he "would very much liked to have kept it in the collection," and if it were at all possible, he would appreciate having it returned.

Nellie Ross personally responded to the letter with uncharacteristic lack of grace. There were no thanks, merely a negative bureaucratic response. Perhaps, in her nineteenth year as Mint Director, she was too tired to care or she was growing weary of the malevolent coin that had dogged every year of her tenure at the Mint.

Just as dutifully, the seventy-seven-year-old director, her blue eyes slightly faded, kept the Secret Service Chief—now U. E. Baughman, another 1933 double eagle investigation veteran—up to date. She pointed out, to cover them all for the record, that a tenth coin had been rumored in Strang's reports and that this must be it. She made no mention of Macallister's claim of even more. Melting the coins would wait, Mrs. Ross cautioned, until a decision was reached in the James Stack case, which continued to sit in the courts like an orphan. She enclosed a copy of Eliasberg's letter, so that facts, and paper, could be added to the fat Secret Service file CO-10468.

Baughman was the Supervising Agent in New York when he was tapped for the post of Chief in 1948. He knew the case well. Eliasberg recalled in his letter that on April 15, 1944, he had purchased the coin for a thousand dollars "from a Philadelphia dealer, whose name I believe was Mr. Reed." Baughman thought back. It was now nearly a decade since the start of it all. On April 15, 1944, Strang had already taken three coins into custody and questioned Ira Reed in depth. The dealer had known the coins were suspect, contraband, and yet he had sold one to an honest man. Baughman shook his head. Ira Reed had nerve.

The Secret Service now held eight 1933 double eagles and the Mint, one—Eliasberg's. It was the only coin missing from his astonishing collection, which was auctioned off decades later for more than forty million dollars.

Farouk's 1933 double eagle remained dully glinting, unadmired, in the blackness of a monolithic steel safe in the Koubbeh Palace—half a world away, and still out of reach.

CHAPTER 16

A Modern Day Aladdin's Cave: The Coin Escapes Again

———◆———

1952. London.

In December, whispers had begun that the Egyptian Army believed that the varied collections amassed by Farouk in addition to those he had inherited from his father would go a long way toward alleviating the aching poverty of the country's people. Even if it were ill-founded rumor, Peter C. Wilson of Sotheby's auction house was canny enough to know it was worth making contact. The potential rewards were enormous. He headed to Cairo immediately.

Through a pair of tiny blue eyes set in a scrubbed pink face and down a long, aristocratic nose, Wilson viewed the world from on high at a commanding six and a half feet. He spoke with the plummy, rolling tones of Eton and Oxford and had an astonishing eye for works of art. His enthusiasm on viewing a great object or painting frequently manifested itself in a sentence beginning with a long "Ooo." Tailored immaculately in dark suits from Savile Row, P. C. W. was no airy aesthete. He would become, to all intents and purposes, titles be damned, Sotheby's. His charm, eye, imagination, and utter ruthlessness when it came to getting property to sell catapulted Sotheby's into preeminence in the once arcane world of art auctions and simultaneously transformed that musty world into big business. Some said for the better, others said for the worse.

P. C. W., who had wartime experience in Military Intelligence—some later gossiped that he may once have been a Russian spy, the unidentified "fifth man" in the circle of Guy Burgess, Kim Philby, Donald Maclean, and Anthony Blunt—had contacts and feelers out around the world.

His timing made Wilson first on the scene in Cairo, but he was not alone. The French competed for the collections through a consortium of auctioneers, and from New York, Parke-Bernet Galleries made a game effort. Even the small guys on the block in the coin world tried to play a hand. Abe Kosoff, the onetime purveyor of fabulous rarities to the deposed monarch, applied on February 3, 1953, to the "Custodian of the Properties of the Ex-King" at Abdine Palace in Cairo. He was informed that he was too late and that the collection was already in liquidation. Kosoff, who had fearlessly bargained with Israel Switt for the only 1933 double eagle he admitted to the Secret Service he had owned, didn't give up.

Successfully dealing with the revolutionary government was in itself an art. The men in charge were suspicious of everyone, including members of their own junta. They were skittish and apt to react adversely to the slightest misinterpreted nuance. In Cairo the odds would seem to have been stacked against Sotheby's, which was having to overcome not only a barrage of competition but also the deep-seated hostility toward the British, always festering but now in full eruption within the government of General Neguib. But the Egyptians had no idea who they were up against.

Peter Wilson was joined by Tim Clarke, a man of average height, ears set at a ninety-degree angle to his head, slicked down but uncontrolled hair, a broad grin, and towering intellect. During the war Clarke's intelligence unit had been posted to Aleppo in Northern Syria, so he knew the area and understood the "workings of the Levantine mind." Between Clarke's clipped cadences and Wilson's considered, imperious drawl, the negotiations went forward. None of the Egyptians in charge would take responsibility for making decisions, and a gargantuan sword of Damocles hung over any decisions, which made both the Egyptian government and Sotheby's very nervous. Through his Italian lawyer, Farouk was making ugly noises about challenging the legality of the sale.

Peter Wilson, blessed with a Machiavellian streak, and Tim Clarke, fully understanding the byzantine ways of the East, were brought into a meeting of the Revolutionary Council, where they explained the legal niceties and huge risks of mounting such a massive project in a climate of uncertainty. The duo suggested some radical changes in Egyptian law and persuaded the council to pass new legislation countering 150 years of the Code Napoleon. Farouk and ninety lesser royal persons were suddenly in the words of the new laws "dispossessed of their property and any further claims against the new state."

P. C. W. would move mountains to get a good sale.

Negotiations dragged and snarled, but in the end, despite the ingrained distrust of and resentment against the British, P. C. W. prevailed. Perhaps it was simply a case of better the devil you know. On February 26, 1953, after a long, complex legal document in English and Arabic was signed, the Ministry of Finance in Cairo officially announced that Sotheby's had been appointed the official advisors for the sale of the ex-king's property. The auctions would not be held in London, however, but in Cairo. It was front-page news throughout the Middle East and Europe.

Abe Kosoff wasn't going down without a fight and kept shooting off missives to Cairo, offering to hold the sale at a convention in Dallas later that year. Even though he received no replies, Kosoff extended a proposal to buy the collection, or parts of it, outright. He later claimed that he had a syndicate willing to pay $890,000. A reply in May from a lieutenant colonel, Director of the Technical Bureau, GHQ Egyptian Armed Forces, informed him the coins would be sold "in a public auction next winter in Cairo." If Kosoff wanted to buy, he would "have to be present in due time."

A "modern day Aladdin's Cave" was to be "thrown open to the world" but not before the grinding, Herculean task of cataloguing the property while navigating the shoals of Egyptian bureaucracy and tetchiness was completed. Sotheby's sent a world-class team of experts to Cairo. When the auction house didn't have specialists of its own, it brought in the best of the world's dealers.

The opportunity to hold and admire great objects wrought by man's genius is every art historian's dream. The riches of Farouk's collections were nearly beyond comprehension, but time was of the essence.

The experts also had to cope with Colonel Mahmoud Younis and Major Gaafir, and liaised with the Egyptian Army. The greatest expert of the twentieth century on the fabulous creations of Carl Fabergé arrived to find a Russian Imperial Easter Egg encrusted with diamonds being used as a football by soldiers. An internationally respected stamp dealer proceeded to catalogue one of the largest collections ever formed, including items purchased from the auction of Franklin Roosevelt's estate in 1946.

Three months was all the time they had to describe the thousands upon thousands of objects, all being catalogued for sale, while committees from the Customs Office, from the Ministry of Finance, and the Assay Office were simultaneously taking detailed inventories and testing the same objects. All of Farouk's ancient works of art were sent to the Cairo Museum, where they paled beside the incomparable holdings already on display and in storage. Nationalism prevailed, and the Egyptians were often undecided about what was to be in the sale. Objects that had already been catalogued one day might, after official reconsideration, be withdrawn the next day.

As spring melted into summer, the sale started to take shape. Extraordinary in size, it was comparable to the dispersals of the Whitehall Palace collection in 1653 and Versailles in 1793. Even though many of the objects might have been deemed vulgarly ostentatious, they were nonetheless of fabulous quality. More than two thousand gold watches were included, along with a staggering array of automata and mountains of silver, paperweights, and gold boxes dripping with jewels. The catalogues were fat, not flimsy.

Into this maelstrom wandered "Uncle" Fred Baldwin, of A. H. Baldwin & Sons, an esteemed firm of London coin dealers, to catalogue Farouk's coins, perhaps the most onerous task of all. Unbeknownst to most numismatists, Farouk's infatuation with coins had been one of the great financial underpinnings of the coin market for the previous decade, and his collection had grown to gargantuan proportions.

Baldwin's family firm had been in the business since 1872, and just as blood-red corpuscles coursed through the average person's veins, the gold, silver, and bronze of numismatics ran through his. The weather was searing, but Uncle Fred, a small, neat mustache nestled comfortably between a sharp nose and thin, determined lips, rolled up his sleeves and got to work.

There were six vaults of coins in the Koubbeh Palace on which Farouk, who paid outrageously high prices, had spent millions of dollars. Each day Baldwin sat down at his work table covered with a gaily colored floral cloth and laid out the coins before him, entering every description by hand into a perfect-bound notebook. Closely eyed by security guards, who were torn between suspicion and boredom, he worked through the hyperbole of the dealers' notes that had accompanied the coins to Farouk. To justify the enormous prices they were charging, dealers frequently described the items to be sold to the young, naive monarch rapturously, if at times fictionally. "I guarantee to Your Majesty that this is the only specimen this side of heaven," Baldwin read scribbled on the envelope of one coin. The florid prose described a coin of which *at least* one other example was then for sale in London.

Lotting the coins into groups as best they could, Baldwin and his brother, Albert, who came out to assist him, were later vilified, somewhat unfairly, by Abe Kosoff for having written a catalogue that "was not an example of expertise or even of good organization." The descriptions of many rare coins were indeed perfunctory, but the collection was monstrous, and included obscure rarities from around the world that none but a specialist in the coinage of that country could have identified. In the end, it was a far from perfect product, but who could have reasonably been expected to do much better under the circumstances?

As the clock relentlessly ticked, the Baldwins had catalogued the rarest of the rare and the most humble and common of specie, in all, approximately 81,000 coins, medals, and banknotes and one "rug woven in the form of a five pound Turkish bank note of the Osmania Government." The sale would include 2,798 lots to be sold over nine days. Some coins glittered as if made yesterday, others were toned rich iridescent hues, and yet others had been laquered, spotted, or mercilessly scrubbed, their value decimated. The robust, suntanned, sixty-three-year-old Fred, who was known to imbibe prodigious quantities of his beloved pink gin (though hopefully not when working), had enjoyed himself enormously, while the forty-one-year-old diabetic Albert was miserable. Perhaps the 1933 double eagle had cast a malefic spell. The younger Baldwin wasted away in the heat, developed massive carbuncles, and was never the same again.

The Palace Collections of Egypt—Farouk's name was expunged—contained 8,852 gold coins, and one of them, which bore no creative description on its protective envelope, was the 1933 double eagle.

When Sotheby's trumpeted the sale to the world's press, few people in Europe or America could have avoided knowing about the sale, even if they had wanted. The story was compelling. Farouk, now in exile in Rome, cavorted with models, starlets, and B-girls to the glee of tabloids around the world, while the proceeds from the sale of his wild extravagances were expected to raise the standard of living in Egypt and build dams and hospitals.

The United States Secret Service read the newspapers too. On Thursday, December 3, 1953, Inspector Russell Daniel sent a memo to Chief Urbanus

E. Baughman along with a clipping from the Washington *Daily News*. The lead read: "The rare coins, stamps and things of beauty (inanimate) that Farouk of Egypt worked so hard to collect are going on the auction block."

Although official United States Government attempts to recover the 1933 double eagle had first been discussed in May, 1944, the war and Egypt's key geographical position in the region had precluded even the most tentative of approaches. On April 28, 1945, the Treasury general counsel's opinion reiterated that "the coin held by King Farouk does not present a problem which this Department should consider at this time."

Those in the Mint would not give up, however, and in the wake of the L. G. Barnard decision in court, the secretary of the Treasury wrote to the secretary of state again on September 14, 1949, asking for permission to request the return of the coin. But in the tense postwar environment, Egypt's strategic importance had grown. With America and the Soviet Union glaring at each other, the iron curtain having descended, Egypt's control of the Suez Canal, and with it the Indian Ocean, made it an ally to be coddled, not nettled. Further weighing that nation's internal stresses—Egypt's humiliating defeat in the Palestine war of 1948–49, the bitterness toward the British, and the 280-pound monarch's drift to a completely detached and sybaritic existence—the Department of State, which took precedence, considered raising the question politically inadvisable and advised the Treasury to drop the matter. It was, after all, only a coin.

Now, however, with the king exiled to *la dolce vita* in Rome, his collection was to be auctioned, and there were no such constraints. Secret Service Inspector Russell Daniel felt that the United States Government was "obligated to place the Egyptian Embassy on notice that the coin is stolen and that title remains with the United States."

Agent Daniel had thought carefully about the matter, and his arguments to the Chief were both reasoned and pragmatic. Even if the present Egyptian government refused to surrender the coin, the inspector felt it was imperative that the record show that they knew the facts. "To fail to do so might place the Secret Service in an embarrassing position," especially, he warned, if the coin were purchased by an American citizen at the upcoming sale and the Secret Service was then forced to recover it on entry into the United States. Daniel took it one harshly logical step further. He predicted that criticism would be bitter, and justifiably so, "from the nine collectors whom we have previously dispossessed of their coins" if no attempt were made to recover Farouk's coin.

Agreement was universal within the Treasury, and for once the gears meshed quickly and easily. The general counsel was asked to draft a Secretary-to-Secretary letter, and within a week a cable was sent to the American Embassy in Cairo over Secretary of State John Foster Dulles's name. The background of the case was outlined and instructions given to contact the Egyptian Government, explain the American case, and retrieve the coin. As yet, however, the United States Government had not seen a catalogue and was still officially unsure if the 1933 double eagle was even in the auction.

They didn't have long to wait. As the catalogues rolled off the presses, the public excitement began to swell. The set of volumes bound in Sotheby's traditional understated, dark green paper covers opened to reveal only a hint of what had been housed in the Koubbeh Palace's four hundred rooms. Dry descriptions describing objects of incomparable opulence let the imaginations of the readers run riot. If only they could have seen what the Egyptians would not allow to be sold.

Farouk's collection of coins lacked little. It ranged from four ancient Roman gold ingots (later withdrawn from the sale) to vast-expanses of nineteenth- and twentieth-century coins in all metals from around the world and 164 platinum coins said to be five times bigger than any previously offered for sale. But it was his United States collection that sent collectors' and dealers' pulses racing. The king did lack the most famous of all United States coins, the 1804 silver dollar, but he had the most renowned of the spurious concoctions produced for personal profit by the men of the Mint. Including the 1884 and 1885 trade dollars and, most famous, the 1913 Liberty Head nickel. The marketing genius of B. Max Mehl, who advertised for decades that he would pay fifty dollars apiece for the nickels (knowing he would never have to ante up—Colonel E. H. R. Green, the son of Hetty Green, "the Witch of Wall Street," then owned all five), got millions of Americans hooked on coin collecting as they assiduously searched through their change in hope of finding one. Mehl created a coveted rarity in the process.

The young monarch's runs of gold coins were crowned by two of Augustus Saint-Gaudens' patterns for the 1907 double eagle. One was an example of the version struck in the extremely high relief that had caused so much consternation and the other was the unique specimen of Gus's preferred design with the Indian Head and standing eagle—ironically said to have been "found among the effects of Charles Barber" after his death in 1917. Farouk's collection was a special one, indeed.

Abe Kosoff got the catalogue. It weighed more than a pound and contained seventy-two pages of third-rate photographs. Perusing it at length, he reckoned there were going to be bargains galore. Kosoff had been thinking of going; now he was sure and set about organizing funds, lining up collectors to represent. And he was still angling to make a private offer.

Hans Schulman, who had provided many coins to the deposed monarch, also got the catalogue. When Farouk went into exile, he owed Schulman $300,000 for unpaid purchases. The lively Dutchman was in the same boat as couturier Christian Dior and jeweler Harry Winston, who were also owed fortunes for lingerie and jewelry. They got the same advice that the ex-king personally gave Schulman over the telephone from Rome: "Hans, your coins are in Cairo; you have to get paid by the Egyptian government. I don't have the coins so I cannot pay you. Good luck." Dior's and Winston's bills got lost in the shuffle. Schulman's pockets were not so deep and he had miles of creditors. He got a lawyer and headed to Cairo.

Dealers and collectors around the world felt their adrenaline levels surge as the sale date drew closer. Each time they looked through the catalogue they discovered a new treasure, something special, something wonderful: for example, lots 344, 345, and 346, three small gold ingots, each a unique denomination—$45.34, $37.31, and $36.55—historic pieces made in California by the State Assayer Frederick Kohler in 1850 while the Gold Rush was still in its infancy and the building of the San Francisco Mint was still two years in the future.

The Egyptians' expectations about what the auction would yield were also growing. Becoming unrealistic, they were bound to be disappointed. Samir Ahmed, the first attache of the Egyptian Embassy, at first refused to give the press an estimate of what the entire auction might bring but then relented and admitted that "$500,000,000 might not be too high." It was.

On January 13, 1954, the Secret Service finally got a copy of the catalogue, which had been issued in November. Agent A. E. Whittaker found what they were looking for in lot 185:

> **Twenty dollars,** 1924, 1924 S, 1924 D, 1925, 1925 S, 1925 D, 1926, 1926 D, 1927, 1927 S, 1928, 1929, 1930 S, 1931, 1931 D, 1932, 1933. *Mostly extremely fine.*

Fred Baldwin had unintentionally camouflaged the '33 with sixteen other double eagles, some rare, others common. His description of their quality, "extremely fine," was standard British nomenclature. An American would have called the coins "uncirculated." Whittaker advised the Chief that the catalogue had received international distribution and that there would be considerable interest in the '33.

GOLD COINS (*continued*)

185 **Twenty dollars**, 1924, 1924 S, 1924 D, 1925, 1925 S, 1925 D, 1926, 1926 D, 1927, 1927 S, 1928, 1929, 1930 S, 1931, 1931 D, 1932, 1933. *Mostly extremely fine.* 17 · 2800

186 **Ten dollars,** first type 1795 *brilliant but light scratches*, 1796 *very fine*, 1797 four stars, *very fine;* second type 1797, six stars, *extremely fine*, 1798-7 four stars, *extremely fine,* 1798-7 six stars, *nearly extremely fine; a nice lot in a fitted case.* 6 520

187 Ten dollars, 1799 two varieties, 1800, 1801, 1803, 1804. *All extremely fine except one 1799 and 1804 which are very fine; a nice lot in a fitted case.* 6 300

188 Ten dollars, 1838 *brilliant proof*, 1839 *extremely fine*, 1839 *different die*, 1840; *last two fine*. 4 195

189 Ten dollars, 1841, 1841 O, 1842 (2) large and small date, 1842 O. *Mostly very fine.* 5 45

190 Ten dollars, 1843, 1843 O, 1844 *extremely fine*. 1844 O, *the others fine.* 4 40

191 Ten dollars, 1845, 1845 O, 1846, 1846 O. *All fine.* 4 35

192 Ten dollars, 1847, 1847 O, 1848, 1848 O. *Very fine.* 4 45

193 Ten dollars, 1849, 1849 O, 1850, 1850 O. *Fine or better.* 4 20

194 Ten dollars, 1851, 1851 O, 1852, 1852 O. *Some very fine.* 4 25

195 Ten dollars, 1853, 1853 O, 1859 O, 1859 S, 1859. *The last extremely fine, others fine.* 5 17

196 Ten dollars, 1854, 1854 O, 1854 S, 1855, 1855 O, 1855 S. *Mostly very fine.* 6 60

197 Ten dollars, 1856, 1856 O, 1856 S, 1857, 1857 O, 1857 S. *Mostly very fine.* 6 60

198 Ten dollars, 1858, 1858 O, 1858 S, 1862 S, 1862. *The last a brilliant proof, others fine.* 5 310

Page of the Farouk Catalogue including lot 185 with the 1933 double eagle noted as "unique."
Fred Baldwin's personal copy, noting Spink's successful bid on behalf of the Norwebs.
Note the number of lots with no buyers' names. (Archives of A. H. Baldwin & Sons Ltd.)

✦   ✦   ✦

One such interested party were the Honorable and Mrs. R. Henry Norweb of Cleveland, Ohio. Both erudite collectors of the first rank, they made a Mutt and Jeff couple. Emery May Norweb was short, slightly round, with dark, widely set eyes and heavy lips. Her husband, Henry, was tall, debonaire, with an immaculately trimmed mustache. He retired in 1948 from the United States diplomatic corps after a long and distin-

217

A Modern Day Aladdin's Cave

guished career. She, the doyenne of Cleveland society, came from a family that owned the *Cleveland Plain Dealer* and whose great wealth came mostly from western mining interests. Together their collections were already among the finest in existence, and they were aggressively accelerating the pace of their acquisitions.

The Norwebs were headed to Cairo via the *Andrea Doria*. They had organized a strategy with David Spink, an English coin dealer. He would do a good portion of their bidding and had already sent to Cairo the head of his foreign coin department, Donald Crowther, a chunky, moon-faced man with deep-set eyes, to examine the entire collection.

As the sale date grew nearer, Leland Howard, who had been appointed Acting Director of the Mint after Nellie Tayloe Ross's retirement in April, 1953, was growing increasingly antsy. Nothing had been heard from Cairo.

The auction was in less than a month's time, and collectors from all over the world were starting to congregate. Sotheby's had organized a special reduced plane fare with B.O.A.C., London to Cairo, round-trip, £162 ($466.50). The Egyptian government set up a "whole new banking and customs department to deal with the occasion." Hans Schulman had prevailed in his battle with the Egyptians and would be given a credit of approximately $300,000 against his purchases at the auction.

Rumors swirled. Despite the Egyptian government's assurances that Farouk's legal position was impotent, word was that Farouk had become a Turkish national and his newly adopted country would seek the return of his collections. Denial. There were stories of injunctions against the sale whistling in the hot winds. Denial. Jewish bidders would not be permitted entry to Egypt. Denial.

With a month to go, State Department wires to the American embassy began to warm. Lest those posted in Cairo think otherwise, "the Treasury Department is seriously concerned at the possibility of the sale of this coin." With no response from the Egyptian government, one of the options discussed was to go public and issue a press release "warning that the coin would be seized if it is brought to the United States." The thought of an "American being victimized into paying a large amount for the coin" and then the government having to seize it was anathema. Leland Howard was frantic, Treasury was worried, and State was in the hot seat.

The exhibition was opened to the public on Sunday, February 14. Marquees were set up in the lush grounds of the Koubbeh Palace. A vaguely surreal atmosphere reigned as a brass band struck up Viennese waltzes and rousing military marches, all accented with delightfully discordant Eastern tonality. Masses of trailing bougainvillea blossoms provided an explosion of almost unearthly color, while the palm trees stood like towering sentinels silhouetted against the deep blues of the sky. The seventy acres of grounds swarmed with armed guards, prospective bidders, and suspicious-looking types in fezes. Some watched the foreigners, hoping for a larcenous opportunity; others from the government watched the villains. Nothing must go wrong. The eyes of the world would be turned to Egypt and its new masters. With servants graciously ministering to the needs of the assembled visitors, it was a snapshot of the last of British colonial Egypt, a picture that would curl, yellow, and fade quickly.

In reality, the exhibition had been organized by the army. Spink, the English coin dealer, had been wise to send his representative ahead to view the coins in privacy and relative comfort. Many of the cases were now nailed shut, and when dealers and collectors asked to examine the larger lots of coins, some of which numbered in the thousands—the coins were tipped out carelessly, dinging and damaging one another. Once inspected, they all had to be carefully, individually counted back into the lot to make sure none had gone astray. For professional dealers who knew what they were looking for, it was fatiguing, tormenting.

The State Department also had sent someone to the exhibition, who heard that the double eagle was still on display at the Koubbeh Palace. One of the American dealers, aware of the coin's murky status, reported the latest word from the Egyptian government: it intended to hold the coin in escrow until the United States came up with the purchase price. Another unfounded rumor, perhaps, but one that the United States consul, Basil Macgowan, dutifully reported back to Washington.

One collector who was also concerned was John Jay Pittman. An Eastman Kodak chemical engineer of modest means, Pittman had an infectious smile, bouncing gait, close-cropped hair, and an amazing eye for detail. He could remember a coin years later from a minuscule blemish. To Pittman, the Farouk auction was the dream of a lifetime, and he determined to go. To finance the trip and his hoped-for purchases, he took a deep breath and a second mortgage on his house. It took him six years to pay it off, and even then he still had to part with some of his hard-fought-for coins. Pittman was also a stickler for the law and he knew the checkered history of 1933 double eagles. He probably took a long, careful look at the '33 with his powerful hand-lens and would have mentally noted even the tiniest of flaws in the soft golden surfaces. Years later he claimed it was he who alerted the government of its inclusion

A Modern Day Aladdin's Cave

because "it was illegally removed from the Mint." Yet neither he nor anyone else at the auction provided a firsthand account of the coin or any distinguishing marks.

Each day the sale neared, there were new whispers, more urgent. The British Museum was buying the entire coin collection. Denial. Farouk was going to be bidding for himself, through a consortium of Italian dealers. Denial. Like dust devils, the rumors sprang up, moaned ominously, twisted into the distance, and died, only to be replaced by others.

A week before the auction, Consul Macgowan communicated that Egypt's largest newspaper, *Al-Ahram,* had reported, "President Mohamed Naguib [*sic*] has approved the withdrawal of an American coin from the auction" and its return. But no such notice had been received by the embassy; perhaps this was just another rumor. Neguib's hold on power was tenuous at present, with Colonel Nasser strengthening his position daily. Where the real power rested was an hour-to-hour affair.

Tuesday, February 23, 1954. Cairo.

On the day before the auction of the coins was to begin (the 1933 double eagle was scheduled to be offered in the first session) there was still no official word on its status. The only exciting news was the offer made by the Egyptians to all bidders who spent at least £5,000 ($14,400) at the auction: they would be permitted access to Farouk's lurid collection of pornography.

The stamps had already been sold, and far from having been a wholesaler's dream, prices had been stiff, in some cases staggering. At the coin exhibition, frantic bidders were having a last-minute view. Tightly clustered groups of dealers and collectors discussed their bidding strategies in a hushed babble of international voices. Now was the time for one-up-manship and posturing. The latest rumble, which wouldn't go away, was that the military was determined that there would be no bargains. Reserves, went the story, had been set on every lot in the sale and at unattainable levels. There was some foundation to the scuttlebutt. As part of his settlement with the military, Hans Schulman had agreed to provide estimates of the minimum acceptable prices for every lot in the sale—but not, said Hans, at outrageously high figures.

At 11:23 A.M., February 23, 1954, the American embassy in Cairo cabled Washington D.C., that the Egyptian Foreign Office had verbally confirmed that Neguib had ordered the withdrawal of the coin pending a final decision on its ultimate disposition. In Washington, the State Department considered these informal assurances satisfactory and chose not to issue any press releases.

But the coin was still on display, gleaming. Those who examined it saw the familiar vision of Liberty, her hair now streaming in the hot desert winds, still proud, still defiant in her battle for existence.

10:00 A.M., Wednesday, February 25, 1954. Cairo.

The echoing, expectant buzz of voices in the foyer of the Koubbeh Palace began to subside. The auctioneer's rostrum, a long, elevated table, was covered in claret-red silk velvet draped in parallel tiers like an upturned cummerbund. Behind it, at an ascending angle, ran the long, grand stairway of *giallo antico* and a host of other multicolored marbles pierced at regular intervals by elaborate bronze fretwork. Maurice George Lee, the auctioneer who readied himself, was not from Sotheby's. He was local, a highly regarded British auctioneer who had lived in Egypt for forty years. Lee knew the local idiosyncrasies and authorities, and they in turn were comfortable with his conducting the sale.

Dapper in a blue three-piece suit and pale oyster-gray tie, Lee took his position at the center of the table, flanked on either side by two Egyptian Ministry men: observers who would record the bids and buyers. Behind them, arrayed below the banister, was another corps of watchers scanning the crowd; some were uniformed, others in mufti, berets, and fezes.

Rows of silk-brocade-upholstered, carved giltwood chairs—Louis Seize in looks, not age—filled the room. In front, a few spindly, marble-topped tables of similar style had been provided for bidders to rest their fat catalogues on; the rest had to make do with their laps. The modest-sized crowd, mostly men and a handful of women, was impeccably dressed, as was fitting for a royal sale in a palace.

With a small red, white, and blue rosette pinned to his lapel, Lee opened the bidding in Arabic and then seamlessly switched to the language of the bidder—English, German, French, Italian, or any other of the seven languages he spoke effortlessly. He waved his ebony-handled, ivory-headed gavel like a wand, and the sale began.

But it began with a whimper. The first four lots were withdrawn, supposedly by order of President Neguib, who resigned from power later that day only to be politically resurrected three days later. When the bidding started in earnest, it went at a good clip. David Spink and Fred Baldwin bought many of the first hundred lots. Those they failed to buy went primarily to Continental dealers and unknown bidders. Other lots did

221

The elegant auctioneer: Maurice George Lee, selling a lot of Farouk's coins.
He conducted the sales in seven languages, and at times, "fussed and strutted."
(Archives of A. H. Baldwin & Sons Ltd.)

not meet their minimum price and were not sold. Lee set a good pace and "excellent prices resulted from spirited bidding."

As the section of United States coins neared, tension heightened. Mrs. Norweb sat knitting furiously, like Madame Defarge, casting a sharp eye to see how the bids that she had given to David Spink for this session would fare.

As the twenty-dollar gold pieces, the double eagles, came up, reported Abe Kosoff, "the auctioneer fussed and strutted." Lot 180 went to Kosoff for £825 ($2,376) which "was a bit more than [he] should have liked to have paid," but he made up for it by buying the next two lots at more acceptable prices. A collector took lot 183, while 184 went unsold.

A session of the Farouk sale in progress. Hans Schulman, who had a $300,000 credit, is shown near right. (Archives of A. H. Baldwin & Sons Ltd.)

At last, lot 185. There was a perceptible creaking of chairs as auction-eer Lee let the air out of the balloon. "The 1933 Double Eagle had been with-drawn and was to be returned to the United States government." It was not unexpected by the audience, but it still felt a sense of disappointment.

The State Department breathed a collective relieved sigh. Mac-gowan wired back to Washington the good news that "the controversial twenty dollar gold piece, 1933 issue" was out of the sale. "Two reliable eyewitnesses," reported it, and the absence of the coin was confirmed by the American citizen who bought the lot—David Spink, who had fended off Abe Kosoff on behalf of the Honorable and Mrs. R. Henry Norweb. At £2,800—more than $8,000—it was still by far the highest price paid in the entire sale, and Spink had been authorized to bid considerably more.

The auction of Farouk's coins continued for eight more days. Even with numerous lots withdrawn and unsold, the total was more than $650,000, by far the most valuable coin sale ever held up to that time. Kosoff reported that "prices were good, competitors keen, participation was not an easy task."

223

A Modern Day Aladdin's Cave

Other parts of the sale ran into stormier waters. In one session Sotheby's had to sit by, scarlet-cheeked, as a mind-boggling ninety-four out of 144 lots were pulled from the auction at the last moment and retained by the Egyptian state. The invidious rumor that had spread prior to the sale, that reserves had been set at astronomical levels, was distressingly true. Lots were opened at prices four and five times more than willing bidders would even contemplate paying.

The entire take for the Palace Collections was a mere $2,250,000, well shy of the half-billion predicted in the press. Collectors were furious. The military remained unmoved. With the exception of the stamp sale, Sotheby's were unpaid for their efforts. There were no winners—except, perhaps, the United States Government. At long last it had Farouk's 1933 double eagle within its reach, although like the fruit above Tantalus, it remained just out of grasp.

Consul Basil Macgowan finally received official word in French, which was still the language of international diplomacy, from the fledging Egyptian Ministry of Foreign Affairs. Its "Note No. 11," written the day after the scheduled sale, confirmed that the 1933 double eagle "by order of the President of the Republic" would not be offered "until a definitive decision shall have been reached on this subject." The minister closed the note with his renewed assurances that the situation would receive the very highest consideration—in due time.

Consul Macgowan kept at it. Dmitri Rizk Hanna, the Acting Director of the Administrative Department of the Ministry of Foreign Affairs, was reminded, prompted, and delicately badgered for an answer on a regular basis. His replies, equally gentle, ever firm, were that the matter remained under consideration. The days ran to weeks, and interest waned, until March 31, 1954, when Hanna reported to the American embassy that "he hoped to have some information within two or three days." And there, abruptly, all correspondence ended. The Egyptian trail to the coin had gone dead.

Tuesday, May 11, 1954. Washington, D.C.

The Secret Service Assistant Chief banged out a paper obituary of the recent Farouk affair on his typewriter to fill some holes in the files. An impassive recitation of the frantic diplomatic cable traffic that had led up to the auction, it affirmed the extraction of the infuriatingly slippery gold coin from the sale and tracked the laconic diminution of questions and responses. As it concerned the most recent whereabout of the coin, at the top of the memo he typed "KEEP ON TOP OF OTHER CORRESPONDENCE." Every incoming agent to the Secret Service was taught that the 1933 double eagles were trouble and on the Most Wanted list, but the case had effectively petered out for now.

Before the Farouk matter had suddenly arisen like an asp from the Egyptian sands, the decade-old case had been stalled. Through 1952 and 1953 the James A. Stack coin languished in the courts in legal limbo. Nothing could be done with any of the '33s in custody until that case was determined, and no one on either side seemed to be in much of a hurry.

Israel Switt and Edward Silver, so long out of the picture, suddenly popped up again in 1953, nearly a decade after Harry Strang's determined investigation had ended. The two men were again applying to the Mint for a scrap-gold license. This aroused Leland Howard, now Acting Director, who was like a bulldog: once he locked onto something, nothing could pry him from it. A Bureau of the Mint field auditor was sent out to check anew on the Jewelers' Row partners. In his opinion, before further consideration was given to granting them the license, the Secret Service might again get involved to "make further efforts to solicit a confession from Switt as to the source of the gold coins traced to him."

Yet Philadelphia's Secret Service Agent in Charge, Fred Gruber, could barely disguise his contempt for the Mint's suggestion in a memo to his Chief, Baughman. It was too little too late, and he knew from bitter experience who he was up against. In light of "Switt and Silver's shrewdness and experience as business men," Gruber wrote, it was highly unlikely that any "further information could be expected voluntarily." The statute of limitations had long since expired, the chance of compelled testimony under oath was a dream of the past, and, closed a clearly disgusted Gruber, "unless otherwise directed, the matter will be considered closed by this office."

Although Farouk's coin was still unrecovered, the Stack case was finally resolved in September, 1955, when it was dismissed with prejudice, and the plaintiff, James A. Stack, who had been dead for four years, was "barred from making any further complaint in the same matter."

The government had prevailed—the Stack coin was theirs. But nobody informed the Bureau of the Mint or the Secret Service, and they didn't learn of the decision until a year later, July, 1956. Now the Mint was eager to have the coins held by the Secret Service turned in for melting. It wanted to close the case.

225

All the lawyers signed off with lightning speed, and on Friday, August 17, 1956, Leland Howard sent orders to the Superintendent of the Philadelphia Mint that the coin Louis Eliasberg had voluntarily surrendered four years earlier was to be destroyed "by the Superintendent of the Melting and Refining Department, in the presence of the Assayer and the Superintendent of the Mint." Certification was to be forwarded to Washington upon completion.

Four days later, in the Treasury Building, the eight remaining 1933 double eagles, eight ounces of gold, each bearing the accursed date on the beautiful, historic design for which Theodore Roosevelt had fought, were turned over by the Secret Service to Mint technicians for melting. The coins that had been "manufactured but not issued," stolen from the Mint—most probably by George McCann, one of its most trusted employees—and recovered from a who's who of wealthy collectors tumbled into the searing heat of the crucible and were gone, reduced to a golden puddle.

Like an execution, the process—which some have considered a crime in itself—was witnessed by Charles R. McNeil, the Assistant General Counsel, who had helped determine the legal position to support the seizures; Robert F. Grube, the Secret Service Special Agent in Charge of the Counterfeit Section; Ida P. Davidson, Leland Howard's assistant; and Timothy J. Quirk, the Technical Consultant to the Mint. Ironically, twenty-three years earlier, Quirk had tested the 1933 double eagle "specials" when the coins had first been struck.

The case was closed technically. But it was left open a crack.

In the passage of time, James G. Macallister, Ira S. Reed, T. James Clarke, James Stack, and Colonel Flanagan had died, and Fred Boyd would die two years later. Williams had sold off his collection, and Barnard had gone broke or mad or both. Switt and Silver stayed in business together, and Izzy got richer and richer. He died in 1990 aged ninety-five, revered as the last of the patriarchs on Jewelers' Row, his obnoxious irascibility—"the customer was never right"—shabbiness, and generosity to charity all part of his legend.

Farouk continued his life in exile in Rome. In March, 1965, after a massive meal, the voluptuary, former monarch, and coin collector sat and relaxed with a fat Havana cigar. His face suddenly went purple, and he pitched "face-down into the leftovers of a meal of oyster and lamb."

Most of the people involved with the 1933 double eagles were gone. All but one of the coins Harry Strang had identified and seized had been melted. But Macallister had said there were more, and King Farouk's vanished coin was still out there somewhere. Reports, embellished tales, and rumors from the legendary Palace sale kept the flame of the mysterious coin flickering, but its whereabouts were completely unknown. It lay somewhere waiting, no doubt, in a plain brown envelope in the airless pitch of a safe deposit box or vault, unacknowledged for its beauty, value, or extraordinary odyssey. There it was swallowed by time, forgotten by most, but not by all.

A Modern Day Aladdin's Cave

PART III

LEGITIMACY

CHAPTER 17

A Double Eagle Reappears

———◆———

April, 1993. London.

———

GRAY AND DANK, APRIL WAS A MONTH OF CHANGES, SOME SUBTLE, some not. The fine, imposing gray building of Spink and Son that wrapped round the corner of Duke and King streets was tall for the neighborhood. Christie's, its richer neighbor to the left, had coveted the real estate for years.

Like an antiques department store, Spink's had picture, furniture, silver and oriental art departments, but was best known for coins and medals.

Upstairs at Spink's, in the coin department, a long, low counter bisected the room, comfortably appointed for clients to wait and chat on one side, an untidy scramble of desks, cabinets, and bookshelves at which the employees worked on the other. There Eric Streiner, an intense American coin dealer with fine red hair, was looking carefully at a group of United States eagles—ten-dollar gold pieces from the 1840s to 1860s. A favored client, he was shown coins that were not available to just anybody. Barely old enough to drink, the New Yorker was the best in the business, and his piercing blue-gray eyes could spot quality with unerring accuracy. His genius was viewed with awe, but his youthful naivete and unyielding honesty made him an occasional target in a business in which piranha are occasionally nibbled on by barracuda, only to become appetizers for a passing shark. Nevertheless, Streiner succeeded, quietly.

Streiner determined that the array of the gold coins laid out before him was splendid, and offered to buy them on the spot. As quickly as his offer was tendered, however, it was rejected. Told that the group had come in through a good client of one of the firm's directors, André de Clermont, Streiner was asked to keep the information to himself, as final arrangements had not yet been made to offer the collection at auction later that year. He nodded. No dealer shared information that might cost him money later, and Streiner very much wanted the coins. He told no one, not even his colleague Steve Fenton, a London coin dealer with whom he was doing considerable business. Eric Streiner was young in years but mature in outlook; he was patient. He believed what he had been told.

After more than a quarter century at Spink's, coin expert André de Clermont was now working for Christie's, the international auction house that had acquired the firm that April. Andrew Weir, the Scottish shipping and insurance company that had owned Spink's for about a decade, had sold out, even though it had once promised that if it ever thought to sell the firm, it would first consult the Spink's Board and give it a say in what happened. They were empty words. De Clermont felt hurt, betrayed, and "completely lied to."

Many thought Christie's had bought Spink's at a fire-sale price solely for the real estate. On top of that de Clermont feared that Christie's had what he called a "youth ethic," and he was in his late forties. De Clermont now answered to a boss ten years his junior. He toughed it out as he considered his future.

In a sense, de Clermont had inherited his position. In 1967, out of college and with no immediate job prospects, he was offered a job in the packing room at Spink's by his uncle, a director of the then family-owned firm. Even with no background in numismatics, de Clermont was quick, learned through osmosis and curiosity, and worked his way up through the ranks in the old apprentice system. In 1981 de Clermont was made a director of the company, in charge of the foreign coin department.

André de Clermont lived near the Thames in one of the best parts of town and at one of the poshest addresses. His clear blue eyes always on the move, he was very smooth and spoke lightly, guardedly, as if there were always secrets just beneath the surface. His humor deflected and protected the depths of what he really knew. His contacts were international but also local. His neighbor, coin dealer Stephen Fenton, visited regularly upstairs to see what was new. De Clermont had little for Fenton at first, but Steve was always interested and always looking for more business. He and de Clermont forged a close professional relationship. They lunched, but their private lives remained private. Both knew the ropes. Each was using the other. It was business as usual.

De Clermont was well suited to be a coin dealer. He offered without giving, said without telling, and shared only those secrets everyone else knew. This temperament also benefited him well for his new area of specialization, Islamic coins, a fresh, fertile ground that had first been sown by Sotheby's in the late 1970s as Arab buyers returned their oil profits to the West. They bought everything wildly for often-inflated prices at auctions, usually in London. By the mid-1980s, the opening thunder of acquisitiveness had abated, but a dull roar continued, especially for coins.

De Clermont didn't wait for the business to come to him but spent years traveling to and from the Middle East, nurturing contacts. He aggressively encouraged new collectors and developed contacts for fresh material to sell them. Along the way he discovered fascinating new leads that had nothing at all to do with Islamic coins.

The coins with which Eric Streiner had been so impressed that April morning had come from just such a source. The news that there were active buyers in London had spread through the Middle East, and purveyors of coins would make regular trips to the English capital to shop their wares. The essence of the souk—to find the best deal—blew from the blistered sands of the Middle East and settled in the shallow dells of London. Relationships were fleeting; loyalty was to the best price.

The months passed, deals came and went, and the time for de Clermont's yearly summer pilgrimage to the United States was at hand.

In August, 1993, the American Numismatic Association held its annual convention in steamy Baltimore, Maryland. Dealers—André de Clermont, Stephen Fenton, and Eric Streiner among them—and collectors from around the world flocked in the thousands. There Streiner discovered that there would be no auction of the eagles after which he had been hankering for months. Spink's had purchased the coins outright and had already resold them to another dealer.

André de Clermont, on behalf of Spink's, said he had bought the group from a self-styled Egyptian coin dealer whose knowledge, de Clermont reckoned, "was pretty minimal." De Clermont recalled that the Egyptian also "had all sorts of memorabilia for tourists: pots, jars, neckties [and] bits of jewelry" for sale. Coins were just one of his many enterprises, which included a travel business and car hire company.

A Double Eagle Reappears

De Clermont had previously dealt with his contact's brother, a Farouk-proportioned individual, now dead, who was reasonably well known to some others in the London coin trade. The man with whom de Clermont now did business "knew a great deal less even than his brother." Used to seeing "predominantly Arab" coins offered by them, de Clermont said he had been fairly staggered by the quality of what the Egyptian dealer had laid out before him. He was first struck that the coins weren't counterfeit, because the Middle East was a hotbed of fakery. The head of the Spink's foreign coin department knew that the dealer was always greedy, so did not "say to him, 'Oh, these are fantastic.'" Instead de Clermont asked for a day to examine them more closely and make a bid, which came to several thousand pounds and was accepted.

Instinctively, de Clermont recalled, he knew that the coins had come from the Farouk sale; it was "the logical thing." Where else? "Who the heavens would have such good coins coming out from Egypt like this," he had thought, and went straight to his copy of the old auction catalogue. It listed about two dozen coins that matched almost perfectly to his new acquisition. All were from lots that had no buyer's name next to them, known or unknown.

As the property of Spink's, the coins fell to de Clermont to sell as he pleased. Rather than offer the coins at public auction, as had been indicated to Streiner, he chose to sell them privately. De Clermont "made a very good profit" and nearly doubled his investment. He sold them for "about $100,000, something like that," to an American dealer, Ed Milas, who owned a large coin dealership in Chicago called RARCOA. It was an interesting choice. While Milas was known in the trade to be extraordinarily wealthy, he also held a fairly significant financial stake in Spink's Zurich operation, which was more a satellite than a wholly owned subsidiary. Christie's had not yet bought Milas out.

In Baltimore a frustrated Eric Streiner took the bad news in stride. He chewed at the corner cuticle of his thumb and considered. He was a fierce competitor and didn't want to lose out on any more deals of this importance. The word was that de Clermont's source had more of the same. If, Streiner reasoned, he himself were in London, he could monitor the situation and make inroads at Spink's. But he wasn't. He needed eyes and ears. He needed Steve Fenton of Knightsbridge Coins. Streiner picked up the telephone.

Fenton had done his time at the Baltimore convention and was weary. He was headed off to cooler weather and a holiday when he got the call. Streiner told him about the coins and that the deal had gone private. Fenton recalled that de Clermont had shown him the eagles when they had just come in and had been told, as had Streiner, that "they would be going in for auction." He hadn't known they had been sold privately, and it was a nasty bit of news at the start of a vacation. Neither dealer was pleased that he had lost out. The coins were good, much too good.

Knightsbridge Coins was an anomaly on Duke Street, St. James's, a short street that runs from Piccadilly and dead-ends at King Street. At one end Fortnum and Mason satisfied the hungers of the belly, at the other, Christie's provided food for the eye. In between, a hiccoughing tumble of Georgian brick and 1970s glass facades housed some of the toniest art dealers in the world.

Tucked in among these decorator-designed environs, each an ode to minimalism, was a shop window dominated by large gold block letters reading, "Coins & Medals Bought and Sold S. Fenton." Within the window, in front of a sun-faded curtain, a heroically austere bust of George Washington looked on impassively at a scantily clad figurine of Una seated provocatively on her Lion. Around them were mahogany coin cabinets, mounted banknotes, and signs: offering to buy—offering to sell.

The proprietor, Stephen C. Fenton, was expansive and well fed, with an easy, disarming smile. His wavy hair, graying at the temples, was brushed back from a high, intelligent forehead. Through a pair of thickish lenses attached to each other by struts of space-age metal and polished to crystalline clarity, he watched the world always objectively, usually suspiciously. It was the nature of his profession. Fenton was born to the business of trading, buying, and selling. He came from the Benardout family of London Oriental rug dealers, and the give-and-take of haggling over a price was like breathing to him, something you just did.

Rugs he had been born to, but coins fascinated him. When he was growing up in Shepherd's Bush, coins transported his imagination back in time and taught him things he didn't learn in school. His mother got him started, plucking coins out of change, and he would follow her around when she visited coin shops. While she chatted, he would stare into the cases at the rows of coins: faces from the past, kings, queens and emperors, people he would never know, but lives that he could share.

By the time he was thirteen he had decided that coins would be his life but not as objects of scholarship. The precocious teenager wanted to be a dealer—selling pennies and shillings, while making pounds in the process. Commerce was in his blood and coins were its medium.

235

At age fifteen Fenton got his wish. It was 1967, and he stood proudly behind a counter at the far back of the ground floor of Harrods, selling coins that the department store received on consignment from a dealer. He was making £6 15s. ($16.50) a week, living at home, and life didn't get much better. His Saturdays were divided among the library of the British Numismatic Society, the coin department of the British Museum, and popping in and out of coin dealer's shops. He was learning about a subject he knew he could never fully conquer—that was part of its appeal; he was teaching himself the trade, which he knew he could master.

But Harrods wasn't in Fenton's future. Nor was a one-week stint working as a modern rug dealer for a distant cousin. Steve wanted coins. He was stubbornly focused on what he felt was his preordained profession, where he knew he would succeed.

None of the big coin dealers to whom he wrote had anything to offer in the way of employment and precious little in the way of encouragement. Then Fate didn't merely smile on him: she positively grinned. Having eagerly answered an ad for an opening as a trainee coin dealer, the sixteen-year-old got to Mayfair Coins before a score of others and exhibited the enthusiasm of the autodidact and a clever, quick eye for minutiae. Fenton got the job.

For seven years, from a small space on Regent Street not far from Piccadilly Circus, Fenton saw collectors, dealers, tourists, and the curious. He bought and sold coins, all the time learning, all the time champing at the bit. A young man in a hurry, he yearned for bigger things, and when he failed to persuade his employers to expand, he quit.

His uncle offered him a tiny space in his rug dealership next to the Rembrandt Hotel, directly across from the Victoria and Albert Museum, and at twenty-three he was in business for himself. He named his shop Knightsbridge Coins and five years later moved to Duke Street in the high-rent district of Mayfair.

Fenton didn't speak in the elegant, richly educated accents of his Duke Street neighbors; his accent was broader, more down to earth. Christie's was just round the corner. Spink's, the largest, most revered name in English numismatics, was his direct neighbor. This proximity to such behemoths worked to his advantage. His shop was Dickensian clutter, a small space entered from a short, dark hall, the cases filled with a jumble of stuff—nothing expensive, nothing rare, few things desirable—except for those who knew to ask. Israel Switt would have felt right at home.

It was a far cry from the order, formality, and grandeur of his larger neighbors. The liveried doormen of these establishments alone could intimidate the smaller sellers, who might not summon the courage to enter those lofty portals. Knightsbridge Coins' closeness to Christie's brought in smaller properties that the international house didn't want to sell, and Spink's ended up being a partner in many transactions.

Stephen Fenton prospered. Although he had a street-level shop, private collectors were not his primary focus. He dealt in wholesale, a more rough-and-tumble existence. Dealer-to-dealer, professional-to-professional transactions were his forte, which made him particularly useful to Spink's. The firm occasionally needed to cloak its involvement in certain significant transactions to protect the privacy of its clients and used Fenton as a go-between with other dealers. Fenton, in turn, developed a growing reputation as a dealer with sources for some terrific material.

While English coins remained his first and foremost specialty, he branched out to countries far from home: Australia, South Africa, and the United States. Fenton made himself known as the biggest buyer of American coins in England. He knew it to be a market of incalculable wealth and wanted to mine its depths. Knowing more about United States coins than the average English dealer but not nearly as much as the smallest American dealer would get him in over his head.

When he returned to London that fall of 1993, Stephen Fenton, his lips drawn thin, confronted André de Clermont—politely; they were, after all, both British. Fenton wanted to know why he, the biggest English dealer in United States coins, hadn't even been offered the chance to tender a bid. Why, after all these years?

De Clermont, always calm, collected, and glib, mollified his old colleague and smoothly told him not to worry. If he didn't explain why Fenton had been left out of the loop, he did reveal that it was a Middle Eastern source and still active. André informed him that a couple of the coins Fenton had recently purchased from Spink's, including one rarity and one fake, had come from his man. He assured Steve that he would bear his old chum in mind in the future.

But in a few months de Clermont quit Spink's. Like a tired tree dropping its autumn leaves, Christie's wanted to shed business and sever links that de Clermont had worked hard to develop over the years. He was particularly distraught at being told that Spink's, because it was Christie's policy, was not interested in continuing with the Middle Eastern business, which was his baby. He decided to face the odds alone. For

A Double Eagle Reappears

years de Clermont had been at the very top of the food chain. Now, set up on his own, he was well known but not well funded and no longer a big fish in the crowded pond.

At first de Clermont set up shop at home, which was no great sacrifice, considering the salubrious neighborhood in which he resided. With his more than a quarter-century of acquaintances and expertise in one of numismatics' most rarified specialties, he started making telephone calls and making the rounds. Islamic coins were nothing but discs of metal covered in squiggles and dots to most professionals, but occasionally they sold for prices in the hundreds of thousands of dollars. De Clermont was now dealing primarily in the hundreds or occasionally thousands of pounds.

Sometime early in 1994, the Egyptian coin dealer who had sold de Clermont the fabulous group of eagles reappeared with a colleague, a young man of about thirty-two or thirty-four who was a jeweler from Cairo. His father had also been a jeweler and the son of a jeweler, and their family, de Clermont learned over time in dribs and drabs, had a number of prominent clients. One of them had been close to Nasser and his tight cadre of colonels and majors that had first overthrown King Farouk in 1952 and then General Neguib in 1954. This young man, recalled André de Clermont, was of medium build, had straight hair, and was clean-shaven, and he "was the source of the coins." The Englishman was delighted. "The [Cairene] and his father, and possibly his grandfather, had all been jewelers to this family . . . a very wealthy and important family." The "Colonel" had died, and now his children were selling. Because of their long-standing familial ties, the jeweler from Cairo was entrusted with discreetly selling parts of their inheritance, jewelry, watches, and coins. Some he sold in London, the rest—most probably including the watches—in Switzerland.

The family name of the dead colonel was not revealed to de Clermont, who knew better than to ask. Neither did he delve into how the colonel had gotten the coins. He was told that the colonel had been a collector who "had acquired a great many coins from the Farouk sale." More than that André de Clermont could only surmise. Maybe the colonel had bought them in the sale; maybe he hadn't. Perhaps they had not been sold at the auction, and he had purchased them after the sale. Maybe, "as one of the people close with Nasser," he was simply given the coins. De Clermont had no idea, and his attitude was similar to that of Israel Switt's nearly sixty years earlier. It didn't really concern him. Only the coins mattered.

When de Clermont decided to forge his own future, one of the first to wish him well was Stephen Fenton. The clever proprietor of Knightsbridge Coins also offered to help out financially, should any interesting bits of business come along—especially, he reminded his old friend, lifting an eyebrow knowingly, if they came from his special contact. It was a welcome offer, since de Clermont no longer had the deep corporate pockets required to compete as successfully or aggressively as he liked.

In August, 1994, the young jeweler from Cairo, now visiting London and dealing directly, contacted de Clermont. De Clermont knew the Egyptian coin dealer who had first introduced them was greedy and also assumed that he might not always be discreet. The jeweler from Cairo must have quietly jettisoned him. Now he had some coins to sell, good ones, another small group of United States coins: a couple of scarce double eagles, one rare, and an odd, small group of pattern coins. Highly prized by collectors and infrequently appearing for sale, one of the group was an 1851 silver dollar struck in nickel—believed to be the only known example.

True to his word and needing the cash flow, de Clermont put in a call to Fenton at his office. The jeweler from Cairo trusted de Clermont and agreed that he could retain the coins to do some research. No doubt de Clermont took them directly to Fenton's shop.

An extension of the upstairs Duke Street clutter, Fenton's private office was not grand. He sat behind a desk blanketed by random sheets of paper at the bottom of a winding, clattering iron staircase. Modern price guides—useful books for a busy dealer—were stuffed helter-skelter onto shelves. Oversized, wildly colored, splendidly fanciful posters devoted to advertising the career of a long-dead magician, one Chung Ling Soo, hung here and there, occasionally askew, some leaning against telephones, the fax machine, and the walls. An Englishman who had imitated and all but stolen the name, personality, and act of a Chinese magician, Ching Ling Foo, he spoke gobbledygook on stage through an interpreter and performed astonishing feats of prestidigitation. One, catching live bullets on a plate, cost him his life during a performance in 1918. Even the great Houdini steered clear of that trick.

Fenton picked up each of the coins separately. He held them lightly between his thumb and finger, turning them with a subtle, well-practiced movement and use of a third finger that was as close as the magic aficionado got to sleight of hand. After carefully examining the coins, Fenton dug a couple of books off the shelves, found a few recent auction catalogues with prices paid, flipped the pages quickly, and made his comparisons. He and de Clermont discussed the coins. They both liked what they saw and agreed on the appropriate price to pay. André would have to come to terms with the jeweler from Cairo, whom he knew to be "capable of being very tough on the price," especially "for a man who supposedly did not know anything about the coins."

Well versed in the art of Middle Eastern negotiating, de Clermont successfully closed the deal, paying cash. De Clermont understood: "Middle Eastern people are generally not trusting of people's checks unless it is a very large transaction; they prefer to work with people's cash. That is their way." Whether the jeweler from Cairo took the cash back to Egypt or "paid it into a bank" in London, de Clermont didn't know. It wasn't his business.

Their first deal was booked on August 3, 1994, for £12,700 ($19,050), the broader-bodied Fenton and the narrower de Clermont were even partners. They sold this first group in America at the annual American Numismatic Association convention, and even though the profit was only a few hundred pounds, it was a good start, and de Clermont started seeing more material from the jeweler from Cairo. The two English dealers were onto a good thing.

The jeweler from Cairo visited more frequently. Like a genie, he would materialize with no warning. Maddeningly, he seemed to know when de Clermont was out of town. But he was apparently loyal and didn't wander from dealer to dealer, as some were wont to do, looking for other offers, playing games. The material he brought was no longer only from the United States but also from Hamburg, Mecklenburg-Schwerin, Italy, Saxony, Brazil, Bavaria, Hanover, Naples, Sicily, Great Britain, and Austria. It was almost always gold, in splendid condition, and proved quite conclusively to both de Clermont and Fenton that the Farouk collection was indeed the source. As they received the coins, the two dealers checked the old, faded, green Sotheby's catalogue that Fred and Albert Baldwin had toiled over in the furnacelike temperatures of Cairo a half-century earlier. De Clermont's copy, which he had bought from Spink's in the 1980s, had been annotated by someone who had attended the sale in 1954; "possibly by David Spink himself." Certainly the marks, bidder numbers, and use of the ancient Spink code COMEANDBUY—each letter consecutively represented by a digit from one to zero (equalling ten), with a couple of personalized twists—should have looked familiar.

Invariably the coins matched up to the descriptions in the catalogue, even though the original envelopes from the sale had been lost. Sometimes entire sale lots were offered to de Clermont intact and agreed perfectly. Other times a few coins from a lot would arrive, to be followed weeks later by more pieces from the same lot. The one constant was that each one of the lots, whether complete or not, that was sold by the jeweler from Cairo matched up only to lots in de Clermont's saleroom copy of the catalogue that had no buyers' names next to them.

The majority of coins that were offered and purchased were of quality, but few were exceptionally rare or important. A smattering had been illustrated in the catalogue, most had not. Nearly all had come from large lots that had contained up to twenty or more coins. The Baldwins had been forced by time, space, and the Egyptian military into combining quantities of coins, even those of stunning rarity, into single lots. Some of these issues were currently trading in the tens or even hundreds of thousands of dollars, and Fenton knew it. Although it was ultimately sold singly in the sale, even the 1913 Liberty Head nickel had been catalogued as part of a lot of 148 other coins and not illustrated. Now, in 1994, it was worth nearly a million dollars.

Individually, the coins could have come from anywhere. Most nineteenth- and twentieth-century machine-made coins were to all intents and purposes anonymous, and the descriptions in the Farouk catalogue were cursory. But, said de Clermont, "It is not the single coin, it is the combination of a group of dates all coming in one," that proved the provenance. If it was a hoax, it was an extraordinarily complicated one. Asked repeatedly by de Clermont about the coins' source, the jeweler from Cairo "always said the same thing, that they were all from King Farouk."

As the offerings became more frequent and the value of the coins increased, Fenton thought it might be easier if he were the banker. He considered it carefully, and one day in 1995 said to André, "Maybe it would be cleaner if I simply pay for everything. You sell the European coins, I will deal with the American coins, and then we can go on a profit share." De Clermont listened. Fenton continued, "If you sell them, you give me half the profit over the cost plus the money I put out." If Fenton successfully sold the pieces in his control, then the same sharing scheme would apply in reverse. It was not an unusual practice in the coin trade. The two men agreed.

Within a year, by mid-1995, their records showed that together they had purchased nearly two hundred coins: United States patterns, including trade and commercial dollars from 1872, 1873, and 1876 and quarter and half eagles struck in copper from 1878; United States double eagles struck in 1920 at San Francisco and at Philadelphia in 1921; half eagles struck between 1851 and 1854; quarter eagles struck between 1834 and 1854. Eighteenth- and nineteenth-century European gold coins included

A Double Eagle Reappears

ducats, guineas, goldgulden, thalers, gold strikings of silver schillings, and unique platinum medals.

De Clermont had consummated approximately fifteen different transactions with the jeweler from Cairo, beginning on August 3, 1994, and extending into 1995, which he and Fenton identified with nearly fifty separate lots from the Farouk sale. They were good coins. It was good business.

The two men pored over the creamy, yellowed pages of de Clermont's copy of the Palace Collection catalogue with increasing interest and diligence and saw the names of the buyers, many legends, most dead: Pittman, Kosoff, Kaplan, Schulman, Baldwin and Spink among them. It was only human to be envious of those who had gone before and had the opportunity to participate in such a fabled event, especially since, to their modern eyes, the prices seemed so cheap. And they could not have helped but come upon the notation at the end of lot 185. Circled, with the word "withdrawn" quickly scratched below, was the entry for the 1933 double eagle. It had vanished without a trace into the sands of Egypt when Stephen Fenton was two years old. But so too—if without fanfare—had the coins that the two dealers were now buying from the Cairo jeweler. Maybe, just maybe, it still existed, ready to wreak havoc again.

Sometime in 1994, André de Clermont first mentioned to Fenton that the 1933 double eagle might become available. Was he interested?

"Of course," was his immediate reply.

A year passed. While they were chatting about the 1954 auction, de Clermont, an easy conversationalist, casually mentioned one day to the jeweler from Cairo that a 1933 double eagle had been in the Farouk collection.

The young jeweler was offhand, dismissive, and "just said, 'Well if it comes, it will come.'"

De Clermont pressed him. "Have you seen that coin?"

No, he said. But, he added, "If it is there, or they offer it to me, I will obviously try to get it."

De Clermont was intrigued. He knew the coin had been pulled from the auction—his uncle had told him so—but, de Clermont claimed, he didn't know why. Even though de Clermont was a "self-described non-expert in United States coins," he still knew the coin was special. Every professional numismatist in the world knew it. Everyone also knew it was illegal to own. But no one really knew why.

In the late summer of 1995, Stephen Fenton got a call from de Clermont. He was stunned by what he heard. De Clermont's man had produced the 1933 double eagle.

Where was it?

London. In his safe deposit box.

Fenton's feet carried him up the winding staircase from his subterranean lair and out the door into Duke Street. He hung a left and marched smartly up to Jermyn Street and hung a right, striding past smart shirtmakers' shops, an antiquities gallery, a heavily aromatic cheese shop, and a few restaurants without paying the slightest heed. At last he arrived at the safe depository in Lower Regent Street, located just steps away from Piccadilly Circus, where Eros, McDonalds, and hordes of roving tourists converged.

The depository was well known to Fenton, who along with many other London-based coin dealers stored his better pieces and overflow from his stock there. It was tightly controlled. Fenton met de Clermont and they found a private cubbyhole in which to examine the coin.

Fenton's eyes grew glassy with excitement as he was handed the coin by his colleague. "It was the most amazing feeling I've ever had with a coin," he recalled. He was mesmerized. A shiver ran through him. He had never seen one before. Who had? Never handled one. Few had. It was legendary.

As Fenton stared at the coin in dazzled awe, de Clermont asked, "What do you think?"

"Wonderful."

It was a breathless, whispered reply. The coin was tantalizing. Absolutely genuine. It glowed with a life of its own. Fenton gazed at the face of Liberty and she gazed back. The small mark across her belly and other minuscule wounds on the soft golden surfaces did not distress him. Virtually all big gold coins bore these birthmarks, which were imparted as they bounced off one another while being made. Liberty had fewer than most. Fenton was captive. He wanted it. He had to have it.

De Clermont showed Fenton the handful of other coins the jeweler from Cairo had given him with the '33. They too were from the United States, but of little if any interest. Fenton barely noticed them. He couldn't take his eyes off the taboo ounce of gold that beckoned alluringly.

He looked up and asked, "What's the price?"

The jeweler from Cairo, who was staying at a hotel in the Bayswater section of London, had told de Clermont when they had met that he wanted $325,000.

A Double Eagle Reappears

Too much, Fenton thought, but didn't say so immediately to de Clermont. It was a great deal of money for a coin in 1995, not world-record level, but stiff.

Did Fenton know the coin was illegal? If he did, his normally rational, calculating, dealer's mind was blinded by the temptation of having what nobody else had. He wouldn't be the first. But still. He had to think it over. The process was a blur. A few years later, Fenton couldn't remember if he had even dickered. He thought he had been asked a price and paid it. He seemed to recall, "It just seemed a fair price." De Clermont had different memories: in fact, a negotiation over price commenced.

The jeweler from Cairo had known that this transaction would take some time. How he had arrived at the asking price was a mystery for a jeweler supposedly untutored in the way of coins. But he was a hard man, a careful man, and must have divined the price from somewhere.

De Clermont now had to act as go-between. Fenton told him that he wanted the coin, but the price was out of the question and made a counter offer well below the asking price. So the traditional game began, Fenton's rug-dealer's blood a good match for the Cairo jeweler's.

Back and forth de Clermont shuttled between the two men. They both trusted de Clermont, and he trusted them, separately. He kept them apart. To introduce them, he felt, would have slightly undermined his own position. The jeweler from Cairo was his source, and he wanted to retain that relationship.

The negotiation lasted a few days. De Clermont went to and fro four or five times. It was more than just throwing a price down. It was a gentle process, usually with some idle small talk and then polite excuses made up for the other man to soften the then proffered offer. The reply was usually considered. This was business and, properly done, an artful science.

At last a bargain was struck. The price: $220,000. The miscellaneous coins were valued together at $10,000; the 1933 double eagle at $210,000. This was not a cash deal.

The size of the transaction precluded de Clermont's financial involvement. Although neither seller nor purchaser knew the other, it was arranged that Stephen Fenton through his Knightsbridge Coins account would wire the funds directly to the Cairo jeweler's account. The transaction would be paid for in dollars.

Tuesday, October 3, 1995. London, England.

Stephen Fenton arranged with his bank to convert £141,706.92 to $220,000 and wire the funds, payable to the Cairo jeweler's account at a branch of the National Westminster Bank in West London. The bank charged Fenton £36.48 to cover its commissions and costs.

Stephen Fenton now owned a 1933 double eagle, perhaps the only one still in existence. Most likely King Farouk's, but there was no paperwork to prove it, though. The catalogue description of the entire lot 185 was cursory, unillustrated, and so there was no catalogue photograph to match. But everything else that the jeweler from Cairo had sold them matched the catalogue descriptions. Forty-one years ago the 1933 double eagle had been removed from lot 185 and disappeared. It was circled and marked in André's catalogue as "withdrawn." The connection was logical. "Yes," said André de Clermont, "it was obviously the Farouk coin."

And it was obviously worth more than Fenton had paid. A significant profit for both dealers could well be in the offing. But this was not like the other transactions that de Clermont had originated and Fenton had bankrolled. They mutually agreed that the fifty-fifty split would not apply to the '33. De Clermont knew Fenton was risking an enormous sum of money on one roll of the dice and he trusted him.

"I will leave it with you" André told Steve. "When you sell . . . tell me and we'll settle something equitably."

Fenton smiled. "André, I'll look after you. You'll do very well if we sell the coin well."

"That's fine with me," replied de Clermont.

As the owner of a 1933 double eagle, Fenton was now one of a handful of men who had shared that privilege—or curse. All had had their gold pieces confiscated. All were dead, their coins melted. This double eagle was the ultimate coin. It was his. It was the only one. The pride of ownership was overwhelming.

Some days, he recalled, he just looked at it and thought he might keep it. Could he share his enthusiasm for the coin with others? Not many—if any. The coin trade in England, America, or anywhere is a sieve. There are secrets, but few are well kept. And Fenton wasn't as wealthy as other collectors before him who had also once owned a 1933 double eagle. Farouk had had untold millions, yet a half-century before had paid only about fifteen hundred dollars for it. Fenton had paid a great deal

A Double Eagle Reappears

more, and although he made a good living, he could not realistically keep the coin. Fenton was not a collector; he was a dealer.

Fenton's mind whirled. Numbers danced in his head. He knew he had to sell it, but didn't know how—or to whom. Regardless, he thought, it had to bring the right price. He would put it on offer. If, like a house in a hot real estate market, it brought the price he asked, he'd sell. If it didn't, he would keep it. He was enthralled, confused. The 1933 double eagle was casting its customary spell, like the Sirens luring the unwary onto the spiny outcrops of calamity.

ILLEGAL TENDER

CHAPTER 18

The Homecoming Deal

———◆———

1995. London.

IT WAS LATE AUTUMN, AND DARKNESS FELL EARLIER AND EARLIER. Stephen Fenton sat in his underground office oblivious to the time of day and thought about his 1933 double eagle. It was a bloody marvelous thing to own, but he knew there were some strings attached to it. Two bibles of the trade, books no dealer could be without, flew warning flags. *The Guide Book to United States Coins* (the "Red Book") said that there had been "none placed in circulation." *Gold Coins of the World* ("Friedberg") said "the coins were not released officially and possession of this one date is illegal." Fenton thought, "That's strange, but obviously a few could have got out." At least one had. He needed help.

Fenton picked up his phone and dialed a number he knew well in Dusseldorf, Germany. His call was to Marc Emory, a multilingual, slightly scruffy American, with a fuzzy beard, a man he considered a friend, personally and professionally. Emory exuded a detached professorial air rather than that of a keen-eyed coin dealer, which is what he was. A representative for Heritage Rare Coins, based in Dallas, Texas, and one of the world's largest firms of coin dealers and auctioneers, Emory was their European eyes and ears. He represented them at foreign auctions but, more important, made contacts at financial institutions, both private and governmental, to see whether there were any coins to be had.

Fenton and Emory had done considerable business together over the years. Fenton, through his contacts around the world, was able to find buyers for some items that Emory and Heritage wanted to sell. He also kept a keen eye out in Britain for coins he thought might be of use to the United States firm. It was a good relationship, a close one.

Stephen Fenton called his old friend of just shy of a quarter-century and discussed the coin. He told him he wanted to sell it but didn't know where to turn. Emory, who Fenton reckoned was an expert in American coins, said he would make a few calls for Steve and get back to him. And as he promised, he got on the telephone.

According to Fenton's recollection, the first person Marc Emory spoke to on his behalf was David Hall, a California coin dealer, who turned down Marc Emory's inquiry. Hall had been dealing in United States coins long enough to know that the 1933 double eagle was forbidden fruit. Undaunted, Emory put in a call to Jay Parrino in Kansas City. Emory did not know Parrino, except by reputation, and Parrino didn't recall meeting Emory but knew he worked for Heritage.

Jasper Parrino—who everyone called Jay—had been a Cub Scout, an enterprising eight-year-old who had taken out ads in *Boy's Life* to sell rare coins to Boy Scouts so they could get their merit badges for coin collecting. Now, forty-two years later, Jay Parrino was an enigma in Hawaiian shirts and polyester pants. Few really knew him. He had been around in the business for forty years, but nobody actually remembered him much before the 1980s. Then, like some slightly pudgy, vaguely olive-skinned god from Olympus, he had suddenly manifested himself with money— tons of it. Five feet seven inches, with black hair and hazel eyes that sparkled when he smiled, which he could well afford to do, Parrino was everywhere and was buying everything. Everything rare. Everything in perfect condition. Everything expensive. He didn't seem to care what he paid as long as he got what he wanted. The coin trade beat a path to his door, offered him their nonpareils at top prices, and wanted to be his best friend.

The Mint, Parrino's aptly named firm, published occasional catalogues offering his rarest of the rare at astonishing, stunning, staggeringly high prices. Not surprisingly, little seemed to sell except for a few pieces every now and then, but not many, and not the truly extraordinary ones. Jay seemed to be perfectly content to sit on a coin for years in a business in which margins were low and regular turnover essential to maintain cash flow.

Nobody in the trade understood it, and they all whispered about it behind his back. What's he up to? How can he afford it? Did he win some lottery? Is he just some rich guy playing a game? Is he nuts? Parrino didn't seem to notice, didn't seem to care, kept buying, and didn't drop his prices.

Cheerful and easy to get along with, Jay grinned obligingly for photographers when he bought world-record-priced coins at auctions, and his stature in the business grew. Other dealers may have gossiped about him, but unlike those of many in the trade, his checks always cleared. In the end, no one really cared where Parrino got his money; they were just jealous because he had more than they had. If a dealer latched on to a new customer with deep pockets, Jay usually had something of interest, and there was always business to be done.

Parrino was receptive to Emory's inquiry and said that he might have a buyer for the coin. He remembered that a dealer from Texas, Jack Moore, whom he had first met around six years before, had asked him "on many occasions" about obtaining a 1933 double eagle for a client. Emory provided Parrino with Stephen Fenton's telephone number and suggested that he deal direct. From that point on, Emory told Parrino, he was no longer involved in the transaction.

Fenton was delighted by Emory's good news, knew Jay's reputation, and thought it sounded like a perfect fit. Emory had done noble service for his English friend but had apparently not warned Fenton about potential pitfalls. Or if he had, Fenton had shaken them off, perhaps naively, perchance over-confident. Or maybe he had become so completely enthralled with the coin that he paid no attention. Curiously too, Emory did not offer the coin to his own company, which certainly had the wherewithal to handle the transaction, or perhaps he had, but Heritage didn't want to take the chance of charred fingers.

Before Jay Parrino could begin to discuss a deal with Fenton, he had to ensure that the Texan was in fact still interested in obtaining the fabled coin. He made a call.

Jack Moore was a marginal coin dealer, who had done time back in the sixties after taking the rap for something foolish his wife had done. She had sold furniture they were leasing and didn't own. Moore told the judge he had done it, got a three-year sentence, spent one in the penitentiary at Huntsville, Texas, and two out on probation with no violations. It was thirty years ago and didn't matter anymore.

But coins did matter to Jack Moore, although he had never spent more than three hundred dollars on a coin for himself. Something about them entranced him. He liked reading about them in the cheap, floppy, newsprint magazines to which he subscribed, articles about Saint-Gaudens' double eagles, Brasher doubloons, 1804 silver dollars, and 1913 Liberty Head nickels. They were the essence of legend—magical, unobtainable objects whose stories made the imagination race.

A West Texas trucker by profession, who since 1961 had sat behind the wheel of the big rigs or worked as a terminal manager, he had been going to coin shows since 1975, buying and selling as a part-time dealer. The camaraderie and noisy halls of coin shows filled with the odors of greasy food, stale cigarettes, and cheap cigars could be seductive. Long aisles of tables on which sat aluminum-sided, thumbprint-smeared, glass-topped cases filled with neat rows or untidy piles of coins could be intoxicating: Within those vitrines lay history, or treasure or profit. Kids and their grandparents hunted for pennies. Wheeler-dealers and collectors swapped tall tales and rumors with people interested in the same things. It was all part of the appeal. Moore loved coins and also saw that a lot of cash changed hands at coin shows. Good money could be made, and that really appealed.

When he retired from trucking in January, 1993, Jack Moore, of Amarillo, Texas, with grandiose ideas, decided he would make his hobby his business and hung out a shingle announcing himself as a rare-coin dealer. Moore started with his personal collection as his stock, with sales of coins he'd had all his life, and in that first year probably made twelve thousand to fourteen thousand dollars. It was a meager harvest, but nevertheless he was a fortunate man. The owner of Groendyke Transport, of Enid, Oklahoma, the trucking company that had employed him for many years, was smitten by coins too. Neither man was very knowledgeable, but Moore and Mr. Groendyke talked coins and in 1990 or 1991 started discussing the possibility of Groendyke putting together a collection of double eagles, just the Saint-Gaudens design from 1907 to 1932. Jack Moore counted up a total of fifty-two combinations of dates, mint marks, and varieties. It was not an impossible task, and it wouldn't be cheap—a million dollars, maybe more—but Mr. Groendyke was wealthy, and Moore was ambitious.

Between 1991 and 1994 Moore started buying Saint-Gaudens double eagles—"Saints" in the trade—for Mr. Groendyke. He was tentative at first, and it was a slow process. During those initial three years, he bought fewer than twenty coins, and not one cost more than six thousand dollars. Moore's boss was generous and paid his employee a commission of between five and ten percent on the coins he bought. Moore traveled to coin shows, popped in on coin dealers, spread the word, and kept an eye out for his boss—his one collector.

In 1994 Jack Moore, the newly minted rare-coin dealer, no longer a trucker, and Mr. Groendyke, still a trucking company owner, "started on it real heavy," and the collection of saints expanded quickly.

Moore traveled the coin-show circuit weekend after weekend. He reckoned he had had his own table on the bourse "five or six hundred" times during his life, occasionally sharing a table with a fellow dealer. But hoofing it from table to table was essential in the coin business, if hard on the legs, hard on the back. Generally wearing cowboy boots and blue jeans with a broad belt cinched by an eye-catching buckle, Moore did what all dealers did: he talked, chatted, bragged, checked out a coin or two, always trying to sell high, buy low. He wasn't very good at it.

He was eking out an existence. His meager library consisted of only about two dozen books, and truth be told, he wasn't very successful. With the exception of that first year, the measly profit which came largely from liquidating his own collection, he never turned a profit in the coin business again—before retiring from the trade in the spring of 1996. All that pretty green cabbage he saw changing hands, all that easy money to be made in coin dealing was not destined for Jack Moore.

But during 1994 and into 1995, Moore was riding high on Mr. Groendyke's wallet, and it seemed that there wasn't a dealer at any table, coin show, or convention in the country, who didn't know that he was putting together a complete set of Saints for his rich client. His client had the money, and he was in the market for the right coins. Coin-business braggadocio: nothing new, whether it comes with a laid-back West Coast shrug, a New York West Side snarl, or a laconic West Texas drawl. Jack Moore fit right in. He was buying good coins for his client, some expensive, and nothing in the self-anointed coin "industry" spoke with greater volume than real buyers.

Many of the coins for which Moore was in the market were not all that rare. In fact, they were dead common, and he could take his pick from hundreds of examples. A common coin of average-quality might cost a few hundred dollars, the great ones a few thousand. Other issues were rare, very rare, in some cases nearly unobtainable.

Along the way, Jack Moore ran into a dealer who frequently had the nearly unobtainable, and then some: Jay Parrino. Moore had acquired one, maybe two double eagles for Mr. Groendyke from Parrino in 1991. Polar extremes of the numismatic world, the Texan had never bought a coin for himself for more than three hundred dollars, and Parrino probably didn't carry coins that cheap. But with Mr. Groendyke's money, Jack Moore had Jay's attention, and they dealt.

The Kansas City dealer's reputation dazzled Moore, as it did so many others. What better way to impress the hell out of Parrino and show him that he wasn't the only high roller in the game than by asking for the one coin he knew Parrino didn't have—couldn't have? So, according to Jay Parrino, sometime around 1991 or maybe 1992, Jack Moore asked Jay if he knew of a 1933 double eagle for sale and said he was interested in purchasing it. Parrino listened, took the trucker at his word, and stored away the query. According to Parrino, Moore repeated his offer on numerous occasions.

At a coin show in Baltimore, in 1993 or 1994, Moore later claimed, Jay Parrino had approached *him* and asked if he "wanted to buy a 1933 twenty-dollar gold piece to put in that set." Parrino told the novice dealer "he knew where one was available."

Jack Moore has professed he was uninterested and said he told Parrino straight out that there "was no reason to buy one" because "it was illegal to own." Such a blunt response should have ended the conversation, especially since they were discussing contraband. But, incredibly, Moore has claimed that Parrino was insistent and pestered him about the subject every time they met, "probably ten times" over the next two years—until November, 1995.

In late November or early December, 1995, Jay Parrino and Stephen Fenton, who had barely met, started to talk about the sale of the 1933 double eagle. At first it was just the two of them. Then each said that others, real or imaginary, had to be consulted. Fenton figured his bargaining position would be stronger if Parrino didn't know he owned the coin, and the Kansas City dealer told him he had to consult his client.

Fenton wanted a great deal of money for the coin or he wouldn't sell. The asking price he came up with, "just picked out of the air," was $750,000. It was not, in 1995, a world record for a coin, but it *was* more than the $725,000 that had been paid in 1979 for a Brasher doubloon, then still the record for a gold coin. It also turned out to be a wholesale price.

From the heartland of America Jay Parrino told Fenton, "Yes, my client is interested." How much?

Sitting in his grottolike office in Duke Street, Fenton took a deep breath and in his lilting way told Parrino his imaginary client wanted $750,000 but that he, Fenton, "wasn't getting rich at the price." Jay said that of course he'd have to talk to his client. Steve understood completely; the curtain was up, they would talk again. The English dealer was patient.

Chairman of the British Numismatic Trade Association, Fenton didn't know that he had just catalyzed a chain of reactions in the United States that would lead to an international firestorm.

On December 8, 1995, Jack Moore got in touch with an old acquaintance of his, Ron Jannings, a retired FBI agent, and told him that he had just been offered a 1933 double eagle that was "available from a foreign owner for $1,500,000." In his own way, Moore explained the background of the coin, its nefarious history, and his involvement. The former agent listened carefully and told him he would contact a Secret Service agent he knew whose bailiwick this was.

Dave Freriks, the Secret Service agent who Jannings called, was nearing retirement—it was a matter of months. He was a burly, sandy-haired, nuts-and-bolts, clear-eyed, button-down sort of guy who had done thirty-two years in the Service: eighteen in Lubbock, Texas, as the Resident Agent in Charge. He didn't know much about coins, but knew that the 1933 double eagle was his responsibility. It was the only coin specifically mentioned in the Secret Service manual, never issued to the public, stolen from the Mint, and seizable as contraband.

Freriks immediately called Jack Moore, set up an appointment, and drove the more than one hundred miles to Amarillo. They met in the back of a restaurant for nearly two hours. Jannings had told Freriks that the informant was a small-time coin dealer. Moore unctuously told the agent "he was knowledgeable concerning numismatic coins." Freriks had no reason to doubt Moore; he didn't know coins and didn't know what further questions to ask.

Jack Moore laid it out. He produced pages from a handful of numismatic publications all noting the questionable legal status of the 1933 Saint-Gaudens double eagle. Moore told Freriks that he may have asked Jay Parrino casually and in jest once or twice about the availability of the coin and that Parrino had advised him that it was illegal to own. Nevertheless, Parrino was now offering Moore an example for $1.5 million.

Jack Moore reeled off a list of gripes, real or imagined, against Parrino and his purported reasons for notifying the officials. He told the Treasury man that he felt he had "been cheated by Parrino in the past out of commission money." According to Moore, there was one deal in which Parrino was supposed to have sent him five thousand dollars, but the Kansas City dealer never sent it and never said anything about it. He didn't like Parrino's attitude: "so high on his coins." He had come to the authorities because he feared Parrino was trying to set him up for dealing in a stolen coin and because he felt Parrino was a black mark on coin dealers and collectors collectively. Dave Freriks took it all in and signed Jack Moore on as a confidential informant. Moore was now referred to in all paperwork as CI 324-15; he was anonymous.

Freriks acted with dispatch—he didn't want the quarry to escape and authorized Moore to make an opening counter offer. It would buy them some time. He told the ex-trucker to counter with $750,000, only half of what Parrino was asking—and, unbeknownst to him, exactly what Fenton wanted. Freriks told Moore that the "transaction should be conducted in the way that coin dealers do transactions" and then he tied some strings to the deal. Moore was to tell Parrino that the buyer's expert would have to see the coin before any money changed hands and that the transaction had to take place in the United States. He also told Moore to tape record the conversations. Moore did—but not all of them.

At 2:50 P.M., on Friday, December 15, 1995, Jay Parrino received a telephone call from Jack Moore—his tape recorder running—who was getting anxious. He had tendered the first counteroffer a few days earlier and hadn't heard back.

Parrino calmed him, "We are working on it. The green part of the deal is what we are working on."

Moore was pleased, but still nervous. Before he had even gotten a counter to his counteroffer, he indicated that he was willing to bump up the price, "Was that price agreeable? If not, maybe I could do something else." Jay explained that he hadn't yet offered the seller a firm price, but what bothered Parrino was where the sale would be consummated.

Moore picked up on Parrino's hesitation immediately. "The coin can't come to here, huh?"

"Uh, huh" was Parrino's affirmative.

But Moore knew his part and played it well. "If they're selling to someone, [they should] take it to the buyer . . . they're, well, collecting the money."

"Well," said Parrino, "they don't want to do that, because it is okay over there, but it's not okay over here."

Moore held his ground, as Freriks had insisted. "I don't know if I could get my person to go overseas or not."

Parrino promised he would talk to his client. The conversation veered off at tangents and then homed back as they played cat and mouse. Moore told Parrino he didn't want to pay $1.5 million and bluntly asked Parrino if he would be making some money on the deal.

Parrino answered with a standard bargaining tactic: "The price I quoted you is the price they quoted me. We haven't really got into negotiations or not. If I'm involved, yeah, I want to make something, but if I'm not involved, I don't care. I don't need to make it."

Agent Freriks had told Moore to do what it took to get the deal, but only in this country. So Moore reiterated to Parrino that "I'm almost certain that my person will not go overseas" and tried offering cash, "the suitcase, or the small briefcase or whatever full of stuff to hand you."

Parrino wanted none of it. There were "reporting requirements here that you don't have over there," he reminded Moore. "It's just a normal deal over there."

Prestige, greed, and the Secret Service would not let this deal go sour. Since Stephen Fenton wanted $750,000 and that had been offered, Parrino was now working on profit. Since Fenton had not expressed any hesitation about bringing the coin into the United States, Parrino was probably using his client's imaginary reluctance to travel as a bargaining chip.

In the late afternoon of December 18, the deal came a great deal closer to fruition. It was snowing in Amarillo when Moore proffered some good news to Parrino over the phone: his "person had agreed to a wire transfer . . . instead of cash, if that would help." Parrino was pleased.

Moore then lowered the boom again. "But, uh, he wants it done here. I mean, he ain't going out of the United States."

Parrino blithely said, "OK." It wasn't going to be a problem.

The tone of the conversation grew lighter. They laughed. But then Parrino got serious. "The only other problem that we've got, Jack, [is that] they're just really firm on their price . . . they're saying that's the number . . . they're not open to a counter . . . I don't know how firm your guy is, but, you, you can't buy it for that . . . they just won't sell it."

Jack Moore responded with what sounded like a surprisingly quick capitulation—after all, it wasn't his money. "So that's the price I gave my guy . . . a million and a half."

"Right. Well," said Parrino, "I think we can do it . . . but are you in there to make some money?"

"Well," came a laconic but avaricious reply, "I wouldn't be doing this if I wasn't going to try to make something on it."

Parrino agreed. He simply wanted to know how high Jack Moore's client was willing to go. He held hard at $1.5 million. Moore really didn't care. He knew all his offers were illusory. He was doing the Secret Service's bidding. He was setting Parrino up for a fall, but not until he was on the plus side of the ledger.

255

Moore told Parrino, "I can get my guy to wire a million and a half, if somebody, and I don't care who, hands me a briefcase with some cash in it."

"I got you," said Jay.

"You understand what I mean?"

"I understand exactly what you mean."

Then Moore abruptly changed the subject. "Okay, and we can talk about that amount later."

Christmas wishes were proffered and returned. But as the conversation wound down, Parrino made it abundantly clear to Moore that price was paramount and firm. He dangled the prospect of a blown deal.

"I think I know who the person is that they're going to offer it to if I don't buy it."

"Oh." A hesitation. "Somebody we both know?"

"Yes . . . He has got somebody who wants it so bad his teeth are rattling. He's asked me for years about it because he knows I know where one is. So, anyhow . . ."

Jack Moore broke in urgently. "Well, don't let it get away, because if worse comes to worst, we may be forced to pay more than a million and a half."

Parrino had succeeded. He calmed Jack Moore and told him, "I'm going to get it locked up some way."

But of course he already had.

The week before Christmas, London was in a festive mood. Regent Street was gaily festooned with twinkling white lights above and pedestrian gridlock below, as determined but cheerful shoppers shuffled along two inches a time from store to store. Office parties were the norm, not the exception, and Stephen Fenton went about his business as usual, ignorant of the bargaining and badinage in which Jack Moore and Jay Parrino were engaged.

The jeweler from Cairo had continued to contact André de Clermont about more coins, and Knightsbridge Coins had purchased even more astonishing prizes. Three gold bars from Brazil as well as three United States pattern coins struck in gold—an eagle from 1868, a half eagle from 1878, and a three-dollar piece from 1865—were all of such rarity that their source, the Farouk sale, was unquestionable; the descriptions were precise, and the American coins had been illustrated in the catalogue. Funds in the amount of $131,500 were wired to the jeweler from Cairo's National Westminster account.

Fenton and Parrino talked occasionally, but Fenton felt they had made a cut-and-dried deal. No lengthy negotiations with Jay over price. No haggling over sale venue. Not even that many phone calls. The point and counterpoint between the two American dealers was their dance alone.

Resident Agent Dave Freriks was also something of a wallflower, privy only to those conversations that were recorded. (Sometimes the little tape machine, curiously, "just didn't work.") But he too was doing some bargaining with Jack Moore. Shortly after the first meeting, the new volunteer, CI 324-15, "inquired as to a fee, an informant fee."

Jack Moore wanted seventy-five thousand dollars for his role. Freriks flatly told him that the Secret Service would pay him nothing like that figure. He offered less, much less. Jack Moore wasn't pleased. He then suggested to the Secret Service man that "maybe he should get it from Mr. Parrino." He felt that it "was his option" to work the deal "so that he would get a payment from Mr. Parrino while working as an informant" in what amounted to a sham transaction.

Freriks sternly told Moore "not to do it and it would be improper just because it's improper." He was emphatic that CI 324-15 "was not to attempt to obtain money from Parrino as part of this transaction." If, however, there was "a separate transaction involving different coins . . . [then] that's their business." Freriks had just left the door ajar.

Christmas came and went. Moore and Parrino chatted, and Moore had his recorder whirring. The deal was getting closer, with nothing but small hiccoughs along the way. It was getting exciting. It was January 3, 1996.

There was some fussing about whether the funds would be wired within or out of the country, but this was essentially not an issue. Nor was a tentative pickup in New York, specifics would be discussed. Parrino would want a receipt. A generic receipt for "one group of gold coins," nothing specific, would be ample. Moore was happy to agree.

Parrino told Moore that his man was coming to New York and would be available between January 16 and 18. He told Moore, "That's the dates. He says he'll come in, do the deal, make a little money, have a little dinner."

"And," Moore reminded Parrino, "I will pick the time and place to meet?"

"Yes," Parrino agreed. He started to speculate on other 1933 double eagles that might exist in other collections. The Kansas City dealer told Jack Moore that "there's another one in New Jersey and there's one other one." Jay hadn't seen it personally but had "heard from a great source that it does exist." He thought there might even be a third—no more. "I think there's three, three uncirculated pieces."

257

They spoke of receipts again and how the coin would be imported into the country. Jack Moore asked Parrino, "Can't you find out from them what it's supposed to say? A group of gold coins . . ."

"Yeah," said Parrino, "but he said, in other words, what they're going to do is they're either going to put it in a roll of common bullion pieces . . . or put it in a set and mislabel it as a '32, or something, ya know."

The conversation flitted from subject to subject: wire transfers, and IRS audits, T-shirts, Concorde, and Egypt. Of this and that and nothing.

"Let's do it," said Jay finally. "It's exciting."

Timing became an issue, and it affected the price. Parrino's man and Jack Moore's man didn't seem to be able to agree. On January 12, 1996, Moore–CI 324-15–told Parrino that "my buyer can't be there next week." He was just too busy, but what about the 24th? Jay was agreeable. Where, he asked?

"He is going to be at the Waldorf-Astoria . . . and that's where he would like to buy the coin."

Parrino was looking at his calendar: "Well, Let's, let's see. Tuesday."

"Isn't that a nice hotel?" Moore asked, "I've never been in it, so . . ."

"Oh," exclaimed Jay, "It's wonderful! Shit, yeah! The Waldorf is gorgeous!"

Moore then said out of the blue, almost tipping his hand, "Let's be realistic, and I'm talking to you on a completely clean line, so you know. You and I both know that it's illegal to own or possess this coin, right?"

Jay disagreed nebulously, said there was legislation in Congress to change its status, and changed the subject. There were certain things you just didn't talk about, especially on the phone.

He laughed it off and said to Jack Moore, "Just drop it."

But the informant, still looking for more ammunition–the tape was running–gaily skipped from one touchy subject to another: "And, and, ah, on, on, on the deal I was talking to you about, what I wanted?"

"Yeah."

"Ah, I've had second thoughts about that. Ah, I don't want it in that form."

"Oh," said Parrino. "You don't?"

"No."

"Okay."

"Because," said Jack Moore, "I'm not going to pay any taxes on what I do. So, so, I want cash. Is that a problem?"

Parrino chuckled: "Yeah. I don't have the cash. We'll work it out, you and I aren't going to have a problem."

But there *was* a new wrinkle. Five days later the two coin dealers spoke again. Now January 24 wasn't going to work, Parrino said, and added, "They want to do the deal in Switzerland."

This was the truth. All the changes of dates were wreaking havoc with Fenton's business schedule. He suggested the Swiss venue to Parrino not to avoid coming to the United States with the contraband coin but because he was scheduled to be there. Traditionally the Basel Coin Fair takes place in the last week of January, and 1996 was no exception. It was arguably the most important event on the Continental numismatic calendar, and Fenton had commitments. If Parrino wanted to buy the 1933 double eagle that week, it had to be in Basel.

Parrino and Jack Moore shuffled leadenly around this issue, about which Parrino did not elaborate. Both men were exasperated. At last a week was agreed on in February, the seventh, eighth, or ninth.

Parrino said that his man was getting nervous; all the changes were bothering him. Jay said that his man now physically had the coin and added, "I think he just wants it out of his hands."

Moore came back at Parrino and said that his guy was also "getting really apprehensive about changing as well." The charade could not last much longer without collapsing in on itself, and both the coin dealers, one big-time, one small-time, knew it.

It was January 21, 1996. They would work it out. But there would be no more taped record for Agent Freriks to follow. He had to rely solely on what Jack Moore told him, and he had already given Jack Moore a very long lead.

Moore was stretching that lead to the limit. On January 23, 1996, he was in Kansas City at Jay Parrino's The Mint. He was making a withdrawal. There were no wires, no tapes running. To all appearances, the Amarillo coin dealer was about to burst through the ethical door that Dave Freriks had accidentally left open about a month earlier.

According to Moore, he had gone to Kansas City at Parrino's suggestion so that they "could discuss the whole deal, and not over the phone." The two men discussed a variety of subjects, including Jay's theory "that he thought it might be the Farouk coin," and came to grips with many details. A date was agreed for the sale of the 1933 double eagle at the Waldorf-Astoria in New York: February 8. The price of the coin increased from $1.5 million to $1.65 million. The Texan said he was asked by Parrino to "write him an invoice for an 1876 Carson City twenty-cent piece, to which he said there was questionable title and," said Jack

Moore, "I did." But Moore had "never owned" such a coin, and The Mint later "advertised the coin for sale for $475,000."

Moore said that in return for writing out the invoice for "$50,000," he received "two checks for $25,000 each, $20,000 in cash, and I don't remember how many krugerrands there were total. It amounted to about $120,000."

Jack Moore left Kansas City with more money than he had ever made from coins in his life and promptly reported it to Agent Freriks. He showed him the checks, he laid out the twenty thousand dollars in cash, and the agent photographed "seventy-five to a hundred" krugerrands. Incredibly, and without substantiation, Moore also claimed to the Secret Service man that Parrino had asked him if he could "launder up to ten million dollars every three months," and that he had hidden "$25 to $35 million . . . in cash, gold, and gold coins." Moore explained to the agent in the motel room where they met that this windfall was all part of a different deal. Freriks must have wanted to believe him. Retirement couldn't come soon enough. He allowed Jack Moore to keep the money but "immediately informed the IRS," as well.

Jay Parrino thought that the payments were all part of the 1933 transaction. He later said that he had "agreed that The Mint would pay Moore part of his commission prior to the closing of the deal." He also claimed that he had "paid Moore more than $150,000, in the form of 165 Krugerrands . . . worth $66,000, two $25,000 checks, $34,000 cash, an antique gun collection, and various additional gold pieces and fractional gold." In exchange, Parrino claimed, Jack Moore left him a "$20 gold piece . . . worth approximately $125,000," as collateral against the advance he had just given Moore. To the contrary, Moore claimed he had left the coin (which he didn't own), "a proof 1907 twenty dollar gold piece," with Parrino "to sell."

On these points the two men would later disagree. At the time, though, regardless of its status—collateral or consignment—they had agreed that the 1907 twenty would be returned to Moore when the sale of the 1933 double eagle at the Waldorf was consummated.

The 1933 double eagle was now priced at $1.65 million, $150,000 more than it had been and exactly the same figure that Parrino claimed he paid Jack Moore.

One thing settled with certainty was that the sting was finally scheduled. The coin that the jeweler from Cairo, André de Clermont, Stephen Fenton, Jay Parrino, Jack Moore, and the Secret Service believed was King Farouk's was finally coming home to the United States.

CHAPTER 19

Put 'Em Up

———◆———

Wednesday, February 7, 1996.

Stephen Fenton was excited. Tomorrow he would sell the 1933 double eagle to Jay Parrino for $750,000. It was the biggest deal of his life, certainly the biggest profit. In anticipation of the trip, he had Jim Brown, his soft-spoken and able assistant for the last twenty-five years, get the paperwork in order.

Brown faxed the required information to the customs broker they had used regularly in the past: Larry Baker at Jet Air Service in New York. The specifics required to facilitate his boss's entry to the States later that day made for very dull reading and didn't require precision. Stephen Fenton would be would be importing "USA Coins—72 Gold—3 Silver—Total: £265,000.00 GB & Australian etc.—22 Gold—6 Silver—Total: £212,000.00." A total of 103 coins with a total declared value of £477,000.00 (approximately $734,000).

Jet Air then filled out the appropriate customs forms and attached a boilerplate letter of its own devising that it had used many times in the past. Its purpose was to fulfill a requirement that would exempt the United States coins from a merchandise processing fee, because they were returning to the country of their manufacture. "The imported items were legal tender U.S. Gold Coins minted by the United States Government between 1830 and 1932." The facts were egregiously misstated. Stephen Fenton was unaware of it at the time but he would later be plagued by endless headaches and heartaches as a result.

Fenton considered his sally to New York just one more business trip. The '33 sale looked good, but Fenton was a realist. There were no guarantees in life. He had witnessed more than one infallible deal evaporate faster than one of Chung Ling Soo's disappearing acts. Even if the '33 fell through, however, he still had the other coins, good coins, to sell while he was in the States.

Although a reluctant flier, Fenton was a regular customer of British Airways. His cherubic face and ingratiating manner made him well known and liked by the ground staff. Booked to fly to New York on BA 003—Concorde, the space-age wonder from the seventies—Fenton was treated with particular deference. He was about as collected as he could be just before any flight. Carrying nearly a million dollars of goods didn't faze him. It was something coin dealers did every day of the week. The 1933 double eagle was no different to him; now it was just merchandise. Normally abstemious, Fenton sat wedged into his seat and sipped champagne. He drank only on planes.

The flight to New York taken by Special Agent R. David Freriks and Confidential Informant Jack Moore on February 6 was not as posh, but the soft drinks were free.

A successful sting is theater. Before any play a run-through is essential, but the sting is a greater challenge. The supporting cast needs to play its roles to perfection so that the stars—Parrino and the unnamed, unknown courier—would carry on naturally and be caught unawares. Agent Freriks and Jack Moore, along with the entire Secret Service team, met at the New York field office to learn their parts.

It was a substantial operation. Two agents were needed to act the part of the buyer and his expert. The room would be wired and have video surveillance, which would need monitoring. Cars were needed to transport the suspects after the arrests were effected. Backup was essential should anything go wrong. Moore, the man in the middle, was getting more and more fidgety; he was, he said, "scared shitless." He reminded Freriks that he had to retrieve a coin from Parrino before the deal went down. He said it was a returned consignment that Parrino hadn't sold. Parrino considered it collateral.

Fenton checked into the Hilton on Sixth Avenue between Fifty-second and Fifty-third streets and met up with his cousin, who had flown over on another flight and who would accompany him the next day. It might be a regular coin sale, but it was for a vast amount of money, and the vulpine dealer knew it didn't pay to be too trusting. Fenton rang Parrino and confirmed the next morning's rendezvous. They would meet in the lobby of the Waldorf-Astoria. Steve and his cousin had an early dinner and turned in. Fenton slept soundly.

Thursday. February 8, 1996. New York City.

When Fenton awakened early, his body clock still on Greenwich Mean Time, he lay in bed for a while and stared emptily at the ceiling.

Special Agent Dave Freriks, Jack Moore, and the rest of the Secret Service team were also up early but didn't have that luxury. They headed over to the Waldorf-Astoria to set the stage and organize the props for the melodrama to be played out in a few hours. About a dozen agents would be at the ready. The technical crew got the room wired, set the video camera in position, carefully showed Jack Moore where it was, and specifically instructed him not to stand in front of it. Business as usual for the Secret Service, but everyone was keyed up.

Fenton slipped on a pair of dark trousers, tucked his Jermyn Street shirt into his waistband, and pulled a black cashmere V-neck sweater over his head. Suits were fine in London, but America was more casual, and he didn't want to stand out while carrying his special cargo. Anonymity was the best security.

He sat and waited a bit. His mouth was slightly dry. He looked around the stark furnishings of the room. He was a little nervous, excited. The size of the transaction gave him slight pause, especially since he was dealing with people he had never met before. His cousin would come along; it was just prudent.

Fenton donned his long charcoal-gray overcoat and went to meet his cousin in the yawning mall the Hilton calls a lobby. Lines of businessmen waited dutifully to check out. Others waited under the grotto-like portico as a steady stream of cabs squealed through, disgorging and engorging passengers simultaneously. Fenton and his cousin caught a taxi quickly for the short ride across town. For all the time he had spent in New York on business, he was unsure where the Waldorf-Astoria was. The 1933 double eagle was sitting safely in a small plastic envelope in one of his pockets.

It was a bright, chilly morning. The sun was low in the east and poured directly into the cab, illuminating it with a hard pale yellow light. Fenton went over the deal again and again. Consciously he wasn't worried, but deep inside he knew there were unanswered questions about the coin. He was doing nothing wrong, he was convinced of it. In truth, no one in the coin business really knew why the '33 was illegal—most thought it was just unissued—and the government had *never* made it clear that it considered this coin stolen property. But the fiery little disc in his pocket had touched the lives of many men, and few had smiled afterward.

Put 'Em Up

Jack Moore was waiting, anxious and scared. It would soon be over. The call would come, the game would be played, and he would walk away a richer man. He already had his piece of the action—$120,000 or $150,000, depending on whose story you believed—and the Secret Service would pay him even more. Greed had put the deal together. Jack Moore would finally get the better of Jay Parrino.

Parrino had dealt in bigger numbers before. He had bought multi-million-dollar collections without batting an eye. At one time or another he reckoned he had handled an example of just about every American coin ever made—but never a 1933 double eagle. He was, as usual, casually dressed. He was staring in the window of the Spy Shop tucked away in the lobby of the Waldorf. He looked at mini-cameras, recording devices, and special briefcases—it was astonishing. He knew 1933 double eagles were contraband but didn't know why—exactly. He had told Moore that there was legislation in Washington, D.C., to make them legal, but he didn't know if there was or wasn't. If he was nervous, it didn't show. It was just business for Parrino.

Fenton's cab pulled up shortly before 9 A.M. in front of the Waldorf-Astoria on Park Avenue between Forty-ninth and Fiftieth streets. The usual crowd hustled and bustled along the avenue. Businessmen and secretaries took quick strides on their way to work, some bundled up against the cold, hunched. Others toughed it out, wearing just their suits, smoking cigarettes as if the glowing red embers would keep them warm. A group of tourists jockeyed with some out-of-town executives in the scrum of a taxi line.

The western facade of the Waldorf stretched skyward and was bathed in deep shadow. An Art Deco palace, all gray stone and geometric angularity, it seemed ominous, looming. Fenton saw the vapor of his breath evaporate under the red heat lamps that lined the underside of the canopy.

The big dealer and his smaller cousin pushed their way through the brushed-steel revolving doors. The Waldorf-Astoria had played home to Herbert Hoover and Colonel James W. Flanagan; James Macallister had kept rooms there, and Abe Kosoff's office had been just down the block. It was serendipitous that the '33 saga would continue in these familiar precincts.

The two Englishmen looked up the short flight of stairs and into the splendid atrium that had been successfully designed to impress. The space was a step back in time. A great tiered chandelier sparkled above a tessellated floor. Four nine-feet-tall inverted bullet-shaped torchères directed light at the ceiling. Extraordinary ironwork—gates and balustrades with simple, clean lines—was visible everywhere. White ties and tails, silk-satin gowns cut on a bias, and the soft click of leather heels would have been more appropriate than the hip-hop dungarees and squeak of tourists' sneakers on the mosaic floors.

Off to one side, in a comfortable chair, sat Jay Parrino. Although they had barely met, the two coin dealers recognized each other instantly. They sat together briefly and chatted. None of the three men had been to the Waldorf before. Together they wandered off in search of the house phone, admiring the palatial public rooms, hushed businesslike splendor, and cascading floral displays. Parrino found the phone and called Jack Moore's room. The informant invited the three men upstairs.

While Parrino, Fenton, and his cousin waited for the elevator, the Secret Service got the tapes running and Moore readied himself.

When the men arrived at Suite 22K2, Parrino knocked.

"Hello, Jack," said Parrino easily as Jack Moore opened the door.

"Jay." He smiled. Moore, outwardly calm and glib; turned his attention to the two Englishmen.

"Hello. Nice to meet ya. How are you guys?"

"Fine," they answered in monosyllabic unison. As he entered, Fenton quickly cast his eyes about the sitting room of the suite. Chairs, sofas, a low table, a few desk lamps made up a pretty ordinary room, and Fenton was not overly impressed. They took their coats off with a minimum of small talk.

Fenton's dark eyes took in the new man, whose full name had not been mentioned. Moore looked about sixty, short and jowly, with shrewd, suspicious little eyes. He was wearing a nondescript shirt, cowboy boots, pressed jeans, a large Western belt buckle. He seemed calm.

"How are you doing?" Moore asked Parrino.

He replied distractedly. "Hangin' in there."

Moore, wearing a gaudy gold ring and a heavy watch, quickly got down to brass tacks. Like a drug dealer, he produced a small electronic scale and said quickly, "Well, I have a little deal here, I thought it might help me. Those are the scales . . . and the real one weighs 33.4."

Fenton had been prepared for this. He took another common double eagle, not the 1933, out of his pocket and slipped it out of its plastic envelope to weigh for comparison; Moore had one as well. Fenton didn't sit down and never took his eyes off the scales.

Moore kept prattling on about his scales. "I got it at one of those Las Vegas shows, and it fluctuates between—" He was interrupted by a sharp clatter. "Did you lay that down on there pretty hard?" he questioned Parrino.

"Yeah," came the sheepish reply. "I kind of dropped it."

"Ah. Turn it off and turn it on again. It should weigh 33.3 or 33.4. So. . . ."

Parrino watched the liquid display numbers bounce around like a slot machine's cylinders until they came to rest. He joked, "Damn, it's real. Well, we're one for one, that's good."

Fenton watched and asked Parrino, "Do you do the authenticating?"

Moore interrupted. "Can we weigh the other one?"

"I suppose we can," said Jay.

"Yeah," said Stephen Fenton. "Well sure, let me get the thing out of here." He had the 1933 double eagle in his hand. It was in a plastic envelope sealed with a single staple. He took out a small penknife and gingerly pried off the folded piece of steel wire.

Moore couldn't contain himself. "I just want to look at it, and then I'm going to call."

"I'm kind of anxious to see it myself," mused Parrino.

"Oh, you haven't seen it?" Moore was surprised.

"No."

Fenton carefully handed Parrino the 1933 double eagle, never taking his eyes off it.

Moore kept his antsy monologue going, but Parrino said little. Fenton said less and his cousin said nothing. Moore was showing off for the audience in the room and for the unseen audience next door that only he knew was there. "I want to look at it with a 20 power . . . I mean the only thing I'd know to look for would be tooling around the date."

Parrino's eyes shone. His heart beat a little faster. He couldn't truly believe what he was holding. "Well," he said with admirable self-control, "this sure is a pleasure . . . I thought I'd handled everything." His eyes took it all in. The mystic date, the forbidden coin. He had one in his hands.

Moore kept talking aimlessly in the background. Parrino automatically answered questions but paid little attention to what was being said. The comfortably heavy piece of gold in his hand had his full attention. Fenton and his cousin barely blinked.

At Moore's insistence, Parrino weighed the coin.

Moore watched the scale: "33.4." He was relieved. He was laughing, giddy: "Now, can I look at it out of that?" It was back in its plastic envelope.

Fenton politely said, "Yeah."

"As long as I just touch the edge." Moore was talking as he looked at the coin with his jeweler's loupe. No one was much listening, but everyone was watching. Moore took in the details of Liberty magnified twenty times, the details of the design sharply delineated, the insignificant imperfections, including a blow to her nose, grotesquely enlarged, the date—the all-important date—filling the field of his eyepiece. Liberty unbound, rushing from the small confines of her gilded frame, the eagle soaring weightlessly: captivating, unsullied by time, and still on the run from the law.

Fenton chatted with Parrino. The two dealers cordially agreed that after handling hundreds of thousands of double eagles during the course of their careers, the 1933 was simply amazing.

Moore interrupted to ask Fenton if he could get him a chair. Now Argus-eyed behind his thick lenses, the English dealer preferred standing. Moore circled round and stood directly in front of the video camera and started talking about the coin he wanted back from Parrino. "I want you to leave that," he said. "I want you to lay that out."

Parrino began to examine the 1933 double eagle again. His eyes glittered with renewed excitement as he finally said to Moore, "You can make your call, I'm just soaking this in."

Turning to Fenton, he said there were "only four [American] coins I've never handled and this is one of them. . . . It's much nicer than I thought."

Moore punched a few buttons on the telephone, "You all just might as well come up," he drawled in an offhand manner. "It's here, and it's real."

They waited and made small talk. Fenton was less tense. It felt like a regular coin deal. Moore got the coin he didn't own back from Parrino and was also more relaxed.

The three started talking about the 1933 double eagle and endless possibilities. They were all abundantly clear about the coin's shadowy legal standing.

"Let me ask you this," the ex-trucker said, setting up Parrino. "Can't we do the deal that you were talking about? Make it legal? We, or he, will pay the fifty grand."

Fenton was confused. Parrino explained. "Well, it's a very interesting thing. What would you feel would happen to the value of this? If it was legalized? I have someone who could do this for fifty thousand dollars. He could do this or he gets nothing and he is the best. He knows all about the coin."

"Double," said Fenton instantly.

"Double the value?" jumped in Moore.

"Oh yes!" Fenton smiled. "I don't think there are really very many out there."

"How many do you think are out there, Jay, besides the two in the Smithsonian?"

"There is one, believe it or not, in New Jersey. Right in Jersey. . . . I haven't seen it, but a good friend of mine has . . . and it's identifiable . . . three little triangle hits right there at the top of the wing. . . . Other than that one, everything else I have ever heard is just rumor."

Moore blurted, "Oh, excuse me, I'm so excited I can't stand it!"

"You should be," said Jay. "What a coin!"

Fenton, at Moore's suggestion, put the 1933 double eagle back in its envelope. They waited and made uneasy banter, small talk. Parrino shared with them his woes about being audited by the IRS for the past "three and a half years" and they "can't find anything."

As Moore asked Parrino about a package he was supposed to have sent, the Secret Service agents in the next room were distracted. "We thought we observed a gun on one of the persons in the room and we were discussing procedure."

Then came a knock at the door.

Moore answered. The two undercover agents had arrived. One of them surreptitiously slipped the deadbolt so the door didn't lock shut.

The shorter of the two said, "Hi, how ya doing?"

Moore introduced him to Fenton. "This is Rock."

"Pleasure," said the Englishman, warily eyeing the newcomers.

The other man, posing as the buyer, was tall and well dressed. He also smelled heavily of cologne. He was abrupt. "We won't be here too long, right?"

Parrino said, "No."

Rock, the "expert," said, "I hope we're not."

Moore was the master of ceremonies. Now in the spotlight, he told the Secret Service expert to weigh the coin. "Feel free. Go ahead. Because you might never in your entire life get a chance to handle one of these. Not many people get to see one."

"That's for sure," Parrino chimed in.

Fenton said nothing. He was vigilant.

The "expert" said, "That the '33 there?"

"It's authentic. Right," said Moore hurriedly.

The "expert" undercover man picked up the coin and examined it with care, not really knowing what he was looking at. His hands shook.

Fenton was instantly alarmed. Something was wrong, he thought. When a man is getting ready to steal a coin, his hands always shake. Fenton was suddenly very alert, on tenterhooks.

"Very nice, very nice," muttered the expert.

Moore was willing the charade to an end. "Well, there is no sense in keeping you any longer. I know you got things to do."

The tall man who smelled of cologne looked at his expert. "You happy with it?"

"I'm happy with it," Rock said.

"We can wire the money," said Moore the informant.

The two undercover agents discussed among themselves what to do next. Fenton's heart was racing. His dark brown eyes never for an instant departed from the 1933 double eagle.

Rock said, "Hey, boss, I don't know if I should be privy to your deal."

"As long as you're convinced," was the terse reply.

"I'm happy," he said. As he was leaving, he said over his shoulder, "Good luck, Jack, see you again."

Fenton felt a sudden calm come over him. He was just starting to exhale. He thought it had all been very strange. Unreal.

Suddenly the door burst open. In rushed men and women with drawn guns.

"Shit!" thought Fenton, "I'm going to be robbed."

The armed intruders, their guns held stiffly out in front of them, started shouting, "Police! Put 'em up! Secret Service! Secret Service!"

Fenton was relieved he wasn't going to be shot. Then his head started to spin. The color drained from his face. It became an out-of-body experience. Fenton was watching it happen to himself.

Moore and the undercover buyer were hustled out of the room. The agents were all wearing dark raid jackets with the words SECRET SERVICE stenciled on them.

The 1933 double eagle disappeared. Fenton had no idea how or where it went. He thought about it but didn't really care. His heart was pounding heavily. His throat was tight, his mouth chalky, breathing rapid. He saw a female agent sitting on the floor, laughing. Felliniesque. He turned to ask his cousin if he was all right and was told harshly to "shut up." He started to think he had been set up. He had no idea by whom. It was all a terrible muddle.

Stephen Charles Fenton, proprietor of Knightsbridge Coins, St. James, London, chairman of the British Numismatic Trade Association, had his arms pulled behind his back and he was handcuffed. The agents draped his coat over his shoulders so that no one would see the steel bracelets. He was led out the door with his cousin and Jay Parrino. To the right, down a long hall, and to the service elevator. Nobody spoke to him.

The elevator opened onto an underground parking area, lit from overhead by strips of harsh, shadowless, fluorescent lights. There was the smell of oil and a gauzy-blue pall of exhaust in the air. The squeal of tires echoed in the distance. Fenton was led out through one of the two open bays and across Forty-ninth Street between Park and Lexington avenues. Dark cars were idling across the street near a battery of four drab green Post Office holding boxes. The female agent opened the door for Fenton and kept his head from hitting the frame.

The cars pulled out and headed west. They turned left on Park Avenue, around and through Grand Central Station, and into the Fourth Avenue tunnel. Fenton was alone with his thoughts. He was terrified. Time collapsed, and suddenly the car pulled into a garage, a security entrance. He was at the New York field office of the Secret Service, 7 World Trade Center, and under arrest.

CHAPTER 20

In Rem

◆

THE SHADE OF HARRY STRANG MUST HAVE SMILED; THE GOLDEN SPOOR had not gone cold. After fifty years, another 1933 double eagle—the evidence indicated Farouk's—had, after casting its cruel spell on a new generation, been brought to ground and seized by the Secret Service. It would be incarcerated for safekeeping in the agency's New York vault in the World Trade Center.

Thursday, February 8, 1996. New York City.

At the Secret Service offices, Fenton was read his Miranda rights, which he waived. It was 11:29 A.M. He was hungry, thirsty and very confused. He would have said anything to stay out of jail. It was his greatest fear. The tale of the coin's purchase he swore to in his statement was eerily similar to that spun for the Secret Service by Israel Switt a half century earlier:

> Anywhere from (5) five to (10) years ago, to the best of my recollection, I purchased a miscellaneous group of gold coins, which could have included hundreds of foreign and British coins. This purchase was made from an individual seller at my store in London. This was a routine transaction, one of possibly dozens made monthly. It was not until after the purchase, upon reviewing the lot of coins that I realized I had a 1933 $20 Gold Coin which I knew to be a better date, an unusual date.

Fenton's account changed from myth to reality as he continued with a reasonably forthright, condensed version of the overture to the transaction and the sting itself. He concluded with his version of the golden troublemaker's legal status:

> As far as I knew, ownership of this coin, 1933 $20 Gold Coin, was no problem in England. But I was not sure of the ownership restrictions in the United States. I never inquired with anybody about any restrictions, if any. Mr. Parrino never offered me any information about the problems of ownership in the United States.

Elsewhere in the building, Jay Parrino was undergoing a similar ordeal. His statement was much more basic. In raw outline he explained his involvement with Jack Moore, Marc Emory, and Stephen Fenton. Parrino concluded with his own self-serving, if confused—but not, at the time, inaccurate—interpretation of the 1933 double eagle's legal status:

> I know of the controversy with the coin but really don't know the particulars. I have never seen one before except in photographs. There was a rumor a few years ago about another one but it was never confirmed. I did not know this was government property just that it was not legal to own, once again, I never knew why.

Stephen Fenton was now recognized by the Secret Service as no mere courier but the owner of the fugitive gold coin. He was escorted, wide-eyed, from the interrogation room to another one, different but the same. There he was closely questioned about his income, wealth, and general business affairs. At last he was introduced to a federal defender: John Byrnes.

Byrnes sat and spoke to Fenton at some length. He explained that the charges were "quite serious," not civil but criminal, and told Fenton that he was not pleased that the coin dealer had already made a statement to the authorities. Steve shook his head in dismay. He tried to explain with contained desperation that he would do or say, virtually anything to be released. He was terrified of being sent to jail. His voice shook, as did his hands. He was a wreck.

Fenton made his preliminary appearance before a judge. The charges were read: He was accused of knowingly attempting to sell stolen United States Government property, a "1933 'Double Eagle' gold coin," for the price of $1.5 million. Fenton was stunned. It was the first time he had ever heard the figure—twice the price he had said he wanted and had negotiated. The government requested that he be held in custody until a bail hearing in a few days' time. Fenton shivered uncontrollably within and started to perspire anew, but Byrnes successfully argued that Fenton was no threat and if the government seized his passport there was nowhere for him to run. It was agreed, and Fenton was flooded with relief. John Byrnes gave the coin dealer a slip of paper with a list of names of criminal defense lawyers. One of them would be Fenton's savior.

Two Secret Service agents, now cordial and cheerful, drove him back to the Hilton, accompanied him to his room and waited in the hall outside while Fenton emptied out his room safe. When he opened the room door, both agents automatically reached for their guns but didn't draw them—just another unsettling moment in a miserably disquieting day. Fenton surrendered his passport, airline ticket, credit cards, and the key to the safe-deposit box that held the other coins he had brought with him. It was 7 P.M.

He had twenty dollars in cash and a piece of paper: Secret Service form SSF 1590. It was a "Receipt for Contraband," made out in his name for "1 One US $20 Gold Coin, 1933." It was a far cry from the $750,000 he had been asking, the $1.5 million Jay Parrino had been firm about, and the $1.65 million Jack Moore had settled on.

The next morning, after a tortured, sleepless night, Fenton made telephone calls to the attorneys on the list that public defender Byrnes had given him. Fenton auditioned each by the sound of his voice, the initial response to his quandary, and the level of sympathy to his plight. One attorney appealed to him instantly, viscerally—Barry Berke.

That afternoon in the looming black glass menhir on Third Avenue that housed the law offices of Kramer Levin Naftalis & Frankel, Fenton was still disoriented, out of focus, but growing angry. As the chairman of the British Numismatic Trade Association he was not only sensitive about his reputation being sullied by the criminal charges hanging over him but worried that he might miss a meeting of the group in London the following week.

Barry Berke was thirty-two years old, a Harvard Law School graduate, very tall, dark-haired, and bore an uncanny facial similarity to a younger, thinner Vice President Al Gore. He had an easy but tight smile, and his eyes, protected by rectangular wire-rimmed glasses, were naturally bright and humorous but could go black and menacing. A white-collar criminal defense lawyer, he had use for the hard stare.

Stephen Fenton got the friendly look and a warm handshake. The litigator questioned Fenton closely and after two hours expressed his opinion that the charges were outrageous. Fenton liked his straight talking and instantly knew he was in good hands.

Berke stood next to Fenton during his arraignment before a United States magistrate judge for the Southern District of New York on Monday, February 12, 1996. Fenton discovered that, according to the United States of America, he, with Jasper Parrino, "unlawfully, willfully, and knowingly would and did embezzle, steal and purloin . . . and negotiate[d] the sale of a 1933 'Double Eagle' gold coin." If convicted, Fenton could face five years in prison and fines of horrendous proportion. Parrino was released on a personal recognizance bond of $500,000; Fenton got off more lightly at a mere $250,000 but had to produce $50,000 to secure the bond. Berke arranged to have Fenton remove four coins from his safe-deposit box, which the Englishman took to Eric Streiner. The New York dealer retained the coins and guaranteed to the government their aggregate value of $80,000. If Fenton scarpered, Streiner reckoned, he was on the hook.

The Secret Service trumpeted the capture of the quarry that had been beyond their long arm for sixty years in a press release that noted their belief that the coin was Farouk's. The story of the sting and the mystery of the 1933 double eagle proved irresistible to the nation's press. Fenton cringed and Parrino was stoic as their names were now popping up in *USA Today*, the *Washington Post, New York Post, New York Daily News,* and *Kansas City Star* as alleged felons.

Stephen Fenton arrived back in London a weary man. As required under the terms of his release, he dutifully surrendered his passport to the United States embassy in Grosvenor Square, at the center of which a statue of Franklin Roosevelt, enfolded in his great cloak, stood sentinel.

On March 4, 1996, a report from the Forensic Services Division of the Secret Service in Washington, D.C. stated that after a side-by-side comparison of the 1933 double eagle seized from Stephen Fenton with the two in the Smithsonian Institution, the coin was, in its opinion, genuine. Three days later, Dr. George E. Hunter of the United States Mint confirmed this finding. The coin was returned to its Secret Service vault in the World Trade Center.

In New York, Barry Berke dived headlong into the inky waters that swirled around the 1933 double eagle. In this he was initially joined by Jay Parrino's attorney, Alan Mansfield, of Greenberg Traurig, and briefly by another lawyer for Parrino, David Krassner. Freedom of Information Act requests were fired off to the United States Mint looking for any scraps of paper that might aid the defense. The responses were pro forma and suggested that the attorneys might do better to investigate the National Archives themselves.

274

Berke's and Mansfield's first onerous task was to convince the government to drop the criminal charges. These implied that Fenton and Parrino had negotiated the sale of the 1933 double eagle with full knowledge that the coin had been stolen from the United States Mint more than a half-century earlier. This was the critical information that the government had never readily disseminated to the public, despite F. C. C. Boyd's suggestion in 1945 that it should do so.

Berke and Mansfield felt that the United States Attorney's Office knew there was no basis for the criminal charges. They leaned hard and in April, 1996, their advocacy prevailed. The criminal charges were dropped.

A civil forfeiture case against the coin was filed by the government in its stead. Forfeiture laws are a muddle. Arcane, they drift back to principles of English common law and admiralty and maritime law. Participants can lay claim to and battle over property that has been seized pending a resolution.

Called an "In Rem" action, a proceeding against a thing, the defendant standing in the dock was now the 1933 double eagle itself. The United States had possession and wanted to keep it. With the criminal consequences having evaporated, or nearly so, Stephen Fenton and Jay Parrino could have scuttled into a corner, licked their wounds, and chalked it up to experience. Neither did—at first.

Fenton, known in the coin trade for his determined, almost bulldog persistence, filed his claim. He kept up the battle because of Berke's sage advice, his own principles, and the $220,000 that was still outstanding. Parrino initially filed his own claim but soon realized the weakness of his position and withdrew. He refused to discuss his involvement with the double eagle again. But that didn't mean he was going away quietly.

On October 20, 1998, Jay Parrino filed suit against Jack Moore, wanting redress for "the advance commission of more than $150,000" he claimed the Amarillo trucker had demanded and that he had paid him for brokering the sale of the 1933 double eagle. Parrino charged that Jack Moore had fraudulently negotiated the "sales commission" when he "knew that the sale was not going to take place."

Moore, who had been paid seventy-five hundred dollars by the United States Secret Service for his involvement and specifically told not to transact any related business with Jay, denied Parrino's allegations. His attorney's response to Parrino's claims cloaked Moore in immunity as having been employed by the Secret Service at the time.

The case never went to trial. On May 5, 2000, the two sides settled. Moore agreed to pay Parrino $140,000. His attempt to play both sides from the middle had failed miserably. And other shenanigans caught up with him as well. Only a year earlier, Jack Moore's old employer, John Groendyke, discovered that Moore, who had shared his love for coins, and whom he had trusted implicitly, had without his knowledge sold his collection of Saints and kept the money. Groendyke sued, and again the ex-trucker from Amarillo was ordered to pay: $1.2 million.

Three, four, five years melted away. Trees were felled and sheets of paper filled with facts, assumptions, arguments, and history grew in their place. Briefs and motions were filed. Berke pushed. The government pushed back. Neither would yield. One judge led to another. Depositions were taken from all and sundry: Dave Freriks, Jack Moore, various Secret Service agents, present and past Mint employees. Parrino refused to relive his role on the record without a promise of immunity. It was not proffered, and he did not talk.

Berke offered suggestions for settlement on a regular basis, almost as a way of making small talk. He offered to have the government buy out Fenton; he offered to have Fenton buy out the government—both suggestions were refused. Berke offered a "Solomonic settlement" to sell the coin and share in the proceeds. A derisory response greeted the proposal.

Four government lawyers dropped by the wayside, and Assistant United States Attorney Jane Levine stepped into the case. Tiny as Berke was tall, Levine was a matter-of-fact New Yorker and sounded like one, mixing an earnest toughness with a dry sense of humor and unwavering focus. With unruly masses of dark Verona-brown ringlets, a small freckled nose, and penetrating dark brown eyes under luxuriant dark brown eyebrows, the New York University law school graduate was a perfect foil for Berke.

Levine had a tougher row to hoe than Berke, who had the entire numismatic industry on his side. Frothing in print and fulminating in private over the excessive zeal of the United States Government's "Gestapo tactics" in tracking down the coin, they lined up to offer their expertise on Fenton's behalf. For many it was seen as a crusade for many other coins of exceptional value and checkered pasts: the 1804 silver dollar, the 1913 Liberty Head nickel, 1885 trade dollar, and thousands of patterns the legitimacy of whose creation has never been fully explained. They felt that if the 1933 double eagle fell to the Feds, then these clandestinely produced coins also could be swept into the government's yawning maw.

They posited and fumed that the Gold Reserve Act of 1934 had been rewritten in 1954 and 1965 and that the ban against owning a 1933 double eagle had been effectively abrogated. Their arguments did not take into account the government's contention that since 1944, the 1933 double eagle had been considered stolen property, gold that had been stolen from the United States Mint and pursued by the Secret Service from the day its loss had been discovered. Despite theories to the contrary, not a shred of unassailable evidence could be produced to prove a single 1933 double eagle had ever legally left government control. This includes the coin that was given an export license before it was discovered that none had been officially issued by the mint.

Jane Levine was a specialist in forfeiture cases and had been a history major in college. Beguiled by the 1933s, Levine looked at the origins of the case from the point of view of those who had lived it and in the process gained enormous respect for the Secret Service's responsibilities. To her, the relentless hunt for the 1933 double eagles had been about security at the Mint, which was not a place from which the country wants to bleed gold.

The Secret Service reports filed by Harry Strang a half-century earlier were a mine of information, and surprisingly much of the contemporary paperwork was intact, spared the wholesale destruction that befell the Mint's archives during the Carter administration, when it was decided that saving space was preferable to saving historical records. But recreating history, arguing on its merits, and proving its accuracy in court was a tall order, especially when all the alleged miscreants and dogged investigators were dead. Two participants, however, very much alive, had not yet been deposed: Stephen Fenton and André de Clermont.

On August 3 and 4, 1999, Fenton was deposed in a two-day baptism by fire. Because he did not have a full waiver of immunity from the federal government for the criminal charges that had been dropped (but could be reinvoked) he spent a great deal of time protecting his right against self-incrimination.

Feisty Jane Levine flicked questions at the thin-lipped Englishman, which Fenton parried with his claim of constitutional rights. She asked a question more than once in different formulas and occasionally got a full answer. She attempted to draw from him his version of the transaction with de Clermont, what he knew about the coin's origin, its legal status, and how the Jet Air Customs papers had not only misstated what he was carrying but understated the value as well. Fenton answered warily, looking for traps, giving little.

Four months later André de Clermont had his turn at the United States embassy in London. De Clermont, too was guarded, but his man-

In Rem

ner was easy. The story that Levine extracted from de Clermont was similar but not identical to Fenton's. The jeweler from Cairo was *his* client and had provided the chain of ownership. Both Levine and Berke agreed that the identity of the Cairo jeweler would be kept confidential, as de Clermont said he wanted to protect his own future business with him.

In answer to Levine's questioning, de Clermont attempted to reconstruct the lots that he and Fenton claimed had come from the Farouk sale. She queried him about his copy of the Farouk catalogue that he believed had been David Spink's own saleroom copy but whose code, he said, he was unable to read. She quizzed him on the fee sharing and what he expected to make from the sale of the 1933 double eagle and drew and twisted him on his familiarity with the coin's notoriety. Finally she pinned him on the fact that for all the minute financial detail between Fenton and de Clermont concerning all the other Farouk purchases, there was nothing comparable in de Clermont's files for one purchase only—the 1933 double eagle.

As the case grumbled inexorably toward trial, Berke relied heavily on the Farouk provenance. He had discovered information that had been lost—unknown—for fifty years: that the Egyptian Legation had been provided an export license for the coin. He also emphasized, but less strenuously, the numismatists' old chestnut: the revocation of relevant aspects of the Gold Reserve Act of 1934. His arguments make for compelling reading, as do Jane Levine's opposition. She told Special Agent Strang's clear and concise tale of the investigation and picked away at the claims of the Farouk provenance, rendering them down to a slurry of hearsay. She disputed the argument that the issuance of the export license metamorphosed stolen property into legal property and interpreted the misstatements on the customs forms that had been prepared by Larry Baker of Jet Air as calculated. The recorded telephone calls between Parrino and Moore appeared to be proof positive that Fenton had intentionally smuggled the 1933 double eagle into the country by falsifying documents, despite Baker's testimony that Jet Air had been using the same forms—wrong as they were—for ages, not only for Fenton, but for other clients as well.

Berke consulted with Egyptian legal scholars on the finer points of Egyptian laws concerning stolen property. Unlike United States law, which precludes good title to stolen property essentially in perpetuity, Egyptian law is based on the thieves' market principle wherein, after a given amount of time, even stolen property is washed clean, and good title may pass.

As the year 2000 wound to a close, after nearly five years of delays, discovery, and depositions, the trial loomed large on the horizon. Both sides were convinced they would win, and both sides realized they could lose, but both were hamstrung by any number of dangling legal issues: how much of the case would be decided by the judge, how much by the jury; and which documents prepared by long-dead Secret Service agents and Mint employees would be allowed into evidence. The judge had been pushing the two sides to settle.

Barry Berke and Jane Levine spoke on an increasingly regular basis, jockeying and playing one-upmanship. During one of these conversations, almost as an aside, Barry Berke said to Jane Levine—or the prosecutor said to the defender—"I can't believe we're not settling." It got them talking earnestly.

The proposal was revived that the government and Fenton split revenues from a sale fifty-fifty. Jane Levine offered to try to sell the idea, which made the rounds at Justice and then headed to the Mint—it was, after all, its coin. But no one in the government wanted to take a firm stand. The law-enforcement side was vehemently against the idea and livid at the prospect that Fenton would profit. When the then director of the Mint was told that it was not an airtight case, however, he decided to settle.

The terms of the settlement were singular. Neither side would keep the coin. It would be sold and the two sides would share the proceeds evenly. Each agreed to one of the other's nonnegotiable points: Fenton ceded title of the coin to the United States Mint, and the Mint agreed that Fenton would have an equal say in the decision-making process that would lead to the coin's sale.

Jane Levine added a warning to the document: "This settlement shall not be deemed to have any precedential significance or affect legal or otherwise, on any other coin of the United States, including any other 1933 double eagle that may exist."

If another '33 appeared, it would be seized. The government's position was crystalline.

The parties signed the document on January 25, 2001. The case was over.

While both Barry Berke and Jane Levine were naturally pleased with the outcome on one level, they were both litigators—gladiators at heart—and frustrated that the case had not gone to court. Berke thought it would have been a corker of a trial and still believes that King Farouk and the export license would have convinced a jury of the coin's legitimacy. Jane Levine also yearned for the cut and parry that would have played out before a judge and jury. She too believes it would have been a killer case, and one in which she would have prevailed.

FDR (with Frank Wilson's Secret Service) after inspecting Fort Knox, April 28, 1943. The coin seized from Stephen Fenton in 1996 was brought to Fort Knox from the World Trade Center for safekeeping only months before September 11. (Franklin Delano Roosevelt Presidential Library)

Almost immediately, days after the settlement, the 1933 double eagle was removed from its holding vault in the Secret Service office at the World Trade Center—only eight months prior to the September 11 attacks that destroyed the buildings. It was first taken to Washington, D.C., where high-resolution scans were done on the coin for identifying purposes. Then it was taken to Fort Knox for safekeeping by the Chief of Mint Police, Dr. William Daddio. There, near the other 445,000 1933 double eagles that had been melted down into bricks in 1937, it sat in America's squat Kentucky safe-deposit box waiting for its future owner.

CHAPTER 21

Auction
and Absolute
Anonymity

———◆———

April, 2001. New York City.

A letter had wandered around Sotheby's for a few days without finding itself a home. Addressed to no one specific, sent from the United States Department of the Treasury, it had been mistakenly directed to the office of Sotheby's treasurer by its mailroom.

Around the country similar envelopes were being opened by coin dealers and auctioneers: Heritage Coins in Dallas, Texas, received one, as did Bowers and Merena Galleries in Wolfeboro, New Hampshire. Others elsewhere were among the chosen few being considered to sell the biggest prize of all: the 1933 double eagle. The scrum would be all out.

The Request for Proposal—a formal letter from the government soliciting competitive bids for the sale of the 1933 double eagle—finally found the desk of Sotheby's Vice Chairman for North and South America, David Redden, on Monday, April 16, 2001. He scanned the letter in his second-floor corner office.

Redden's soft, silvery hair and hooded hazel eyes gave a calm impression, but those who worked with him knew otherwise. Like Subrahmanya, the Hindu god with six faces and twelve arms, Redden and his activities were all a simultaneous blur. He was a visionary and enthusiast, in perpetual motion and seldom on time for any appointment.

After more than twenty-five years at Sotheby's, Redden had conceived and brought to fruition a number of sales that had utterly riveted the attention of the American and world's press and public. These were not sales of mere multimillion-dollar Picassos or van Goghs but events that sizzled and popped with general interest. Redden had spent years negotiating with Russian authorities and succeeded in securing great artifacts from the nascent days of the space race. He had sold not only a piece of the moon—proving Redden's theory that "true collecting is not about the actual possession of objects" but a conceptual thing—but a machine *on* the moon (delivery was the responsibility of the purchaser). A hunter of the fabulous, clad in a gray suit and black-tasseled loafers even while in the Dakota Badlands, Redden presented himself to a Native American in blue jeans and a bolo tie and came away with a national treasure: "Sue," the biggest and best *Tyrannosaurus rex* ever discovered. Its sale to Chicago's Field Museum was international front-page news, and the $8.4 million skeleton subsequently became Chicago's unofficial mascot. Capturing imaginations was what David Redden did best.

Redden's eyes scanned the page quickly. He was not a coin expert, and the timing was awkward. The coin department, Sotheby's second oldest, was being closed after 246 years in an effort to tighten the corporate belt. New York's was already shuttered, and London's had one sale left. It had been one of the departments in Redden's division, and all he had left was a long-tenured and beleaguered consultant who habitually wore red socks. Redden put in a call to him and faxed the letter. By the time the two men had finished talking, Redden's eyes were aglitter. Sotheby's simply had to have the 1933 double eagle.

Redden next put in a call to Stack's. Harvey Stack, a big, gregarious man with a small gray mustache who carried his seventy-plus years lightly, and his son, Larry, a bearlike man with a bushy brown beard, were the second and third generations of the firm whose auction of Colonel Flanagan's collection a half-century earlier had started the merry-go-round. Sotheby's and Stack's were already preparing a proposal together on another extraordinary coin collection, and so a similar arrangement was instantly agreed upon for the 1933 double eagle. They were the only two firms ever to have offered a 1933 double eagle at auction (and to have had them withdrawn) and so, thought Larry Stack, it would be poetic justice if together they now prevailed.

The reaction around the country was electric. Every firm that had been invited to the first round—a written proposal was due within days—ached to make it to the second, when "three to five offerors" would be "invited to present oral presentations to supplement their proposals." It was a time of hard decisions and tentative, sometimes diplomatic calls.

The United States Mint and the Fenton-Berke partnership had jointly arrived at the determination of which companies would receive invitations to the ball. It was a marriage of convenience, uneasy at times. The Mint's procurement officer sent out six to eight solicitations for the first round. Fenton suddenly had lots of best friends. He was circumspect, but he would take calls. He would listen, perhaps make a suggestion, and was ever polite, but he could promise nothing.

The Mint had one set of ideas about selling the coin, and Fenton and Berke had others. They were not always in accord. Decisions, cloaked by confidentiality agreements, had to be made, both sides had an even say, and the five years of litigation hadn't necessarily endeared one side to the other. Things could get tense, and word was it did.

Before 5:30 P.M. on Wednesday, April 25, 2001, every one of the firms that had been asked to tender proposals to the United States Mint in the wink of an eye did so. All had labored many hours to produce so compelling an argument on paper that they would be allowed to make their pleas in person. Each felt that it could best serve the needs of the Mint and Fenton; each believed its method of marketing the best; each stretched and offered the best financial terms it could; and each expressed its nearly mystical awe of the coin—which none had even seen. After the first round cuts and oral presentations had been made the waiting game brought anxiety to all the competitors.

In late June, David Redden received the call from the contracting officer from the United States Mint asking if Sotheby's would like to tender a contract for the sale of the 1933 double eagle. Sotheby's and Stack's had won. But there was no celebrating. The decision was still shrouded in secrecy, and negotiations over the contract could always go wrong.

In the small world of auctions, going after expensive property and persuading the owners to sell is one of the most exciting challenges as well as one of the most creative aspects of the business. Addressing all aspects of the sale and crafting the appropriate legal language was a protracted process, but in January, 2002, the signatures were finally affixed to the sales contract. A new chapter began.

A sale date of July 30, the day before the opening of the American Numismatic Association convention in New York City, was agreed, as was the published estimate: $4 million to $6 million. It was a world-record level. The then current record for a coin was $4,140,000 for the finest known 1804 silver dollar. Sotheby's and Stack's had argued for a lower number, not wanting to scare off potential bidders; instead, a published reserve, or minimum selling price, of $2.5 million was also agreed and felt to be reasonable and achievable.

The coin would not be kept at Sotheby's but would be moved from Fort Knox to West Point, which was more accessible from New York City. Any public exhibitions required United States Mint Police in attendance. The United States Government would not represent the 1933 double eagle as being provably the Farouk specimen, and any and all written materials, including the manuscript for the auction catalogue being jointly researched by Sotheby's and Stack's experts, had to be submitted to all parties for review. The catalogue stated that this '33 was the only example the government ever intended to authorize for private ownership and that any other examples that might exist were also government property and subject to seizure, a point that was regularly stressed to the press.

Getting the word out to the public in a controlled manner was the first concern. The news of the auction was released exclusively to the Associated Press on February 6 and run the next day. A firestorm of interest exploded. The papers loved the story and it ran around the world.

On Monday, March 18, 2002, the 1933 double eagle arrived at Sotheby's from its holding cell at West Point, with its gun-toting minders from the Mint Police. It was the first time the auctioneers had seen the coin they had fought so hard to secure for sale. Each person in the room who handled the coin, however briefly, experienced the same jolt of excitement that had surged through Steve Fenton in that London vault. It was just a coin, but it was different. And seemed to exude an electric life force of its own. The next day it glittered in its television debut on the *Today* show.

In the coming months the coin was displayed at Sotheby's to a cross-section of potential buyers, during other exhibitions, and Stack's got in touch with their special clients, as well. Always guarded by the Mint's men in blue, in early June it arced across the country to the Long Beach Coin Expo in California, where, beneath a revolving six-foot-diameter enlargement, the 1933 double eagle made its numismatic debut. Mint Director Henrietta Holsman Fore and Larry Stack unveiled the coin, while masses of the curious came from far and wide and waited patiently in line to look at the infamous coin. Finally toward the end of June, the

'33 was briefly exhibited at the Federal Reserve Bank of New York, in the same vaulted halls that had echoed with the ring of returned gold coins in March, 1933. In just over a month it would be chaperoned to Sotheby's where it could rest secure that its sixty-nine year odyssey as a fugitive from the United States government would at last be over.

Tuesday, July 30, 2002. New York City. Late afternoon.

Auction, when properly done, is an art. It is the perfect fusion of business and theater and is more riveting than theater because it is so unpredictable. Five minutes before the auction was to begin, charged ions seemed to leap from body to body. Excitement was palpable. It was standing room only, and there was not much of that. Those with reserved seats were quickly seated.

Although the curtain was soon to rise, hard business decisions were still being made. To be permitted to bid, prospective buyers had had to submit their financial bona fides well in advance. Not all had, and earlier in the day with only a few hours remaining Sotheby's and Stack's had to decide on whom it was worth taking a gamble. Sotheby's knew its client base, and for those few the decision was cut-and-dried. Larry Stack knew the numismatic dealers and collectors. But few had ventured into this lofty troposphere before. Only one coin had ever exceeded the $2.5 million published reserve price, and only three or four coins had even broached the million-dollar mark.

Stack was read the names in David Redden's office. The air conditioning was having a hard time keeping up with the unyielding heat, and the big man had slight beads of perspiration following his hairline. He leaned forward in his chair, which creaked slightly. His navy blue tie, decorated with little hockey players, dangled. His forearms were on his thighs. Some of the individuals in question, he was convinced, would eventually pass muster. On hearing the names of one or two others, he bobbed his head emphatically—on their wherewithal he would bet his reputation. But at the mention of another pair he winced involuntarily. Then at the sound of another name he growled menacingly through his beard and shook his head vehemently.

Other names were completely unknown to either Stack's or Sotheby's. Twelve bidders were ultimately approved.

One prospective bidder was not an American, but a Bahamian financial portfolio manager who read seven newspapers a day. Most of them had

The 1933 double eagle on exhibition at Sotheby's New York, July 30, 2002, guarded by the United States Mint Police. The crowds would grow. The box to left was one of those used to "mail" the melted gold coins to Fort Knox in 1937. (Author)

carried articles about the 1933 double eagle, and they intrigued him. An investment wizard, he was in his mid-thirties and hadn't collected or even much thought about coins since he was a kid. He had known nothing of the history of the notorious coin until he had read the recent press accounts, but the more he read, the more the '33 fascinated him. He had checked out the Sotheby's website and decided about a week before that he wanted to own the coin, "for its uniqueness, its history, the fact it was the only one." It was not an impulse, but he wanted that coin and no other. He contacted a disbelieving friend who he wanted to have bid for him at the auction.

The coin sat in isolated splendor, a round disk of gold protected by a rectangular piece of black plastic. Lights from within the case made it shimmer; aimed spotlights from the ceiling above made it dance. The stand on which it sat was swaddled in black velvet.

On opposite walls flanking the coin were two framed certificates, which some wags jested were worth more than the coin itself. Both awaited the Mint Director's signature. One was the Transfer of Sale, elaborately engraved. The other, less ornate, was a Certificate of Monetization. This document was alchemical. It would transform the 1933 double

ILLEGAL TENDER

eagle, still a piece of chattel in the eyes of the government, into an authorized coin, making it legal to own and, if one were so inclined, legal to spend. For this the United States Government insisted that regardless of the price paid at the auction, the new owner would have to tender an additional twenty dollars to the United States Mint. This was to balance the books when they finally legalized the coin. It also tipped the balance of the fifty-fifty split twenty dollars in the government's favor.

A group of businessmen, coin dealers, one of whom wore a short brown crew cut, walked determinedly over to the coin and had a long, hard look at it. They spoke to one another, smiling and nodding as they did. This group had tendered a $4 million cash offer to Stephen Fenton and the Mint when the settlement had been announced. Now, on behalf of the same unnamed client, who was said to own a baseball team, they were going to give the 1933 double eagle another try. They had arranged with Sotheby's for a private skybox above the seething crowd, where they could bid by telephone in complete anonymity.

Dwight Manley, once a coin dealer, now a sports agent, collector, and entrepreneur, glided through the fray, smiling at people he knew. He already owned a 1913 Liberty Head nickel that had cost him $1.84 million, and the fact that the 1933 double eagle was a "legal" rarity appealed to him. Only in his thirties, he had been thrilled by coins since he had been a kid. He saw them as "connections to ancestors—real links, in that they and we see the same item." He was willing to bid $3 million, but one never knew what would happen at an auction.

Elsewhere in the growing crowd was a businessman and philanthropist who had carefully concealed his blue bidder's paddle in a large white envelope. A white-haired man, not tall, in his mid-seventies, who carried himself with athleticism and wore a blue suit, white shirt, and red patterned tie, he was well known to the numismatic fraternity. He had a tough, George Raft style of talking and owned remarkable collections, which he was famously reluctant to discuss. Coins were only a portion but a passion. Those few who had some insight into what his collections held would never have anticipated his interest in the 1933 double eagle, but he was drawn to the coin because of its fascinating history. He joined the ranks of other collectors, of whom it is said they pay ten percent for the object and ninety percent for the story.

Another prospective bidder, a well-known coin collector, venturing far from his acknowledged specialties, wanted to examine it closely and wanted no one to see his interest. The long, tall case in which the coin reposed was opened and the coin removed. It was taken to him quickly on another floor of the building by the Mint Police and was soon returned to its altar.

A bidder from out West looked at the 1933 double eagle with mixed feelings. Once a coin dealer, he had sought and found much greener pastures, but as soon as he had heard the coin was going to be sold, he knew he had to have it. To him it had always been "untouchable, unobtainable . . . the ultimate coin." He looked at it now, minutes before the auction was to begin, a "little nervous." He only collected rarities, and he had an absolutely rock-solid number in his head. Although pride of ownership was involved, he was in it strictly for investment. At his price he thought he could double his money in a few years.

Director of the National Collector's Mint Barry Goldwater, Jr., looked very much his father's son. Grey-haired, with craggy features and a determinedly square jaw, the company he headed had created and was aggressively marketing on television and in print a "tribute" reproduction of the 1933 double eagle for $19.95 each. With a cohort from his company, he was planning to bid on the object of their accolade. Always good for sales.

One man unknown to all, cloaked in anonymity, wandered over to the display case. He looked at the coin and left. Its story fascinated him. He had no other coins. He said nothing and disappeared into an elevator.

In Sotheby's book department Senior Vice President Selby Kiffer looked out his window. The sky looked gritty, an ugly luminescent green, at the end of another day of an interminable heat wave. He had no particular urge to jostle with the sweaty commuters at the height of the rush hour and was staying late for the 6:00 P.M. auction to watch the fun. During his nineteen years at Sotheby's, Kiffer had catalogued an astonishing array of historical icons, including a leaf from Lincoln's House Divided speech, a copy of the first printing of the Declaration of Independence, and the *Tyrannosaurus rex* named Sue. Redden knew Selby was staying and had asked him if he would like to be on the telephone with a bidder in one of the private boxes. Kiffer said sure.

This bidder was new to Sotheby's and seemingly new to auctions. He had only registered to bid as the clock was running out. To David Redden the process of bidding at auction was automatic, like a heartbeat. But to the gentleman just introduced to him it was not. Redden took time and carefully walked him through every step. He also assured him that he would have a senior member of Sotheby's staff on the other end of his telephone.

Selby Kiffer reached for the phone on his desk as it rang. It was his man. The voice on the phone was direct and businesslike. Its owner wanted to run through the process again and get a sense of what the bidding increments would be and how much time he would have to make up his mind. With a sale of this magnitude, the auctioneer allowed greater leeway and would be patient–to a point. If the voice wanted to bid, all he had to say was "go," or "yes," or "bid." If he cared to, he could give Kiffer a firm figure and then take over himself if it exceeded that number. Kiffer would make sure that David Redden would see his hand in the air.

The voice on the phone was not nervous, but Kiffer sensed that it was fearful of something going wrong in the process. The voice wanted to get things right.

By 5:00 P.M. a sense of anticipation was filling the seventh floor. The lights were on in the saleroom itself. Screens to the right and left of the auctioneer's podium glowed with massive images of the coin. The raptor on the reverse sailed to the left. Liberty strode forward, oblivious to the date at her side that had made her very existence a challenge. Three hundred gray-cushioned folding chairs had been set up but barely filled a quarter of the airplane hangar of a space. A few collectors sat down and waited. The first ten rows had been reserved. Sotheby's had organized a seating plan so that the registered bidders would not be denied a seat and David Redden would have a map of where they were sitting. Redden looked over the room, was satisfied, and excused himself. He disappeared into his office to prepare some notes for his opening remarks.

Stephen Fenton circulated, looking surprisingly relaxed and cool, even though his nerves had been badly rattled during the last few weeks. An Egyptian journalist had telephoned Fenton and informed him that the fate of the 1933 double eagle remained unresolved. As in 1954, before the Farouk auction, the coin would be withdrawn. This time the coin was going to be claimed by Egypt as having been stolen from Farouk's collection. Fenton immediately passed the word on to Barry Berke, who got on to Jane Levine, and she to her contact. As far as they could determine it was all just rustling in the wind, with no substance. One law-enforcement official quipped, "Stolen from Farouk? It was stolen from us first–they can get in line."

A young man in the crowd looked out of place, thoroughly lost. His clothes were dark with sweat, half the suffocating New York weather, half preauction nerves. "You're kidding!" he had said the day before and had laughed in shock when his friend, the young Bahamian financier, had told him that he was going to bid on the 1933 double eagle and wanted him to execute his bids on the floor, while he would be at the other end of the cell phone. Now he was at Sotheby's. He worked at a financial institution in New York, but knew no one in the crowd. He looked at his cell phone and kept checking it. He had never been to Sotheby's before. Neither he nor his client had ever bid at an auction before. He took a deep breath that didn't seem to fully fill his lungs and exhaled slowly. He stood in the first row behind the seated throng. Apprehensive. He tinkered with his phone yet again.

With the coin in the center of the stage, spotlighted, David Redden climbed into the auctioneer's podium and scanned the room. To his right the massed bank of cameras and reporters was cordoned in behind velvet ropes. The hot lights were switched on.

To Redden's left was a long, elevated wood-paneled desk on which banks of telephones were concealed behind a raised barrier. Here Harvey and Larry Stack sat next to each other. The younger, bearded coin dealer checked his scribbled notes, punched up a long distance number and waited for an answer. His father cast an appraising eye over the crowd and was pleased with what he saw.

A few chairs down on the same bank, further from the auctioneer, Selby Kiffer, took his seat and immediately called his man in a private box above the sale room. The connection was fine. Kiffer's large dark eyes absorbed images of the mob.

Above, in the private boxes, Stephen Fenton and Barry Berke waited expectantly. In other boxes, behind curtains drawn completely or partly, prospective bidders weighed up their respective chances. Each had his own reasons for wanting the coin, and some couldn't even fully explain it to themselves. Each had a numbered blue plastic paddle more suited to a game of ping-pong than raising bids into the millions of dollars. Standing toward the back, a man nervously double-checked his cellphone connection. His stomach felt hollow.

The room was filled with hundreds of gawkers, some said six hundred, some eight hundred: Twelve individuals had been cleared to bid. Both numbers were impressive.

A telephone rang in the legal department on the eighth floor of Sotheby's. The voice on the other end was from the United States Federal Government. Representations from the Egyptian government had just been received, asking that the sale be stopped. The Egyptians had been told the request was too little and too late. The sale would continue.

It was 6 P.M.

"My name is David Redden." The room fell quiet. The American with an English accent continued, "And I shall be your auctioneer this

The saleroom, July 30, 2002, moments before the auction began. (Author)

evening. Seldom do we have a single-lot sale, so this will not be a long sale, but it will be a *great* moment."

The audience listened politely, shifting slightly in their seats, as Redden graciously acknowledged all the individuals who had helped out on the project. By law, he ran through the conditions of sale: an additional 15 percent buyer's premium would be added to the hammer price, as would the extra twenty dollars to pay for monetization, but no sales tax would be charged, as the coin was being sold by the United States Government.

"So." He paused. Faces turned to him, rapt. "And I need to begin the sale with two million five hundred thousand dollars . . . two million five hundred thousand dollars. . . ."

Redden looked to his right and, as he had been told to expect, saw the flicker of blue rising.

"Two million five hundred thousand dollars—to Barry Goldwater, Jr., National Collector's Mint . . ."

The reserve had been met and technically the coin was sold. It was already the second most expensive coin in the world.

Larry Stack was on the phone, whispering to his client, as his eyes sped over the crowd.

"Two million five hundred thousand dollars," Redden repeated thrice.

291

Hands went up round the room in unison. Redden picked them off. "Two million six hundred."

"Two million seven hundred on the telephone." It was a bid from a skybox.

It was back to the floor. Manley was thinking, waiting. Goldwater's hand was in the air.

"Two million eight—on the right."

The man from out West jumped in; up went paddle 102. "Two million nine hundred thousand, on the center aisle now . . ."

Immediately, "At three million dollars on the telephone, now . . ."

Redden was looking to the bank of phones. Someone from the bid department had her hand in the air. The out-of-sight coin dealers were having their bid relayed. Stack was talking to his client. Kiffer was keeping the voice in the action. Manley was out.

The man from the West's paddle went up again. "Bidding at three point one million . . ."

"At three million two hundred thousand dollars . . ." It was Goldwater again.

Redden repeated. He repeated again and again.

Then once more, on the phone. "Three million three hundred thousand dollars now . . . At three million three hundr—" A man in the front row made a move to bid but did not.

"Four hundred thousand dollars now . . ." from another place. Only Redden saw it.

Heads in the crowd swiveled left and right to see where the bids were coming from.

Another came and went. More hands were up. Then down. Goldwater was back in at "Three million six hundred . . . Three million six hundred thousand . . ." Redden kept the cadence.

Then Kiffer heard the voice in the phone. His hand shot up. Redden caught it as his eyes moved relentlessly over the sea of faces.

"Three million seven hundred thousand . . . at three million seven hundred thousand—far telephone, left . . . At three million seven hundred thousand . . ."

"Three million eight hundred thousand . . ."

Immediately: "Three million nine hundred thousand." Goldwater again.

Redden slowed his tempo, enunciating each word for dramatic effect.

Kiffer's man said, "Bid." Like a marionette's, the senior vice president's hand went up.

"At FOUR million dollars on the telephone now, at four million dollars now, bidding at FOUR MILLION . . ."

The 1933 double eagle was already the most valuable coin in the world. It had taken about a minute and a half. The crowd was watching, anticipating, not bidding, but part of the drama nonetheless. The men who had come to bid, wealthy men who made instant business decisions, sat in their chairs and thought.

Redden repeated his mantra: "At four million dollars." His eyes were taking it all in, his peripheral vision picking out intended motion from the blur of casual movement. The refrain of his bid continued.

"Four million ONE hundred thousand . . ." The National Collector's Mint was still in. Goldwater's face looked rocky—determined.

"Bid." Kiffer's hand was up. Redden saw it. Another hundred thousand dollars was chalked up. He repeated it matter-of-factly, almost conversationally. Over Redden's left shoulder a tote board ticked over the bids in dollars, euros, and pounds sterling. Stephen Fenton could watch his wealth grow in real terms.

Harvey Stack, an auctioneer himself, cast a practiced eye over the room. Larry Stack talked to his client but did not move. A couple of the bidders looked irresolute. One or two others discussed what to do. They did nothing.

The man in the back, who had been fussing with his cell phone, had it pressed to his ear. Suddenly his paddle, 111, shot up.

Redden nabbed the bid. "Four million THREE hundred thousand, in a *new* place, standing at the back. . . ." There was increased excitement in his voice. "At four million three hundred thousand dollars, now . . . ," his voice warbled, "at four million three hundred thousand dollars, now . . ."

"At four million four hundred thousand—telephone." The voice in Selby's ear was back.

"At four million four . . ."

Redden didn't finish. Goldwater again "At four million five . . ." He repeated it over and over.

"Four million *six* hundred . . ." Selby.

"Four million *seven* hundred." The bid was eclipsed. Stack was whispering furiously to his client, his eyes riveted on the mob. Most hands were in their laps. Firmly. Redden scanned with mechanical efficiency as he kept crooning his bid. Goldwater and his compatriots were shaking their heads. It looked like they were out.

"Four million eight hundred thousand . . ." Redden fairly whispered, acknowledging Kiffer's hand. He kept his voice low—drawing in the audi-

Auction and Absolute Anonymity

ence. The battery of cameras to the side ran, aimed, and reaimed as the bids rippled from one end of the room to the other.

"Four million nine hundred thousand . . . at four million nine hundred thousand, standing . . ." The cell phone man was staring straight at Redden. Heads in the front of the room were pivoting like owls', peering over shoulders to see where the action was.

Redden, *sotto voce,* "At four million nine hundred thousand . . . at four million nine hundred thousand, standing center . . ."

"At FIVE MILLION dollars now on the phone." Redden jolted the room like Haydn's Surprise Symphony. As he repeated the figure, light applause crackled in the room; it grew. Redden continued, unaffected. It was three minutes since the opening bid.

The white-haired collector, the dealers in the skybox, Dwight Manley, and the man from out West were out. Barry Goldwater, Jr., and the National Collector's Mint were out. Others made motions of intent but never followed through. It was beginning to look like a two-man game.

"Five million . . . one hundred thousand dollars . . . in the center back."

The voice in Selby's ear said, "Bid."

"At five million *two* hundred thousand dollars, at five million two hundred thousand dollars, on my left . . ."

The man in the back of the room was murmuring into his cell phone. The man in the Bahamas had only planned to go to "five million and change," now he was considering stretching a bit. The eyes of the room bored in on his agent. Few people looked at the auctioneer. Redden, looked elsewhere, scanning raptorlike for the flicker of a bid. He intoned the bid twice more.

The cell-phone hand went up.

"At five million, THREE HUNDRED THOUSAND dollars . . ."

Quickly. "Bid." Selby.

"Five million—four hundred thousand dollars . . ."

The man on the cell-phone was not as sure. Not as quick on the trigger. The Bahamian had been slightly distracted. He was trading after-hours equities simultaneously.

Redden chanted, "Five million four hundred thousand dollars, now . . . at five million four hundred thousand . . . at five million four hundred thousand—on my left . . ."

Suddenly: "Five million five HUNDRED thousand . . ."

The voice, ever businesslike, instantly crackled in Kiffer's ear. He nodded at Redden.

"Five million SIX HUNDRED thousand," he acknowledged and repeated it.

Everyone was a participant, willing the bids higher. Hundreds of onlookers shared the nervous excitement.

Redden's voice began to trail away again, then—

"At five million—SEVEN—HUNDRED—thousand," he woke up the room, fairly roaring the bid, and then dropped his voice as he repeated it.

The voice told Kiffer, "That other guy is coming awfully close to owning this coin."

"Well," said Kiffer, "so are you."

"Bid."

Kiffer nodded again.

"Five million," Redden hesitated briefly, "*eight* hundred thousand . . . At five million eight hundred thousand dollars, now—on my left . . . Five million eight hundred . . ." he paused again.

The man on the cell phone responded positively.

"Five million nine hundred" three times.

"SIX—MILLION—DOLLARS." Redden's voice soared; he called out each word clearly.

Applause burst out again, nearly drowning out Redden's "On my left . . ."

The crowd quieted.

"At six million dollars now," quickly but distinctly, "at six million dollars on the left, at six million dollars, now."

"Six million ONE hundred thousand dollars" came the response relayed by a nod of the head from the standing man. He didn't have long to enjoy his supremacy.

"Six million—TWO—hundred thousand dollars." Again Kiffer.

Coin dealer Eric Streiner was standing almost next to the man on the cell phone as he muttered urgently into the little piece of plastic. Streiner had never seen the man before and wondered who he was. Redden began to slow his pace. He was acutely attuned to the limits of bidders. It was mystical. A good auctioneer frequently had a better idea of when the bidders would drop by the wayside than they did themselves.

"At SIX—MILLION—TWO—HUNDRED—THOUSAND—DOLLARS—AT—SIX—MILLION—TWO—HUNDRED—THOUSAND—DOLLARS . . ." It looked as though the cell phone man was fading, and then—

"Six million THREE hundred thousand dollars." Redden's speech became increasingly deliberate, sensing that the battle of these two titans was slowing. The auctioneer kept flicking his eyes over the crowd for telltale movements that might indicate a new player—or the return of an old one.

Kiffer waved his hand defiantly.

"At six million FOUR–HUNDRED–THOUSAND–DOLLARS . . . At six million FOUR . . . HUNDRED . . . THOUSAND . . . DOLLARS." Redden began a slow diminuendo. "At six million four hundred thousand dollars."

The Bahamian was already well over his predetermined limit, and for a coin he had never seen. But it was the only coin he had ever wanted to own. He'd give it another go—just one. The man on the cell phone nodded from the rear. But Redden saw a resigned look on his face.

"SIX MILLION FIVE HUNDRED THOUSAND DOLLARS now . . . thank you . . ."

There was little hesitation. The voice in Selby's ear was determined. "Bid," it said. He did.

"Six million SIX hundred thousand, at six million six hundred thousand dollars, now . . . at six million six hundred thousand dollars . . . at six million six hundred thousand dollars, on the left." Redden looked to the rear—the man on the cell phone shook his head. The crowd was still willing on the grudge match. Redden's hooded eyes looked round: "At six million six hundred thousand dollars . . . at six million six hundred thousand dollars." Everybody in the room looked to see if there was more. "At six . . . million . . . six . . . hundred . . . thousand . . . dollars, on my left, all the way left," he was ever so slow and deliberate, "six million six hundred thousand dollars." He looked up with a twinkle in his hazel eyes and asked as his voice rose, "Anyone else?"

Selby had the phone pressed to his ear. Larry Stack watched from his phone. Steve Fenton and Barry Berke looked down from on high. The Mint Director watched keenly. The cameras still churned. Reporters started straining against the velvet rope. The white-haired man and all the other prospective bidders still had a chance. . . .

"Six million six hundred thousand dollars. Fair warning. On my left. On the telephone. Fair warning," he repeated, "at six million six HUN-DRED thousand dollars . . ."

BANG!

The vice chairman of Sotheby's brought the hammer down hard, and a roar went up. The room erupted into cheers. Some, including Redden's wife, his daughter, Clare, and a blond-haired woman in a white linen dress, stood and applauded. The entire room was clapping loudly now, and soon they all stood. It had taken six minutes and twenty-one seconds.

"Congratulations," whispered Selby Kiffer to the voice on the phone.

"Remember," came the reply, "Absolute anonymity."

To the hammer price was added the fifteen percent buyer's premium—and of course the extra twenty dollars. The total was $7,590,020. The price was astonishing, breathtaking, historic. Of the millions upon millions American made works of art ever sold at auction, only twenty paintings and four objects—including a copy of the Declaration of Independence—had brought more than the 1933 double eagle.

Barry Berke and Stephen Fenton cheered along with the crowd. As they stood side by side and looked down on the crowd, Fenton remembered. "Do you know, Barry," he said with a smile, "the first time you stood beside me was at the bail hearing." Berke smiled back.

It was chaos below. Reporters descended on Kiffer, badgering him for the name of his client. Because Selby was from the book department, the rumor quickly spread that it was one of his collectors. Kiffer at first refused to acknowledge even the sex of the bidder, but at some point slipped and mentioned that the purchaser was American. Beyond that his lips were sealed.

Washed-out, exhausted, the man on the cell phone was suddenly accosted by a mob of coin dealers proffering their cards and wanting his custom. Three women asked him if he was single.

Larry Stack was grinning broadly and gave the smiling David Redden a hearty pump of the hand and the red-socked consultant a rib-crushing bear hug. It was bedlam. Redden was under siege in the podium by well-wishers and reporters alike. The *New York Times* wanted to know. But the voice on the phone had been adamant. "Absolute anonymity."

Amid the immediate postsale confusion, Sotheby's personnel set up a long table at the front of the auction room immediately below the ounce of gold that was now worth just shy of $7.6 million. Behind the table, Mint Director Henrietta Holsman Fore, resplendent in a silk taffeta gown, and then Assistant Mint Director David Pickens stood in the lee of the human maelstrom that surged round the room. Before them were the two certificates wanting signatures.

Cameras rolled. Cameras flashed. A crush of people closed in. Among them was a face that only David Redden knew—and whose voice would have been instantly recognizable to Selby Kiffer.

First the Certificate of Transfer was signed. The anonymous owner would get the certificate when he paid for the coin.

Next was the Certificate of Monetization. David Redden ceremonially tendered a twenty-dollar bill to Mint Director Fore. Smiling broadly,

297

she spoke a few well-chosen words and swiftly applied her signature to the document. When she was done she displayed it to the cameras while the applause mounted to a soaring crescendo.

At last, a 1933 double eagle—this single 1933 double eagle—was no longer chattel, it had been issued by the United States Government. It had taken sixty-nine years, sixty-five since the first had been made available to unsuspecting collectors by Israel Switt. For fifty-nine years it had been on the run, wanted by the Secret Service. Now with the flourish of Mrs. Fore's pen, this one 1933 double eagle was officially a coin.

Illegal tender no more.

Epilogue:
The 1933 Yeti

———◆———

EVEN THOUGH THE OWNER DID NOT REVEAL HIMSELF TO THE WORLD, which ached to know who bought the 1933 double eagle, he had decided to share it. Through Sotheby's he graciously agreed to a long-term loan of at least four years to the American Numismatic Society's exhibition of coins within the secure precincts of the extraordinary palazzo that houses the Federal Reserve Bank of New York, appropriately located at 33 Liberty Street. There, collectors, sightseers, the curious, and school-children would be able to gaze upon the storied gold piece.

In Egypt, the Minister of Culture Farouk Hosni, and Zahi Hawass, the Secretary-General of the Supreme Council of Antiquities had both been involved in official overtures to "repatriate" the 1933 double eagle. "We left no stone unturned in our attempt to recover this most valuable coin in the world," said Hosni to *Al-Ahram* after the auction. The legal papers proving Egypt's right to the coin "were sent to U.S. Customs, Interpol and other U.S. bodies in an attempt to stop the sale. "All were turned down." Hawass blamed it on "loopholes of the old [Egyptian] antiquities laws . . . that made it impossible to recover."

The absolutely anonymous man who won the privilege of owning the only legal 1933 double eagle and the young financier from another country who had come so close were both captivated by its extraordinary odyssey. Months later, the Bahamian still regretted not having come away with the only coin he wanted to own. But both men, along with McCann, Switt, Strang, Macallister, Boyd, Farouk and Fenton and the rich cast of support-ing players are now part of the powerful mystique of the 1933 double eagle—and they too will be the subject of speculation and rumor for years to come.

The 1933 double eagle is the Yeti—the abominable snowman—of coins. For years shadowy sightings of other examples have been reported with varying degrees of credibility. Numismatics is a field that has frequently been awash in scuttlebutt, gossip, and innuendo. Some settle in comfortably to become part of the rich oral history of the field. Differentiating the kernels of truth from the cobs of myth is not just a challenge but part of the entertainment. Determining the absolute truth is well-nigh impossible for the average Joe, and in the case of the 1933 double eagle, even the highly trained professionals of the Secret Service could not fully satisfy their curiosity in the pursuit of justice.

No one except those who took part in each scene of each act of the drama will ever know for sure what happened. So many men had convenient bouts of amnesia, wove fiction, or unabashedly stonewalled. James G. Macallister, who earnestly tried to help Harry Strang, provided him with the most tantalizing clue of all: that Switt had owned twenty-five and sold only fourteen.

Despite some modern complaints that the Secret Service investigation was over-vigorous, this last clue was never pursued, aggressively or otherwise. Strang reported bluntly and repeatedly on the many suspects' implausible, unreliable statements and their utter contempt for the truth. Even if they weren't all criminals, neither were they choirboys. But in the end their equivocation succeeded in preventing the discovery of the source of the coins. With hopes of prosecution quashed by the statute of limitations, all that was left to the government was recovery of the coins.

But were there more than Strang had identified? The unexpected appearance in 1952 of Louis Eliasberg's tenth coin proves that there were. And are there *still* more? Most knowledgeable professionals in the coin trade believe that there are indeed other 1933 double eagles out there. But the harsh light of international publicity cast on Stephen Fenton's coin has made those other coins even more dangerous to own. It would be well nigh impossible now—unlike Stephen Fenton and Jay Parrino—not to know (or even *claim* not to know), that the United States Government considers these objects stolen property. F. C. C. Boyd's concern that collectors be informed of the 1933 double eagles' status has at last been answered.

But what *about* others?

Surprisingly, there have been few sightings over the decades, and even fewer of any veracity, but enough rumor to make things interesting.

300

A Diplomatic Coup?

The purchase of lot 185 by the Norwebs at the Egyptian Palace sale in 1954 led to a rumor that swirled most alluringly within the trade—and along coin show bourses—in the weeks and months leading up to the auction in 2002.

Despite the announcement in 1954 that the coin had been withdrawn from the sale, some now believed that the truth was otherwise: that the Egyptians had agreed to the statement solely for consumption by the general public and the United States Government and that those attending the sale, or at least some of them, knew better. R. Henry Norweb had a long and distinguished career in diplomacy, and he had important contacts. If he had so desired, went the rumor, the courtly career diplomat, who had served under every president from Wilson through Truman, could have arranged for the coin to have been part of his purchase. Why else, they postulated, would the Egyptians have simply ignored the United States' request that the coin be returned? And why else would the United States have not pressed its case harder? Collusion for the privileged few was the answer. Then, the story continued, when the Norwebs died in the early 1980s the coin was sold privately and disappeared—seemingly the fate of all 1933 double eagles.

This rather appealing story is easily dispelled. In 1991 the children of R. Henry and Emery May Norweb gave the purchase ledgers of the remarkable collection their parents had amassed to the American Numismatic Society in New York City. There the smallish, neatly bound volumes reside on the sliding shelves of the library's incomparable archival collections. On page 82, listed under item 7950, there is a note that lot 185 purchased at the Farouk sale contained only sixteen coins. The seventeenth coin—withdrawn—was the 1933 double eagle.

But then, some conspiracy theorists propounded, would they record an illegal coin? And others asked, was this coin spirited overseas after the Norwebs' deaths, only to return to the United States in Stephen Fenton's pocket? And, if not the Norwebs, the theorists then asked, what about Schulman, Spink, or Kosoff?

No facts, just groundless fantasy.

Grabbing at Reeds

If Israel Switt and Edward Silver had sold only fourteen of the twenty-five 1933 double eagles they had, what happened to the remaining eleven?

Switt, as reported by Macallister, said that Silver was keeping two for his daughter. If true, these have never surfaced.

Those who knew Izzy Switt well said that the investigation into the '33s soured him on coins and from that point on his involvement was ever more tangential. He might have cut his losses and simply melted the remaining pieces in 1944, when the Secret Service investigation got hot. Or, never one to pass up a profit, he might have sold them all at a discount—perhaps to Ira S. Reed, it has been speculated.

Reed's involvement was never satisfactorily accounted for by the Secret Service. It was established that he continued to dissemble, only admitted to bits and pieces of the truth when pressed hard, and even during the investigation sold one of the coins to unsuspecting Louis Eliasberg. He repeatedly tantalized Strang and Drescher with fragmentary hints that he had handled more than could be accounted from Israel Switt's nine admitted coins. Well after Reed retired from the coin business in 1947 and died seven years later, a curious rumor cropped up.

Sometime in the 1970s or 1980s, Israel Switt, shrunken with age but still doing business from within the grimy, yellowed windows of his seedy shop on Jewelers' Row in Philadelphia, got in touch with a coin dealer of his acquaintance. He liked this dealer about as much as Izzy could like anybody, and they were accustomed to going next door from time to time for roast beef sandwiches. But as much as Switt might enjoy the dealer's company personally, he did very little business with him. For one thing, his stock of coins had greatly dwindled over the years, and for another, this coin dealer had once haggled over a price—the one unforgivable sin. Switt hadn't kicked him out of the shop, but nor had he offered him another choice deal.

Between bites of his roast beef sandwich, Israel Switt came right out with it. Would the coin dealer be interested in handling a 1933 double eagle? The dealer stared in stunned disbelief. It was not, said the leathery old jeweler quickly, something that he personally owned. He was inquiring on behalf of the owner, a relative or close acquaintance of Ira Reed. The coin dealer blanched.

Of course, Switt—who probably knew more about the *verboten* status of the coin than anyone else alive—said he didn't want to get the coin dealer into trouble. Izzy told him that if he was interested, the sale had to take place out of the country, preferably in Switzerland. The dealer nodded thoughtfully and promised to consider it. Nothing more was said about it. The two men munched on their sandwiches.

The coin dealer was uneasy. He'd done substantial deals before, but this was walking the knife edge of the law. Unsure, he spoke to one or two trusted colleagues, who had no qualms about offering their one-word opinions. "Radioactive," said one. "Poison," said the other. His mind instantly made up, the coin dealer called Switt and flatly refused the offer of handling such tainted goods. Izzy didn't argue. He'd been down this path before. He understood perfectly.

There was no sale. And that 1933 double eagle vanished—if it had ever existed.

A Whole Bag

When the United States weaned itself off the gold standard and called back privately owned gold, it did not apply the same standards to all entities. Most especially the government, which now owned the gold itself, could do as it liked. Over the years in the natural course of international trade, there was need for gold to be used in payment for debt. Generally these payments were in bar form, but before Roosevelt's gold purges, these payments were frequently made in coin. Thousands upon thousands of bags of gold coin were used and frequently recycled.

If a foreign country that had received United States coin in payment was now in debt, its payment would frequently take the same form, and the coins would be returned to the United States. Once the melting of gold coins was ordered in 1934, ideally these coins upon their return to within American borders would be rendered into ingots and any future payments made in that form. But that was not always the case.

Hundreds of thousands of bags of United States gold coins remained scattered around the world in central banks. Beginning in the 1950s, the numismatic value of some of these coins became known to the central banks holding them. Many holdings were then assiduously searched, and coins of considerable rarity and value made their way into the markets. None was a 1933 double eagle.

There are those who fervidly believe that within some of these dwindling golden caches are bags that conceal these forbidden coins. Some have intimated they know where they are. But these theories belie certain facts. The Mint's own records account for all the 1933 double eagles having traveled mere feet, not thousands of miles, from the vaults to the melting pots in 1937. The 1933 double eagles simply never left the building until, in their new, glowing, bricklike form, they were sent on their way to eons of storage in Fort Knox.

If there is a whole bag out there, it would miraculous, but it is unlikely—to say the least.

Scattered about the Country?

Shortly before being interrupted by the Secret Service in Suite 22K2 of the Waldorf-Astoria, Jay Parrino mentioned that he had reliable information that there was a 1933 double eagle in New Jersey, one with three identifiable marks on the reverse. Other examples have been variously rumored to exist in Chicago, the Northeast, and the Midwest. No one has ever claimed to have seen them—but some have claimed to have known someone who has.

The Ocean's Bounty

The late Walter Breen, one of the most talented researchers American numismatics has known, was a prodigious writer and blessed with a fecund imagination—or maybe he knew something. He wrote in 1988: "At least one other was reportedly flung into the ocean to avoid seizure, prior to 1956." One hopes the water was shallow.

A Handful

Another legend has been reported by Q. David Bowers, an esteemed gentleman and numismatist of more than fifty years' standing in business. An "old-timer" on the West Coast told him that he had once, back in the 1940s or 1950s, held four 1933 double eagles in his hand. One of the four was purportedly sold and was said to have ended up in Switzerland, where there have been repeated sightings of 1933 double eagles for over a half century; these have been occasionally accompanied by a dealer's claim to have physically handled a single example in a Swiss bank vault.

The other three have never been seen or reported.

The Mystery Coin

While they may contain a whiff or two of fact, most of the myths, legends, and wishful thinking above are of gossamer and dissipate on closer inspection. There is, however, one saga that has been told a hundred times by twice as many voices. It too has been overlain with labyrinthine versions in some cases, but overall it seems to have the essence of truth.

In the late 1940s or early 1950s a rich southern California collector, like Croesus, coveted gold. He longed for the rarest and wanted the best available. Price was immaterial. The California sun a half century ago was less dimmed by smog than it is today, and coins in those halcyon days were cheap by today's standards. With the means and desire, a spectacular collection could be assembled in a relatively short time. The collector had both.

While he was partial to all gold coins, he was utterly captivated by double eagles. Perhaps it was because of the glorious history of the denomination, born of necessity by the California Gold Rush and later to bear Saint-Gaudens' imagery, the most inspired numismatic designs in America's history. But maybe it was more visceral, perhaps he was simply impressed by their size: big, solid, and heavy. Regardless, he made it his aim to assemble the finest, most complete set in existence.

To help him achieve his goals he enlisted the aid of a transplanted New York dealer, Abe Kosoff. In 1948 the dark, good-looking coin dealer had moved west, leaving the New York offices of his firm, the Numismatic Gallery, in the capable hands of Abner Kreisberg, a charming, bright-eyed man with a good sense of humor and a jaunty bow tie. Kosoff opened a shop in Beverly Hills on Wilshire Boulevard. Not the superchic shopping district it is today, it was far humbler, with a relaxed, small-town feel. Where haute couture is now sold to movie stars and moguls at breathtaking prices there was a hobby shop selling balsa wood airplanes, model kits, and kites, a pet shop, and other everyday stores.

Abe Kosoff was a pioneer in the West Coast market. There the abundant sunshine made things grow and gave Abe his perpetual tan. The movie industry, real estate explosion, and oil salted the area with men of means who needed a hobby. Kosoff was there to fill the void, and he was spectacularly successful. He had East Coast sources for coins and West Coast clients to sell them to. Abe Kosoff was canny, energetic, and mixed in well with various levels of California society.

He had also known Israel Switt and bought coins from him. According to the Secret Service investigation, these had included two 1933 double eagles, a claim that Kosoff adamantly denied. Abe told Special Agent Milton Lipson in April, 1944, very specifically, that "the truth of the matter" was that he had only sold a single example, which he had unsuccessfully tried to sell a second time. They believed him.

But in 1982, the snowy-haired Abe Kosoff, now an old timer and lauded as the "dean of numismatics," recalled it differently. The Secret Service agents, wrote Kosoff in his regular column in the hobby standard, *Coin World,* "asked for the names and addresses of the collectors to whom I had sold the 1933 Double Eagles. I suggested that I would prefer to contact them, refund their money and get the coins back and the agents agreed after contacting their head office. I proceeded and indeed obtained the return of the coins which I had sold."

Kosoff continued, "I truly cannot remember just how many there were, two or three or four."

But Abe's claims and the official records disagree. Abe Kosoff returned no 1933 double eagles to the Secret Service, and none was seized from him.

Did Abe lie to the Secret Service in 1944? Or was Kosoff, in 1982, simply weaving another myth?

Regardless, the wealthy collector—by some accounts a real estate baron—had finally realized his goal with the able, vigorous help of Kosoff. He had put together a nearly complete set of double eagles, one of the finest known, and it included a 1933 double eagle, quite possibly supplied by Kosoff. For some years the collector continued to acquire gold coins, but over time he began to tire of the metal's endless glitter and looked to expand his collecting into other, more challenging areas. Bored, he looked to sell his collection of double eagles. It was the 1970s, and a group of three dealers helped broker the transaction.

The collection that had taken the southern California collector years or perhaps decades to assemble found a larger-than-life Texan who had the same goals but who wanted a leg up. He bought the whole collection, then one of the finest, and made it better still.

The Texan had oil money, an expansive personality, a sharp collector's eye, a gambler's gut instincts, and a long, close friendship with Jack Daniels. He continued to collect, improve, and expand. He added greater, rarer, and better coins to those he already had. As finer double eagles became harder and harder to find, he moved on to other denominations. He always used the same technique: buy an intact collection and improve it. He might one day have put together the finest collection ever formed, but he never got the chance. While still a young man, he dropped dead. It was the late 1970s.

Mike Brownlee, a dealer who also hailed from Texas, shared the late Texan's taste for coins, living large, and amber-colored liquid. A stocky man, with dark hair atop a round head, Brownlee had oddly sad eyes. He maintained a stable of clients that was the envy of the trade, but now he had lost one of his brightest stars and offered to help out the estate.

A list of the collection had been prepared and circulated among to a number of coin dealers in New York City. One of them was former big-band saxophone player Lester Merkin, a kindly, soft-spoken man, with slightly protuberant eyes. He liked his Scotch with water, his cigarettes without filters, and always dressed like the gentleman he was. Lester

Merkin dealt in knowledge, had a reputation for probity, great taste in coins, and was enormously successful. Merkin showed the list to a few other people, and all commented on one outstanding feature—the list of double eagles included the untouchable 1933. Maybe it was a simple typographical error, but Merkin passed the word on, just in case. The Texan's estate had no idea of the illicit nature of the coin. Mike Brownlee, of course, was keenly aware of its awkward inclusion and without letting on about the bigger issues, politely offered to make it go away.

Here the film slips its sprockets and the story goes wildly out of kilter. Chronology gets jumpy and muddled. In late 1978, 1979, 1980 or possibly earlier—accounts differ widely—Brownlee was said to have offered the coin in New York City to a number of coin dealers, one of whom expressed interest. But knowing the deep pools of doubt that surrounded the coin, the dealer first consulted with attorneys to see what the law actually said. The research took time, but the answer was predictable. The 1933 double eagle was illegal to own, and the dealer prudently passed on the transaction.

Not one to waste time, Brownlee apparently found someone else who was interested and willing to take a chance. But not before the coin had made its way around the country and was shown to a cadre of numismatists. One well-respected dealer, Fred Weinberg, recalled at Sotheby's Beverly Hills offices in 2002 that he had seen the coin as a young man, he thought in 1977 or 1978, at the now long-defunct firm Numismatics Limited, and all he did was "stare at the date." Another veteran dealer, Kenneth Goldman, remembered Mike Brownlee coming up to him at a convention in Long Beach, also in seventies but perhaps a year or two earlier, saying "Wanna see a coin that'll stop the show?" The young dealer, then in his mid-twenties, was dumbfounded by what tumbled out of the small brown envelope and into his hand. Brownlee said, "Now remember, you can't even tell your mother what you saw!"

During these jumbled peregrinations, the 1933 double eagle found new ownership. It was not sold but traded for another coin, also a double eagle, one that had been struck at the United States Mint in New Orleans in 1856, a few of which survived, most badly battered and worn. This example, with limpid mirrorlike surfaces, was undoubtedly the finest in existence and had previously been offered to a select few for around a quarter-million dollars.

A deal was struck: from whom to whom is unknown. A courier was found, the mystery coin handed over—in the Pelham section of the Bronx goes one version—and shipped to Switzerland.

And like the Farouk coin, it disappeared.

Epilogue

The "MYSTERY COIN." Previously unpublished anonymous photographs of a 1933 double eagle (developed in October, 1980, as seen from the Kodak logo on the backs of the prints). It is not the $7,590,020 coin, nor is it either of the two examples in the Smithsonian Institution. Its whereabouts are unknown.
(Anonymous)

The End

In the days, weeks, and months leading up to the auction at Sotheby's—and even today—swirling lazily, whispered rumors and theories have claimed that it was this mystery coin, and not Farouk's, that Stephen Fenton and Jay Parrino were arrested with at the Waldorf-Astoria. Well-regarded coin dealer Ron Gillio, was shown a 1933 double eagle by the late Mike Brownlee in Zurich in 1977 or 1978. One dealer claimed to have seen the Farouk coin in London in 1984. And Ken Goldman was positive the coin sold at Sotheby's was *not* the same as the mystery coin he saw many years earlier. But no one else was sure.

But just as there is no absolutely unassailable proof that the Fenton coin is King Farouk's—and not the mystery coin—there is none to prove that it isn't. Indeed, the king's onetime ownership seems more secure than ever. Fenton's and de Clermont's sworn beliefs, their source, and his name on the wire transfer certainly lends credence, as does the Egyptian government's official interest in the coin. But still, there are questions. And, as always, rumors.

And then there were the photographs.

A quarter-century ago, as a coin dealer's lawyers profoundly considered the legality of that mystery coin, some snapshots of it were taken. Those photographs, which were printed in October, 1980—as indicated by the Kodak marks on the back of the images—are of neither of the two coins in the Smithsonian Institution. Nor are they of the coin that Stephen Fenton was arrested with, which was sold by Sotheby's and Stack's in July 2002 for $7,590,020.

They are proof that there are others—or at least one other—out there.

And it—or they—are all *still* . . .

Illegal Tender.

Author's Note

Until February, 2002, when Sotheby's and Stack's announced the auction of the 1933 double eagle, there were few people outside numismatic circles who knew or cared about the history, or what was *thought* to be the history, of this single gold coin.

Within coin collecting circles it was generally assumed that a few of the coins had legitimately slipped into circulation despite the government's arguments to the contrary. It was also assumed that the government's sole cause for rounding them up and tarring them illegal was as part of the FDR's general recall of all gold coins and abandonment of the gold standard. As his laws were rewritten and over the next half century and private ownership of gold once again legalized, it was theorized, in numismatic circles, that this would similarly legitimize ownership of any 1933 double eagles that might, somehow, have eluded the keen eyes of the Secret Service.

I, too, accepted this interpretation of history until the United States Government signed a contract with Sotheby's to sell the coin at auction and enormous piles of legal documents, depositions, and archival Secret Service reports were made available to Sotheby's and Stack's for research.

What a shock it was. I was Sotheby's Special Consultant on the auction, and when those of us charged with researching the story for the auction catalogue read these documents, we were in unanimous and virtually instantaneous agreement that the long-accepted assumptions bore little relationship to what had actually happened seventy years previously. The legality of the 1933 double eagle no longer hinged on legal subtleties and oral tradition. It had been the target of a serious Secret Service investigation that had concluded that all of the 1933 double eagles had been *stolen* from the United States Mint. *That* was the reason for the sixty years of unrelenting attention.

But the reason for the half-century of numismatic misunderstanding was quite simply the government's fault: it never explained to the coin-collecting fraternity that the 1933 double eagle was deemed illegal because it was stolen property. Had it done so, Steve Fenton would undoubtedly have avoided the coin like the plague—and I would have had no book.

Pockets of American numismatics are conservative, insular, and protective of their own, like any other tight-knit community of enthusiasts. They are comfortable with the richly textured lore of the pursuit and wary of new interpretations of accepted history, especially—and not altogether unreasonably—if they might have a negative bearing on private ownership. The colorful tradition of Mint employees and their covert activities providing an underground railway for coins to collectors has been seen as unofficial rather than illegal; and indeed the hobby is richer for these individuals' success. But as a result, a skeptical, at times uneasy, relationship between numismatists and the government, and by extension, the Mint, developed. Some coin people feared that a reinterpretation and rigorous enforcement of the laws might make certain coins that have been traded as collectibles for well over a century illegal, but the 1933 double eagle remains the *only* coin on the Secret Service's Most Wanted list.

Over the days and months that followed the auction in 2002, I told anyone who would listen that I was writing a book on the subject. To those who said they had information or even photographs I gave my card and I hoped they would send me information. Some did, anonymously. All were keen to help, but most decidedly so were the skeptics, who hoped that I would now tell the *real* story and uncover the truth as they believed it. Their insistence that the traditional view of a legitimate release was correct and that the new story—the theft—was balderdash made me dig for information like the dickens. A new smoking gun, another exit—perfectly legitimate—from the Mint, or official malfeasance could only make the book more interesting to read. Looking for these wisps of evidence certainly made the research more enjoyable.

By the time it came to sit down and put words on paper, seemingly a million F.O.I.A. requests later, I had accumulated tens of thousands of pages of information (my office floor exists somewhere beneath them), and my library shelves sagged with the bound additions. Much vastly enjoyable time was spent digging through papers, files, and otherwise ignored archival data: material that was assembled, in part, from the National Archives, the Library of Congress, the Franklin D. Roosevelt Presidential Library, Federal Reserve Bank of New York Archives, and Dartmouth College Library to name but a few. Interviews with participants, descendants and acquaintances of participants provided life and pointed me in new, unimagined directions. Trips to Philadelphia, tracking down where the participants lived and did business, and my time spent at the Community College of Philadelphia (housed in the old Mint Building, where four of the original vault doors are still hanging on their hinges) were a joy, as I was able to see where it all happened. Undoubtedly one of the most fascinating and useful archival caches was that of Secret

Author's Note

Service and Treasury Department reports and internal memoranda that had been compiled in the 1940s and 1950s when the investigation was launched. (These were an integral part of the discovery process for both sides of the Fenton case. It is the first time, I believe, that such a complete file of a Secret Service investigation has ever been made so accessible.) Without these documents, tightly written with a wealth of detail and without bombast, though with the human touch (there are ample typographical and spelling errors) the story would not have been as rich.

As I had no predetermined conclusion, I let the documented facts be my guide—always wanting more, and they did not disappoint. But the information gleaned from vintage foolscap must be read in the context of the period in which it was written, and so I gobbled up contemporary views of the events of 1933 and on from newspapers and memoirs by those who lived through those tumultuous days. We forget that before FDR gold was money, not mere ornament, and the initial actions of his administration were among the most dramatic, even drastic, of any president in American history. The discovery of the disappearance of gold, not mere coins, from the Mint in 1944 was viewed as an important transgression, certainly embarrassing, and it was the Secret Service's responsibility, part of its mandate, to track the gold down, even during a world war.

My eyes opened wider during the research, and I have made every effort to leave no stone unturned or theory uninvestigated, and after more than two years consumed by a single coin—a single story, rather—I hope I have managed to narrate its odyssey accurately. If there is new documentary evidence, I look forward to seeing it and incorporating it into any future edition that might, by luck, be issued. The epic—and controversy—of the 1933 double eagle is a continuing one.

As the strands drew together, I found myself facing a story that was not cold history. My research introduced me to wonderfully colorful individuals from the long gone and near past. Whether their actions were right or wrong or open to interpretation made no matter. They were characters from a play in the theater of history. Rather than give a mere recitation of names, dates, facts, and figures, I have tried to recreate the story as it happened, each act performed on a different stage by new players, but all coming to the same dramatic conclusion.

One way or another the adventure of discovery was great fun. To those who offered their help, ideas, information, and most of all, their challenges that spurred me along I can express only gratitude. For the mistakes, hopefully few, I apologize, but take full responsibility.

Author's Note

Abbreviations

---◆---

ADC: André de Clermont

AEW: A. E. Whittaker

AGS: Austin G. Sutterfield

ASG: Augustus Saint-Gaudens

AUSA: Assistant United States Attorney

CBR: Charles B. Rich

DT: David Tripp

EHD: Edwin H. Dressel

ES: Eric Streiner

FDR: Franklin Delano Roosevelt

FDRPL: Franklin Delano Roosevelt Presidential Library

FDRP: Franklin Delano Roosevelt Papers

FJW: Frank J. Wilson

FLH: F. Leland Howard

FRBNYA: Federal Reserve Bank of New York Archives

FWG: Fred W. Gruber

GCD: George C. Drescher

HEG: Herbert E. Gaston

HHPL: Herbert Hoover Presidential Library

HJS: Harry J. Stein

HWS: Harry W. Strang

IOC: Inter-Office Communication

IOM: Inter-Office Memorandum

IR: Intermediate Report

JAS: James A. Stack

JJMcG: John J. McGrath

JJO'C: Joseph J. O'Connell, Jr.

JM: Jack Moore

JP: Jay Parrino

LC: Library of Congress

LRS: Lawrence R. Stack

ML4: Dartmouth College Library, Rauner Special Collections Library, Augustus Saint-Gaudens Papers, ML4, and locator number

MR: Memorandum Report

NAB: National Archives Building, Washington, D.C.

NACP: National Archives at College Park, Maryland

NARA: National Archives and Records Administration

NARA (CCP): National Archives and Records Administration Mid Atlantic Region (Center City Philadelphia)

NTR: Nellie Tayloe Ross

NYT: The *New York Times*

OF: Official File (FDR)

PPF: President's Personal File (FDR)

PSF: President's Secretary's File (FDR)

RD: Russell Daniel

RDF: R. David Freriks

RG: Record Group

RJG: R. J. Grant

RWR: Ralph W. Robuck

SA: Special Agent

SAIC: Special Agent in Charge

SF: Stephen Fenton

TR: Theodore Roosevelt

UEB: Urbanus E. Baughman

USSS: United States Secret Service

WHW: William Hartman Woodin

313

Notes

◆

Prologue

Page xiv: *"Does your record"*: Telegram. F. Leland Howard (FLH), Director, Bureau of the Mint to the Superintendent of the United States Mint, Philadelphia, March 18, 1944. National Archives and Records Administration (NARA). Records of the United States Mint at Philadelphia, Record Group (RG) 104, Entry 702. National Archives and Records Administration Mid Atlantic Region (Center City Philadelphia) (NARA CCP).

Chapter 1: The Artist, the President, and the S.O.A.B.

Page 3: *"I think," "Would it"*: Theodore Roosevelt (TR) to Leslie Mortier Shaw, December 27, 1904. *Letters of Theodore Roosevelt,* ed. Elting E. Morison. Vol. 4, Letter 3414, p. 1088.

Page 4: *"pet baby"*: Letter, TR to Augustus Saint-Gaudens (ASG), January 6, 1906. ML4 16:37.

Page 4: *AIA dinner:* American Institute of Architects, January, 11, 1905. Dartmouth College, Rauner Special Collections Library, Augustus Saint-Gaudens Papers, ML4, 59:2

Page 4: *"capital should"*: Charles Moore, *The Promise of American Architecture,* 1905, p. 6.

Page 5: *sharp, curling:* Francis Grimes, "Reminiscence." ML4, 44:11.

Page 6: *"always overworked"*: James E. Fraser, "Reminiscence." ML4, 44:9.

Page 6: *"in a serious," "home"*: Fraser, "Reminiscence." ML4, 44:9.

Page 6: *"never seemed"*: Francis Grimes, "Reminiscence." ML4, 44:11.

Page 6: *"dashed out"*: Fraser, "Reminiscence." ML4, 44:9.

Page 6: *fragile temperament:* Draft Letter, Augusta Saint-Gaudens (Gussie) to Dr. Sir William Osler, August, 1907. ML4, 14:42.

Page 6: *cab built, home to:* Letter, ASG to Gussie. January 12, 1905. ML4, 28:8.

Page 6: *"better than ever"*: Letter, ASG to Gussie, January 8, 1905. ML4 28:8.

Page 7: *twelve small: Official Functions, The White House, 1904–05,* NAB, RG 42 Entry 159, Vol. 4.

Page 7: Oscar Straus's brother, Isidor, and wife, Ida, perished famously on the *Titanic* in 1912. Oscar Straus was appointed Secretary of Commerce and Labor in 1906–the first Jew in American history to join the Cabinet.

Page 7: *chicken sandwiches:* Alice Roosevelt Longworth, *Crowded Hours,* pp. 161–162.

Page 7: *"banal character"*: Augustus Saint-Gaudens: A Master of American Sculpture, Exhibition Catalogue, p. 78.

Page 8: *capable of: Augustus Saint-Gaudens: A Master of American Sculpture,* Exhibition Catalogue, p. 78.

Page 8: *"competent"*: Don Taxay, *United States Mint and Coinage,* p. 287.

Page 8: *"Roosevelt was like"* Cass Gilbert, *The American Architect,* Dec. 10, 1919, p. 710.

Page 8: *"Barber is"*: Letter, ASG to Louis Saint-Gaudens, January 14, 1905. ML4 32:42.

Page 8: *"Mr. Straus"*: Archibald Roosevelt address at the New York Numismatic Club, December 14, 1934, *Numismatist,* February, 1935, p. 103.

Page 8: *"employed for," "to be"*: Letter, TR to Shaw, January 16, 1905. Morison, ed., *Letters,* Vol. 4, Letter 3438, p. 1103.

Page 9: *"What would"*: Letter, TR to ASG, January 17, 1905. Theodore Roosevelt Papers, Manuscript Division, Library of Congress (LC), Washington DC.

Page 9: *"In the matter"*: Letter, ASG to TR, January 20, 1905. ML4, 16:36.

Page 9: *"began with"*: Fraser, "Reminiscence." ML4, 44:9.

Page 9: *April:* ASG Diary, ML4, 53:3.

Page 10: *"state $5000," "the same design"*: Letter, ASG to Mint Director Roberts and TR, July 10, 1905. ML4, 78:2.

Page 10: *"I make"*: J. Fraser, "Reminiscence," ML4, 44:9.

Page 10: *"calluses"*: J. Fraser, "Reminiscence." ML4, 44:9.

Page 10, 11: *modest suggestion, "Would it"*: Letter, TR to ASG, November 6, 1905. ML4, 16:36.

Page 11: *a few:* Letter, ASG to Mrs. MacDowell, November 10, 1905. ML4, 12:36.

Page 11: *"the authorities"*: Letter, ASG to TR, November 11, 1905. LC.

Page 11: *"a living"*: Letter, ASG to TR, November 11, 1905. LC.

Page 11: *"summoned all"*: Letter, TR to ASG, November 14, 1905. ML4, 16:36.

Page 11: *"How would"*: Letter, TR to ASG, November 14, 1905. ML4, 16:36.

Page 11: *"a trial"*: Letter, ASG to Secretary Shaw (copy to TR) January 2, 1906. ML4, 16:37.

Page 12: *"pet baby," "crack-brained"*: Letter, TR to ASG, January 6, 1906. ML4, 16:37.

Page 12: *"by increasing"*: Letter, ASG to TR, January 9, 1906. LC.

Page 12: *before proceeding:* Letter, Secretary Shaw to ASG, January 16, 1906. NARA RG 104, Entry 628, NARA (CCP).

Page 13: *"There was no one"*: F. Grimes, "Reminiscence." ML4, 44:11.

Page 13: *Janvier:* Letter, ASG to TR, June 28, 1906. LC.

Page 13: *"nailed here"*: Letter, ASG to John LaFarge, June 13, 1906. ML4, 11:37.

Page 13: *"I direct"*: Letter, TR to Secretary Shaw, Sept. 11, 1906. Morison, ed., *Letters,* Vol. 5, Letter 4044, pp. 405–406.

Page 14: *"these dies," "I suppose I shall"*: Letter, TR to ASG, December 20, 1906. ML4, 16:37.

Page 14: *who returned:* Letter, ASG to Mint Superintendent Landis, March 13, 1907. NARA RG 104, Entry 628, NARA (CCP).

Page 15: *check for:* Letter, Mint Director Roberts to Superintendent US Mint, July 25, 1907. NARA RG 104, Entry 628, NARA (CCP).

Page 15: *Mint's own:* Letter, Superintendent Landis to Director Leach, April 20, 1908; letter, Charles O. Brewster to Superintendent Landis, April 22, 1908. NARA RG 104, Entry 628, NARA (CCP). Letter, Brewster to Gussie, April 23, 1908. ML4, 3:2.

Page 15: *"how much relief"*: Letter, ASG to TR, May 23, 1907. LC.

Page 15: *"His sickness"*: Homer Saint-Gaudens, ed., *The Reminiscences of Augustus Saint-Gaudens,* p. 359.

Page 15: *"I am so glad"*: Letter, Frances Grimes to Barry Faulkner, undated, circa August 1907. ML4, 48:1.

Page 16: *fist down on his desk:* Frank Leach, *Recollections of a Mint Director,* pp. 101–2.

Page 16: *"doing a," "walls and"*: Leach, *Recollections,* p. 35.

Page 17: *"to flake:"* Leach, *Recollections,* p. 48.

Page 17: *"All you"*: Leach, *Recollections,* p. 102.

Page 18: *"all day"*: Letter, C. E. Barber to Superintendent Landis, November 23, 1907. NARA RG 104, Entry 628. NARA (CCP).

Page 18: *"Saint-Gaudens gave us"*: Glenn Brown, *American Architect,* December 10, 1919, p. 716.

Chapter 2: Swift and Staccato Action: The Great Depression

Page 19: *"The country was dying"*: Presidential Address: Franklin Delano Roosevelt (FDR), May 7, 1933 (reprinted in *On Our Way,* The John Day Company, 1934, p. 70).

Page 20: *"orgy of mad"*: David M. Kennedy, *Freedom from Fear,* p. 35.

Page 20: *directly attributed:* Kennedy, *Freedom,* p. 73.

Page 20: *"primary cause"*: Kennedy, *Freedom,* p. 71.

Page 21: *"economic interdependence"*: H. Hoover in Kennedy, *Freedom,* p. 71.

Page 21: *bank failures:* Horace White, *Money and Banking,* p. 671.

Page 21: *"Wherever possible"*: FDR, *Public Papers and Addresses,* vol. 2, p. 29.

Page 21: *"refugee" gold:* Kennedy, *Freedom,* p. 76.

Page 21: *"a loose cannon"*: Kennedy, *Freedom,* p. 76.

Page 21: *Charles Merrill:* A number of these hoards remained untouched for decades, and only in recent years have found their way back to the United States, where the coins have been fed into the hands of collectors and a new generation of gold bugs.

Page 22: *"great void"*: Arthur M. Schlesinger, Jr., *Age of Roosevelt, Crisis of the Old Order,* p. 456.

Page 22: *"the bony hand"*: Raymond Moley, *After Seven Years,* p. 140.

Page 22: *"for nearly two"*: FDR, *Public Papers and Addresses,* p. 26.

Page 22: *"Roosevelt's alter"*: Kennedy, *Freedom,* p. 124.

Page 22: *"found it impossible"*: Moley, *After,* p. 143.

Page 23: *"the best-informed"*: White, *Money and Banking,* p. 529n.

Page 23: *"cocked his head," "swell"*: Moley, *After,* p. 121.

Page 24: *"heroic jobs"*: Moley, *After,* p. 123.

Page 24: *"as obviously its"*: Letter, Herbert Hoover to FDR, Franklin Delano Roosevelt Papers (FDRP), President's Personal File (PPF) 820, Franklin Delano Roosevelt Presidential Library, Hyde Park, New York (FDRPL).

Page 24: *"the breaking point"*: Moley, *After,* p. 140.

Page 24: *"a very early"*: Letter, Herbert Hoover to FDR, February 17, 1933. FDRP, PPF 820, FDRPL.

Page 24: *"Roosevelt was . . . unmoved"*: Moley, *After,* p. 141.

Page 24: *"an oversight"*: Moley, *After,* p. 142.

Page 24: *"the fire"*: Letter; FDR to Herbert Hoover, February 20, 1933. FDRP, PPF 820 FDRPL.

Page 25: *"details of the inaugural"*: Moleys *After,* pp. 142 and 143.

Page 25: *"It was Will"*: Moley, *After,* p. 143.

Page 25: *The Internal Revenue:* *Philadelphia Inquirer,* March 1, 1933.

Page 25: *A single taxpayer: NYT, Book Review,* February 19, 1933, p. 24.

Notes

Page 25: *"wobbling"*: Moley, *After*, p. 140.

Page 25: *"obliteration"*: Moley, *After*, p. 140.

Page 26: *"147 pages"*: Letter, Woodin to FDR, July 5, 1933. FDRP, PPF 258, FDRPL.

Page 26: *"invoke emergency powers"*: Moley, *After*, p. 146.

Page 27: *"I shall be waiting"*: Moley, *After*, p. 146.

Page 27: *"Still the talk"*: Moley, *After*, p. 146.

Page 27: *"thing is bad," "Will you come"*: Moley, *After*, p. 147.

Page 27: *"We had forgotten"*: Moley, *After*, p. 148.

Page 27: *"the gold withdrawals"*: Moley, *After*, p. 147.

Page 27: *"bowed under," "week of"*: Moley, *After*, p. 148.

Page 28: *"so grim as"*: New York Times *(NYT)*, March 5, 1933.

Page 28: *"the time to speak"*: FDR Inaugural Address, March 4, 1933 (reprinted in *On Our Way*, pp. 255–261).

Page 28: *"They know only the rules"*: FDR Inaugural Address, March 4, 1933 (reprinted in *On Our Way*, pp. 255–261).

Page 28: *"the money changers"*: FDR Inaugural Address, March 4, 1933 (reprinted in *On Our Way*, pp. 255–261).

Page 28: *"only a foolish"*: FDR Inaugural Address, March 4, 1933 (reprinted in *On Our Way*, pp. 255–261).

Page 28: *"We must act"*: FDR Inaugural Address, March 4, 1933 (reprinted in *On Our Way*, pp. 255–261).

Page 29: *"his reassuring confident"*: NYT, March 5, 1933.

Page 29: *"at the head"*: NYT, March 5, 1933.

Page 29: *"the new President"*: NYT, March 5, 1933.

Page 29: *"Franklin D. Roosevelt March"*: Letter, FDR to (WHW) William Hartman Woodin January 27, 1933. FDRP, PPF 258, FDRPL.

Page 29: *"prearranged signal"*: NYT, March 5, 1933.

Page 29: *"Why can't we"*: NYT, March 5, 1933.

Page 30: *intended to invoke:* Moley, *After*, p. 148.

Page 30: *"This Act gave"*: FDR, *Public Papers and Addresses*, p. 26.

Page 30: *"on the dubiousness"*: Moley, *After*, p. 148.

Page 30: *"We considered"*: Harold Ickes (Ickes), *Secret Diary of Harold Ickes: The First Thousand Days (The Secret Diary)*, p. 3.

Page 30: *At the Mint:* Memo, Superintendent US Mint Philadelphia Edwin H. Dressel (EHT) to Mint Director Nellie Tayloe Ross (NTR), March 21, 1944.

Page 31: *"broke in with"*: Moley, *After*, p. 149.

Page 31: *"prevent complete chaos"*: FDR, *Public Papers and Addresses*, vol. 2 p. 28.

Page 31: *"swift and staccato"*: Moley, *After*, p. 151.

Page 31: *"just before midnight"*: Ickes, *The Secret Diary*, p. 3.

Page 32: *"Whereas"*: FDR, *Public Papers and Addresses*, pp. 24–25.

Page 32: *"like throwing"*: News-Week, March 11, 1933.

Page 32: *"Special trust accounts," "safe depository"*: NYT, March 6, 1933, p. 1.

Page 33: *"Not once did"*: Time, March 20, 1933, p. 8.

Page 33: *"we were facing"*: Moley, *After*, p. 151.

Page 33: *"a man-to-man"* Moley, *After*, p. 151.

Notes

Page 33: *"a message instilling"*: Letter, Freeman Gosden and Charles Correll to FDR, March 5, 1933. FDRP, PPF 3795, FDRPL.

Page 33: *"decidedly effective"*: Telegram, Steven Early to Freeman Gosden and Charles Correll, March 6, 1933. FDRP, PPF 3795, FDRPL.

Page 33: *"We [the Treasury] can issue"*: Moley, *After*, p. 152.

Page 34: *"was far from well"*: Moley, *After*, p. 163.

Page 34: *"Capitalism was saved"*: Moley, *After*, p. 155.

Chapter 3: Gold Rush in Reverse

Page 35: *"It is ridiculous"*: NYT, March 6, 1933.

Page 35: *"a protection"*: NYT, March 6, 1933.

Page 35: *"a technical"*: New York Daily News, March 6, 1933.

Page 35: *"noted banking," "Some persons"*: NYT, March 6, 1933.

Page 35: *"as long as"*: Complete Roosevelt Press Conferences, Vol. 1, Number 1, March 8, 1933.

Page 36: *"The actual monetary"*: White, *Money and Banking*, pp. 80–82.

Page 36: *"United States," "I realize"*: Ickes, *The Secret Diary*, p. 23.

Page 36: *"Mr Secretary"*: FDR, *On Our Way*, p. 61.

Page 36: *"broke every," "the dictatorial"*: New York Daily News, March 6, 1933.

Page 38: *"The President"*: Letter, Secretary of the Treasury to Director of the Mint Bureau, March 6, 1933. FDRP, OF 21, FDRPL.

Page 38: *Identical orders:* Emergency Banking Instructions, WHW to Treasurer of United States, March 6, 1933. FDRP, OF 21, FDRPL.

Page 38: *Federal Reserve:* Emergency Banking Instructions, WHW to Federal Reserve Banks, March 6, 1933. FDRP, OF 21, FDRPL. In February 1933, the Federal Reserve Bank of New York paid out or earmarked $72 million in gold coin, while receiving less than $1.4 million. In March, the tables started to turn with $78.8 million paid out (in the first few days of the month) and $108.8 million received. In April *no* gold coins were paid out, and $35.2 million was received. Gold Disbursements, 1927–1954. 252.1 Federal Reserve Bank of New York Archives (FRBNYA).

Page 38: *"officials . . . working at"*: NYT, March 8, 1933.

Page 39: *"Authorized to issue"*: Wire, Assistant Secretary of the Treasury James H. Douglas to Treasury Dept. to Philadelphia Mint, March 8, 1933. NARA RG 104, Entry 702, NARA (CCP).

Page 39: *"Issue of gold"*: Wire, Assistant Secretary of the Treasury James H. Douglas to Philadelphia Mint, April 12, 1933. NARA RG 104, Entry 702, NARA (CCP).

Page 39: *"If a depositor"*: Letter, R. J. Grant to Lewis A. Froman, March 15, 1933. NARA RG 104, Entry 702, NARA (CCP). Lewis Froman was an economics professor at the University of Buffalo (and later President of Russell Sage College). His inquiry was specifically related to his revision of Horace White's *Money and Banking*, and it was Froman's opinion that "The last country holding to the full [gold] standard was the United States, but it suspended in March, 1933." (p. 83).

Page 39: *"No gold or gold certificates"*: R. J. Grant to F. H. Jackson, March 17, 1933. NARA RG 104, Entry 702, NARA (CCP).

Page 39: *"all those who"*: NYT, March 8, 1933.

Page 40: *"found their supply"*: NYT, March 9, 1933.

Page 40: *"came with," "few odd coins"*: *NYT,* March 10, 1933.

Page 40: *"I do not know"*: *NYT,* March 10, 1933.

Page 41: *"any and all," "an equivalent"*: Henry Morgenthau Diary, Book 1, Treasury Department Chronology of Gold Actions. FDRPL. The new legislation even affected foreign diplomats. The Councellor of the Panamanian Consulate asked to keep her salary ($2,500), paid in gold (as her government had no paper money of its own). The U.S government found she was under its jurisdiction and denied her request. Correspondence, March 10 and November 24, 1933. C.262.2A, FRBNYA.

Page 41: *"gold stampede"*: *NYT,* March 11, 1933.

Page 43: *"little smiling"*: *NYT,* March 11, 1933.

Page 43: *"there were no orders"*: *NYT,* March 11, 1933.

Page 44: *"unmanufactured gold"*: Regulation Number 25. FDRP, OF 21, Box 1, FDRPL. *NYT,* March 14, 1933.

Page 44: *affidavit:* Even the need for minuscule amounts of gold required these documents to be filled out. J. Brown, a gilder on Fulton Street in New York City, purchased two pennyweights of gold, worth $2.67, to continue his work on April 25, 1933. C.262.2A, FRBNYA.

Page 44: *"The fellow who"*: *NYT,* March 15, 1933.

Page 44. *"An Italo-American"*: *NYT,* March 19, 1933.

Page 44: *"The enclosures speak"*: FDR to Treasury, March 23, 1933. FDRP, OF 21, FDRPL.

Page 44: *enormous burdens: NYT,* March 19, 1933.

Page 45: *controlled, "He's too busy"*: *Roosevelt Presidential Press Conferences,* Vol. 1, Number 1, March 8, 1933.

Page 45: *"Off the record"*: *Roosevelt Presidential Press Conferences,* Vol. 1, Number 3, March 15, 1933.

Page 45: *"One of the curiosities"*: *NYT,* March 19, 1933.

Page 45: *his difficult problems, "luncheon," "Instead"*: *NYT,* March 23, 1933.

Page 46: *"slated to be"*: *NYT,* March 23, 1933.

Page 46: *"Executive Order"*: FDR to Homer Cummings, April 3, 1933. FDRP, OF 294, FDRPL.

Page 46: *"many persons"*: *Public Papers and Addresses,* Vol. 2, Number 32 (p. 110).

Page 46: *"special value"*: *Public Papers and Addresses,* Vol. 2, Number 33 (p. 111).

Page 47: *"Beer is legal" NYT,* April 6, 1933.

Page 48: *"right arm"*: Harold A. Williams, *Robert Garrett and Sons: Origin and Development, 1840-1965:* Baltimore, Privately printed, 1965, p. 42.

Page 49: *"It might be interesting," "In reference to"*: The Garrett Archives, Dealer Correspondence, The American Numismatic Society, New York.

Chapter 4: Just a Factory: Making Money

Page 53 *February 18:* The [Coiner's] Daily Process Record, Gold, 1929-1933. NARA RG 104, Entry 691, NARA (CCP).

Page 53: *In 1922:* Letter, P. A. Kearney (Coiner, San Francisco Mint) to M. J. Kelly (Superintendent, San Francisco Mint), September 28, 1922. NARA RG 104, Entry 740, NARA (CCP).

Page 54: *size of a:* James Young, *United States Mint at Philadelphia,* p. 35.

Page 56: *March 1:* Cashier's Daily Statement of Receipts, Disbursements and Balances, March 1, 1933. NARA RG 104, Entry 330, National Archives at

Notes

College Park (NACP). Analysis of 1933 eagle coinage: Memo, FLH to FJW, April 11, 1944. According to the Cashier's Daily Statement, Pomerantz tendered a total of $30. What other coins he received on March 1 is unclear from the records.

Page 56: *One hundred had:* Cashier's Daily Statement of Receipts, Disbursements and Balances, January 19, 1933. NARA RG 104, Entry 330, National Archives at College Park (NACP).

Page 56: *Mint tour:* Young, *United States Mint at Philadelphia,* p. 55.

Page 57: *sixty-five thousand:* The [Coiner's] Daily Process Record, Gold, 1929–1933. NARA RG 104, Entry 691, NARA (CCP).

Page 57: *"cherry red":* Letter, P. A. Kearney (Coiner, San Francisco Mint) to M. J. Kelly (Superintendent, San Francisco Mint), September 28, 1922. NARA RG 104, Entry 740, NARA (CCP).

Page 58: *pair of mechanical:* Young, *United States Mint at Philadelphia,* p. 52.

Page 59: *Over the weekend:* U.S. Mint Service Form 270, shipping report, March 6, 1933, signed H. A. Powell and Edwald F. McKernan. NARA RG 104, Entry 702, NARA (CCP).

Page 60: *"it was business":* Philadelphia *Inquirer,* March 7, 1933.

Page 60: *These sacks were printed:* Information from United States Mint, Philadelphia, Department of Exhibits and Public Services.

Page 61: *"was always customary":* Memo, Helen C. Moore to file, September 25–26, 1945. NARA RG 104, Entry 702, NARA (CCP).

Page 61: *"forwarded to the Director":* Anonymous essay, "Our Coining Department," Bureau of the Mint, undated, c. 1913. NARA RG 104, Entry 740, NARA (CCP).

Page 62: *Mint's regulations:* Leach, *Recollections,* p. 97. (Reprinted from *Recollections of a Newspaperman,* 1917.) Regulations regarding ban on release of coinage prior to positive "Special Assay" report being received by Mint, confirmed orally to author, November 6, 2002, by Dr. George E. Hunter, retired Assistant Director for Process Control and Quality Assurance, United States Mint.

Page 62: *Pyx Box: Numismatist,* March 1934, p. 18.

Page 62: *"then the employees":* Anonymous essay, "Our Coining Department," Bureau of the Mint, undated, c. 1913. NARA RG 104, Entry 740, NARA (CCP).

Page 62: *$8,890,540:* U.S. Mint Shipping Clerk's records. Recapitulation of Gold Coin Shipped from January 1, 1932 to December 31, 1932. NARA RG 104, Entry 702, NARA (CCP).

Page 63: *445,500 pieces:* The Federal Reserve could not have guessed that in the first two months of 1933 alone, before FDR closed the sluices, the growing panic would require the Mint to ship more than three million double eagles–none dated 1933–to slake the seemingly unquenchable thirst of banks, businesses, and hoarders.

Page 63: *There had been ten deliveries:* Compiled from Cashier's Daily Statements and US Mint breakdown in a memo to the Director of the Mint, March, 1944.

Page 63: *In all, only two:* In theory, with the first delivery Powell would have opened a bag of 250 double eagles, selected the two "special" coins, which were immediately dispatched to Washington, and an additional one of every one thousand for the Pyx Box. Thus, on March 15, a total of twenty-seven pieces would have been removed, the bag resealed and stored with the bulk of the just-delivered coins in the Cashier's Working Vault. With each of the succeeding nine deliveries the procedure should have been repeated identically, depending on its size; always with two specials removed and one of every thousand coins. With the tenth and last delivery on May 19, the Cashier should have broached and resealed ten bags in making his sampling–not only two.

Page 64: *"hoarding [had] become"*: Speech, FDR, c. March 15, 1933.

Page 65: *Cage Number 1:* Vault Custodian Edward McKernan's records. Abstracted by United States Mint personnel for report to Director of the Mint (NTR), March 21, 1944 (for forwarding to the United States Secret Service). Report signed by Helen C. Moore, Acting Superintendent US Mint at Philadelphia. Report of the Settlement Committee to EHD, March 23, 1937. NARA RG 104, Entry 703, NARA (CCP).

Page 65: *Vault Custodian:* Manuscript abstract of page 373, McKernan's ledger. Transcribed, c. March, 1933. NARA RG 104, Entry 702, NARA (CCP).

Chapter 5: The Great Melt and the Great Escape

Page 67: *"Ever feminine" NYT,* Obituary, December 21, 1977.

Page 67: *"As long as":* NYT, Obituary, December 21, 1977.

Page 68: *"It all sounded":* NYT, Obituary, December 21, 1977.

Page 68: *"I am deeply":* Letter, NTR to FDR, April 28, 1933. FDRP, OF 21E, FDRPL.

Page 68: *six individuals:* One was the Hon. William Ashbrook, who also served on the 1908 Assay Commission that tested the *first* Saint-Gaudens double eagles. On March 20, 1908, he purchased a high relief ("second coinage") $20 from the Mint for $20 plus postage (10¢). Letter, Ashbrook to

Landis. NARA RG 104, Entry 628, NARA (CCP).

Page 69: *"commission adjourned":* Proceedings of the Annual Assay Commission, 1934, Wednesday, February 14, 1934.

Page 70: *February 20:* Cashier's Daily Statement of Receipts, Disbursements and Balances. NARA RG 104, Entry 330, NACP.

Page 70: *"All gold":* Gold Reserve Act of 1934, Section 5.

Page 71: *"to proceed":* Wire, NTR to Mint Superintendents, August 4, 1934. NARA (CCP) RG 104.

Page 71: *which was recorded:* Receipt, T. Belote, Smithsonian Institution, October 11, 1934.

Page 72: *"not all been melted":* Numismatist, March, 1936, p. 178.

Page 72: *"with former values":* Abstracted by United States Mint personnel for report to Director of the Mint Ross, March 21, 1944 (for forwarding to the United States Secret Service). Report signed by Helen C. Moore, Acting Superintendent US Mint at Philadelphia.

Page 72: *Between February:* Vault Custodian's record, photostat copy made from original, April 18, 1944. Attached to United States Secret Service Intermediate Report (IR), Special Agents Harry W. Strang (HWS) and George C. Drescher (GCD) to Secret Service Chief Frank J. Wilson (FJW), April 21, 1944.

Page 73: *"It has been reported"*. Lee F. Hewitt, *Numismatic Scrapbook,* April, 1937, p. 75.

Chapter 6: A Double Eagle Flies to Cairo

Page 77: *Girls who worked:* David Brinkley, *Washington Goes to War,* p. 107.

Page 77: *combined the charm:* Brinkley, *Washington Goes to War,* p. 106.

Page 78: *$1,575:* USSS Document, undated, c. 1944.

Page 78: *$1,440:* Brinkley, *Washington Goes to War,* p. 107.

Page 78: *sensational $100,000:* John Adams, *United States Numismatic Literature,* Vol II, p. 56. Adams reports the figure as $1,000,000, a typographical error.

Page 78: *average Egyptian:* T. Cliff, *Neither Washington nor Moscow,* London, Bookmarks, 1982.

Page 78: *Gold Reserve Act of 1934:* Section 3.

Page 79: *including the denomination:* Treasury Document, TGL-11: NARA RG 56, NACP.

Page 79: *"representation that":* Treasury Inter-Office Memo, January 5, 1938. To Mr. Pehele from Mr. Rupert. Signed and initialed by NTR. NARA RG 56, NACP.

Page 79: *gross appetite:* Hugh McLeave, *The Last Pharaoh,* p. 150.

Page 79: *aspirin bottles:* Frank Hermann, *Sotheby's,* p. 342.

Page 80: *the British Museum:* Hermann, *Sotheby's,* p. 342.

Page 80: *"brushed off":* Hans Schulman in Abe Kosoff, *Abe Kosoff Remembers,* p. 94.

Page 80: *"completely different":* Schulman in Kosoff, *Abe Kosoff Remembers,* pp. 93–94.

Page 81: *dictated a letter:* "[was the 1933 double eagle] of recognized special value to collectors of rare and unusual coin immediately prior to the issuance of the Order of the Secretary of the Treasury of December 28, 1933, and has been of such special value at all times subsequent thereto[?]; and was [it] of such special value immediately prior to the issuance of the Executive Order of April 5, 1933, and has been of such special value at all times since such date[?]" Letter, NTR to T. Belote,

February 25, 1944. United States of America vs. A $20 Gold Coin, known as a 1933 "Double Eagle" U.S. District Court, Southern District of New York, 96 Civ. 2527.

Page 81: *"The reply":* Handwritten note on Letter, NTR to T. Belote, February 25, 1944. USA vs A $20 Gold Coin.

Page 82: *up to 1916:* The striking of proofs recommenced in 1936.

Page 82: *"Twenty Dollar":* Letter, M. M. O'Reilly to T. H. Lillard, January 9, 1934. NARA RG 104, Entry 235, vol. 573, NACP.

Page 83: *"a $3 set":* Numismatic Scrapbook, January 1943, p. 55.

Chapter 7: A Routine Inquiry

Page 85: *a Haitian tomtom:* Letter, James Wainwright Flanagan to FDR. FDRP, PPF 6000, FDRPL.

Page 86: *"Announcement Extraordinary":* Numismatist, January, 1944, p. 54.

Page 86: *"The Excessively Rare":* Stack's, *The Col. James W. Flanagan Collection of Gold Coins,* March 23, 1944.

Page 87: *No double eagles: Annual Report of the Director of the Mint,* 1934, Addenda, p. 61.

Page 87: *445,500: Annual Report of the Director of the Mint,* 1933, p. 6.

Page 89: *ten-page memorandum:* March 21, 1944, Report from Philadelphia Mint to Director of the Mint, Washington, D.C. NARA RG 104, Entry 702, NARA (CCP).

Page 89: *"Miss McNutt":* Telegram, FLH to E. Kehr. March 22, 1944. NARA RG 104, Entry 702, NARA (CCP).

Page 90: *nickel stogies:* Frank Wilson and Beth Day, *Special Agent,* p. 38.

Page 90: *Sarouk rug:* Wilson and Day, *Special Agent,* p. 94.

Page 90: *going up for sale, "close friend":* March 22, 1944, United States Mint, Memo to File: USA vs A $20 Gold Coin.

Page 90: *"Proud custodian":* Michael F. Reilly, *Reilly of the White House,* p. 4.

Page 90: *bulletproof limousine:* Brinkley, *Washington Goes to War,* p. 88.

Page 91: *"Frank J. Wilson":* Wilson and Day, *Special Agent,* p. 71.

Page 91: *Albatross:* Wilson and Day, *Special Agent,* p. 94.

Page 91: *26,470:* Annual Report of the Secretary of the Treasury, 1945, p. 259.

Page 92: *headed to Stack's:* USSS Inter-Office Memorandum (IOM), HWS to FJW, March 27, 1944.

Page 92: *"Scarcely 50 paces":* Stack's Promotional Flyer, undated, c. late 1940s.

Page 94: *2 P.M.:* Receipt, signed by Harry W. Strang, Treasury Form 1544, March 24, 1944.

Page 94: *"James G.":* USSS IOM, HWS to FJW, March 27, 1944.

Page 95: *"and found to":* USSS IOM, HWS to FJW March 27, 1944.

Page 95: *"New York dealer":* USSS IOM, HWS to FJW March 27, 1944.

Page 95: *vice president:* Stack's, John J. Ford, Jr. Collection, October 14, 2003, pp. 13–15.

Page 96: *maintained a separate:* History of the New York Numismatic Club, New York, 1992, privately published. p. 49.

Page 96: *"to him that":* USSS IOM, HWS to FJW March 27, 1944.

Page 97: *did not recall to whom:* USSS IOM, HWS to FJW March 27, 1944.

Page 97: *At 2 P.M.:* Receipt, signed by Harry W. Strang, Treasury Form 1544, March 25, 1944.

Chapter 8: Assistance, Resistance, and Stalemate

Page 99: *"freely discussed":* USSS IOM, HWS to FJW March 27, 1944. Strang's report reads "1935" but this is clearly a typographical error; the 1935 convention was held in Pittsburgh.

Page 100: *"temporary assignment":* USSS Inter-Office Communication (IOC), SA McGrath to FJW March 28, 1944.

Page 100: *"Reference to":* USSS Teletype, FJW to McGrath, March 27, 1944.

Page 100: *well-known:* USSS IOC, HWS/George C. Drescher (GCD) to FJW March 29, 1944.

Page 102: *1886:* R. C. Davis, *Coin Collectors Journal,* May, 1886.

Page 102: *"The coins":* Numismatist, 1910.

Page 102: *"While Woodin":* USSS IOC, HWS/GCD to FJW, March 29, 1944.

Page 102: *"whether he had":* USSS IOC, HWS/GCD to FJW, March 29, 1944.

Page 103: *"intimated that":* USSS IOC, HWS/GCD to FJW, March 29, 1944.

Page 103: *Macallister's family:* Personal recollection to DT, J. T. Macallister, February 26, 2003.

Page 105: *Israel Switt:* USSS IOC, HWS/GCD to FJW, March 29, 1944.

Page 105: *"no 1933 double":* USSS Intermediate Report, HWS/GCD to FJW, May 12, 1944.

Page 105: *Berenstein had:* Numismatist, February, 1936, p. 145.

Page 105: *elusive 1933:* Numismatist, October, 1938. p. 854. Specifically the 1933 Eagle was given to the American Numismatic Association whose coins were loaned to the Smithsonian until the ANA established its own museum (today in Colorado Springs).

Page 106: *"It became apparent":* USSS IOC, HWS/GCD to FJW, March 29, 1944.

Page 106: *"An old lady"*: USSS IOC, HWS/GCD to FJW, March 29, 1944.

Page 106: *"In view of"*: USSS IOC, HWS/GCD to FJW March 29, 1944.

Page 107: *"a very interesting"*: Letter, F. C. C. Boyd to J. M. Haley, March 31, 1944.

Page 107: *his salary:* Jack Collins, Washingtonia Catalogue, F. C. C. Boyd Collection Introduction, 1991.

Page 108: *shown it off:* USSS Inventory (Form 1544).

Page 108: *New York Numismatic Club:* Boyd showed the coins at the March 12, 1937, meeting. *Numismatist,* April, 1937, pp. 312 and 330.

Page 108: *There were more: Numismatic Scrapbook,* April, 1937, p. 75.

Page 108: *"the last of"*: *Numismatist,* October, 1938, p. 854.

Page 108: *Fred Boyd's wife exhibited: Numismatist,* November, 1939, p. 916.

Page 108: *In February, 1941: Numismatist,* February, 1941, p. 126.

Page 109: *"any time you"*: Letter: J. M. Haley to F. C. C. Boyd, April 5, 1944.

Page 110: *"as far as I know"*: Treasury Department Inter-Office Memo, FLH to FJW, March 30, 1944.

Page 111: *Israel Switt: Philadelphia Inquirer,* Obituary, January 19, 1990. Anonymous interviews with author, February 25, 2003, and April 1, 2003.

Page 111: *on Monday morning:* USSS Intermediate Report (IR), HWS/GCD to FJW, April 1, 1944.

Page 112: *two or more:* Israel Switt sworn statement, March 30, 1944.

Page 112: *"I do not"*: Israel Switt sworn statement, March 30, 1944.

Page 112: *"On my oath"*: Israel Switt sworn statement, March 30, 1944.

Page 112: *an unusually:* USSS IR, HWS/GCD to FJW, March 29, 1944.

Page 113: *nothing of interest:* USSS IR, HWS/GCD to FJW, April 1, 1944.

Page 113: *"I never had"*: Israel Switt sworn statement, March 30, 1944.

Page 113: *have any of:* Israel Switt sworn statement, March 30, 1944.

Page 114: *"his memory was"*: USSS IR, HWS/GCD to FJW, April 1, 1944.

Chapter 9: The Crooked Cashier

Page 115: *Reception Room:* U.S. Mint, Second Floor Assignment Plan, c. 1900. NARA RG 104, Entry 211A, NARA (CCP).

Page 116: *to install a:* Report, Helen C. Moore, Acting Superintendent, Philadelphia Mint to Director of the Mint. March 21, 1944, NARA RG 104, Entry 702, NARA (CCP).

Page 117: *representing the superintendent:* USSS IR, HWS/GCD to FJW, March 29, 1944.

Page 117: *bag of:* USSS IR, HWS/GCD to FJW, March 29, 1944.

Page 117: *charged to Edwin Dressel:* Treasury Memorandum to file, intitialed A.R., January 20, 1942. NARA RG 104, Entry 703, NARA (CCP).

Page 118: *Finally, in 1945:* Letter, Ross to Edwin H. Dressel (EHD), February 3, 1945. NARA RG 104, Entry 703 NARA (CCP).

Page 118: *a veteran: Philadelphia Inquirer,* May 30, 1940.

Page 118: *controlled the:* USSS Report, HWS/Charles B. Rich (CBR) to FJW, October 13, 1944.

Page 118: *"was their"*: USSS IR, HWS/GCD to FJW, April 21, 1944.

Page 118: *"lost"*: USSS IR, HWS/GCD to FJW, April 21, 1944.

Page 118: *superintendent:* Memo, FLH to FJW, April 23, 1945.

Page 118: *then Assistant:* USSS IR, HWS/GCD to FJW, April 21, 1944.

Page 118: *"a crook"*: USSS IR, HWS/GCD to FJW, April 21, 1944.

Page 118: *"wastage"*: USSS IR, HWS/GCD to FJW, April 21, 1944.

Page 118: *"Four Horsemen"*: USSS Report, HWS/CBR to FJW, October 13, 1944.

Page 119: *$2,421.79:* USSS Summary and Final Report, HWS/CBR to FJW, November 24, 1944.

Page 120: *$170.73:* USSS Summary and Final Report, HWS/CBR to FJW, November 24, 1944.

Page 120: *"A 71-year-old,":* Numismatist, July 1939, p. 549.

Page 120: *"immediately went"*: Memo, EHD to Secretary of Treasury, July 15, 1941. NARA RG 104, Entry 703, NARA (CCP).

Page 121: *ferret out: Philadelphia Inquirer,* May 30, 1944.

Page 121: *"As an aid"*: Memo, Comptroller General of the United States to Secretary of the Treasury, from July 15, 1941. NARA RG 104, Entry 703, NARA (CCP).

Page 121: *"defalcations"*: Letter, EHD to NTR, August 5, 1941. NARA RG 104, Entry 703, NARA (CCP).

Page 121: *"$16.75"*: Letter, EHD to NTR, January 15, 1944. NARA RG 104, Entry 703, NARA (CCP).

Page 121: *$1.50:* Letter, NTR to EHD, July 6, 1942. NARA RG 104, Entry 703, NARA (CCP).

Page 121: *"George A. McCann"*: Court Document, District Court of the United States for the Eastern District of Pennsylvania, June 6, 1940, Criminal Case 8618. NARA RG 21, NARA (CCP).

Page 122: *"held in the"*: Philadelphia Inquirer, March 25, 1941.

Page 122: *"Section 19"*: Taxay, *U.S. Mint and Coinage,* p. 67.

Page 122: *about two years:* USSS Memo, SA Connors to FJW, April 3, 1944.

Page 122: *had given:* USSS Demo, SA Connors to FJW, April 3, 1944.

Page 122: *"purchased it from"*: USSS Memo, SA Connors to FJW, April 3, 1944.

Page 123: *he was not positive:* USSS Memo, SA Oates to FJW, April 4, 1944.

Page 124: *"Mr. Mehl"*: USSS Memo, SA Oates to FJW, April 4, 1944.

Page 125: *"the time element"*: USSS IR, HWS/GCD to FJW, April 7, 1944.

Page 126: *"more or less"*: USSS IR, HWS/GCD to FJW, April 7, 1944.

Page 126: *"admitted a close"*: USSS IR, HWS/GCD to FJW, April 7, 1944.

Page 126: *"was a coin collector"*: USSS IR, HWS/GCD to FJW, April 7, 1944.

Page 126: *"was said to"*: USSS IR, HWS/GCD to FJW, April 7, 1944.

Page 126: *"was familiar"*: USSS IR, HWS/GCD to FJW, April 7, 1944.

Page 126: *"had many activities"*: USSS IR, HWS/GCD to FJW, April 7, 1944.

Page 127: *"persons wishing coins"*: USSS IR, HWS/GCD to FJW, April 7, 1944.

Page 127: *"wished to secure"*: USSS IR, HWS/GCD to FJW, April 7, 1944.

Page 127: *"Reed promised"*: USSS IR, HWS/GCD to FJW, April 7, 1944.

Page 127: *"endeavoring to cultivate"*: USSS IR, HWS/GCD to FJW, April 7, 1944.

Page 127: *in the regular:* USSS IR, HWS/GCD to FJW, April 7, 1944.

Page 127: *"running his hands"*: USSS IR, HWS/GCD to FJW, April 7, 1944.

Page 128: *"could permit," "[I] regarded"*: USSS IR, HWS/GCD to FJW, April 7, 1944.

Chapter 10: Working the List

Page 129: *"Anything else"*: Henry Morgenthau Diary, Book 718, pp. 30–31, FDRPL.

Page 129: *sent a memo*: USSS IOC, FJW to Fred W. Gruber (FWG), June 3, 1944.

Page 129: *"You might be"*: Henry Morgenthau Diary, Book 718, pp. 30–31, FDRPL.

Page 130: *"Henry the Morgue"*: Reilly, *Reilly of the White House,* p. 10.

Page 130: *"What did they"*: Henry Morgenthau Diary, Book 718, pp. 30–31, FDRPL.

Page 130: *"during the year"*: Letter, Morgenthau to Howe, February 6, 1934. FDRP, OF 21E, FDRPL.

Page 130: *"who was honest"*: Reilly, *Reilly of the White House,* p. 10.

Page 130: *"I would love"*: Letter, Morgenthau to Howe, February 6, 1934. FDRP, OF 21E, FDRPL.

Page 130: *"In compliance"*: Memo, Asst. US Treasurer to USSS FJW, April 6, 1944.

Page 131: *The two agents:* USSS IOC, FWG to FJW, April 12, 1944.

Page 131: *"1933 Double Eagle"*: USSS IR, HWS/GCD to FJW, April 13, 1944.

Page 132: *"D-E No. 1"*: USSS IR, HWS/GCD to FJW, April 13, 1944.

Page 134: *"as past experiences"*: USSS IR, HWS/GCD to FJW, April 21, 1944.

Page 134: *"I would take," about $250.00:* Sworn statement, Charles Rumpp, May 31, 1940, NARA RG 104, Entry 703, NARA (CCP).

Page 136: *"No subsequent"*: USSS IR, HWS/GCD to FJW, April 21, 1944.

Page 136: *"I can recall"*: Sworn statement, Charles Rumpp, May 31, 1940. NARA RG 104, Entry 703, NARA (CCP).

Page 136: *Louis Frizzle:* USSS IR, HWS/GCD to FJW, April 21, 1944.

Page 137: *"on at least"*: USSS IR, HWS/GCD to FJW, April 21, 1944.

Page 137: *"the 1933 Double"*: USSS IR, HWS/GCD to FJW, April 21, 1944.

Page 137: *"ordinarily have any"*: USSS IR, HWS/GCD to FJW, April 21, 1944.

Page 137: *instructed him in:* USSS IR, HWS/GCD to FJW, April 28, 1944.

Page 138: *"He admitted"*: USSS IR, HWS/GCD to FJW, April 28, 1944.

Page 138: *"about"*: USSS IR, HWS/GCD to FJW, April 21, 1944.

Page 138: *April 26, 1937:* Memo, EHD to Secretary of Treasury, July 15, 1941, p. 8. NARA RG 104, Entry 703, NARA (CCP).

Page 139: *"direct knowledge"*: USSS IR, EWS/GCD to FJW, April 21, 1944.

Page 139: *"a personal"*: USSS IR, HWS/GCD to FJW, April 21, 1944.

Page 139: *"was not a vigilant"*: USSS IR, HWS/GCD to FJW, April 21, 1944.

Page 139: *"that in view"*: USSS IR, HWS/GCD to FJW, April 21, 1944.

Page 140: *Charles M. Williams:* The earliest Secret Service reports confused Charles Williams with his father, Frank.

Page 140: *"first tried"*: USSS Memorandum Report (MR), RWR to FJW, April 14, 1944.

Page 141: *"upon learning"*: USSS MR, RWR to FJW, April 22, 1944.

Page 141: *in 1942:* USSS MR, STG to Supervising Agent Chicago, April 22, 1944.

Page 141: *no intention of:* USSS MR, Austin G. Sutterfield (AGS) to Supervising Agent, Louisville, KY, April 24, 1944.

Page 142: *"taken up by"*: USSS MR, STG to Supervising Agent Chicago, April 22, 1944.

Page 142: *"hold the coin,"*: Letter, J. Bell to FJW, April 18, 1944.

Page 142: *"Mr. Bell was," "from Mr. Reed"*: USSS MR, STG to Supervising Agent Chicago, May 20, 1944.

Page 142: *Abe Kosoff:* Throughout all the Secret Service internal memoranda and reports Kosoff's name was misspelled Kasoff.

Page 142: *"right around the"*: Kosoff, *Abe Kosoff Remembers*, p. 14.

Page 142: *"I'd play"*: Interview with DT, 2003.

Page 143: *"was the main"*: USSS Report, SA Milton Lipson to FJW, April 24, 1944.

Page 143: *he was aware:* USSS Report, Lipson to FWJ, April 24, 1944.

Page 143: *"was not so"*: USSS Report, Lipson to FWJ, April 24, 1944.

Page 144: *"an unbalanced"*: USSS Report, Lipson to FWJ, April 24, 1944.

Page 144: *"the truth"*: USSS Report, Lipson to FWJ, April 24, 1944.

Page 144: *"All these," "for some time," "some of"*: USSS Report, Lipson to FWJ, April 24, 1944.

Page 144: *"off the record," 33 double:* USSS Report, Lipson to FWJ, April 24, 1944.

Page 144: *"coin dealers'"*: Kosoff, *Abe Kosoff,* p. 27.

Page 144: *"seen the"*: USSS Report, Lipson to FWJ, April 24, 1944.

Page 145: *$150 and $175:* J. Barnet advertisement, *Numismatist,* April, 1938, p. 373.

Page 145: *$80 and $85:* H. Grunthal advertisement, *Numismatist,* May, 1942, p. 419.

Page 145: *"rode the hobby"*: New Netherlands Catalogue, 47, April 19, 1956.

Chapter 11: Wondering about Woodin

Page 147: *insisting on payment:* Letter, J. F. Bell to FJW, April 18, 1944.

Page 147: *"that some arrangement"*: Letter, Greenhill & Greenhill to J. Maloney, April 18, 1944.

Page 147: *"A criminal investigation"*: Letters, FJW to Greenhill & Greenhill, April 29, 1944 and FJW to J. F. Bell, May 1, 1944.

Page 148: *"serious consideration"*: USSS IOC, FJW to FWG, Phila., April 26, 1944.

Page 148: *"five coins," "knowing wink"*: USSS IR, HWS/GCD to FJW, March 29, 1944.

Page 148: *authority:* USSS IR, HWJ/GCD to FJW, March 29, 1944.

Page 149: *"musical or mystical"*: Letter, W. W. Rowe (grandson) to author, February, 13, 2003.

Page 149: *"a playboy who"*: Letter, W. W. Rowe to DT, February, 13, 2003.

Page 149: *London* Times: "Town Topics," anonymous magazine article, undated, post-1921, p. 60.

Page 149: *"forbade any member"*: "Town Topics," anonymous magazine article, undated, post-1921, p. 60.

Page 149: *"hard, dirty and"*: "You Can't Boss Others Unless You Can Boss Yourself," Harry A. Stewart. Unknown magazine article, September, 1922.

Page 149: *his teachers, Billy:* "You Can't Boss Others Unless You Can Boss Yourself," Harry A. Stewart. Unknown magazine article, September 1922.

Page 149: *Gutenberg Bible:* Letter, W. W. Rowe to author February 13, 2003.

Page 150: *remarkable collection:* Letter, W. W. Rowe to author, February, 13, 2003.

Page 150: *"Coins are the metallic"*: Edgar H. Adams and William H. Woodin,

United States Pattern Trial, and Experimental Pieces, 1913, Introduction.

Page 150: *"the finest collection":* Letter and attachment, William Wirt Mills to Professor Bradley Stoughton, December 14, 1933. FDRP, PPF 258, FDRPL.

Page 151: *"A man of":* "Town Topics," anonymous magazine article, undated, post-1921, p. 60.

Page 152: *more than fifty:* Letter and attachment, William Wirt Mills to Professor Bradley Stoughton, December 14, 1933. FDRP, PPF 258, FDRPL.

Page 152: *"a large, imposing":* Letter, W. W. Rowe to author, February, 13, 2003.

Page 152: *on the site: Toledo Times,* March 2, 1930.

Page 152: *of $8 a: San Francisco Californian,* February 6, 1930.

Page 152: *twelfth floor, $310,000: Toledo Times,* March 2, 1930.

Page 152: *"endeavoring to create it":* Woodin, *Syracuse University Alumni News,* June, 1933.

Page 152: *"director over": Syracuse University Alumni News,* June, 1933, p. 9.

Page 152: *"We are not": Time,* March 20, 1933, cover.

Page 153: *"Is the bill": Time,* March 20, 1933, p. 9.

Page 153: *"Some People Get All the Breaks":* by Cecil Jensen, undated, c. March-April, 1933 (W. H. Woodin, III).

Page 153: *"gold coin having":* Executive Order, April 5, 1933. FDRP, OF 229, FDRPL.

Page 154: *Sicilian, "defiant pompadour":* Arthur S. Schlesinger, *The Coming of the New Deal,* p. 435.

Page 154: *near-titan:* Schlesinger, *The Coming of the New Deal,* p. 435.

Page 154: *"quite legally":* Schlesinger, *The Coming of the New Deal,* p. 435.

Page 154: *"preferred list," "good, sound":* Schlesinger, *The Coming of the New Deal,* p. 436.

Page 154: *"House of Morgan":* Schlesinger, *The Coming of the New Deal,* p. 436.

Page 154: *"Discredited":* FDRP, OF 21, FDRPL.

Page 154: *"a class audience":* FDRP, OF 21, FDRPL.

Page 154: *"We are still":* Letter, Dr. C. S. Horton to FDR, May 26, 1933, FDRP, OF 21, FDRPL.

Page 154: *ashamed of:* Letter, W. W. Rowe to DT, February, 13, 2003.

Page 154: *"told the President":* Ickes, *Secret Diary,* p. 45.

Page 154: *"many people":* Schlesinger, *The Coming of the New Deal,* p. 437.

Page 154: *"Will Woodin is":* Memo, Steve Early to FDR, June 30, 1933. FDRP, PPF 258, FDRPL.

Page 155: *"feared the end":* Moley, *After,* p. 252.

Page 155: *"through the insistence," "This old boy":* Letter, WHW to FDR, July 5, 1933. FRDP, PPF 258, FDRPL.

Page 155: *"after a severe":* Letter, WHW to FDR, October 31, 1933. FRDP, PPF 258, FDRPL.

Page 155: *"been away":* Ickes, *Secret Diary,* p. 92.

Page 155: *"dangerous and probably":* Letter, WHW to FDR, October 27, 1933. FDRP, PPF 258, FDRPL.

Page 156: *The pages:* Figures from Cashier's Daily Statement of Receipts. NARA RG 104, Entry 330, NACP.

Page 157: *"of the improbability":* USSS IR, HWS/GCD to FJW, April 7, 1944.

Page 157: *silver certificate:* William H. Woodin III, personal recollection to DT, December, 2002.

Page 157: *"retained a quantity"*: USSS IR, HWS/GCD to FJW, May 5, 1944.

Page 158: *"Fred C. C. Boyd," "no 1933"*: USSS IR, HWS/GCD to FJW, May 5, 1944.

Page 159: *"Peter Pan," "held the controls"*: Moley, *27 Masters of Politics,* p. 186.

Chapter 12: The Red-Headed Philadelphia Sucker and the Deacon

Page 161: *"the coin held by"*: USSS OM, SAIC Whitman to FJW, June 15, 1944.

Page 162: *Chief got Strang:* USSS IR, HWS/GCD to FJW, May 5, 1944.

Page 162: *official records:* Internal memo and attachments, to Chief of Secret Service from US Treasurer's Office, June 30, 1944.

Page 162: *Childs:* Childs' coin, purchased on May 13, 1932, remained in the family until August, 1999, when it was sold at auction for $25,300. In the same collection was the finest known 1804 dollar which sold for a then-world record $4,140,000.

Page 163: *May, 1936:* USSS IR, HWS/GCD to FJW, June 23, 1944.

Page 163: *"red-headed"*: USSS IR, HWS/GCD to FJW, May 19, 1944.

Page 163: *"from Switt for"*: USSS IR, HWS/GCD to FJW, May 5, 1944.

Page 164: *records for 1937:* USSS IR, HWS/GCD to FJW, April 28, 1944.

Page 164: *Kosoff had conferred:* USSS IR, HWS/GCD to FJW, April 28, 1944.

Page 164: *"the ninth coin"*: USSS IR, HWS/GCD to FJW, April 28, 1944.

Page 164: *make himself available:* USSS IR, HWS/GCD to FJW, April 28, 1944.

Page 164: *one of the:* USSS IR, HWS/GCD to FJW, April 28, 1944.

Page 164: *"he [was] positive"*: USSS IR, HWS/GCD to FJW, April 28, 1944.

Page 164: *"was the first"*: USSS IR, HWS/GCD to FJW, April 28, 1944.

Page 164: *"gold-buying"*: USSS IR, HWS/GCD to FJW, May 5, 1944.

Page 165: *$758,003.23:* Mint Records, NARA RG 104, Entry 702, NARA (CCP).

Page 165: *"actually brought"*: USSS IR, HWS/GCD to FJW, May 5, 1944.

Page 165: *Melting Room:* Conversation with DT, April 1, 2003.

Page 165: *"While Switt and"*: USSS IR, HWS/GCD to FJW, May 5, 1944.

Page 165: *far below that:* USSS Summary and Final Report, HWS/CBR to FJW, November 24, 1944.

Page 165: *The Switts:* Conversation with author, April 1, 2003.

Page 166: *"he had paid"*: USSS IR, HWS/GCD to FJW, May 5, 1944.

Page 166: *"brought to the attention"*: USSS IR, HWS/GCD to FJW, May 5, 1944.

Page 166: *requested that any:* USSS IR, HWS/GCD to FJW, May 12, 1944.

Page 167: *"promised to consult"*: USSS IR, HWS/GCD to FJW, May 12, 1944.

Page 167: *sought to convey:* USSS IR, HWS/GCD to FJW, May 12, 1944.

Page 167: *"attitude was anything"*: USSS IR, HWS/GCD to FJW, May 12, 1944.

Page 167: *"they had not"*: USSS IR, HWS/GCD to FJW, May 12, 1944.

Page 167: *"intimated"*: USSS IR, HWS/GCD to FJW, May 12, 1944.

Page 167: *"used all of"*: USSS IR, HWS/GCD to FJW, May 12, 1944.

Page 168: *"on each occasion"*: USSS IR, HWS/GCD to FJW, May 12, 1944.

Page 168: *"My partner Ed"*: USSS Summary Report, HWS/GCD to FJW, July 15, 1944.

Page 168: *"was keeping two"*: USSS IR, HWS/GCD to FJW, May 12, 1944.

Page 168: *"that no 1933"*: USSS Summary Report, HWS/GCD to FJW, July 15, 1944.

Page 168: *"melted up a whole"*: USSS Summary Report, HWS/GCD to FJW, July 15, 1944.

Page 168: *intention to interview, all possible*: USSS IR, HWS/GCD to FJW, May 5, 1944.

Pages 168, 169: *clerical capacity, a four-family apartment house*: USSS IR, HWS/GCD to FJW, May 5, 1944.

Page 169: *business grossed*: USSS IR, HWS/GCD to FJW, May 19, 1944.

Page 169: *four or five*: USSS IR, HWS/GCD to FJW, May 19, 1944.

Page 169: *denied knowing*: USSS IR, HWS/GCD to FJW, May 19, 1944.

Page 169: *"had seen McCann"*: USSS IR, HWS/GCD to FJW, May 19, 1944.

Page 169: *"financial interest in"*: USSS IR, HWS/GCD to FJW, May 19, 1944.

Page 170: *"determine if they"*: USSS IR, HWS/GCD to FJW, May 19, 1944.

Page 170: *"It was obvious"*: USSS IR, HWS/GCD to FJW, May 19, 1944.

Page 170: *"declined to permit"*: USSS IR, HWS/GCD to FJW, May 19, 1944.

Page 170: *"profess[ed] to keep"*: USSS IR, HWS/GCD to FJW, May 5, 1944.

Page 171: *on April 15, 1944*: Letter, Louis E. Eliasberg, Sr., to FLH, September 4, 1952.

Page 172: *"original circulation"*: USSS IR, HWS/GCD to FJW, May 12, 1944.

Page 172: *paid Switt by*: USSS IR, HWS/GCD to FJW, May 19, 1944.

Page 172: *"he [had] evidently paid"*: USSS IR, HWS/GCD to FJW, May 19, 1944.

Page 172: *"no record in"*: USSS IR, HWS/GCD to FJW, May 19, 1944.

Page 172: *"the name of"*: USSS IR, HWS/GCD to FJW, May 12, 1944.

Page 172: *"for 1937 to 1943"*: USSS IR, HWS/GCD to FJW, May 12, 1944.

Page 172 *"engaged in"*: USSS IR, HWS/GCD to FJW, May 12, 1944.

Page 172: *Switt purchased*: USSS IR, HWS/GCD to FJW, May 12, 1944.

Page 172: *Reed Baby Cottage*: Ira Reed obituary, *Philadelphia Inquirer*, October 22, 1954.

Page 173: *"past developments"*: USSS IR, HWS/GCD to FJW, May 12, 1944.

Page 173: *court testimony*: USSS IR, HWS/GCD to FJW, May 30, 1944.

Chapter 13: Grounds for Recovery

Page 175: *"without the characteristic"*: Letter, Landis to FDR, May 10, 1944. FDRP, PPF 8586, FDRPL.

Page 176: *"pressed for the delivery"*: Letter, Greenhill & Greenhill to FJW, May 15, 1944.

Page 176: *"advice in the"*: Treasury Department, IOC, from JJO'C to HEG, May 4, 1944.

Page 176: *"particular attention"*: Treasury Department, IOC, from JJO'C to HEG, May 4, 1944.

Page 176: *"Whosoever"*: Excerpt, Section 48, Criminal Code (U.S.C., title 18, sec. 101). Treasury Department, IOC, from JJO'C to HEG, May 4, 1944.

Page 177: *"it was unnecessary"*: Treasury Department, IOC, from JJO'C to HEG, May 4, 1944. O'Connell cited "Lewis v. Hudspeth (1939 C.C.A. 10th Circ.) 103 F. (2d) 23."

Page 177: *"were stolen," "not lost"*: Treasury Department, IOC, from JJO'C to HEG, May 4, 1944.

Page 178: *"an intent to"*: Treasury Department, IOC, to HEG, May 4, 1944. O'Connell cited "Section 4 of the Gold Reserve Act of 1934, and U.S. vs 98 $20 U.S. Gold Coins (1937) 20F. Supp. 354."

Page 178: *"that they acquired"*: Treasury Department, IOC, from JJO'C to HEG, May 4, 1944.

Page 178: *"based on the"*: Treasury Department, IOC, from JJO'C to HEG, May 4, 1944.

Page 178: *"title to personal"*: Treasury Department IOC, JJO'C to HEG, May 4, 1944: O'Connell cited "Ventress v. Smith (1856) 10 Pet. 16; Murray v. Lardner (1864) 2 Wall. 110; Dows v. National Bank (1875) 91 U.S. 618; Bozeman Mortuary Assn. v. Fairchild (Ky. 1934) 66 S.W. (2d) 756."

Page 178: *"even if acquired," "rare coin"*: Treasury Department, IOC, JJO'C to HEG, May 4, 1944: O'Connell cited "Holly v. Domestic and Foreign Missionary Soc. (1889) 92 F. 745 affd 180 U.S. 284; State Bank v. United States (1885) 114 U.S. 401: Annotations 25 LRA (NS) 632, LRA 1917A 707."

Page 178: *"only partly"*: Treasury Department, IOC, from JJO'C to HEG, May 4, 1944.

Page 178: *"been exported to"*: Treasury Department, IOC, from JJO'C to HEG, May 4, 1944.

Page 178: *"it would be"*: Treasury Department, IOC, JJO'C to HEG, May 4, 1944.

Page 179: *"do anything which"*: USSS IR, HWS/GCD to FJW, May 30, 1944.

Page 179: *business integrity*: USSS IR, HWS/GCD to FJW, May 30, 1944.

Page 179: *gold dealings*: USSS IR, HWS/GCD to FJW, May 30, 1944.

Page 179: *operated a melting*: USSS IR, HWS/GCD to FJW, May 30, 1944.

Page 179: *"that he [had]"*: USSS IR, HWS/GCD to FJW, May 30, 1944.

Page 180: *"he denied"*: USSS IR, HWS/GCD to FJW, June 23, 1944.

Page 180: *"the correct"*: USSS IR, HWS/GCD to FJW, May 30, 1944.

Page 180: *"keen delight," entirely recovered*: Letter, FDR to Farouk, June 5, 1944. PPF 8586, FDRP, FDRPL.

Page 181: *"famous American"*: Wilson and Day, *Special Agent*, p. 94.

Page 182: *$2,421.79, $3,087.84, financial worth*: USSS Summary Report, HWS/GCD to FJW, July 15, 1944.

Page 182: *"statements with"*: Treasury Memorandum to file, initialed A.R., January 20, 1942. NARA RG 703, NARA (CCP).

Page 182: *false*: Treasury Memorandum to file, initialed A.R., January 20, 1942. NARA RG 104, Entry 703, NARA (CCP).

Page 182: *explained the source*: Treasury Memorandum to file, intitialed A.R., January 20, 1942. NARA RG 104, Entry 703, NARA (CCP).

Page 182: *"personal transactions"*: Treasury Memoradum to file, intitialed A.R., January 20, 1942. NARA RG 104, Entry 703, NARA (CCP).

Page 183: *financial numbers*: USSS Report, HWS/GCD to FJW, June 23, 1944.

Page 183: *"held a Power"*: USSS Report, HWS/GCD to FJW, June 23, 1944.

Page 183: *were using a*: USSS Report, HWS/GCD to FJW, June 23, 1944.

Page 183: *"Recordak"*: USSS Report, HWS/GCD to FJW, June 23, 1944.

Page 184: *circulated in*: USSS Report, HWS/GCD to FJW, June 23, 1944.

Page 185: *"Surely by this"*: Letter, Greenhill & Greenhill to FJW, July 23, 1944.

Page 185: *Pepper wrote Wilson*: Letter, Hon. Claude Pepper to FJW, August 2, 1944.

Page 185: *"recent victories," "still cherish[ed]"*: Letter, Farouk to FDR, August 5, 1944. FRRP, PSF 28, FDRPL.

Page 185: *"advance any"*: USSS IOC, FWG to FJW, October 10, 1944.

Page 185: *"intimated that"*: USSS IOC, FWG to FJW, October 10, 1944.

Chapter 14: A Clumsy Liar

Page 187: *real estate business:* USSS IR, HWS/CBR to FJW, October 13, 1944.

Page 188: *"custody at any"*: USSS IR, HWS/CBR to FJW, October 13, 1944.

Page 188: *had the only:* USSS IR, HWS/CBR to FJW, October 13, 1944.

Page 188: *"they were placed"*: USSS IR, HWS/CBR to FJW, October 13, 1944.

Page 188: *"At no time"*: USSS IR, HWS/CBR to FJW, October 13, 1944.

Page 188: *"he had no"*: USSS IR, HWS/CBR to FJW, October 13, 1944.

Page 188: *merely relaying:* USSS IR, HWS/CBR to FJW, October 13, 1944.

Page 188: *he had never:* USSS IR, HWS/CBR to FJW, October 13, 1944.

Page 188: *"professed to have"*: USSS IR, HWS/CBR to FJW, October 13, 1944.

Page 188: *"carte blanche," held the only key:* USSS IR, HWS/CBR to FJW, October 13, 1944.

Page 188: *January 27, 1942:* Letter, Director of the Mint to Superintendent, U.S. Mint, Philadelphia, (with enclosed letters). NARA RG 104, Entry 703, NARA (CCP).

Page 189: *retirement funds:* USSS IR, HWS/CBR to FJW, October 13, 1944.

Page 189: *$6,500:* McCann continued to battle over the $6,500 over the next five years. The tit-for-tat series of suits and countersuits that he instigated was finally dismissed on October 24, 1947. NARA RG 104, Entry 703, NARA (CCP).

Page 189: *extremely agitated:* USSS IR, HWS/CBR to FJW, October 13, 1944.

Page 189: *first allegation:* USSS IR, HWS/CBR to FJW, October 13, 1944.

Page 189: *According to:* USSS IR, HWS/CBR to FJW, October 13, 1944.

Pages 189, 190: *"McCann said," "certified to"*: USSS IR, HWS/CBR to FJW, October 13, 1944.

Page 190: *"the representative"*: USSS IR, HWS/CBR to FJW, October 13, 1944.

Page 190: *"in the interest"*: USSS IR, HWS/CBR to FJW, October 13, 1944.

Page 190: *"that McCann's health"*: USSS IR, HWS/CBR to FJW, October 13, 1944.

Page 190: *direct contradiction:* USSS IR, HWS/CBR to FJW, October 13, 1944.

Page 191: *death of Fred Chaffin:* Philadelphia Inquirer, June 18, 1936.

Page 191: *"accumulated"*: USSS IR, HWS/CBR to FJW, October 13, 1944.

Page 191: *the Four Horsemen:* USSS IR, HWS/CBR to FJW, October 13, 1944.

Page 192: *"redeemed his"*: USSS IR, HWS/CBR to FJW, October 20, 1944.

Page 192: *Ziegler had died: Philadelphia Inquirer,* February 16, 1938.

Page 192: *power of attorney:* USSS IR, HWS/CBR to FJW, October 20, 1944.

Page 192: *"gave direct lie"*: USSS IR, HWS/CBR to FJW, October 20, 1944.

Page 193: *"could not have"*: USSS IR, HWS/CBR to FJW, October 20, 1944.

Page 193: *"had the only"*: USSS IR, HWS/CBR to FJW, October 20, 1944.

Page 193: *"that his records"*: USSS IR, HWS/CBR to FJW, October 20, 1944.

Page 193: *"in turn call"*: USSS IR, HWS/CBR to FJW, November 4, 1944.

Page 193: *"to obtain"*: USSS IR, HWS/CBR to FJW, November 4, 1944.

Page 194: *"definite decision," "that the Government"*: USSS IR, HWS/CBR to FJW, November 4, 1944.

Page 194: *"no account"*: USSS IR, HWS/CBR to FJW, November 4, 1944.

Page 194: *"a coincidence," "unauthorized"*: USSS IR, HWS/CBR to FJW, November 4, 1944.

Page 195: *"if divided," little opportunity*: USSS IR, HWS/CBR to FJW, November 4, 1944. The regulations allowed a legal tolerance of one ounce per thousand.

Page 195: *"for the purpose"*: USSS IR, HWS/CBR to FJW, November 4, 1944.

Page 195: *97.9 percent: Annual Report of the Secretary of the Treasury, 1945,* p. 259.

Page 196: *"set forth"*: Letter, FWG to G. Gleeson, December 18, 1944.

Page 196: *"any criminal"*: Letter, FWG to G. Gleeson, December 18, 1944.

Page 196: *"We are awaiting," "an opinion"*: Treasury Department Memo, FJW to Mr. McNeill, January 17, 1945.

Chapter 15: Seizures, Suits, and Surrender

Page 197: *"were showing"*: FDRP, *The President's Trip to the Crimea Conference and Great Bitter Lake, Egypt, January 22 to February 28, 1945.* OF 200 4E, FDRPL.

Page 198: *"in hopes of"*: Bishop, *FDR's Last Year,* p. 299.

Page 198: *"he could not"*: John Gunther, *Roosevelt in Retrospect,* p. 360.

Page 198: *"conversation"*: Bishop, *FDR's Last Year,* p. 441.

Page 199: *"greatest enthusiasm"*: Letter: S. Pinkney Tuck to FDR, April 3, 1945, FDRP, PSF 28, FDRPL.

Page 200: *"coins were embezzled"*: Letter, HEG to 1933 double eagle owners of record, May 15, 1945.

Page 200: *Criminal Code:* Section 48 (U.S.C. title 18, sec. 101); Letter, HEG to 1933 double eagle owners of record May 15, 1945.

Page 200: *"retention"*: Letter, HEG to 1933 double eagle owners of record May 15, 1945.

Page 200: *"It is possible"*: USSS Summary and Final Report, HWS/CBR to FJW, November 24, 1944, p. 5.

Page 201: *F. C. C. Boyd: NYT* Obituary, September 9, 1958.

Page 201: *"I do not care"*: Letter, F.C.C. Boyd to HEG, May 31, 1946.

Page 201: *"for the American"*: USSS Memo to file, June 21, 1945. Boyd meant *Numismatist.*

Page 201: *"any other coins," "the proper"*: USSS Memo to file, June 21, 1945.

Page 201: *to surrender:* USSS MR, RWR to FJW, June 5, 1945.

Page 201: *wired Williams:* USSS MR, RWR to FJW, June 21, 1945.

Page 202: *"numismatic circles"*: Letter, HJS to HEG, May 19, 1945.

Page 202: *"one coin of"*: Letter, HJS to HEG, May 19, 1945.

Page 202: *permissive seizure:* USSS Memo, JJMcG to FJW, June 22, 1945.

Page 202: *L. G. Barnard:* USSS Initial Report, AGS to FJW, June 8, 1945.

Page 203: *"declaratory judgment"*: USSS Initial Report, AGS to FJW, June 8, 1945.

Page 203: *"under protest," "right to"*: Letter, JAS to Treasury Department, June 20, 1945.

Page 203: *"that's bad"*: Memo to File: Helen G. Moore, September 26, 1945, NARA RG 104, Entry 702, NARA (CCP).

Page 204: *exchanged for gold:* Abstract Cashier's Daily Settlement Log, March 7, 1933–April 12, 1933. Prepared by E.G.S. for Barnard trial, June 16, 1947. NARA RG 104, Entry 703, NARA (CCP).

Page 204: *"while the Department"*: Letter, General Counsel Treasury Dept to Harry J. Stein, July 3, 1946.

Page 204: *Wilson's retirement:* Wilson and Day, *Special Agent,* p. 233.

Page 205: *Barnard stipulations:* USA vs. Barnard, Stipulation. The stipulation that the weight of the gold coins "was the same as the weight of the bars" after melting, was neither strictly accurate, nor hideously wrong either. When gold is melted, there are natural losses, acceptable at the Mint to a tolerance of one thousandth of an ounce. These parameters had been met and bettered.

Page 205: *in good faith:* USA vs. Barnard, Answer of Defendant, filed Sept. 6, 1945.

Page 205: *minted:* USA vs. Barnard, Answer of Defendant, filed Sept. 6, 1945.

Page 205: *"money or currency":* USA vs. Barnard, Opinion, July 22, 1947.

Page 205: *later went broke:* Kosoff, *Coin World,* March 24, 1982.

Page 206: *"intelligent":* Barrie St. Clair McBride, *Farouk of Egypt,* p. 149.

Page 206: *"In the palace":* McBride, *Farouk of Egypt,* p. 186.

Page 207: *"Let us spare":* McBride, *Farouk of Egypt,* p. 195.

Pages 207, 208: *there was a cloud, "very much":* Letter, LEE to LFH, September 4, 1952.

Chapter 16: A Modern Day Aladdin's Cave: The Coin Escapes Again

Page 210: *"Custodian of":* Kosoff, *Abe Kosoff,* p. 57.

Page 210: *in liquidation:* Kosoff, *Abe Kosoff,* p. 57.

Page 210: *"workings of":* Frank Hermann, *Sotheby's: Portait of an Auction House,* p. 343.

Page 211: *"dispossessed":* Hermann, *Sotheby's,* p. 341.

Page 211: *$890,000:* Kosoff, *Abe Kosoff,* p. 59.

Page 211: *"in a public," "have to":* Kosoff, *Abe Kosoff,* p. 57.

Page 211: *"modern day," "thrown open":* Hermann, *Sotheby's,* p. 343.

Page 211: *had to cope:* McBride, *Farouk of Egypt,* p. 209.

Page 212: *committees:* McBride, *Farouk of Egypt,* p. 211.

Page 213: *"I guarantee":* Personal correspondence: D. J. Crowther to DT, August 20, 2002.

Page 213: *"example of expertise":* Kosoff, *Abe Kosoff,* p. 63.

Page 213: *"rug woven":* Sotheby's, *The Palace Collections of Egypt,* 1954, lot 2640 (sold: £23).

Page 213: *robust, suntanned:* Edward Baldwin correspondence with DT, May 19, 2003.

Page 213: *raise the standard: Washington Daily News,* December 2, 1953.

Page 214: *"The rare coins": Washington Daily News,* December 2, 1953.

Page 214: *"the coin held":* USSS IOM, AEW to UEB, January 15, 1954.

Page 214: *return of the coin:* Treasury Department Memorandum, Counsel Hugo A. Ranta to Secret Service Assistant Chief Harry Edward Neil, December 23, 1953.

Page 214: *Department of State:* Treasury Department Memorandum, Counsel Hugo A. Ranta to Secret Service Assistant Chief Harry Edward Neil, December 23, 1953.

Page 214: *"obligated to":* USSS Memo, RD to UEB, December 3, 1953.

Page 214: *present Egyptian, "To fail":* USSS Memo, RD to UEB, December 3, 1953.

Page 214: *"from the nine":* USSS Memo, RD to UEB, December 3, 1953.

Page 215: *"found among the effects":* Letter, E. H. Adams to J. W. Garrett, Sept. 11, 1933, American Numismatic Society Archives.

Page 216: *"Hans, your":* Schulman in Kosoff, *Abe Kosoff,* p. 94.

Page 216: *"$500,000,000"*: *Washington Daily News.* December 2, 1953.

Page 216: *"extremely fine"*: Sotheby's, *The Palace Collections of Egypt,* 1954, lot 185.

Page 216: *considerable interest:* USSS IOM, AEW to UEB, January 15, 1954.

Page 218: *"whole new"*: Hermann, *Sotheby's,* p. 343.

Page 218: *"the Treasury"*: State Department Wire, Washington D.C. to Cairo, January 27, 1954.

Page 218: *"warning that"*: State Department Wire, Washington D.C. to Cairo, January 27, 1954.

Page 218: *"American being"*: State Department Wire, Washington D.C. to Cairo, January 27, 1954.

Page 219: *was still on display:* State Department Wire, Cairo to Washington, D.C., February 11, 1954.

Page 219: *the purchase:* State Department Wire, Cairo to Washington, D.C., February 11, 1954.

Page 219: *John Jay Pittman:* Bob Korver, *Coin World,* June 3, 2002, p. 114.

Page 220: *"it was illegally"*: Pitman in Korver, *Coin World,* June 3, 2002, p. 114.

Page 220: *"President Mohamed"*: State Department Wire, Cairo to Washington, D.C., February 17, 1954.

Page 220: *Schulman had agreed:* Schulman in Kosoff, *Abe Kosoff,* p. 94.

Page 220: *ordered the withdrawal:* State Department Wire, Cairo to Secretary of State, February 23, 1954.

Page 221: *The first four:* A. Kosoff, *Numismatist,* April 1954, p. 340.

Page 222: *"excellent prices"*: A. Kosoff, *Numismatist,* April 1954, p. 340.

Page 222: *"the auctioneer"*: A. Kosoff, *Numismatist,* April 1954, p. 340.

Page 222: *"was a bit more"*: A. Kosoff, *Numismatist,* April 1954, p. 340.

Page 223: *"The 1933 Double Eagle"*: A. Kosoff, *Numismatist,* April 1954, p. 340.

Page 223: *"the controversial"*: State Department, Foreign Service Despatch, Consul Basil F. Macgowan Cairo to State Department, Washington D.C., February 25, 1954.

Page 223: *"Two reliable"*: State Department, Foreign Service Despatch, Consul Basil F. Macgowan Cairo to State Department, Washington D.C., February 25, 1954.

Page 223: *"prices were"*: A. Kosoff, *Numismatist,* April 1954, p. 341.

Page 224: *sit by:* Hermann, *Sotheby's,* p. 344.

Page 224: *"Note No. 11"*: State Department Wire, Cairo to Washington D.C., February 26, 1954.

Page 224: *"by order of"*: State Department Wire, Cairo to Washington D.C., February 26, 1954.

Page 224: *"he hoped to"*: State Department Wire, Cairo to Washington D.C., March 31, 1954.

Page 225: *"Keep on top"*: USSS Memo to file, May 11, 1954.

Page 225: *"make further"*: USSS Memo, FNG to UEB, December 15, 1953.

Page 225: *"Switt and Silver's"*: USSS Memo, FNG to UEB, December 15, 1953.

Page 225: *"barred from"*: USSS Memo, SA George J. Shersen to UEB, August 15, 1956.

Page 225: *Mint was:* USSS Memo, UEB to SAIC NY AEW, July 27, 1956.

Page 226: *"by the Superintendent"*: Letter, FLH to Superintendent Philadelphia Mint, August 17, 1956.

Page 226: *"manufactured but not issued"*: U.S. Mint Certificate of Destruction, August 21, 1956.

Page 226: *"face-down"*: *New York Herald Tribune,* March 19, 1965.

Chapter 17: A Double Eagle Reappears

Page 231: *was looking:* Conversations, Eric Streiner with author 2002–2004.

Page 232: *thought to sell:* United States of America, vs. A $20 Gold Coin; known as a 1933 "Double Eagle," U.S. District Court, Southern District of New York, 96 Civ. 2527 (AKH): Deposition, ADC, January 18, 2000, p. 17.

Page 232: *"completely lied":* Deposition, ADC, January 18, 2000, p. 18.

Page 232: *"youth ethic":* Deposition, ADC, January 18, 2000, p. 18.

Page 233: *"was pretty":* Deposition, ADC, January 18, 2000, p. 52.

Page 233: *"had all sorts":* Deposition, ADC, January 18, 2000, p. 53.

Page 234: *"knew a great":* Deposition, ADC, January 18, 2000, p. 52.

Page 234: *"predominantly Arab":* Deposition, ADC, January 18, 2000, p. 48.

Page 234: *was always:* Deposition, ADC, January 18, 2000, p. 50.

Page 234: *"say to him":* Deposition, ADC, January 18, 2000, p. 50.

Page 234: *several thousand:* Deposition, ADC, January 18, 2000, p. 51.

Page 234: *"the logical":* Deposition, ADC, January 18, 2000, p. 51.

Page 234: *"Who the":* Deposition, ADC, January 18, 2000, p. 51.

Page 234: *"made a very":* Deposition, ADC, January 18, 2000, p. 77.

Page 234: *doubled:* Deposition, ADC, January 18, 2000, pp. 77–80.

Page 234: *"about $100,000":* Deposition, ADC, January 18, 2000, p. 77.

Page 235: *they had, "they would be":* United States of America, vs. A $20 Gold Coin, known as a 1933 "Double Eagle," U.S. District Court, Southern District of New York, 96 Civ. 2527 (AKH):

Deposition, Stephen Fenton (SF), August 4, 1999, p. 217/8.

Page 235: *Stephen C. Fenton:* Interview, SF to David Tripp (DT), January 14, 2003.

Page 237: *one rarity:* A 1909-O half eagle, from Farouk lot 265. Deposition ADC, January 18, 2000 (as lot 165 in error). Confirmed by SF to DT. The fake was an 1849 Massachusetts & Co. $5 (these are believed to have been made by Stephen Nagy in the early twentieth century). Interview, SF to DT, January 14, 2003.

Page 237: *sever links:* Deposition, ADC, January 18, 2000, p. 19.

Page 237: *because it:* Deposition, ADC, January 18, 2000, p. 21.

Page 237: *in continuing:* Deposition, ADC, January 18, 2000, p. 21.

Page 238: *Sometime early:* Deposition, ADC, January 18, 2000, p. 70.

Page 238: *about thirty-two:* Deposition, ADC, January 18, 2000, p. 75.

Page 238: *medium build:* Interview, ADC to DT, November 20, 2003.

Page 238: *"was the source":* Deposition, ADC, January 18, 2000, p. 71.

Page 238: *"The [Cairene]":* Deposition, ADC, January 18, 2000, p. 73.

Page 238: *The "Colonel":* Deposition, ADC, January 18, 2000, p. 72.

Page 238: *a collector:* Deposition, ADC, January 18, 2000, p. 73.

Page 238: *"had acquired":* Deposition, ADC, January 18, 2000, p. 72.

Page 238: *"as one of":* Deposition, ADC, January 18, 2000, p. 74.

Page 239: *be discreet:* Deposition, ADC, January 18, 2000, p. 76.

Page 239: *1851:* Lot 1744 in the Farouk catalogue, it was catalogued as one of two known. Currently considered "unique," Judd (2003 edition), p. 61, no. 133.

Page 240: *"capable of," "for a man"*: Deposition, ADC, January 18, 2000, p. 107.

Page 240: *"Middle Eastern"*: Deposition, ADC, January 18, 2000, p. 135.

Page 240: *"paid it"*: Deposition, ADC, January 18, 2000, p. 135.

Page 240: *£12,700:* Deposition, ADC, January 18, 2000, Receipts Book, Exhibit BB.

Page 240: *was only:* Deposition, ADC, January 18, 2000, p. 104.

Page 240: *"possibly by David Spink"*: Deposition, ADC, January 18, 2000, p. 62.

Page 241: *"It is not"*: Deposition, ADC, January 18, 2000, p. 172.

Page 241: *"always said"*: Deposition, ADC, January 18, 2000, p. 172.

Page 241: *"Maybe it," "If you sell"*: Deposition, ADC, January 18, 2000, p. 141.

Page 242: *nearly fifty:* Including all, or portions of lots 184, 252, 274, 277, 713, 737, 739, 745, 756, 783, 1565, 1895, 1986, etc.

Page 242: *1994:* Interview, ADC to DT, November 20, 2003.

Page 242: *the 1933, "Of course"*: Interview, SF to DT, January 14, 2003.

Page 242: *"just said"*: Deposition, ADC, January 18, 2000, p. 228.

Page 242: *"Have you seen"*: Deposition, ADC, January 18, 2000, p. 229.

Page 242: *"If it is"*: Deposition, ADC, January 18, 2000, p. 249.

Page 242: *"self-described"*: AUSA Jane Levine in Deposition, ADC, January 18, 2000, p. 251.

Page 243: *mesmerized:* Interview, SF to DT, January 14, 2003.

Page 243: *Bayswater:* Interview, ADC to DT, November 20, 2003.

Page 244: *"It just seemed"*: Deposition, SF, August 4, 1999, p. 255.

Page 244: *different memories:* Deposition, ADC, January 18, 2000, p. 255.

Page 244: *slightly undermined:* Deposition, ADC, January 18, 2000, p. 255.

Page 245: *wire the funds:* Knightsbridge Coins Purchase Number 11720. USA v. 1933 $20: Supplemental Motion for Summary Judgement, March 17, 2000, Exhibits C & D.

Page 245: *"Yes"*: Deposition, ADC, January 18, 2000, p. 258.

Page 245: *mutually agreed:* Deposition, ADC, January 18, 2000, p. 262.

Page 245: *"I will leave it"*: Deposition, ADC, January 18, 2000, p. 262–264. (The verbatim transcript was without common conjunctions that have been provided in the text for clarity.) Following the auction, Fenton compensated de Clermont for an undisclosed figure.

Page 245: *thought he might keep it:* Interview, SF to DT, January 14, 2003.

Chapter 18: The Homecoming Deal

Page 247: *"none placed"*: R. S. Yeoman, *A Guide Book of United States Coins,* 48th edition, 1995, p. 223.

Page 247: *"the coins"*: Robert Friedberg, *Gold Coins of the World,* 6th edition, 1992, p. 670.

Page 247: *"That's strange"*: Deposition, SF, August 4, 1999, p. 247.

Page 248: *According to, David Hall:* Interview, SF to DT, January 14, 2003.

Page 248: *recall meeting:* United States of America, vs. A $20 Gold Coin, known as a 1933 "Double Eagle," U.S. District Court, Southern District of New York, 96 Civ. 2527 (AKH). Declaration in opposition to Summary Judgement, exhibit TT: Sworn Affidavit, J. Parrino (JP), February 8, 1996.

Page 248: *worked for:* Sworn Affidavit, JP, February 8, 1996.

Page 248: *Boy's Life:* JP in *Kansas City Star,* February 14, 1996.

Page 249: *stature in: Kansas City Star,* February 14, 1996.

Page 249: *remembered that a dealer:* Jay Parrino's the Mint L.L.C. vs. Jack R. Moore (JM), U.S. District Court for the Western District of Missouri, 98-1105-CV-W-8-BC-SOW-ECF, October 20, 1998.

Page 249: *"on many":* JP vs. JM, Complaint, p. 2.

Page 249: *he was no longer:* Sworn Affidavit, JP, February 8, 1996.

Page 249: *sold furniture:* United States of America, vs. A $20 Gold Coin, known as a 1933 "Double Eagle," U.S. District Court, Southern District of New York, 96 Civ. 2527 (AKH): Deposition Jack Moore (JM), December 16, 1997, p. 44.

Page 249: *three hundred dollars:* Deposition, JM, December 16, 1997, p. 18.

Page 250: *He liked:* Deposition, JM Moore, December 16, 1997, pp. 66–67.

Page 250: *since 1961:* Deposition, JM, December 16, 1997, p. 13.

Page 250: *1975:* Deposition, JM, December 16, 1997, p. 13.

Page 250: *buying and selling:* Deposition, JM, December 16, 1997, p. 14.

Page 250: *loved coins:* Deposition, JM, December 16, 1997, p. 235.

Page 250: *Good money:* Deposition, JM, December 16, 1997, pp. 235–236.

Page 250: *January, 1993:* Deposition, JM, December 16, 1997, p. 48.

Page 250: *with sales of:* Deposition, JM, December 16, 1997, p. 23.

Page 250: *probably made:* Deposition, JM, December 16, 1997, p. 16.

Page 250: *1990 or 1991:* Deposition, JM, December 16, 1997, p. 24.

Page 250: *Between 1991:* Deposition, JM, December 16, 1997, p. 25 *ff.*

Page 250: *than twenty:* Deposition, JM, December 16, 1997, p. 26.

Page 250: *six thousand dollars:* Deposition, JM, December 16, 1997, p. 27.

Page 250: *five and ten:* Deposition, JM, December 16, 1997, p. 26.

Page 251: *"started on it":* Deposition, JM, December 16, 1997, p. 24.

Page 251: *"five or six":* Deposition, JM, December 16, 1997, p. 235.

Page 251: *about two:* Deposition, JM, December 16, 1997, p. 67.

Page 251: *wasn't very successful:* Moore said that "I guess I invested in the wrong [coins]" and wasn't a "good businessman." Deposition, JM, December 16, 1997, p. 236.

Page 251: *turned a profit:* Deposition, JM, December 16, 1997, pp. 48–51.

Page 251: *one, maybe two:* Deposition, JM, December 16, 1997, p. 69.

Page 252: *1991 or maybe 1992:* "Several years ago (4 or 5)." Sworn Affidavit, J. Parrino, February, 8, 1996.

Page 252: *knew of a, interested in purchasing:* Sworn Affidavit, J. Parrino, February 8, 1996.

Page 252: *on numerous occasions:* Parrino vs. Moore, Complaint, p. 2.

Page 252: *At a coin:* Deposition, JM, December 16, 1997, p. 71.

Page 252: *"wanted to buy":* Deposition, JM, December 16, 1997, p. 71.

Page 252: *"he knew":* Deposition, JM, December 16, 1997, p. 74.

Page 252: *"was no reason":* Deposition, JM, December 16, 1997, p. 74.

Page 252: *"it was illegal":* Deposition, JM, December 16, 1997, p. 74.

Page 252: *"probably ten":* Deposition, JM, December 16, 1997, p. 75.

Notes

Page 252: *"just picked":* Interview, SF to DT, January 14, 2003.

Page 252: *"Yes, my":* Interview, SF to DT, January 14, 2003.

Page 252: *"wasn't getting":* Interview, SF to DT, January 14, 2003.

Page 253: *"available from":* United States of America, vs. A $20 Gold Coin, known as a 1933 "Double Eagle," U.S. District Court, Southern District of New York, 96 Civ. 2527 (AKH): Deposition R. David Freriks (RDF), March 17, 1998, p. 170 and exhibit 27.

Page 253: *a small-time:* Deposition, RDF, March 17, 1998, p. 209.

Page 253: *"he was knowledgeable":* Deposition, RDF, March 17, 1998, p. 210.

Page 253: *casually and:* Deposition, RDF, March 17, 1998, exhibit 27. Deposition, JM, December 16, 1997, pp. 165–166.

Page 253: *once or twice:* Deposition, RDF, March 17, 1998, exhibit 27. Deposition, JM, December 16, 1997, pp. 167–168.

Page 253: *illegal to own:* Deposition, RDF, March 17, 1998, p. 34. Deposition, JM, December 16, 1997, p. 169.

Page 253: *"been cheated":* Deposition, RDF, March 17, 1998, exhibit 27.

Page 253: *there was one deal:* Deposition, JM, December 16, 1997, p. 226.

Page 253: *"so high":* Deposition, JM, December 16, 1997, p. 226.

Page 253: *feared Parrino:* Deposition, RDF, March 17, 1998, exhibit 27 and Deposition, Moore, December 16, 1997, p. 173.

Page 254: *felt Parrino was:* Deposition, RDF, March 17, 1998, exhibit 27.

Page 254: *$750,000:* Deposition, RDF, March 17, 1998, pp. 37–40.

Page 254: *"transaction should":* Deposition, RDF, March 17, 1998, p. 38.

Page 254: *buyer's expert, the transaction:* Deposition, RDF, March 17, 1998, p. 37–40.

Page 254: *tape recorder:* Deposition, JM, December 16, 1997, pp. 152–156. Deposition, RDF, March 17, 1998, pp. 291–292.

Page 254: *"We are":* USSS Taped Conversation, JM and JP, December 15, 1995.

Page 255: *any hesitation:* Interview, SF to DT, January 14, 2003.

Page 255: *"person had agreed":* USSS Taped Conversation, JM and JP, December 18, 1995.

Page 256: *Three gold bars:* Transaction, November 6, 1995. Described as Farouk lots: 16, 18, 25, 312, 315, 324–326, 357, 358 (part), 362, USA v. 1933 $20: Motion for Summary Judgement, February 1, 2000, Exhibit BB.

Page 257: *cut-and-dried deal:* Interview, SF to DT, January 14, 2003.

Page 257: *"just didn't":* Deposition, JM, December 16, 1997, p. 154.

Page 257: *"inquired as to":* Deposition, RDF, March 17, 1998, p. 196.

Page 257: *seventy-five thousand dollars:* Deposition, RDF, March 17, 1998, pp. 196–200.

Page 257: *"maybe he should":* Deposition, RDF, March 17, 1998, p. 197.

Page 257: *"was his option":* Deposition, RDF, March 17, 1998, p. 199.

Page 257: *payment from:* Barry Berke in Deposition, RDF, March 17, 1998, p. 199.

Page 257: *"not to do it":* Deposition, RDF, March 17, 1998, p. 202.

Page 257: *"not to attempt":* Deposition, RDF, March 17, 1998, p. 203.

Page 257: *"a separate transaction":* Deposition, RDF, March 17, 1998, p. 203.

Page 257: *"one group of":* USSS Recorded telephone conversation, JP and JM, January 3, 1996. USA v. 1933 $20. Opposition for summary judgement, exhibit QQ.

Page 257: *coming to:* USSS Recorded telephone conversation, JP and JM, January 3, 1996. USA v. 1933 $20. Opposition for summary judgement, exhibit QQ.

Page 257: *"That's the dates," "I will pick":* USSS Recorded telephone conversation, JP and JM, January 3, 1996. USA v. 1933 $20. Opposition for summary judgement, exhibit QQ.

Page 257: *"Yes," "there's another one":* USSS Recorded telephone conversation, JP and JM, January 3, 1996. USA v. 1933 $20. Opposition for summary judgement, exhibit QQ.

Page 258: *"Can't you find":* USSS Recorded telephone conversation, JP and JM, January 3, 1996. USA v. 1933 $20. Opposition for summary judgement, exhibit QQ.

Page 258: *"Let's do it":* USSS Recorded telephone conversation, JP and JM, January 3, 1996. USA v. 1933 $20. Opposition for summary judgement, exhibit QQ.

Page 258: *"my buyer":* USSS Recorded telephone conversation, JP and JM, January 12, 1996. USA v. 1933 $20. Opposition for summary judgement, exhibit QQ.

Page 258: *"He is going":* USSS Recorded telephone conversation, JP and JM, January 12, 1996. USA v. 1933 $20. Opposition for summary judgement, exhibit QQ.

Page 258: *"Let's be":* USSS Recorded telephone conversation, JP and JM, January 12, 1996. USA v. 1933 $20. Opposition for summary judgement, exhibit QQ.

Page 258: *legislation:* USSS Recorded telephone conversation, JP and JM, January 12, 1996. USA v. 1933 $20. Opposition for summary judgement, exhibit QQ.

Page 258: *"Just drop":* USSS Recorded telephone conversation, JP and JM, January 12, 1996. USA v. 1933 $20. Opposition for summary judgement, exhibit QQ.

Page 258: *"on the deal":* USSS Recorded telephone conversation, JP and JM, January 12, 1996. USA v. 1933 $20. Opposition for summary judgement, exhibit QQ.

Page 259: *"They want to do":* Recorded telephone conversation, JP and JM, January 17, 1996. USA v. 1933 $20. Opposition for summary judgement, exhibit QQ.

Page 259: *changes of dates:* Interview, SF to DT, January 14, 2003.

Page 259: *not to avoid:* Interview, SF to DT, January 14, 2003.

Page 259: *"I think he":* USSS Recorded telephone conversation, JP and JM, January 21, 1996. USA v. 1933 $20. Opposition for summary judgement, exhibit QQ.

Page 259: *"getting really":* USSS Recorded telephone conversation, JP and J. Moore, January 21, 1996. USA v. 1933 $20. Opposition for summary judgement, exhibit QQ.

Page 259: *"could discuss the":* Deposition, JM, December 16, 1997, p. 199.

Page 259: *"that he thought":* Deposition, JM, December 16, 1997, p. 128.

Page 259: *"write him an":* Deposition, JM, December 16, 1997, p. 175 and exhibit 29.

Page 260: *"never owned":* Deposition, JM, December 16, 1997, p. 175.

Page 260: *"advertised the coin":* Deposition, JM, December 16, 1997, p. 175.

Page 260: *"$50,000":* Deposition, JM, December 16, 1997, p. 175.

Page 260: *"two checks for":* Deposition, JM, December 16, 1997, p. 175 and exhibit 30.

Page 260: *"seventy-five to":* Deposition, RDF, March 17, 1998, p. 222.

Page 260: *"launder up"*: Deposition, JM, December 16, 1997, p. 231.

Page 260: *$25 to $35 million:* Deposition, JM, December 16, 1997, p. 232.

Page 260: *motel room:* Deposition, RDF, March 17, 1998, p. 222.

Page 260: *"immediately informed"*: Deposition, RDF, March 17, 1998, p. 232.

Page 260: *"agreed that"*: JP vs. JM, Complaint, p. 3.

Page 260: *"paid Moore more"*: JP vs. JM, Complaint, p. 4.

Page 260: *"$20 gold"*: JP vs. JM, Complaint, p. 4.

Page 260: *"a proof 1907"*: Deposition, JM, December 16, 1997, p. 218.

Page 260: *"to sell"*: Deposition, JM, December 16, 1997, p. 218.

Chapter 19: Put 'Em Up

Page 261: *"USA Coins"*: Fax communication, Knightsbridge Coins to Jet Air, February 7, 1996 (1:28 P.M.). USA v. 1933 $20. Motion for summary judgement, exhibit B.

Page 261: *"The imported items"*: (Undated) Jet Air Service to U.S. Customs Service, re entry #609-0253275-7. USA v. 1933 $20. Motion for summary judgement, exhibit GG.

Page 261: *Fenton considered:* Interview, SF to DT, January 14, 2003.

Page 262: *"scared shitless"*: Deposition, JM, December 16, 1997, p. 240.

Page 263: *slipped on:* Interview, SF to DT, January 14, 2003.

Page 263: *little nervous:* Interview, SF to DT, January 14, 2003.

Page 263: *unanswered questions:* Phone conversation, SF to DT, January 17, 2004.

Page 264: *Spy Shop:* USSS "The Waldorf Tape," February 8, 1996. USA v. 1933 $20. Opposition for summary judgement, exhibit QQ.

Page 264: *legislation:* USSS Recorded telephone conversation, J. Parrino and JM, January 12, 1996. USA v. 1933 $20. Opposition for summary judgement, exhibit QQ.

Page 265: *"Hello, Jack"*: USSS "The Waldorf Tape," February 8, 1996. USA v. 1933 $20. Opposition for summary judgement, exhibit QQ.

Page 265: *Moore looked:* Interview, SF to DT, January 14, 2003.

Page 265: *"How are you doing?"*: USSS "The Waldorf Tape," February 8, 1996. USA v. 1933 $20. Opposition for summary judgement, exhibit QQ.

Page 265: *"33.4"*: The statutory weight of a double eagle is 33.436 grams.

Page 267: *It felt:* Interview, SF to DT, January 14, 2003.

Page 267: *"Let me ask you"*: USSS "The Waldorf Tape," February 8, 1996. USA v. 1933 $20. Opposition for summary judgement, exhibit QQ.

Page 268: *"We thought"*: Deposition, RDF, March 17, 1998.

Page 268: *"Hi, how ya doing?"*: USSS "The Waldorf Tape": February 8, 1996. USA v. 1933 $20. Opposition for summary judgement, exhibit QQ.

Page 268: *hands always shake:* Interview, SF to DT January 14, 2003

Page 269: *"Very nice"*: USSS "The Waldorf Tape," February 8, 1996. USA v. 1933 $20. Opposition for summary judgement, exhibit QQ.

Page 269: *"Shit"*. Interview, SF to DT, January 14, 2003.

Page 269: *"Police"*: USSS "The Waldorf Tape," February 8, 1996. USA v. 1933 $20. Opposition for summary judgement, exhibit QQ.

Page 269: *relieved:* Interview, SF to DT, January 14, 2003.

Notes

Chapter 20: In Rem

Page 271: *Fenton was read:* Interview, SF to DT, January 14, 2003.

Page 271: *"Anywhere from":* United States of America v. A $20 Gold Coin, known as a 1933 "Double Eagle," U.S. District Court, Southern District of New York, 96 Civ. 2527 (AKH). Declaration in opposition to Summary Judgement, exhibit TT: Sworn affidavit, Stephen Fenton, February 8, 1996.

Page 272: *"As far as I knew":* Sworn affidavit, SF, February 8, 1996.

Page 272: *"I know":* Sworn affidavit, JP, February 8, 1996.

Page 272: *"quite serious":* Interview, SF to DJ, January 14, 2003.

Page 272: *"1933"* Complaint, in violation of 18 U.S.C. § 371. United States of America v. Jasper Parrino and Stephen C. Fenton, Southern District of New York, February, 1996.

Page 272: *the first time:* Deposition, Fenton, August 3, 1999, p. 167.

Page 273: *"1 One US":* SSF 1590, receipt dated February 8, 1996.

Page 273: *liked his straight:* Alison Frankel, *American Lawyer,* p. 93.

Page 274: *"unlawfully":* USA v. Jasper Parrino and Stephen C. Fenton.

Page 274: *$250,000, surrendered his passport:* Interview, SF to DT, January 19, 2003, and ES conversations with author, 2002–2004.

Page 274: *press release:* USSS News Press Release, February 12, 1996.

Page 275: *October 20, 1998:* JP vs. JM, Complaint, paragraphs 25, 26, 35, 46, 51.

Page 275: *seventy-five hundred dollars:* Deposition, JM, December 16, 1997, p. 233.

Page 275: *$140,000:* JP vs. JM, Judgement filed May 8, 2000.

Page 276: *"Solomonic":* Frankel, *American Lawyer,* p. 95.

Page 278: *toward trial:* USA v. $20, Claimant Stephen C. Fenton's Motion for Summary Judgment, February 1, 2000; Government's Opposition to Motion for Summary Judgment, March 3, 2000.

Page 278: *thieves' market:* Interview, Barry Berke to DT, January 14, 2003.

Page 279: *got them talking:* Interviews, Barry Berke, Jane Levine, David Pickens, William Daddio, Greg Weinman to DT, 2002–2004.

Page 279: *"This settlement shall":* USA v. 1933 double eagle, settlement January 25, 2001.

Chapter 21: Auction and Absolute Anonymity

Page 282: *"true collecting":* Robert Lacey, Sotheby's–Bidding For Class, p. 301.

Page 283: *"three to five":* Department of the Treasury, Request for Proposal, April 11, 2001.

Page 283: *5:30 P.M.:* Department of the Treasury, Request for Proposal, April 11, 2001.

Page 284: *The catalogue:* Sotheby's/ Stack's, auction catalogue, July 30, 2002, p. 12.

Page 286: *"for its uniqueness":* Interview, underbidder with DT, June 18, 2003.

Page 287: *"connections to":* Interview and correspondence, Dwight Manley with DT, May 9, 2003.

Page 287: *ten percent:* Response to DT's questionnaire, April 14, 2003.

Page 288: *"untouchable, unobtainable":* Interview with DT, May 9, 2003.

Page 288: *"little nervous":* Interview with DT, May 9, 2003.

Page 288: *This bidder:* Interview, Selby Kiffer and David Redden to author, May 28, 2003, and later.

Page 289: *"Stolen from"*: Interview with DT, September, 2002.

Page 289: *"You're kidding"*: Interview, underbidder to DT, June 18, 2003.

Page 295: *"That other guy"*: Interview, Selby Kiffer to DT, May 28, 2003.

Page 297: *"Remember," "Absolute anonymity"*: Interview, Selby Kiffer to DT, May 28, 2003.

Page 297: *"Do you know"*: American Lawyer, p. 70.

Epilogue: The 1933 Yeti

Page 299: *"We left"*: Al-Ahram Weekly On-line, Issue 598, 8-14 August 2002.

Page 299: *"loopholes"*: Al-Ahram Weekly On-line, Issue 598, 8-14 August 2002.

Page 301: *item 7950:* Norweb Purchase Ledgers, American Numismatic Society Archives.

Page 302: *Sometime in:* Interview with DT, March 27, 2003.

Page 303: *Thousands upon:* Some gold coin held in earmarked accounts (it was stipulated that these had to exist prior to March 6, 1933) at the NYFRB could, on receipt of a Treasury license, be exported. But the foreign earmarked account was fully depleted by April 30, 1935. Gold Disbursements, 1927-1954. 252.1 and Applications for gold license, A-H. C.262.2A, FRBNYA.

Page 304: *"At least one"*: Walter Breen, *Walter Breen's Complete Encyclopedia of United States and Colonial Coins,* 1988, p. 576.

Page 304: *A Handful:* Conversations and correspondence, Q. David Bowers with DT, July 31, 2002, December 31, 2003, January 20-25, 2004.

Page 305: *"the truth"*: USSS Report, SA Milton Lipson to FWJ, April 24, 1944.

Page 305: *"asked for"*: "Kosoff Commentary," Coin World, March 24, 1982, p. 28.

Page 306: *"I truly"*: "Kosoff Commentary," Coin World, March 24, 1982, p. 28.

Page 307: *"stare at"*: Interview, Fred Weinberg to DT, February 24, 2003.

Page 307: *"Wanna see"*: Interview, Kenneth Goldman to DT, January 22, 2004.

Page 308: *Ron Gillio:* Interview and correspondence with DT, February 3, 2004.

Selected Bibliography

◆

Adams, John W. *United States Numismatic Literature*. Vol. 1, *Nineteenth Century Auction Catalogues*. Mission Viejo, Calif.: George Frederick Kolbe, 1982.

——. *United States Numismatic Literature*. Vol. 2, *Twentieth Century Auction Catalogues*. Crestline, Calif.: George Frederick Kolbe, 1990.

Adelson, Howard L. *American Numismatic Society 1858-1958*. New York: American Numismatic Society, 1958.

Akers, David W. *United States Gold Coins: An Analysis of Auction Records*. Vol. 6, *Double Eagles, 1849-1933*. Englewood, Ohio: Paramount, 1982.

——. *United States Gold Patterns*. Racine, Wis.: Western Publishing Co., 1975.

American Numismatic Association. *Numismatist,* various vol. Federalsburg, Md.: 1909, 1910, 1932-1956.

Anonymous. *Facts about New York*. New York: Sun Printing and Publishing Association, 1927.

——. *History of the New York Numismatic Club, 1908-1991*. Union City, N.J.: privately printed, 1992.

——. *Souvenir and Easy Guide to New York*. New York: Manhattan Postcard Publishing Co., Inc., 1954.

[Baldwin, Fred and Albert Baldwin], cataloguers. *The Palace Collections of Egypt: Catalogue of the Important and Valuable Collection of Coins and Medals*. London: Sotheby & Co., 1954.

Baughman, U. E. and Leonard Wallace Robinson. *Secret Service Chief.* New York: Harper & Brothers, 1962.

Bishop, Jim. *FDR's Last Year: April 1944-April 1945*. New York: William Morrow & Co., 1974.

Bowen, Walter S. and Harry Edward Neal. *The United States Secret Service*. Philadelphia: Chilton Co., 1960.

Bowers, Q. David. *Abe Kosoff: Dean of Numismatics*. Wolfeboro, N.H.: Bowers and Merena Galleries, 1985.

——. *The History of United States Coinage As Illustrated by the Garrett Collection*. Los Angeles: Bowers and Ruddy Galleries, 1979.

——. *Louis E. Eliasberg: King of Coins*. Wolfeboro, N.H.: Bowers and Merena Galleries, 1996.

——. *The Rare Silver Dollars Dated 1804 and the Exciting Adventures of Edmund Roberts*. Wolfeboro, N.H.: Bowers and Merena Galleries, 1999.

——. *United States Gold Coins: An Illustrated History*. Los Angeles: Bowers and Ruddy Galleries, 1982.

——. *Virgil Brand: The Man and His Era*. Wolfeboro, N.H.: Bowers and Merena Galleries, 1983.

Breen, Walter. *Walter Breen's Complete Encyclopedia of U.S. and Colonial Coins*. New York: F. C. I. Press and Doubleday, 1988.

Brinkley, David. *Washington Goes to War*. New York: Alfred A. Knopf, 1988.

Chernow, Ron. *The House of Morgan*. New York: Simon and Schuster, 1990.

Christopher, Milbourne. *Houdini: The Untold Story*. New York: Thomas Y. Crowell Co., 1969.

Davis, Allen F. and Harold D. Woodman (eds.). *Conflict or Consensus in American History*. Boston: D. C. Heath and Co., 1966.

de Hureaux, Alain Daguerre (ed.). *Augustus Saint-Gaudens 1848-1907: A Master of American Sculpture*. Toulouse, France: Somogy Editions d'Art, 1999.

Dolkart, Andrew S. *Guide to New York City Landmarks*. Washington, D.C.: Preservation Press, 1992.

Dorman, Michael. *The Secret Service Story*. New York: Delacorte, 1967.

Dryfhout, John H. *The Work of Augustus Saint-Gaudens*. Hanover and London: University Press of New England, 1982.

——. *Augustus Saint-Gaudens: The 1907 United States Gold Coinage*. Cornish, N.H.: Eastern National, 2002.

Duffy, Henry J. and John H. Dryfhout. *Augustus Saint-Gaudens: American Sculptor of the Gilded Age*. Washington, D.C.: Trust for Museum Exhibitions, 2003.

Edel, Leon. *Henry James: The Master*. Philadelphia: J. B. Lippincott Co., 1972.

Evans, George G. (ed.). *Illustrated History of the United States Mint*. Philadelphia: George G. Evans, 1885.

Fante, John. *1933 Was a Bad Year*. Reprint, London: Canongate Books, 2001.

Frankel, Alison. "The Coin Chase." *American Lawyer,* March 2003.

Gatewood, Willard B. "Theodore Roosevelt and the Coinage Controversy." *American Quarterly* 18 (Spring 1966): 35-51

Gilbert, Cass. "Roosevelt and the Fine Arts." *American Architect* CXVI, no. 2294 (December 10, 1919): 708-722.

Gunther, John. *Roosevelt in Retrospect*. New York: Harper & Brothers, 1950.

Hagedorn, Hermann. *The Roosevelt Family of Sagamore Hill*. New York: Macmillan, 1954.

Hermann, Frank. *Sotheby's: Portrait of an Auction House*. New York and London: W. W. Norton & Co., 1980.

Hodder, Michael and Q. David Bowers. *The Norweb Collection: An American Legacy*. Wolfeboro, N.H.: Bowers and Merena Galleries, 1987.

Ickes, Harold L. *The Secret Diary of Harold L. Ickes: The First Thousand Days, 1933-1936*. New York: Simon and Schuster, 1953.

James, Henry. *The Henry James Letters*. Vol. 4, 1895-1916. Leon Edel (ed.). Cambridge: Belknap Press of Harvard University Press, 1984.

James, William. *The Correspondence of William James*. Vol. 3. Ignas K. Skrupskecis and Elizabeth M. Berkeley, (eds.). Charlottesville and London: University Press of Virginia, 1996.

Judd, J. Hewitt. *United States Pattern, Experimental and Trial Pieces*. 6th ed. Racine, Wis.: Western Publishing Co., 1977.

Kennedy, David M. *Freedom from Fear*. New York and Oxford: Oxford University Press, 1999.

Kosoff, Abe. *Abe Kosoff Remembers: 50 Years of Numismatic Reflections*. New York: Sanford J. Durst, 1981.

Lacey, Robert. *Sotheby's–Bidding for Class*. London: Little Brown, 1998.

Leach, Frank A. *Recollections of a Mint Director*. Reprint, Wolfeboro, N.H.: Bowers and Merena Galleries, 1987.

Mansfield, Peter. *The British in Egypt*. New York: Holt, Reinhart and Winston, 1972.

McBride, Barrie St. Clair. *Farouk of Egypt*. South Brunswick and New York: A. S. Barnes, 1968.

Selected Bibliography

McLeave, Hugh. *The Last Pharoah: Farouk of Egypt.* New York: McCall, 1970.

Melanson, Philip H. and Peter F. Stevens. *The Secret Service: The Hidden History of an Enigmatic Agency.* New York: Carroll & Graf, 2002.

Miller, Nathan. *Theodore Roosevelt: A Life.* New York: William Morrow & Co., 1992.

Moley, Raymond. *After Seven Years.* New York: Harper and Brothers, 1939.

——. *27 Masters of Politics: In a Personal Perspective.* New York: Funk & Wagnalls, 1949.

Morris, Edmund. *Theodore Rex.* New York: Random House, 2001.

Morris, Sylvia Jukes. *Edith Kermit Roosevelt: Portrait of a First Lady.* New York: Coward McCann & Geoghegan, 1980.

Olson, James S. (ed.). *Historical Dictionary of the New Deal: From Inauguration to Preparation for War.* Westport, Conn.: Greenwood Press, 1985.

Powers, Lyall H. (ed.). *Henry James and Edith Wharton, Letters, 1900–1915.* New York: Charles Scribner's Sons, 1990.

Raymond, Wayte (ed.). *Standard Catalogue of United States Coins and Currency.* Various eds. New York: Wayte Raymond, 1935, 1936, 1937, 1938, 1939, 1940, 1942, 1946.

Roosevelt, Alice Longworth. *Crowded Hours.* New York: Charles Scribner's Sons, 1933.

Roosevelt, Franklin, D. *Looking Forward.* New York: John Day Co., 1933.

——. *On Our Way.* New York: John Day Co., 1934.

——. *Public Papers and Address of Franklin D. Roosevelt: With a Special Introduction and Explanatory Notes by President Roosevelt.* Vol. 2, *The Year of Crisis: 1933.* Comp. S. I. Rosenman. New York: Random House, 1938.

——. *Complete Roosevelt Presidential Press Conferences.* Vol. 1–2. New York: DeCapo Press, 1972.

Roosevelt, Theodore. *Theodore Roosevelt's Letters to His Children.* New York: Charles Scribner's Sons, 1919.

——. *Letters.* 8 vols. Ed. Elting E. Morison and John Blum. Cambridge, Mass.: Harvard University Press, 1951–1954.

——. *The Autobiography of Theodore Roosevelt.* Centennial Ed. Ed. Wayne Andrews. New York: Charles Scribner's Sons, 1958.

Saint-Gaudens, Augustus. *The Reminiscences of Augustus Saint-Gaudens.* Ed. Homer Saint-Gaudens. London: Andrew Melrose, 1913.

Saint-Gaudens, Homer. "The Later Works of Augustus Saint-Gaudens." *Century Magazine,* March 1908: 695–714.

——. "Roosevelt and Our Coin Designs." *Century Magazine,* April 1920: 721–736.

Schlesinger, Arthur M., Jr., (ed.). *Almanac of American History.* New York: Bramhall House, 1983.

Schlesinger, Arthur M., Jr. *The Crisis of the Old Order.* Boston: Houghton Mifflin, Riverside Press Cambridge, 1957.

——. *The Coming of the New Deal.* Boston: Houghton Mifflin, Riverside Press Cambridge, 1959.

——. *The Politics of Upheaval.* Boston: Houghton Mifflin, Riverside Press Cambridge, 1960.

Smith, Pete. *American Numismatic Biographies.* Rocky River, Ohio: Gold Leaf Press, 1992.

Sotheby's/Stack's. *1933 Double Eagle: Auction Catalogue.* New York: Sotheby's, July 30, 2002.

Selected Bibliography

Stadiem, William. *Too Rich: The High Life and Tragic Death of King Farouk.* New York: Carroll & Graf, 1991.

Stern, Michael. *Farouk: Uncensored.* New York: Bantam Books, 1965.

Straus, Oscar S. *Under Four Administrations.* Boston and New York: Houghton Mifflin Co., 1922.

Strouse, Jean. *Morgan: American Financier.* New York: Harper Perennial, 2000.

Taxay, Don. *Counterfeit, Mis-Struck and Unofficial U.S. Coins.* New York: Arco, 1963.

——. *The U.S. Mint and Coinage.* New York: Arco, 1966.

Tharp, Louise Hall. *Saint-Gaudens and the Gilded Era.* Boston and Toronto: Little, Brown & Co., 1969.

United States Mint. *Annual Report of the Director of the Mint.* Washington, D.C.: United States Government Printing Office, 1932, 1933, 1934.

United States Treasury. *Annual Report of the Secretary of the Treasury on the State of the Finances.* Washington, D.C.: United States Government Printing Office, various eds. 1932–1945.

Vermeule, Cornelius. *Numismatic Art in America: Aesthetics of the United States Coinage.* Cambridge: Belknap Press of Harvard University Press, 1971.

Wagenknecht, Edward. *The Seven Worlds of Theodore Roosevelt.* New York: Longmans, Green & Co., 1958.

White, Horace. *Money and Banking.* 6th ed. Ed. Charles S. Tippets and Lewis A. Froman. Boston: Ginn and Co., 1935.

Wilkinson, Burke. *Uncommon Clay: The Life and Works of Augustus Saint Gaudens.* San Diego, New York, and London: Harcourt Brace Jovanovich, 1985.

Wilson, Frank J. and Beth Day. *Special Agent.* New York: Holt, Reinhart and Winston, 1965.

Yeoman, R. S., Lee F. Hewitt, and Charles E. Green. *Handbook of United States Coins.* 2d, 3rd, and 4th eds. Racine, Wis.: Whitman Publishing, 1942, 1944, 1945.

Young, James Rankin. *United States Mint at Philadelphia.* Anneville, Pa.: A. G. M. Heister, 1903.

Archives, Court Documents and Manuscript Collections

Federal Bureau of Prisons, Washington, D.C.

George C. Drescher Papers, Herbert Hoover Presidential Library, West Branch, IA.

Federal Reserve Bank of New York Archives, New York.

John Work Garrett Numismatic Archives, American Numismatic Society, New York.

Louis M. Howe Papers, Franklin Delano Roosevelt Library at Hyde Park, N.Y.

Henry Morgenthau, Jr., Papers, Franklin Delano Roosevelt Library at Hyde Park, N.Y.

Norweb Family Numismatic Archives, American Numismatic Society, New York

Eleanor Roosevelt Papers, Franklin Delano Roosevelt Library at Hyde Park, N.Y.

Franklin D. Roosevelt Papers, Franklin Delano Roosevelt Library at Hyde Park, N.Y.

Theodore Roosevelt Collection, Harvard University Library, Cambridge, Mass.

Theodore Roosevelt Papers, Library of Congress, Washington, D.C.

Augustus Saint-Gaudens Papers, Rauner Special Collections, Dartmouth College Library, Hanover, N.H.

Oscar S. Straus Papers, Library of Congress, Washington, D.C.

Selected Bibliography

United States Bureau of the Mint, National Archives at College Park, Maryland, and Mid Atlantic Region, Center City, Philadelphia, Pennsylvania

United States Department of the Treasury, National Archives at College Park, Maryland

United States District Court for the District of New Jersey, National Archives and Records Administration, Northeast Region, New York City, New York

United States District Court for the Eastern District of Pennsylvania, National Archives and Records Administration, Mid Atlantic Region, Center City, Philadelphia, Pennsylvania

United States District Court for the Southern District of New York, New York, New York

United States District Court for the Western District of Missouri, Kansas City, Missouri

United States District Court for the Western District of Tennessee, Western Division, Memphis, Tennessee

United States Office of Public Buildings and Grounds, National Archives Building, Washington, D.C.

Newspapers and Periodicals

Al-Ahram

American Numismatic Society Magazine

Coinage

Coin World

Evening Star, Washington, D.C.

Life

News-Week

New York Daily News

The New Yorker

New York Herald Tribune

New York Post

New York Times

Numismatic News

Numismatic Scrapbook

Numismatist

Philadelphia Inquirer

Time

Washington Daily News

Washington Times

Acknowledgments

———◆———

I can no longer count the number of people to whom I have spoken, formally or informally, about this remarkable tale. Astonishingly, only one or two were reluctant to speak at all. Many more people unselfishly helped me track down a tiny lead, a minor character who may have ended up on the cutting room floor—or explained a fine point of history that had been beyond my understanding. I salute them all.

I had not met Stephen Fenton or his attorney, Barry Berke, before that day in May when all the interested auction houses were pitching woo at the U.S. Mint to get the right to sell the coin. I got to know them both during the auction process, and for their cooperation on the book my gratitude knows no bounds. Steve patiently listened and responded to my questions both in London and New York. He answered all my questions unhesitatingly. He was uncomfortable in reliving a dark day in his life as I walked him through the day of his arrest, but he persevered with good humor. His insight and experience as the ultimate insider in the modern story was more than beneficial: it was essential. Barry Berke was another savior. He graciously allowed me extraordinary access to his files on the case—from the old Secret Service reports to modern depositions—which after five years of litigation were mountainous. Barry was also willing to sit with me while I asked him naive questions about the legal process, played devil's advocate to my theories, and shared his inner thoughts about the case as it had meandered through the judicial system.

Assistant United States District Attorney Jane Levine responded cheerfully to my varied queries. My first call to her in February, 2002, asking for the supporting exhibits from the case, was met with new levels of insight from her perspective, followed by copies of the Secret Service reports and Treasury memos galore.

Sotheby's Vice Chairman David Redden, who wields a mighty auctioneer's gavel, has been a marvelous friend for thirty years and loved the idea of the book from day one. He has peppered me with questions and suggestions and opened the doors for me to talk with a number of the bidders, most especially the mysterious underbidder; and, under a continued cloak of strict anonymity, he has acted as amanuensis for the buyer as well.

His assistant, Debbie Moerschell was always there and ever patient. Selby Kiffer was the man on the phone with the "absolutely anonymous" buyer and took the time from his hectic schedule to relate the tale from his end. Matthew Weigman and Lauren Gioia from Sotheby's press office were, during the lead-up to the sale a continuing delight to work with, always pulling some new and unexpected press coverage from their hat. During the writing of the book they always found time to get me the information I needed and have been unstinting in their support.

At Stack's, Harvey Stack was a godsend. Having been brought up in the coin business since he was a pup, he personally knew many of the dealers and collectors who have long since departed, and I spent many delightful hours, hounding him with questions and reveling in a world long gone. There were some scoundrels then too. He also knew and described Harry Strang to me, giving a face and personality to a name. To his junior partner, son, and my great old friend Larry Stack I am beholden. He called regularly to see how I was bearing up under the pressure and offered any and all assistance. And when I asked for something, it seemed to arrive even before I had put the phone down. There was highly informed input when needed from all at Stack's: Mike Hodder was enormously generous, and, as ever, knows the story back to front; as do his colleagues David Alexander, and Vicken Yegparian.

Dave Bowers, a friend for a quarter-century, shared his 1933 stories and opinions with me selflessly. He might not necessarily agree with all my conclusions, but he forced me to look where I might not have thought to look, and I am grateful. Eric Streiner shared his memories of the first flight of eagles at Spink's as the modern chapter opened. André de Clermont spoke to me about his reminiscences of the jeweler from Cairo and beyond.

From the world of numismatics I cannot even begin to give thanks to all those who gave of their time, information, reminiscences, or theories, some not even aware I was listening: Edward Baldwin, Mitch Battino, Ruth Bauer, Donald Crowther, John Dannreuther, Harry Forman, David Ganz, Martin Gengerke, Ron Gillio, Kenneth Goldman, David Hall, Robert W. Julian, Kevin Lipton, Dwight Manley, Eric P. Newman, Tom Noe, Paul Nugget, Donn Pearlman, Ed Reiter, Armen Vartian, Fred Weinberg, the late Lester Merkin (who always knew something), and a passel of anonymous others.

I am grateful to the descendants of those individuals who graciously spoke or corresponded with me and provided papers. Not all wish their names acknowledged, but all of their help has been invaluable: Frederick C. C. Boyd III, James T. Macallister, Woody Rowe, William H. Woodin III, and others.

From the United States Mint, the gracious director, Henrietta Holsman Fore, has always been keenly interested in the story, while Greg Weinman and Bill Daddio provided me with much insight and history. Tim Grant in Philadelphia was another boon to my research. David Pickens and Dr. George Hunter, former members of the Mint, also shared their wisdom with me.

Dr. Thomas Hawk from the Philadelphia Community College provided me with a stage on which the drama unfolded as he gave me a tour back into time, in the old Mint building and allowed me access with my clumsy camera.

Research institutions and individuals galore gave so generously. The American Numismatic Society: Ute Wartenberg (always encouraging), Francis Campbell (ever responsive), Robert Hoge, and Sebastian Heath. The Smithsonian Institution: Doug Mudd. The FDR Library at Hyde Park: Bob Clark (special thanks). The United States Secret Service: Mike Sampson. The Federal Reserve Bank of New York Archives: Rosemary Lazenby (a marvel), Joseph Komljenovich. The Saint-Gaudens National Historic Site: Henry Duffy. Dr. Wallace Dailey, Curator, Theodore Roosevelt Collection. Sarah Hartwell, Dartmouth College Library. Wayne DeCesar, NARA, Archivist, Civilian Records. Frank B. Arisman (remarkable friend and photographer), Fred Bauman, Matthew DiBiase, Gail Farr, Doran Ghatan, Bill Golder, Jack Klein, Donald G. Partrick, Robert A. G. A. Scott, Michael Shadix, Dr. Aggie Stillman, Olivette Taylor, Stephen Tebo, Ken Weiderhorn, and many more.

Cathy Melocik, generous friend, my pre-editor copyeditor, allowed me to submit a much cleaner product than I would have ever been capable of and saved me much embarrassment.

This book would simply not exist were it not for a wonderfully serendipitous cascade of events that followed an off-hand remark made by me to my wife, Susan, during dinner on a winter's eve in 2002, as I was working on the auction catalogue for the sale of the 1933 double eagle. In seeing the intricacy and richness of the story, and already in its thrall, I said, "There's too much for a catalogue. This could be a book." Susan peered up from the other end of the table, took a sip of her wine, and said, "Call Larry."

Larry Ashmead, the legendary editor, a good friend and neighbor, agreed that there was a book in this phenomenal tale and graciously inflicted me on one of his former assistants, now literary agent, Scott

351

Waxman. Scott too was hooked and set me to work writing a proposal. This to my amazement found me my wonderful, patient, understanding, dare I say saintly, editor, Leslie Meredith.

Larry has been a constant cheerleader and fount of wisdom during my first, tenuous, foray into publishing. To Scott, a simple "thank you" would not suffice for having had to deal with a difficult, self-doubting, first-time, tetchy, know-it-all author. I've made him gray before his time.

The story of the 1933 double eagle is a great one, but not necessarily the easiest to tell, and I am grateful to all at the Free Press for taking a chance on me. The well-tempered and wondrous Leslie Meredith, my editor and savior, has performed a Herculean task, unbending my tortured prose and gently, firmly, keeping me on track through a century of events while asking questions I should have thought of myself. I can't believe my good luck. I must also thank her assistant, Stephen Karam (and his predecessor, Dorothy Robinson), whose unenviable task was chasing me down, with great humor, for all the stuff I hadn't yet done and probably still haven't! Michele Jacob, publicity manager, has creatively helped find new ways to spread the word about the book.

My sister, Suzanne Jurmain, an author herself, was always there to listen to her little brother and haul him through the shoals of a first book. I regret that my first editor, from my youth, my mother, never got to see the book. And I am deeply saddened that my father, Paul Tripp, a wonderful writer, was not there to answer his son's questions. He was so excited when he learned that I had sold the book, had planned to attend the auction of the coin, and I was looking forward to his sage advice, but the Moirae intervened and Atropos cut his thread—all too soon.

Finally there is my wife, Susan. It was her "Call Larry" that started it all, and without her there would be nothing. Susan was *the* research assistant, endnote organizer, permissions maven, photo editor, first reader (and re-reader), cook (supreme), and kept a frequently wobbly writer pedaling forward. I don't know how she did it. This book is hers.

Index

---◆---

Page numbers in *italics* refer to illustrations.

353

357

last letter to T. Roosevelt by, 15
as master of low relief, 11
memorial meeting for, 18
preliminary double eagle design of,
    10
World's Columbian Exposition Pre-
    sentation Medal and, 8
Saint-Gaudens, Homer, 15
Saint-Gaudens, Louis, 8
San Francisco earthquake of 1906, 16
San Francisco Mint, 16–17, 53, 68, 71, 192,
    216
Schulman, Hans, 80, 81, 216, 218, 220,
    223
scrip (emergency money), 32, 33
Secret Service, xiv, xv, 91, 92, 100, 201,
    214, 216, 225, 253, 255, 260, 263,
    264, 271, 275, 277, 298
    Forensic Services Division of, 274
    form SSF 1590 of, 273
    Jews in, 143
Senate, U.S., 29, 33
Senate Banking and Currency Commit-
    tee investigation, 153–54
September 11, 2001 terrorist attacks, 280
Settlement Committee, 65, 117, 139, 140,
    190
Shapiro, Jake, 97
Shaw, Leslie Mortier, 3, 4, 7, 8, 11
Sherman Monument, 11
Silver, Edward, 113, 165, 166, 168, 169,
    182, 185, 187, 193, 195, 225, 226,
    301
    bank withdrawals of, 183–84
    McCann's connection to, 183–84
    melting of gold by, 179
silver dollar (1804), 86, 191, 215, 284
silver dollar, nickel (1851), 239
silver trade dollar (1884), 100–101, 191,
    215
silver trade dollar (1885), 100–101, 191,
    215
Sinnock, John, 53
Smith, Al, 22
Smith, R. H., 94, 99
Smith and Son, 108–9
Smithsonian Institution, 53, 71, 73, 81,
    89, 105, 125, 138, 178, 188, 195, 205,
    274
"Some People Get All the Breaks"
    (Jensen), 153
Sotheby's, 213, 215, 218, 221, 224, 233,
    281–82, 283, *286,*
    accusations of collusion against, xv
    arrival of double eagle at, 284
    collection of, 240
    Farouk Collection sale of, 209–24

2002 auction at, xv–xvii, 285–98, *291*
South Philadelphia National Bank, 183
Soviet Union, 214
speakeasies, 45
special trusts accounts, 32
specie, *see* coins
speculation, 20
Spink, David, *217,* 218, 219, 221, 222, 223,
    240, 278
Spink and Son, 231, 232, 233, 234, 236,
    237, 238
    codename, 240
Spy Shop, 264
Stack, Harvey, 282, 290, 293
Stack, James, 109, 122–23, 133, 203, 206,
    208, 226
    lawsuit of, 205–6, 225
Stack, Joseph, 86, 93–94
Stack, Larry, 284, 285, 290, 291, 292, 293,
    296, 297
Stack, Morton, 86, 93–94
Stack's, 85, 92–93, 95, 99, 143, 282, 283,
    284, 285
Stalin, Joseph, 197
*Standard Catalogue of United States
    Coins,* 184
Stanford, Leland, 48
State Department, U.S., 179, 214, 218,
    219, 220–21, 223
Statute of Limitations, 196
steel industry, 20
Stein, Harry J., 202–3, 204, 205
Steinhardt, Laurence A., 83
Stimson, Henry, *177*
stocks, in Great Crash, 20
Strang, Harry W., 92, 93, 99–100, 110–19,
    122, 125–27, 134, 136, 138–40, 142,
    145, 148, 155, 157, 158, 161, 162,
    164–73, 175, 179, 181, 182, 185,
    192–96, 225, 226, 271, 277, 278
    Carey interviewed by, 139–40
    charting of known coins by, 131–33,
        136–37
    final report to Wilson by, 194–96, 200
    Macallister interviewed by, 105, 162,
        164
    McCann interviewed by, 187–90
    Nagy interviewed by, 101–2
    Reed interviewed by, 102–3, 147,
        170–72
    seizures of double eagles by, 94, 95,
        97, 201–3, 208
    Silver interviewed by, 169–70
    Stack's suit against, 205–6
    SwITT interviewed and investigated
        by, 111–14, 165–66, 167
Straus, Oscar, 7

361

Index

363

ABOUT THE AUTHOR

DAVID TRIPP is a numismatic consultant, art historian, writer, and cartoonist. He was formerly the Director of the Coin, Tapestry, and Musical Instrument Departments at Sotheby's New York for much of the 1970s. After leaving Sotheby's he became a numismatic consultant, advised on many of the most valuable and famous collections ever sold, and wrote award-winning catalogues for a number of record-breaking auctions. He has continued to consult for Sotheby's and was a leading member of the team that brought the 1933 double eagle to sale in July, 2002.

Trained as an archaeologist, he has degrees from New York University and the Institute of Archaeology at London University and spent three seasons excavating in Italy and England, where he was the site photographer.

Raised in New York City, Tripp—the son of Paul Tripp, the creator of *Tubby the Tuba* and a pioneer in early children's television—appeared on television, film, and records as a child. David Tripp is also a cartoonist, whose work has appeared in *Punch* and whose featured strip, *Sadie,* has appeared in *Cat Fancy* magazine since 1985. He is married, has two cats—who act as gag writers for his strip—and lives in Columbia County, New York.

Printed in the United States
By Bookmasters